ORGANIZATIONS
Structure and Process

RICHARD H. HALL
University of Minnesota

Prentice-Hall, Inc., Englewood Cliffs, New Jersey

PRENTICE-HALL SERIES IN SOCIOLOGY
NEIL J. SMELSER, Editor

ISBN: 0–13–642033–8

Library of Congress Catalog Card Number: 78–173426

10 9 8 7 6 5 4 3 2

Printed in the United States of America

PRENTICE-HALL INTERNATIONAL, INC., LONDON
PRENTICE-HALL OF AUSTRALIA, PTY. LTD., SYDNEY
PRENTICE-HALL OF CANADA, LTD., TORONTO
PRENTICE-HALL OF INDIA PRIVATE LIMITED, NEW DELHI
PRENTICE-HALL OF JAPAN, INC., TOKYO

To Sherry

Contents

v

Preface

We live in an organizational world. Birth and death are usually organizationally located. We use organizations to make war. In some cases we use organizations to make love. Almost everything in between has organizations as a central or important component. In an industrialized, urbanized, technological society they are the place of employment, the source of education and inspiration, and a major focus of recreation for the individual. They are agents of and resisters of social change.

In the past decade the amount of discussion and research about organizations has increased exponentially. The discussions of organizations have been focused around what they do to and for society and the individual. Research has been directed toward these issues and also toward an understanding of the organization itself.

This book is designed to reflect these recent developments. The first concern is to understand the *nature* of organizations. We will be concerned with what an organization is trying to *accomplish* and ways in which its *performance can be assessed*. We will then examine the rather extensive amount of information available about the *structure* of organizations. This information is coming increasingly from *comparative* studies which deal with relatively large numbers of organizations in a variety of settings. A decade ago, there was little other than case study evidence available. From a concern with structure the focus will shift to a concern with *process*. Here the information is really less substantial than that dealing with structure, but we are able to deal with some certainty with issues such as *power, communications,* and *decision making,* These processes are at the heart of organizational change. They are also the point at which the individual can have the greatest input. The last section deals with a topic that only recently has come into its own as a research subject—the relations between *organizations* and their *environments.*

We will look at the manner in which the environment affects the organization and then turn around and examine the manner in which organizations affect their environment. These topics have received scant attention in the past.

This book is an attempt at understanding organizations as organizations. That is, it treats organizations, rather than the individuals of which they are comprised, as the subject of discussion. This consciously *sociological approach* to organizations is not meant to diminish in any way the importance of the individual—his contribution will be noted continuously in the chapters that follow, but rather to indicate the manner in which organizational factors must be understood if the organizations that are so important in our lives are to be analyzed, manipulated, or survived.

Before this book was begun, lengthy discussions with several friends in the field led me to the conclusion that it was premature to write a book on the sociology of organizations, given the existing conceptual and empirical shortages. A reading of the book will indicate that this conclusion is in part correct. There are areas in which the empirical evidence is scanty or nonexistent. The conceptual framework suffers because of this and contains statements that are educated guesses or poorly supported lines of thought.

But, despite these problems, I feel some sense of closure on the completion of the work. We have fairly consistent information about organizational structures at present. This fits in well with the evidence available about processes internal to the organization and its transactions with its environment. The shortage of empirical information regarding processes and transactions makes these areas stand out as the ones in which evidence is most needed. They are also the areas in which current research seems to be most interested. If this is the case, there is hope for the future.

The purpose of the book is to analyze organizations. It is hoped that this analysis will serve and be relevant to three audiences. For the practitioner in the organization, this may be in the form of new insights into why things happen the way they do and how certain actions might be encouraged or resisted. For the student, perhaps the book will provide integration in his attempts to understand the organizational literature. For my fellow organizational analysts, I hope that the holes in the analysis will serve as research issues for future work.

My intellectual debts are probably most accurately reflected in the citations made throughout the book. It will be evident that while the conceptual model is somewhat eclectic, it fits the basic "systems" perspective. Particular sections have benefited heavily from work with John Clark and David Hickson. James Price, Jerald Hage, and Neil Smelser provided understanding critical assistance. Alan Lesure, formerly of Prentice-Hall, Inc., was supportive and patient with the book. My colleagues at the University of Minnesota and the National Science Foundation, were consistently supportive. The preparation of the manuscript could not have been accomplished without the prompt and cheerful help of Rose Mary Florek, Kay Kuusisto, and Polly Hardy, who had to work in a disjointed time and space context. My family was just what a family should be during both the stressful and the happy moments associated with the writing of a book.

part one

THE NATURE OF ORGANIZATIONS

INTRODUCTION

Western society has been characterized as an "organizational society" [1] and its population as "organization men." [2] Modernizing nations utilize organizations as a major tool in the development of their political, economic, social, and military systems. While the ideas of organizational societies and organization men convey strong suggestions of negative consequences for the societies and men involved, the terms are descriptively accurate. We live in a world surrounded by and made up of organizations.

These organizations take many forms and represent the crosscutting and conflicting value systems within a society. In a period of rapid social change and evident social conflict, organizations are a major contributing factor both to change and conflict and to resistance to change and conflict. The United States government, the Black Panthers, the United States Army, Students for a Democratic Society, the International Business Machine Corporation, the Roman Catholic Church, the Ku Klux

[1] Robert Presthus, *The Organizational Society* (New York: Alfred A. Knopf, Inc., 1962).

[2] William H. Whyte, Jr., *The Organization Man* (New York: Simon & Schuster, Inc., 1956).

Klan, the University of Minnesota, the First National Bank, and the myriad of other organizations in which people work, participate, and believe represent a dominant component of contemporary society.

THE GOAL OF THE BOOK

The primary purpose of this book is to analyze organizations. This in itself is a legitimate academic purpose. But the analysis should also contribute to our understanding of the world around us, not only in regard to the operation of organizations and their members, but also in terms of the impact of organizations on their environments and the environments' impact on the organizations.

The overall perspective that will be taken is one of change. But first we will examine organizations as rather static entities, thus allowing the analysis of organizational processes and change to proceed from a common basis.

Every social phenomenon is static at a particular point in time. The forms taken by each can be compared at this point in time. A static analysis also allows some determination of which organizational characteristics are interrelated, and this approach provides indications of why and how organizations reached their present forms. Historical and experimental evidence allows further understanding of the dynamics of organizational development and change. From this analysis of organizations as entities at a point in time, the focus will shift to processes internal and external to organizations that affect their behavior and that of their members.

Organizations do not operate in a vacuum. They affect their environments and are affected by them. It is quite clear that organizations are in constant interaction with other organizations, clients and customers, and general societal conditions. At the same time, organizations themselves influence general social change. They can be agents of change; they can also obstruct potentially beneficial or harmful changes. Later we will examine the conditions under which organizations play these roles and the consequences of their actions.

This brief discussion has implied that organizations are concrete entities. Human experience verifies this. Organizations are something that pervade human life, from birth and the hospital to death and the mortuary, and almost everywhere in between. While everyone is familiar with organizations, we can add clarity to the discussion if we use a commonly agreed-upon definition for the balance of this analysis.

DEFINITIONS

Discussions of definitions are capable of being quite deadly; but they are also capable of yielding a good deal of insight into the phenomena under investigation.[3] And they provide a basis for understanding the approach taken by their developer in his own discussion of these phenomena.

WEBER.   Like any field of study, and like organizations themselves, the analysis of organizations has a tradition, one that in many ways centers around Max Weber. Weber has become known in the field primarily because of his discussions of bureaucracy, a topic we will discuss later, but he also concerned himself with the more general definitions of organizations. Weber first of all distinguishes the "corporate group" from other forms of social organization. The corporate group is a "social relationship which is either closed or limits the admission of outsiders by rules, . . . so far as its order is enforced by the action of specific individuals whose regular function this is, of a chief or 'head' and usually also an administrative staff." [4]

This aspect of the definition contains a number of elements requiring further discussion, since they are basic to most other such definitions. In the first place, organizations involve social relationships. That is, individuals interact within the organization. These individuals are not simply in random contact, however, as the reference to closed or limited boundaries suggests. The organization (corporate group) includes parts of the population and excludes others. The organization itself thus has a boundary. A major component of this definition, the idea of order, further differentiates organizations from other social entities. Interaction patterns do not simply arise; there is a structuring of interaction imposed by the organization itself. This part of the definition also suggests that organizations contain a hierarchy of authority and a division of labor in carrying out their functions. Order is enforced with specific personnel designed to perform this function.

To the idea of the corporate group, Weber adds some additional

[3] James G. March and Herbert A. Simon with Harold Guetzkow, in *Organizations* (New York: John Wiley & Sons, Inc., 1958), p. 1, suggest that definitions of organizations do not serve much purpose. I disagree.

[4] Max Weber, *The Theory of Social and Economic Organization*, trans. A. M. Henderson and Talcott Parsons (New York: The Free Press, 1947), pp. 145–46. Weber also has a specific definition of organizations: "A system of continuous purposive activity of a specified kind" (p. 151). This is actually too concise for this discussion.

criteria for organizations. In organizations, interaction is "associative" rather than "communal." [5] This differentiates between the organization and other social entities such as the family, which would share the other, aforementioned characteristics. Weber also notes that organizations carry out continuous purposive activities of a specified kind.[6] Thus, organizations transcend the lives of their members, and they have goals, as the "purposive activities" phrase suggests. Organizations are designed to do something. Weber's early inclusion of this idea has been followed up by most organizational analysts.

Weber's definition has served as the basis for many others, in part because it is close to reality. His focus is basically on legitimate interaction patterns among organizational members as they pursue goals and engage in activities.

BARNARD.   A different focus has been taken by Chester Barnard and his followers. While in agreement with Weber on many points, Barnard stresses a different basis for organizations. His basic definition of an organization is "a system of consciously coordinated activities or forces of two or more persons"; [7] that is, activity accomplished through conscious, deliberate, and purposeful coordination. Organizations require communications, a willingness on the part of members to contribute and a common purpose on the part of the members. Barnard stresses the role of the individual. It is he who must communicate and be motivated. It is he who must make decisions. While Weber emphasizes the "system," Barnard is concerned with members of the system. The relevance and implications of these contrasting approaches will be taken up at a later time.

Organizations and Social Organization

One of the major problems in discussing or thinking about organizations is that the very term is so similar to the broader term of "social organization." Most analysts conceive of social organization as the "networks of social relations and the shared orientations . . . often referred to as the social structure and culture, respectively." [8] Social organization

---

[5] *Ibid.*, pp. 136–39.

[6] *Ibid.*, pp. 151–52.

[7] Chester I. Barnard, *The Functions of the Executive* (Cambridge, Mass.: Harvard University Press, 1938), p. 73.

[8] Peter M. Blau and W. Richard Scott, *Formal Organizations* (San Francisco: Chandler Publishing Co., 1962), p. 4. For a recent overview of the scope of social organization, see Marvin E. Olsen, *The Process of Social Organization* (New York: Holt, Rinehart & Winston, Inc., 1968). Olsen defines social organization as "the process of merging social actors into ordered social relationships, which become infused with cultural ideas."

is the broader set of relationships and processes of which *organizations* are a part. The analysis of social organization can be at the macro or total societal level, or the micro or interpersonal or intergroup level. Analyses of dyads or triads carried out in an experimental setting, for example, contribute to the understanding of social organization. Organizations, as we are using the term here, are part of the more general social organization, being affected by it and, reciprocally, affecting it in turn.

OTHER DEFINITIONS. Some writers have attempted to alleviate these terminological problems by adding the adjective "complex," "large-scale," or "formal" as a prefix to organizations. Peter M. Blau and W. Richard Scott, for example, note that:

> Since formal organizations are often very large and complex, some authors refer to them as "large-scale" or as "complex" organizations. But we have eschewed these terms as misleading in two respects. First, organizations vary in size and complexity, and using these variables as defining criteria would result in such odd expressions as a "small large-scale organization" or a "very complex complex organization." Second, although formal organizations often become very large and complex, their size and complexity do not rival those of the social organization of a modern society, which includes such organizations and their relations with one another in addition to other nonorganizational patterns. (Perhaps the complexity of formal organizations is so much emphasized because it is man-made, whereas the complexity of societal organization has slowly emerged, just as the complexity of modern computers is more impressive than that of the human brain. Complexity by design may be more conspicuous than complexity by growth or evolution.)[9]

While few would argue with Blau and Scott's points regarding the difficulties in the use of "complex" or "large-scale," the same criticism of "formal" as a prefix can be made. Organizations also vary in terms of their formalization, and we would thus have to talk about more or less formal formal organizations, which is not a great leap forward. With these considerations in mind, the simple term "organization" will be used here. "Social organization" will refer to the broader context.

The discussion becomes more concrete when we consider Amitai Etzioni's and W. Richard Scott's definitions and examples. Etzioni states:

> Organizations are social units (or human groupings) deliberately constructed and reconstructed to seek specific goals. Corporations, armies, schools, hospitals, churches, and prisons are included; tribes, classes, ethnic groups, and families are excluded. Organizations are characterized by: (1) divisions

---

[9] Blau and Scott, *Formal Organizations*, p. 7.

of labor, power and communication responsibilities, divisions which are not randomly or traditionally patterned, but deliberately planned to enhance the realization of specific goals; (2) the presence of one or more power centers which control the concerted efforts of the organization and direct them toward its goals; these power centers also continuously review the organization's performance and re-pattern its structure, where necessary, to increase its efficiency; (3) substitution of personnel, i.e., unsatisfactory persons can be removed and others assigned their tasks. The organization can also recombine its personnel through transfer and promotion.[10]

Scott's definition contains some additional elements. He says:

. . . organizations are defined as collectivities . . . that have been established for the pursuit of relatively specific objectives on a more or less continuous basis. It should be clear, . . . however, that organizations have distinctive features other than goal specificity and continuity. These include relatively fixed boundaries, a normative order, authority ranks, a communication system, and an incentive system which enables various types of participants to work together in the pursuit of common goals.[11]

This definition appears to correspond with reality quite well. However, two problems that are evident in this and the other definitions concern the place of goals in the nature of organizations and the issue of the distinctiveness of boundaries. It is clear that a widely varying proportion of organizational activity is unrelated to goals.[12] Perhaps it is preferable to say that organizations are established for the pursuit of goals but engage in activities that may or may not be related to them. This acknowledges the role of goals, but at the same time points to the importance of other activities that are not goal-related.

The problem of the distinctiveness of the boundary is evident in some easily recognized cases. The local political party, for example, often has a small paid staff to answer phones, collect mail, and so on. However, the power really belongs to nonpaid members of the organization, some of whom may not even be known to the paid members. During election campaigns, the membership in the organization swells rapidly as people are enlisted to make telephone calls, deliver posters, and make speeches. This addition of voluntary and part-time personnel

[10] Amitai Etzioni, *Modern Organizations* (Englewood Cliffs, N.J.: Prentice-Hall, Inc., 1964), p. 3.

[11] W. Richard Scott, "Theory of Organizations," in Robert E. L. Faris, ed., *Handbook of Modern Sociology* (Chicago: Paul McNally and Co., 1964), p. 488.

[12] For a concise statement of this position, see Alvin W. Gouldner, "Organizational Analysis," in Robert K. Merton, Leonard Broom, and Leonard S. Cottrell, Jr., *Sociology Today* (New York: Basic Books, Inc., 1959), pp. 405–6.

really throws the boundary issue up into the air. Many similar kinds of organizations could be identified—religious, fraternal, and others. These voluntary organizations may in this way be so different from other organizations that they form a uniquely distinct type. (This issue will be discussed in the section on typologies.) Organizations dealing with emergencies often have their ranks expanded by volunteers—even those with very distinct boundaries, such as police or fire departments. This unusual type of case calls for a further provisions of openness in the definition.

Then again, none of the definitions discussed has included the organization's environment, a point that should be made explicit in the definition, since environmental considerations play a major role in what goes on in organizations. The conception of environment to be used here includes everything "outside of" a particular organization. Climatic and geographic conditions, other organizations, the state of the economy, and the stage of development of the nation—these are but a few of the environmental factors that all organizations must face and try to contend with.

Environmental factors affect organizations from two directions. The environment affects what goes into an organization, since environmental factors are a major part of its input. The organization, as described in the definitions above, then does something with this input, producing an output. The output goes back into the environment, thus again affecting the organization as the output is consumed, utilized, and evaluated in the environment.[13]

With all these considerations in mind, the definition of organizations to be used in this analysis can now be stated. *An organization is a collectivity with relatively identifiable boundary, a normative order, authority ranks, communications systems, and membership coordinating systems; this collectivity exists on a relatively continuous basis in an environment and engages in activities that are usually related to a goal or a set of goals.*

This definition is admittedly cumbersome. But the discussion thus far has indicated the reasons for this. Organizations are complex entities that contain a series of elements and are affected by many diverse factors. To convey an understanding of the nature and the consequences of these internal and external factors is the task of the remaining chapters of this book. Before turning to the analysis itself, however, an important but often overlooked question must be asked.

---

[13] This discussion and terminology correspond to that of James D. Thompson, *Organizations in Action* (New York: McGraw-Hill Book Company, 1967), pp. 19–20; and Daniel Katz and Robert L. Kahn, *The Social Psychology of Organizations* (New York: John Wiley & Sons, Inc., 1966), pp. 16–17.

ARE ORGANIZATIONS REAL?

This question probably seems inane at first glance; it was stated at the outset that organizations are all around us and that we are a part of them most of our lives. But a second look at the question will reveal a very basic issue: whether or not organizations are anything more than individuals who have come together in an interaction system.

Many organizational analysts say that organizations can be understood only by taking the interaction perspective; [14] that is, that since humans make decisions and react to situations, the actions and reactions of individuals form the heart of the organization, and therefore nothing in an organization can be understood apart from the individuals involved. Blau provides a good example of this perspective when he states:

> Within the organization, indirect exchange processes become substituted for direct ones, although direct ones persist in interstitial areas, such as informal cooperation among colleagues. The development of authority illustrates the transformation of direct into indirect exchange transactions. As long as subordinates obey the orders of a superior primarily because they are obligated to him for services he has rendered and favors he has done for them individually, he does not actually exercise authority over the subordinates, and there is a direct exchange between him and them, of the type involving unilateral services. The establishment of authority means that normative constraints that originate among the subordinates themselves effect their compliance with the orders of the superior—and indirect exchanges now take the place of the former direct ones. The individual subordinate offers compliance to the superior in exchange for approval from his colleagues; the collectivity of subordinates enforces compliance with the superior's directives to repay its joint obligations to the superior; and the superior makes contributions to the collectivity in exchange for the self-enforced voluntary compliance of its members on which his authority rests.[15]

Blau then goes on to note that:

> . . . in return for offering services to clients without accepting rewards from them, officials receive material rewards from the organization and col-

14 Herbert A. Simon makes a succinct statement of this position when he warns against reifying the concept of organization—". . . treating it as something more than a system of interacting individuals." In Simon, "On The Concept of Organizational Goal," *Administrative Science Quarterly*, Vol. 9, No. 1 (June 1964), 1. The position taken here is the exact opposite. The organization is not reified, because it is reality.

15 Peter M. Blau, *Exchange and Power in Social Life* (New York: John Wiley & Sons, Inc., 1967), p. 329.

league approval for conforming with accepted standards. The clients make contributions to the community, which furnishes the resources to the organization that enable it to reward its members.[16]

Blau's analysis places primacy on the interaction between individuals as the heart of the organization. The position taken in this book is that this is an incomplete view of organizations in two ways.

Organizations and the Individual

In the first place, individuals in organizations frequently behave *without* engaging in direct or indirect exchange. When the captain of the defensive platoon of a football team shouts "Pass!" both the linemen and defensive backs react immediately in terms of their stance and entire approach to the play. When an item to be charged in a department store costs more than $100, the clerk routinely calls the credit office to check the credit of the prospective purchaser. Both these illustrations involve routine learned behavior. Although the learning has taken place in a direct interaction situation, the actual behavior takes place without mental reference to the interaction process. It has become a learned stimulus–response type of mechanism, with the intervening interaction variable deleted as a consideration. Much behavior in organizations is of this type. The organization trains, indoctrinates, and convinces its members to respond on the basis of the requirements of their position. This response becomes quite regularized and routinized and does not involve the interaction frame of reference.

The argument that behavior in organizations is organizationally based, rather than individually or interactionally, is not intended to mean that *all* behavior in organizations is so determined. Rather, the intent here is to demonstrate that organizational factors play an important part in determining how an individual will act in a variety of situations. The particular impact of organizational factors will vary according to the situation. In some situations, organizational factors are dominant; in others, individual or interaction effects. Even in the case of individually or interactionally based behavior, however, organizational considerations play a role. In discussing the factors that contribute to the kinds of role expectations one organization member holds toward another (role expectations play a vital role in any interaction situation), Robert Kahn et al. note:

To a considerable extent, the role expectations held by the members of

16 *Ibid.*, p. 330.

a role set—the prescriptions and proscriptions associated with a particular position—are determined by the broader organizational context. The organizational structure, the functional specialization and division of labor, and the formal reward system *dictate the major content of a given office.* What the occupant of that office is supposed to do, with and for whom, is given by these and other properties of the organization itself. Although other human beings are doing the "supposing" and rewarding, the structural properties of organization are sufficiently stable so that they can be treated as independent of the particular persons in the role set. For such properties as size, number of echelons, and rate of growth, the justifiable abstraction of organizational properties from individual behavior is even more obvious.[17] [Italics added]

In answer to the question posed at the beginning of this section, therefore, we can say at this point that organizations are real. They are real to the extent that strictly organizational factors account for part of the behavior of individuals at all times in organizations. The exact proportion of the variation in individual behavior accounted for by the organizational factors, as opposed to interactional or individual factors, cannot be exactly specified at the present time. The position taken here is that organizational factors can account for *all* the variation in behavior in some circumstances (this is the purpose of training and indoctrination programs in many kinds of organizations). In others, organizational factors interact with other behavioral determinants. It is hoped that research in organizations will begin to provide data regarding the conditions under which these factors operate. At present, unfortunately, the analysis must rest on these verbal descriptions.

Organizations as Actors

The treatment of organizations as realities has thus far been concerned with the behavior of individuals. An even more basic issue is whether or not organizations have an existence of their own, above and beyond the behavior and performance of individuals within them. The question becomes, "Do organizations act?" The answer is again in the affirmative and is the second reason that viewing organizations just as interacting individuals is too narrow a conceptualization.

Some characteristics of the definitions discussed above provide indications of the existence of organizations. The fact that organizations persist over time and replace members suggests that they are not dependent on particular individuals. When a new member enters an organization, he

---

[17] Robert L. Kahn, Donald M. Wolfe, Robert P. Quinn, J. Dieddrick Snock, and Robert A. Rosenthal, *Organizational Stress* (New York: John Wiley & Sons, Inc., 1964), p. 31.

is confronted with a social structure—which includes the interaction patterns among organizational members and these members' expectations, toward him—and a sct of organizational expectations for his own behavior. It does not matter who the particular individual is; the organization has established a system of norms and expectations to be followed regardless of who its personnel happen to be, and it continues to exist regardless of personnel turnover. This is not to suggest that personnel do not have an impact on organizations. Rather, the contributions of individuals are incorporated into the organizational system. But the system persists over time and across individuals.

There is another sense in which organizations have an existence. When we think about decision making, it is typically at the level of the individual using a variety of techniques to arrive at a decision. Many decisions in organizations, however, are organizational decisions. That is, the organization has set the parameters for decision making and the individual simply follows the procedures that have been prescribed for him. These rather programmed types of decisions are usually at a low level. But more important decisions about future organizational directions and policies are also strongly influenced by organizational factors. The whole area of tradition and precedent, power position within the organization, and the organization's relationship with its environment have an impact on how individuals within the organizational hierarchy make decisions on behalf of the organization. Organizational considerations thus pervade the decision-making process.

When we hear statements such as "It is company policy," "Z State University never condones violence," or "Trans–Rhode Island Airline greets you with a smile," these are recognizable as being about organizations. Organizations do have policies, do and do not condone violence, and may or may not greet you with a smile. They also manufacture goods, administer policies, and protect the citizenry. These are organizational actions and involve properties of organizations, not individuals. They are carried out by individuals, even in the case of computer-produced letters, which are programmed by individuals—but the genesis of the actions remains in the organization.[18]

18 A basic difficulty in answering the question of whether or not organizations are real is methodological in nature. Since we tend to think of information about organizations as coming from individuals, it is difficult to conceptualize organizations as entities. Paul F. Lazarsfeld and Herbert Menzel ("On the Relationship Between Individual and Collective Properties" in Amitai Etzioni, ed., *Complex Organizations: A Sociological Reader* [New York: Holt, Rinehart & Winston, Inc., 1961]; See also Allen H. Barton, *Organizational Measurement* [New York: College Entrance Examination Board, 1961] for a related discussion) have developed a framework from which distinctions between individual and collective (organizational) properties may be drawn. They note that information from individuals can be utilized to determine organizational properties by using averages, standard

Organizational characteristics are of vital importance in regard to the behavior of individuals in organizations. That is, if organizations have characteristics of their own, and if organizational characteristics affect the behavior of members apart from the members' own contributions to their behavior, then organizational characteristics must be understood if we are to understand human behavior in general.

PERSPECTIVES ON ORGANIZATIONS

Let us begin our analysis of organizations by examining the different perspectives on organizations that are dominant in the field.[19] The topic could have been "theories of organizations," since this is the term usually given to the discussion that follows. It is clear, however, that the field of organizations does not have a theory, or even a set of theories, in the sense of a set of empirically verified propositions that are logically linked. We do have a number of perspectives or conceptualizations that are becoming increasingly crystallized and increasingly based upon previous research; they are therefore subject to empirical investigation.

The purpose of this section is to identify the major perspectives on organizations, trace their origins and current status, and attempt their

---

deviations, correlation coefficients, and other such figures. Information about the relationships between members of the organization also describes the organization. Information can also be gathered that is *not* dependent upon individuals. Information bearing directly on organizational characteristics can be obtained from records, informants, national data sources, etc. The informants may be organizational members, but they relate characteristics of the organization and not of themselves. This approach can be seen in the recent work of: Peter M. Blau, "The Hierarchy of Authority in Organizations," *American Journal of Sociology*, Vol. 73, No. 4 (January 1968), 453–67; Peter M. Blau, Wolf V. Heydebrand, and Robert E. Stauffer, "The Structure of Small Bureaucracies," *American Sociological Review*, Vol. 31, No. 2 (April 1966), 179–91; D. S. Pugh, D. J. Hickson, C. R. Hinings, and C. Turner, "Dimensions of Organizational Structure," *Administrative Science Quarterly*, Vol. 13, No. 1 (June 1968), 65–105; Marshall W. Meyer, "Two Authority Structures of Bureaucratic Organization," *Administrative Science Quarterly*, Vol. 13, No. 2 (September 1968), 211–28; Meyer, "Automation and Bureaucratic Structure," *American Journal of Sociology*, Vol. 74, No. 3 (November 1968), 256–64; Meyer, "Expertness and the Span of Control," *American Sociological Review*, Vol. 33, No. 6 (December 1968), 944–51; Richard H. Hall, J. Eugene Haas, and Norman J. Johnson, "Organizational Size, Complexity, and Formalization," *American Sociological Review*, Vol. 32, No. 6 (December 1967), 903–12; and William A. Rushing, "The Effects of Industry Size and Division of Labor on Administration," *Administrative Science Quarterly*, Vol. 12, No. 2 (September 1967), 273–95.

[19] We are not alone in shying away from "theories" and using "perspectives." Charles Perrow, in *Organizational Analysis: A Sociological Perspective* (Belmont, Calif.: Wadworth Publishing Co., Inc., 1970), adapts the same strategy.

integration. We will have to be rather abstract at first, returning to more concrete terms as the specific topics are discussed. A fairly large amount of recent literature has attempted to develop some order within the world of organizational theories.[20] We will not dwell on the historical antecedents of the various perspectives, even though this can be a rewarding experience. The current status of a set of ideas appears to be a much more relevant basis for discussion, since this is the foundation on which research and practice are based.

The major perspectives to be dealt with can be placed in two basic categories—a somewhat oversimplified method, but a useful way to conceptualize past and present thought. These basic approaches are those that view the organization as an *open system* or as a *closed system.*[21] Several other perspectives to be included in the discussion can in general be subsumed under the open- or closed-system perspectives, but have unique characteristics that deserve separate examination.

The Organization as a Closed System

The closed-system model views organizations as instruments designed for the pursuit of clearly specified goals. Organizational arrangements and decisions are geared to goal achievement and are directed toward making the organization more and more rational in the pursuit of its goal. This perspective is traditionally tied to Max Weber's early writings on bureaucracy. While Weber has been overly criticized for ignoring factors that would deflect an organization from a pure closed system, much of his writing is concerned with how organizations can structure themselves for the utmost rationality.

Weber's ideal type of bureaucracy is one in which the goals and purposes are clear and explicit. Organizational rules, procedures, and regulations are derived from the goals in a manner that says, "If this is the goal, then this is the most rational procedure for achieving it." The tasks to be performed in the achievement of the goal are subdivided among the members of the organization so that each member has a limited sphere of activity that is matched to his own competency. Of-

---

20 See, for example, Paul R. Lawrence and Jay W. Lorsch, *Organization and Environment: Managing Differentiation and Integration* (Cambridge: Harvard Graduate School of Business Administration, 1967), pp. 159–210; Derek S. Pugh, "Modern Organization Theory: A Psychological and Sociological Study," *Psychological Bulletin,* Vol. 66, No. 21 (October 1966), 235–51; David J. Hickson, "A Convergence in Organizational Theory," *Administrative Science Quarterly,* Vol. 11, No. 2 (September 1966), 224–37; and Thompson, *Organizations in Action.*

21 This distinction and terminology follows Thompson, *Organizations in Action,* pp. 4–7.

fices (positions) are arranged in a pyramidal hierarchy, with each office having more authority than those below it. Decision making is based upon officially established rules and criteria that are attached to the position. If, at a particular level, a decision is required that is beyond the realm of that position, it is passed up to the next level. Members participate in the organization on the basis of contractual (written or otherwise) agreements, and the participation is based upon remuneration, which is typically in the form of a wage or salary. (Voluntary organizations are obviously another matter. They have not been examined carefully from this perspective.) The person fills the office or position, so that in an important way it does not matter who the person is, since his behavior is guided by the organizationally established normative order. Selection for membership is based on the person's technical competence—the combination of the individual's skills and the requirements of the position determining who shall be employed and in what position. Interpersonal relationships are maintained on an impersonal basis, so that socio-emotional elements do not intrude into organizational operations.

It has been demonstrated that these elements do not appear together in reality.[22] It is also clear that this is too limited a perspective on organizations from any other bases. Nonetheless, this approach to organizations persists in the literature. A recent example is Jerald Hage's attempt to develop an "axiomatic theory of organizations." [23] The variables selected for inclusion in the theory and the indicators used to measure these variables reflect a closed-system approach.

Hage considers four organizational ends or goals.[24] The first is adaptiveness, or flexibility, and is to be measured by the number of new programs per year and the number of new techniques adopted per year. Flexibility in other contexts usually refers to adaptation to external influences or other disturbing factors, and Hage suggests that environmental influences are important. At the same time, however, new programs and new techniques can be developed on the basis of internal considerations. The second organizational end is production, or effectiveness, measured by the number of units produced per year and the rate of increase in number of units produced per year. This is clearly an internal consideration. The third goal is efficiency, or the cost factor, and is measured by the cost per unit of output per year and the amount of idle resources per year. The final end is job satisfaction, or morale. This is measured by the employee's satisfaction with working conditions and

[22] See Richard H. Hall, "The Concept of Bureaucracy: An Empirical Assessment," *American Journal of Sociology*, Vol. 69, No. 1 (July 1963), 32–40.

[23] Jerald Hage, "An Axiomatic Theory of Organizations," *Administrative Science Quarterly*, Vol. 10, No. 3 (December 1965), 289–320.

[24] *Ibid.*, p. 293.

by the rate of turnover in job occupants per year. These ends involve more than just output; basically, they reflect internal organizational factors, with only minimal concern paid to external considerations. They are also part of a conceptual model that views the organization as a system in and of itself.

The "closedness" of this approach is emphasized when the means to these ends are discussed. Hage gives four organizational means.[25] The first is complexity, or specialization, which is measured by the number of occupational specialties and the level of training required for them. Complexity is necessary because "organizations must divide work into jobs in order to achieve their specific objectives." This statement is, of course, extremely close to Weber's position. The second means is centralization, or hierarchy of authority, and is measured by the proportion of occupations or jobs whose holders participate in decision making and the number of areas in which they participate. The third means area is formalization, or standardization, which involves the number of jobs that are codified and the range of variation allowed within jobs. The final means is stratification, or the status system. This is measured by the differences in income and prestige among jobs and the rate of mobility between low- and high-ranking jobs or status levels. These means, as might be expected, are totally internal to the organization.

From these ends and means, Hage develops a set of propositions and corollaries, indicated in Table 1–1. Whether or not these are empirically valid is not the issue at this point. What is important is the perspective taken that organizations can be understood on the basis of these basically internal factors.[26] As we shall demonstrate, many of the factors that Hage labels as means are in fact related. The ends part of the equation is probably too internally oriented to satisfy most organizational analysts. At the same time, Hage's supporting evidence is strong and provides partial substantiation for the propositions and corollaries he derives. Undoubtedly, however, factors other than the means and ends discussed have an effect on them.

Organizations are not closed systems for the sake of being closed systems. It is at this point that the idea of rationality within the closed system must be introduced. The closed-system perspective is a way of approaching and optimizing organizational rationality—linking means to ends. Thompson catches the essence of this point when he notes, "The rational model of an organization results in everything being functional—making

25 *Ibid.*, pp. 293–94.

26 It should be noted that most of Hage's research does not rely exclusively on the closed-system approach. See, for example, Michael Aiken and Jerald Hage, "Organizational Interdependence and Intra-organizational Structure," *American Sociological Review*, Vol. 33, No. 6 (December 1968), 912–29.

TABLE 1–1 MAJOR PROPOSITIONS AND COROLLARIES OF THE THEORY

Major Propositions:
  I. The higher the centralization, the higher the production.
  II. The higher the formalization, the higher the efficiency.
  III. The higher the centralization, the higher the formalization.
  IV. The higher the stratification, the lower the job satisfaction.
  V. The higher the stratification, the higher the production.
  VI. The higher the stratification, the lower the adaptiveness.
  VII. The higher the complexity, the lower the centralization.

Derived Corollaries:
  1. The higher the formalization, the higher the production.
  2. The higher the centralization, the higher the efficiency.
  3. The lower the job satisfaction, the higher the production.
  4. The lower the job satisfaction, the lower the adaptiveness.
  5. The higher the production, the lower the adaptiveness.
  6. The higher the complexity, the lower the production.
  7. The higher the complexity, the lower the formalization.
  8. The higher the production, the higher the efficiency.
  9. The higher the stratification, the higher the formalization.
  10. The higher the efficiency, the lower the complexity.
  11. The higher the centralization, the lower the job satisfaction.
  12. The higher the centralization, the lower the adaptiveness.
  13. The higher the stratification, the lower the complexity.
  14. The higher the complexity, the higher the job satisfaction.
  15. The lower the complexity, the lower the adaptiveness.
  16. The higher the stratification, the higher the efficiency.
  17. The higher the efficiency, the lower the job satisfaction.
  18. The higher the efficiency, the lower the adaptiveness.
  19. The higher the centralization, the higher the stratification.
  20. The higher the formalization, the lower the job satisfaction.
  21. The higher the formalization, the lower the adaptiveness.

Limits Proposition:
VIII. Production imposes limits on complexity, centralization, formalization,
      stratification, adaptiveness, efficiency, and job satisfaction.

Source: Jerald Hage, "An Axiomatic Theory of Organizations," Administrative
Science Quarterly, *Vol. 10, No. 3 (December 1965), 300.*

a positive, indeed an optimum, contribution to the overall result. All
resources are appropriate resources, and their allocation fits a master
plan. All action is appropriate action, and its outcomes are predictable." [27]

[27] Thompson, *Organizations in Action,* p. 6.

A Critique of Closed-System Perspective

The organization, approached from this viewpoint, must make a perfect link between ends and means. It can do so internally within the closed-system perspective. It can arrange itself so that the conditions Thompson suggests can be achieved. Obviously, this is more easily said than done. In developing his critique of the rational model, Thompson says that in order to be as rational as possible, organizations must "buffer" themselves from environmental influences, anticipate those environmental changes that cannot be buffered against, and ration their resources when the environmental influences cannot be controlled.[28] This suggests strongly that *organizations are forced to move away from a purely rational model*. It also brings up the importance of environmental factors as they impinge upon the organization, a point that will be taken up shortly. Before turning to the external situation and its impact on the organization, let us look at two "internal" factors that diminish the utility of the closed-system approach.

Stanley H. Udy, Jr. has identified a series of "bureaucratic" characteristics and shown the manner in which they are or are not associated with each other.[29] In keeping with Weber's own terminology, Udy refers to the "rational bureaucracy" in his approach. Udy's research demonstrates that bureaucratic elements in an organization are not necessarily related to rationality. Using data from 150 organizations engaged in the production of material goods in 150 nonindustrial societies, Udy found that while the bureaucratic elements he identified were related to each other, they were not related to the characteristics that he termed rational. He concludes, "Bureaucracy and rationality tend to be mutually inconsistent in the same formal organization." [30] Udy means that the presence of a hierarchy or a specialized administrative staff is not related to a performance emphasis or other indicators of an emphasis on goal attainment. Increased bureaucratization, then, does not lead to greater rationality, at least to the extent that many proponents of the closed-system model would have us believe.

My own research on contemporary organizations leads to a similar conclusion. I found that the bureaucratic elements were basically unrelated to each other.[31] These findings suggest that when organizations

[28] *Ibid.*, p. 19.
[29] Stanley H. Udy, Jr., " 'Bureaucracy' and 'Rationality' in Weber's Organization Theory," *American Sociological Review*, Vol. 24, No. 6 (December 1959), 791–95.
[30] *Ibid.*, p. 794.
[31] Hall, "Concept of Bureaucracy."

are viewed as closed systems, elements within the system are not necessarily arranged in a neat, harmonious fashion. Instead, weak and negative relationships are found among elements that are supposed to be related to each other. The approach that both Udy and I used is in essence an examination of the relevance of the closed-system approach by determining how elements of the system interrelate. The findings from both sets of studies suggest that the closed system cannot be viewed as being closed unless a chaos perspective toward the social order is taken. That is, given the weak and negative relationships among elements, the nature of organizations must be accounted for by factors other than those internal to the system itself. If this were not the case, assuming that organizations will attempt to minimize conflicts and disharmonies between elements, there would be strong pressures to bring these elements into harmonious and nonconflictive relationships with each other. This is not to say that simply identifying the factors contributing to these relationships will eliminate conflicts and disharmonies within organizations. This is not the case, nor, as we shall see, is it necessarily desirable to do so. Rather, these data suggest that the search for the bases of organizational structures and processes must include more than just elements within the organization itself.

The second factor internal to the organization that throws doubt on the total utility of the closed-system approach is the nature of the organizational members themselves. The closed-system approach tends to assume that people will act in accordance with the organization's desires. Most of the time, this is probably the case. However, there is enough deviation from norm and role expectations to make the idea of organizational members as well-oiled machines extremely naive.

James March and Herbert Simon's discussion of the shortcomings of viewing humans as machines in a closed-system perspective has become a classic in the field.[32] March and Simon note that an individual must be motivated to participate and produce in the organizational setting. The individual is confronted with a series of action alternatives that he could pursue. Each of these alternatives has consequences for the individual, and the consequences in turn are valued differentially by him. These values are affected by the identification patterns of the individual. For instance, he can identify with his own work group, which may or may not have values that coincide with those of the organization. The individual is also confronted with the dynamics of the group, perhaps in a situation in which competition is required by the organization or develops on its own. In either case, individual behavior is different from what it would be under conditions of cooperation.

[32] March and Simon, *Organizations*, pp. 34–171.

At the same time, the individual has external sources of identification, such as his family, union, or professional organization. The recent literature on professionals in organizations strongly suggests that membership in a profession strongly influences the individual employed in an organization.[33] He brings his professional values with him into the organization, and if the organization wants him to do something that is in violation of his professional norms and values, he is apt to reject or substantially alter the organizational requirements. The professional or trade union member is usually in the "enviable" position of being able to leave an organization for another very readily, because there are probably many other organizations ready and willing to pay for his services.

The organization member can also identify with the organization itself. This is fine, but only up to a point. If it is carried too far, or if the identification is with organizational means and not ends, it can be dysfunctional for the organization as well as for the individual. Merton's concept of the bureaucratic personality, with its rigid adherence to rules, inflexibility with clients, and absence of adaptability, and Victor Thompson's concept of "bureaupathology," with many of the same characteristics, are indicative of the manner in which overadherence to and identification with organizational means can deflect the individual from the behavior that is most beneficial to the organization.[34]

March and Simon also point out that there are limits to the individual's cognitive abilities, thus restricting the extent to which he can make rational decisions in or out of the organizational context. March and Simon propose that decisions are *satisficing*, rather than optimal.[35] That is, given the limitations of the human being, even if he is assisted by computers, the decisions that are made in an organization are not as optimal as they would be if humans had access to, and the ability to interpret, all relevant information before making a decision. The norm of rationality itself cannot therefore be viewed as a set standard, but rather as a guideline from which deviation is expected.

The criticism of the closed-system perspective thus far has concentrated on factors that limit its utility from within the organization. As I implied earlier, the major problem with this approach is that it tends to ignore external considerations. Katz and Kahn state:

---

[33] See, for example, William Kornhauser, *Scientists in Industry* (Berkeley: University of California Press, 1963), and *Administrative Science Quarterly*, Vol. 10, No. 1 (June 1965), entire issue.

[34] Robert K. Merton, "Bureaucratic Structure and Personality," *Social Forces,* Vol. 18, No. 4 (May 1940), 560–68; and Victor Thompson, *Modern Organizations* (New York: Alfred A. Knopf, Inc., 1961), pp. 152–77.

[35] March and Simon, *Organizations,* pp. 140–41.

The major misconception is the failure to recognize fully that the organization is continually dependent upon inputs from the environment and that the inflow of materials and human energy is not constant. The fact that organizations have built-in protective devices to maintain stability and that they are notoriously difficult to change should not obscure the realities of the dynamic interrelationships of any social structure with its social and natural environment. The very efforts of the organization to maintain a constant external environment produce changes in organizational structure. The reactions to changed inputs to mute their possible revolutionary implications also results in changes.[36]

Katz and Kahn go on to note that there are additional misconceptions inherent in the closed-system model. They mention that there are more ways than one to produce a given outcome, and thus internal arrangements could vary rather widely to give rise to a common end. They also suggest that it is erroneous to view environmental influences as "error variances." [37] The environmental factors cannot be controlled in research or practice. Further, the closed-system approach ignores the importance of feedback for the information system of an organization.

Experience and practice in organizations indicate that the environment *does* play a major role in what happens within an organization. Since both input and output are directly related to the environment and are major components to be included in any analysis, the closed-system perspective is, almost by definition, inadequate for a comprehensive understanding of organizations. From an empirical standpoint, too little of the variance within organizations is explained by internal factors. But despite all these shortcomings, the perspective persists in the literature and in practice, apparently for the reason that the closed-system approach does explain some of what organizations do. Organizations do try to maximize rationality, even if they are aware that they can attain only "satisficing" decisions. They do try to buffer, level, and smooth out environmental fluctuations. Since organizational actions are at least partially based on a closed-system perspective, it is a necessary component of the organizational analyst's repertoire, even though he recognizes that the technique will not be totally successful. Furthermore, the relationships found by Udy and Hall and suggested by Hage, whether positive or negative, are relationships. That is, an increase or decrease in the intensity of one internal factor is related to an increase or decrease in the intensity of another. Whether the source of the change is internal or external to the organization is thus irrelevant if the relationship is predictable. Predictable relationships are a prerequisite for theory or practice. The closed-system perspective would seem to be a similar

36 Katz and Kahn, *Social Psychology of Organizations*, p. 26.
37 *Ibid.*, p. 27.

prerequisite for the insights provided by other perspectives. With this in mind, let us examine the open-system perspective.

The Organization as an Open System

The distinction between the closed- and open-system approaches to organizations has its modern roots in the work of Alvin Gouldner. Gouldner distinguished between the "rational" and "natural-system" models of organizations, the terms largely corresponding to our closed- and open-system perspectives, respectively. Gouldner describes the open-system approach as follows:

> The natural-system model regards the organization as a "natural whole," or system. The realization of the goals of the system as a whole is but one of several important needs to which the organization is oriented.[38]

One of these important needs is survival, which can lead to neglect or distortion of goal-seeking behavior. Organizational changes are seen as relatively unplanned, adaptive responses to threats to organizational equilibrium. The organization is seen as emergent, with organizational goals playing a relatively minor role in the directions in which the organization emerges. The natural-system approach also stresses the interdependence of the parts of organizations, noting that even a planned change in one part will have important, and usually unanticipated, ramifications for the rest of the system.

Gouldner's major concern is with developments within the organization that deflect it from the rational model. In a sense, this approach still views the organization as a closed system, since the emphasis is on developments and attempts to maintain homeostatic conditions within the organization. Gouldner hints at the importance of environmental factors but does not develop this consideration very far. It is clear from studies such as Michel Crozier's analysis of two French organizations that the *general environment* surrounding an organization has a tremendous impact on how it is structured and operated, as well as on the goals it purports to seek.[39] The role of *other organizations* on the behavior of a focal organization has been clearly documented in the analyses of William Evan, Litwak and Hylton, and others.[40] Organizations are con-

[38] Gouldner, "Organizational Analysis," p. 405.

[39] Michel Crozier, *The Bureaucratic Phenomenon* (Chicago: The University of Chicago Press, 1964).

[40] William M. Evan, "The Organization-Set," in James D. Thompson, ed., *Approaches to Organizational Design* (Pittsburgh: University of Pittsburgh Press, 1966), pp. 173–91; and Eugene Litwak and Lydia F. Hylton, "Interorganizational

fronted from inside and outside with conditions that lead to the "natural" forms of development described by Gouldner. Survival is thus based on adaptation to both internal and external forces.

The open-system perspective has been more fully developed in the work of Katz and Kahn. They suggest nine common characteristics shared by all open systems:

1. *The importation of energy.* New supplies of energy are brought into the organization in the form of people and materials. This energy is supplied by other organizations or the general environment.
2. *The through-put.* This is simply the work that is done in the system (organization). The input is altered in some way as materials are processed or people are served.
3. *The output.* Whatever emerges from an organization is utilized, consumed, rejected, etc., by the environment.
4. *Systems as cycles of events.* Products sent into the environment are the basis for the source of energy for the repeating of the event. Industry uses labor and materials to produce a product that is sold. The income derived is used to buy more materials and labor. The voluntary organization can do something for its members that leads them to continue to contribute energy to the organization. In both cases the importation of new energy into the organization triggers a new cycle. Each cycle may be composed of subsystems or be a part of a larger system. At the same time, the cycles themselves are affected by changes in the total system.
5. *Negative entropy.* Organizations attempt to import more energy than they expend. Energy can be stockpiled to avoid the condition of using more energy than is imported. (The latter situation leads to organizational death.)
6. *Information input, negative feedback, and the coding process.* The information coming into an organization is coded and selected so that the organization is not inundated with more than it requires. Information provides signals from the environment, and negative

---

Analysis," *Administrative Science Quarterly,* Vol. 6, No. 4 (March 1962), 395–420. See also Burton R. Clark, "Interorganizational Patterns in Education," *Administrative Science Quarterly,* Vol. 10, No. 2 (September 1965), 224–37; Harold Guetzkow, "Relations Among Organizations," in Raymond V. Bowers, ed., *Studies on Behavior in Organizations: A Research Symposium* (Athens, Ga.: University of Georgia Press, 1966), pp. 13–44; Sol Levine and Paul White, "Exchange and Interorganizational Relationships," *Administrative Science Quarterly,* Vol. 5, No. 4 (March 1961), 583–601; and Roland L. Warren, "The Interorganizational Field as a Focus for Investigation," *Administrative Science Quarterly,* Vol. 12, No. 3 (December 1967), 369–419.

feedback indicates deviations from what the environment desires. It is a control mechanism.

7. *The steady state and dynamic homeostasis.* Systems tend to maintain their basic character, attempting to control threatening external factors. As growth and expansion occur, basic system characteristics tend to remain constant. Under conditions of extreme growth or expansion, a new character may develop that will serve as a new homeostatic basis.

8. *Differentiation.* There is a tendency toward elaboration of roles and specialization of function.

9. *Equifinality.* Multiple means to the same ends exist within organizations. As knowledge increases, the number of relevant means may be reduced, but there will still be more than one way to accomplish objectives.[41]

The Katz and Kahn approach is built around the general systems model that is increasingly finding favor in many disciplines.[42] Although some of the terminology and concepts are obviously difficult to operationalize and use, the development of their system demonstrates the essence of the open-system approach. Organizations are affected by what comes into them in the form of input, by what transpires inside the organization, and by the nature of the environmental acceptance of the organization and its output. Understanding organizations involves much more than understanding goals and the arrangements that are developed for their accomplishment. At a later point, we will consider in depth the nature of the impact on organizations of both internally and externally based influences. Meanwhile, we must recognize the open-system perspective for its relevance in directly specifying these elements as important for organizational analysis.

A Critique of the Open-System Perspective

The open-system model is obviously much broader in its conceptual scope than is the closed-system approach This breadth is vital for better understanding and operation of organizations. At the same time, as Etzioni suggests, the model is much more "exacting and expensive" when used for research.[43] Few researchers have the tools or the ability to take

41 Katz and Kahn, *Social Psychology of Organizations,* pp. 19–26.
42 See Walter Buckley, *Sociology and Modern Systems Theory* (Englewood Cliffs, N.J.: Prentice-Hall, Inc., 1967); and Walter Buckley, ed., *Modern Systems Research for the Behavioral Scientist* (Chicago: Aldine Publishing Company, 1968).
43 Etzioni, *Modern Organizations,* p. 17.

into account all the various components that must be included in even a relatively simple open-system model. The measurement of the various forms of inputs and the consequences of outputs has not been even moderately developed. For the practitioner, a full utilization of the model involves the comprehension and evaluation of the multiple factors that impinge upon his organization. March and Simon have stated that decision making in organizations is based on "bounded rationality." When the full implications of the open-system perspective are taken into consideration, the bounds on rationality become even more apparent.

The open-system perspective suggests that rationality within organizations is or can be drastically impaired and also that events occur without organizational intent—that there is a crescive development of interaction patterns, norms, and structure that occurs apart from the officially intended system. A total acceptance of the open-system approach, especially as proposed by Gouldner, would make it appear that there is actually little need for organizations at all, since things just seem to happen. Rather obviously, this is too extreme a position. The very nature of organizations signifies that they do accomplish certain things. They do alter their inputs and produce outputs and make decisions; and these things are done on a relatively predictable and relatively stable basis. The Katz and Kahn notion of cycles of action suggests that organizational work is not composed of random actions. A basic question, therefore, is: Can the open-system and the closed-system perspectives be reconciled? Can the insights provided by each be combined in some way to yield more insights than does either perspective taken alone? At least partial answers to these questions are provided by James Thompson's recent work.

Thompson develops a set of propositions that describe how organizations act (or should act), given the fact of external and internal constraints on rationality. These propositions specify what organizations can do, in the face of threats to rationality, to stay as rational as possible. For example, "The more sectors in which the organization subject to rationality norms is constrained, the more power the organization will seek over remaining sectors of its task environment." [44] If an organization is constrained in one area, it will seek to reduce constraints in others, giving it more power in the total system than if it did not make such

[44] J. Thompson, *Organizations in Action*, p. 32. The concept of task environment was first proposed by William R. Dill to indicate those components of the environment that are significant or potentially significant for goal setting and goal attainment. The task environment, according to Dill, includes customers, suppliers, competitors, and regulatory groups. See Dill, "Environment as an Influence on Managerial Autonomy," *Administrative Science Quarterly*, Vol. 2, No. 4 (March 1958), 409–43.

an attempt. For example, during an inflationary cycle, an organization with rising costs will seek power to increase its income through raising the prices for its goods and services. This is essentially a trade-off situation. The organization that is unable to gain power in other sectors and is thus totally dominated by the situation around it cannot operate in a rational manner. Most organizations have areas in which their own discretion can operate and therefore can subject themselves to the norm of rationality.

Thompson develops similar propositions about most areas of organizational operations. The content of these propositions is subject to empirical verification, but for our purposes, it does not really matter if the propositions are valid or not. What is important is that they form a basis for bringing the insights of the closed- and open-system approaches together. In essence, *organizations attempt to be rational, controlling their internal operations and environment to the greatest extent possible, but never achieving a totally closed, rational system.* The degree to which the organization is successful in achieving rationality is dependent upon the strength of the internal and external pressures and the organization's capability of control.

Some Other Perspectives

The two basic perspectives we have discussed are the major frameworks upon which most of the writings on organizations can be arranged. Since organizational analysis crosses traditional academic and practice lines, there are additional groupings of perspectives that should be noted. Several schools of thought are identifiable, and we will attempt to show the commonalities and differences between them. Some writers, such as Lawrence and Lorsch, attribute the differences to the analyst's own experiences in organizations; [45] others link them to variations in training and discipline. Derek Pugh has provided a categorization of these schools that will be the basis for the present discussion.[46] The six approaches are management theory, structural theory, group theory, individual theory, technology theory, and economic theory.

Management theory has been largely derived from practicing managers who have attempted to put their experiences on paper for the benefit of other practitioners. The major representatives of this approach are Henri Fayol, Lyndall F. Urwick, Luther Gulick, James Mooney, and

---

[45] Lawrence and Lorsch, *Organization and Environment,* pp. 159–84.
[46] Pugh, "Modern Organization Theory."

Frederick W. Taylor.[47] These writers have offered numerous prescriptions on how organizations ought to be set up for maximum productivity and efficiency. Their major concern has been with principles of specialization, hierarchical arrangements, delegation of authority and responsibility, span of control, and the arrangement of organizational subunits.

These authors, concerned with getting the most out of the organization and its employees, attempt to develop techniques that are applicable to all organizations. They suggest, for example, that "each five to six workers . . . need one first line supervisor; every six first line supervisors, and hence, every forty workers, need one second line supervisor, and so on." [48] Various principles of specialization are offered, such as by purpose, process, clientele, or geographical concentration.

Management theory is in many ways a specialized instance of the broader closed-system approach and has been criticized on many of the same grounds. The nature of the specialization within an organization can be affected by the general culture in which the organization is found, the kinds of personnel employed, the availability of personnel, and the restrictions imposed by labor legislation and union contracts. Management theory tends to ignore or oversimplify the motivations of all levels of employees, assuming at the extreme that all organization members should be viewed as extensions of the machines with which they are working, in the case of manual workers, or as guided solely by job descriptions, in the case of higher-level employees. These writers also assume only one type of authority—that based on hierarchical position. The role of expertise is almost totally ignored or is assumed to coincide perfectly with position.

A more basic problem with this approach is highlighted by Pugh when he states

> The . . . difficulty with management theorists, particularly the common sense ones, is that not being scientists, their statements do not have sufficient precision to enable crucial experiments to be undertaken to test their validity. This is their attraction for the layman, since the proverbs appear to be wise and true for all occasions. But scientific statements are precisely *not* true for *all* occasions, and it is an integral part of the process of science to look for occasions for which they are not true. A scientific hypothesis is essentially a

---

[47] Henri Fayol, *General and Industrial Management* (London: Sir Isaac Pitman, 1949); Lyndall F. Urwick, *The Elements of Administration* (London: Sir Isaac Pitman, 1947); Luther Gulick and Lyndall F. Urwick, eds., *Papers on the Science of Administration* (New York: Institute of Public Administration, Columbia University, 1937); James D. Mooney and Allan C. Reilly, *Onward Industry!* (New York, Harper & Row, Publishers, 1931); and Frederick W. Taylor, *Principles of Scientific Management* (New York: Harper & Row, Publishers, 1911). Pugh places Taylor in another category, but he is as easily and more traditionally placed here.

[48] Etzioni, *Modern Organizations*, p. 23.

falsifiable statement. When the statements of the management theorists are subject to the same scrutiny, and attempts made to operationalize them, it is usually found that they do not stand up to such analysis very well.[49]

Pugh then goes on to note that the proverb, "Increased specialization will lead to greater efficiency," sounds fine, but the basis for specialization remains unspecified.

Etzioni pinpoints the difficulties inherent in this approach when he raises the questions: "Take, for example, building missiles for military use. Should the missile program be assigned to one branch of the armed forces or all three, since missiles can be used on land, sea, and air? Should we have a single missile force because all missile-building requires a common fund of knowledge? Should we build a number of different regional forces because some missiles are built for Europe's defense and some for U.S. defense?" [50]

Management theorists do deal with issues that are central to the understanding of organizations. Their treatment, however, is insufficiently based in reality. While the theorists themselves have real experiences that serve as the basis for their own formulations, the generalizability and basis for the formulations is highly suspect. Since management theory is in many ways a very specific form of the closed-system perspective, it suffers from the same weaknesses.

Structural theorists are the next group identified by Pugh.

> Regularities in such activities as task allocation, the exercise of authority, and coordination of function are developed. Such regularities constitute the organization's structure, and sociologists have studied systematic differences in structure related to variations in such factors as the objectives of ownership, geographical location, and technology of manufacture, which produce the characteristic differences in structure of a bank, a hospital, a mass production factory or a local government department.[51]

Weber, of course, is identified most closely with this approach in his discussions of bureaucracy. Later examinations of the extent to which organizations do or do not conform to the bureaucratic model are in the structuralist tradition.

The major problem in the utilization of the structuralist approach appears to be due to historical developments within the field of organizational analysis itself. Many earlier studies that have become "classics" in their own right came to the justified conclusion that the pure bureau-

---

[49] Pugh, "Modern Organization Theory," p. 238.

[50] Etzioni, *Modern Organizations,* p. 24.

[51] Pugh, "Modern Organization Theory," p. 239. The work of Pugh et al., which will be discussed in some detail later, falls in this category for the most part.

cratic model, when applied to real organizations, led to a whole series of dysfunctions.[52] These dysfunctions exist at both the organizational and individual behavior levels. In retrospect, it is not surprising that there are differences in power among organizational subunits, that some tasks cannot be organized in the same way as other tasks within the organization, or that individuals may overconform to rules and procedures. If organizational structure is assumed to be based only on the bureaucratic model, the structuralist approach is certainly a dead-end street. If, on the other hand, variations in structure are assumed and the sources of variations can be pinpointed, the structuralist approach remains a relevant component for organizational analysis. Burns and Stalker and Lawrence and Lorsch have demonstrated rather clearly that major differences in structure are related to environmental, technological, and internal considerations.[53] These differences are also related to organizational effectiveness.

Pugh points out that the traditional structuralist approach does not take the individual and his motivations and contributions to the organization into consideration. The individual is assumed to be "programmed into" appropriate organizational behaviors. Here again this may have been the case in the past. Few contemporary analysts ignore the individual. He is considered in conjunction with the other factors that are significant for understanding organizations. Organizational structure is one of these factors.

Using just one structural yardstick, whether it be the bureaucratic model or anything else, is clearly rather futile. At the same time, the past misuse of the structural approach should not result in its dismissal for the present analysis. Like management theorists, structural theorists have been the victims of some of the shortcomings of the closed-system approach. In the present analysis the structuralist approach will remain as one of the important and powerful tools, because structural regularities are an important contributor to the differences between organizations.

Partially as a reaction to an extreme emphasis on structure and partly from its own impetus, the third school of theorists, the *group theorists,* arose. Elton Mayo, who directed the now famous (or infamous, depending on one's point of view) Hawthorne studies, and Kurt Lewin and his associates, who followed up with research, are most directly responsible

---

[52] See, for example, Phillip Selznick, *TVA and the Grass Roots* (New York: Harper Torchbook Edition, 1966); Alvin W. Gouldner, *Patterns of Industrial Bureaucracy* (New York: The Free Press, 1954); and Merton, "Bureaucratic Structure and Personality."

[53] See Tom Burns and G. M. Stalker, *The Management of Innovation* (London: Tavistock Publications, 1961); and Lawrence and Lorsch, *Organization and Environment.*

for, and advocates of, this approach.[54] The major premise of this set of theorists is that the work group exerts a tremendous amount of influence on individual behavior, overriding both the organizationally based norms and the individual's own predispositions. Some of the principal conclusions from this approach are:

> . . . the amount of work carried out by a worker is determined not by his physical capability but by his social capacity; non-economic rewards are most important in the motivation and satisfaction of workers, who react to their work situations as groups and not as individuals; the leader is not necessarily the person appointed to be in charge, informal leaders can develop who have more power; the effective supervisor is "employee-centered" and not "job-centered," that is, he regards his job as dealing with human beings rather than with the work; communication and participation in decision making are some of the most significant rewards which can be offered to obtain the commitment of the individual.[55]

These findings, which are correct to some degree for all organizations, have been taken as the basis for an overall organizational theory and also for many prescriptions on how managers ought to manage and how organizations ought to organize.[56] But there are several drawbacks to this use. Foremost is the fact that there is contradictory evidence in regard to group vis-à-vis individual or organizational bases for behavior.[57] Under some conditions, the factors that seem to be the major determinants of behavior are the exact opposite of what the group theorists propose. Pugh points out that these theorists have ignored the important dimension of power in organizational relationships.[58] The evidence used as the basis of the approach comes largely from case studies, and these case studies, according to Lawrence and Lorsch, have generally been carried out in organizations that would provide support for the group theorists' perspective.[59] The group theorists argue that

[54] See Elton Mayo, *The Human Problems of Industrial Civilization* (New York: The Macmillan Company, 1933); Fritz J. Roethlisberger and William J. Dickson, *Management and the Worker* (Cambridge, Mass.: Harvard University Press, 1939); and Kurt Lewin, "Forces Behind Food Habits and Methods of Change," *Bulletin of the National Research Council*, 108 (1943), 35–65.

[55] Pugh, "Modern Organization Theory," p. 241.

[56] See, for example, Rensis Likert, *New Patterns of Management* (New York: McGraw-Hill Book Company, 1961), and Douglas McGregor, *The Human Side of Enterprise* (New York: McGraw-Hill Book Company, 1960).

[57] For a particularly devastating critique of the major empirical basis for this perspective, see Alex Carey, "The Hawthorne Studies: A Radical Criticism," *American Sociological Review*, Vol. 32, No. 3 (June 1967), 403–16.

[58] Pugh, "Modern Organization Theory," p. 241.

[59] Lawrence and Lorsch, *Organization and Environment*, pp. 179–82. This is not meant to imply that the researchers "stacked" their data. It rather represents the kinds of organizations that are receptive to research by university-based scholars.

organizational theory ought to be built around the concept of the group and its effects on the individual and on his behavior in the organization. The group and the processes of group interaction become tools for better organizations, management, and in the long run, society, according to this perspective. This approach does ignore many other highly salient factors, and therefore it cannot stand alone as an organizational theory. But the findings of the research and the perspective taken do contribute to our overall understanding of organizations and thus must be incorporated in any form of systematic overview that is taken.

The next set of theorists is also concerned with the individual, in this case as an individual. Pugh labels as *individual theorists* those who focus their major concern upon the individual and his predispositions, reactions, and personality within the organizational setting.[60] A basic issue in such an approach is the nature of the view of personality that is taken. On the one hand are those of a psychoanalytical bent who see organizations as staffed by members with varying kinds of relationships to their parents, and who, acting in a continual state of development, behave in organizations on the basis of their individual predispositions alone. Others, such as Maslow and Herzberg, view the organization as a means of providing the individual with a set of rewards of varying levels of satisfaction, with the implication that organizations should continually attempt to provide members with the highest (self-growth and self-development) level of motivation and reward possible.[61] While these and other such approaches to individual personality contain elements of plausibility, they have not been sufficiently documented with empirical evidence to allow their total acceptance as the final theory of personality. More important for our purposes, they obviously ignore or totally discount the impact of organizational, wider societal, and generally, even group influences on individual behavior.

The work of March and Simon, a modern classic in the field of organizations, utilizes the individual perspective. They regard the organization as a set of individuals engaged in the decision-making process. While they recognize the importance of organizational constraints on the decision-making process, their framework is built around individual motiva-

---

[60] See Chris Argyris, *Understanding Organizational Behavior* (Homewood, Ill.: Dorsey Press, 1960), and *Integrating the Individual and the Organization* (New York: John Wiley & Sons, Inc., 1964). Barnard, *Functions of the Executive*, could also be placed in this category. Much of this writing could also be placed under the "management theory" rubric, again indicating the difficulties and overlap inherent in attempts to classify multidisciplinary approaches to organizations.

[61] See Frederick Herzberg, Bernard Mausner, and Barbara Snyderman, *The Motivation to Work* (New York: John Wiley & Sons, Inc., 1959); and Abraham H. Maslow, *Eupsychian Management* (Homewood, Ill.: Richard D. Irwin, Inc., 1956).

tions. Their important discussion of the "cognitive limits on rationality" is at the individual psychological level, with important organizational modifiers such as hierarchical and task differentiation.[62] The potential from such an approach is great. It has not been realized to its fullest because of the absence of an empirically grounded set of psychological principles around which individual behavior can be organized. Nevertheless, any total analysis of organizations must include the individual human element. Too frequently, sociologists tend to assume that individual differences are randomly distributed and therefore do not matter in their analyses. The viewpoint to be taken here is that they do in fact matter. Although the focus will not be psychological and there will be little mention of the individual as an individual, the impact of different types of individuals will be included in the perspective developed. In our discussion of types of individuals, the primary focus will be on occupational types, and differences will be considered within a narrow range of variation. Since there is not yet a firm basis on which to align individual differences, it seems appropriate to note that they do exist and make a difference, but not to try to account for every possible individual permutation.

The next perspective is represented by the *technology theorists*. Much of the gist of this approach will be discussed in the chapter on typologies, with the implication that technology is a major factor in the development and form of organizations. Technology is part of the environment, in that organizations can bring technological developments into their systems.[63] It is also part of the internal system of the organization. Woodward's work graphically illustrates the influence of differing forms of technological systems on organizational structure. Thompson's concern with the "core technology" of the organization also emphasizes the importance of this variable, as does Perrow's analytical framework.[64] As would be expected, technology will be included as a component of the perspective to be advanced here. It cannot be given a primary position in the analysis, however, since technology is in interaction with organizational structure, group structure, individual factors, and so on. The work of Trist and his associates has demonstrated that the technical system of an organization interacts with the ongoing social system.[65] In

---

62 March and Simon, *Organizations*, pp. 136–71.

63 See Lawrence and Lorsch, *Organization and Environment*.

64 By "core technology," Thompson means the operations within the organization, or what the organization does, regardless of its nature.

65 E. L. Trist and K. W. Bamforth, "Some Social and Psychological Consequences of the Longwall Method of Goal-Getting," *Human Relations*, Vol. 4, No. 1 (February 1951), 3–38; and F. E. Emery and E. L. Trist, "The Causal Texture of Organizational Environments," *Human Relations*, Vol. 18, No. 1 (February 1965), 21–32.

their studies of coal mining operations, these researchers from the Tavistock Institute conclude that a changed technical system does not immediately alter the organization. It has an effect, but the effect is moderated by what has existed before. The introduction of a similar technological change in an organization with a different basis would have different results. From this standpoint, technology will be a major determinant of the nature of organizations, but not *the* determinant.

The final set of theorists considered by Pugh is the *economic theorists.* This approach typically uses business firms as its basis, but the ideas can be extended to other organizational forms. The basic premise in this perspective is that the organization is an active participant in the economic process, seeking to enhance its position and make economically sound (rational) decisions. Much of the work in this area is an attempt to specify how economically rational decisions can be made under conditions of psychological and sociological variations.[66]

Despite the fact that it is based on simulation models that lack empirical verification,[67] the approach is valuable because it forces the organizational analyst, and particularly the sociologist, to pay attention to economic factors. At face value, economic factors are important to organizations simply as a survival requisite, but they are too often ignored in organizational analyses. It is true that we have no clear understanding of the exact role that economic factors play. If too much attention is given to such factors, many of the dangers of an overly rational view of organizations come into play. If they are ignored, an important component is eliminated. Again, additional information is needed.

A final perspective should be included in this section. The role of *power* as a component of organizational analysis is properly emerging in the literature.[68] Power, including economic power, is clearly an important variable both within the organization and in terms of the organization's transactions with its environment. The allocation of resources and the decision-making process are intimately intertwined with the power process. The organizational structure itself is a power arrangement. While power can be subsumed under some of the other perspectives already mentioned, it is important in its own right. From this perspective, organizations can be viewed as social systems in which power arrangements determine a major part of what occurs. Power struggles

---

[66] See Richard M. Cyert and James G. March, *A Behavioral Theory of the Firm* (Englewood Cliffs, N.J.: Prentice-Hall, Inc., 1963).

[67] Pugh, "Modern Organization Theory," pp. 247.

[68] Amitai Etzioni, in *A Comparative Analysis of Complex Organizations* (New York: The Free Press, 1961), uses power as a major basis for his analytical scheme. For a recent summarization and some empirical studies of the power variable, see Mayer N. Zald, *Organizational Power* (Nashville, Tenn.: Vanderbilt University Press, 1969).

alter these arrangements and are an ongoing part of the organizational system.

Having reviewed the various perspectives that are taken toward organizations and critically evaluated their strengths and weaknesses, we shall try to assemble the information into a coherent whole. Obviously, a simple perspective is empirically untenable and inappropriate. Instead, we must try to incorporate the most relevant components of the various approaches discussed into a working perspective on organizations.

THE PERSPECTIVE OF THIS ANALYSIS

The perspective to be taken in the present analysis is probably already evident from the discussions and criticisms that have been presented. The closed-system perspective, under which most aspect of the management, economic, and structuralist theories can be subsumed, has been shown to be inapplicable in practice because of the many factors that deflect from a total emphasis on and total program built around goal attainment. The open-system approach, which would include most aspects of the group, individual, technological, and power theories, calls attention to the factors affecting organizations in such a way that a focus on attempts at goal attainment would miss most of what goes on in organizations. Interactions between an organization and the relevant components of its environment should be added to the list of factors that would keep an organization from being a totally closed system. At first glance, then, the important deflections that arise when the components of the open-system perspective are considered would seem to negate most of the closed-system approach. But, as Thompson in particular has cogently shown, organizations do in fact try to behave rationally in the face of the multiple conflicting pressures and thus will attempt to control those aspects of their existence, both internal and external, that impinge upon their rational pursuit of goals.

This is only partially adequate as an overall perspective on organizations, however. At times the norm of rationality is not part of the picture. The history of labor–management relations, for example, is filled with cases in which the owner of a small industry has closed the business rather than give in to what he considers unreasonable demands. From the union's viewpoint, the same kind of behavior is evident—demanding something that cannot be achieved, thus forcing the total operation to cease, at least at the particular organization in question. The issue of rationality is further clouded when we consider the fact that organizations can pursue multiple and at times contradictory goals. A case in which an organization is pursuing goals that, while not mutually exclusive, are incompatible given finite resources is the controversy regarding expenditures for the U.S. space program at a time when several domestic areas appear to need large financial outlays.

The Thompson perspective is, therefore, highly relevant when rationality norms are operative. When they are not, one is forced back to some form of the open-system perspective. The organization seeks to survive in whatever way it deems appropriate. Whether it survives or not, as in the case of the small industry and, some would say, the U.S. government, seems largely based on the amount of power the organization has and can retain. Organizations respond to immediate threats to them from within and without. If these can be handled within a rationality framework, the Thompson perspective is highly useful. If, on the other hand, the threat is viewed as severe by the decision makers within the organization, rationality norms may no longer operate and survival norms will become the most salient ones. (Note that survival in this case may be entirely directed away from the original path the organization would pursue if it were truly goal-seeking or rational.)

The key to the point at which rationality norms cease to operate appears to be the power or perceived power of the threat to the organization.[69] When the threat is strong or is perceived to be strong, organizational resources will be deployed to reduce the power of the threat. If the threat is reduced, under norms of rationality, the organization will return to its former employment. This assumes, of course, that the goals themselves do not change under periods of survival pressures. If they do, the changed deployment to achieve a new goal or set of goals will still represent operation under norms of rationality.

The perspective that has been derived, therefore, is that organizations do operate generally under norms of rationality. Under pure rationality norms, the organization's energies would be deployed as illustrated in figure 1–1. Since it has been amply demonstrated in the discussion that

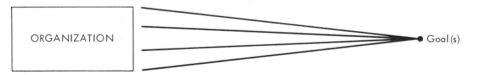

FIG. 1–1   Deployment of Organizational Structure and Processes
Under Pure Rationality Model

69 When decisions between alternative goals within the organization are made, the power process is also operative. See Aaron Wildavsky, *The Politics of the Budgetary Process* (Boston: Little, Brown and Company, 1964), for a discussion of the political processes involved in determining federal budgets.

both external and internal considerations lead to a deflection from the closed rational system, organizations under most conditions will deploy themselves in the manner indicated in figure 1–2. Under severe external

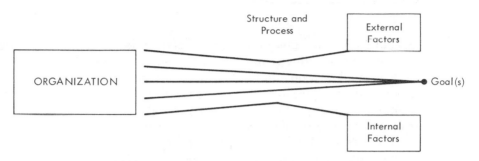

FIG. 1–2   Deployment of Organizational Structure and Processes
Under Typical Open System Model

threat, the deployment will be in the form indicated in figure 1–3. The power of the external and internal pressures and threats is the key variable. Unfortunately, there are no systematic measures available of the power of such threats. The security of the threat is a matter of decision making within the organization. The decision-making process itself is carried out under less than fully rational conditions.

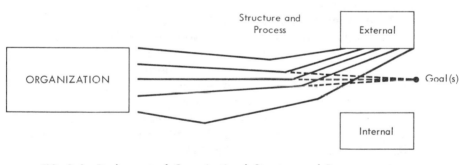

FIG. 1–3   Deployment of Organizational Structure and Processes
Under Powerful Threat Conditions (External)

Figure 1–2 indicates how organizations actually operate under most conditions. The figure is truncated, in that it ignores the transactions at the input and output ends of what the organization does and the feedback mechanisms from these transactions, as well as from those occurring within the system itself—all of which are important factors. Nevertheless, figures 1–2 and 1–3 do illustrate the distillation of the perspectives that have been discussed and that will be followed in the analysis.

SUMMARY AND CONCLUSIONS

Organizations are ubiquitous in society; everyone is familiar with them. But despite this familiarity, the understanding of them is not sufficient to allow people in organizations to realize their own desires, to allow the organization to achieve its goals, nor to allow organizations to accomplish all they could for society. By introducing a definition, noting organizational reality, and deriving a perspective, we hope to raise the level of understanding. Clearly, the sociological view is an incomplete one, but taken in conjunction with other approaches it contributes to a better understanding of organizations and, perhaps, a better society.

A major consideration in the discussion has been the fact that while organizations are goal-seeking entities, many of their energies are deflected from goals as they react to internal and external pressures. The test of this perspective, as well as of the others presented, lies not in logic, but in empirical reality. Enough case studies exist to demonstrate that the perspective makes some sense, but there is not enough evidence to tell us when and why and how it operates. The true test of the perspective lies in research and practice. A partial test will be presented in the chapters that follow.

The plan for the rest of the book is quite simple. In the next chapter we will consider the issue of organizational typologies, and the discussion will enable us to begin to pinpoint the variables that appear to be critical for organizational analysis and thus also for typologies. We will then look carefully at the issue of organizational goals and effectiveness. Organizational structure is the next topic; it will be shown that structure is crucial in determining what actually happens in an organization. We will then turn to the processes within an organization, analyzing those that are most crucial for its operations. Finally, we will consider how the organization interacts with its environment and how organizations are related to social change.

TYPES OF ORGANIZATIONS

2

The United States Department of Justice and the University of Minnesota; the Hennepin County Democratic-Farmer-Labor Party and the Mattachine Society; the General Motors Corporation and the Edgeworth Sand and Gravel Company; the Church of Jesus Christ of the Latter Day Saints and Seagram's Distilling Company. Are these organizations alike or different? What makes them that way? What are the critical *organizational* characteristics that distinguish one from the other or that make them part of the same class of organizations? These are some of the questions that will concern us in this chapter. We will also concern ourselves with the variables that appear to be critical for developing a meaningful typology (or typologies) of organizations. In so doing we will get a clearer picture of the variables that are critical for organizational anaysis.

THE NEED FOR CLASSIFICATION

Discussions of typologies can seem entirely academic.[1] As a matter of fact, they are not. Man must classify phenomena in order to be able to

---

[1] Many analyses of organizations (e.g., that of March and Simon) do not deal with the problem of typologies. This approach, while treating organizations as a

think about them. He must have some framework by which to view the world around him, or else he is surrounded by an unordered kaleidoscope of stimuli, rendering him unable to function at all. The same is true for people working in, around, and on organizations. The organization member makes many decisions that are based on an implicit categorization of organizations. The decision to take a job involves (in good times) the distinction of whether or not the organization is a good place to work; the distinction among sales, production, or administrative organizations might also be a factor.

Organization executives are usually concerned with how to organize for effectiveness, and this too involves a classificatory mode of thought. In an electronics manufacturing firm, for example, rapid expansion forced the issue of reorganization to the forefront. The executives of this company decided to structure the greater part of the organization like a university, rather than like a traditional manufacturing firm. The organization was heavily involved in research and development (even the salesmen participated in the development process), and it was felt that more would be gained from the scientists and engineers if they could work in a semi-collegial setting rather than in a more rigid hierarchy. In this case, the executives classified the organization before they made their decision. Their classification was on the basis of the nature of the work to be performed, rather than the more simplistic profit–nonprofit distinction that could have been made.

The same kinds of classification must be made by the union organizer who is interested in hospital workers. He must classify the nature of their work and organization. In this case much of the work is factory-like. Similarly, some religious organizations are arranged more like military units than like other religious organizations, and decisions are made accordingly. Classification is thus necessary for all those in contact with an organization, particularly those in decision-making positions.

Organizational analysts are well aware of the need for typologies. But at the same time, they are convinced that the relatively simple, prima facie typologies probably add more confusion than clarity. Charles Perrow, for example, notes:

> . . . types of organizations—in terms of their functions in society—will vary as much within each type as between types. Thus, some schools, hospitals,

---

generic entity, makes generalizations difficult, since it is not clear how one set of findings might apply in another situation. For the purposes of the discussion that follows, we will assume that the terms *classifications, typology,* and *taxonomy* are synonomous, even though in a strict sense they are not. For a discussion of this, see Tom Burns, "The Comparative Study of Organizations," in Victor H. Vroom, ed., *Methods of Organizational Research* (Pittsburgh: University of Pittsburgh Press, 1967), p. 119.

banks, and steel companies may have more in common, because of their routine character, than routine and nonroutine schools, routine and nonroutine hospitals, and so forth. To assume that you are holding constant the major variable by comparing several schools or several steel mills is unwarranted until one looks at the technologies employed by the various schools or steel mills.[2]

While we may argue about Perrow's emphasis on technology as the key variable, his point is very important. It is *organizational characteristics* that should serve as the classificatory basis. The great danger in most classificatory schemes is oversimplification. They are based on a single characteristic. Typologies thus derived ". . . can be expanded indefinitely as some new factor is seized upon to indicate an additional class."[3] Such problems with typologies are not limited just to the study of organizations. Tom Burns notes, ". . . the history of sociology, from Montesquieu through Spencer, Marx, and up to Weber himself, is littered with the debris of ruined typologies that serve only as the battleground for that academic street-fighting that so often passes for theoretical discussion."[4]

Typologies that end in debris did not stop at Weber's era. The fact is that there is not a generally accepted typology of organizations, is in spite of the general agreement that a good typology or set of typologies is desperately needed. While simple typologies can be used for limited analyses, such as comparing organizations on the basis of their turnover rates, growth rates, or rates of investment in research and development, classifications of this sort have only a limited usefulness.[5] We end up knowing only one thing about organizations, not understanding them in their rich complexity.

The essence of the typological effort really lies in the determination of the critical variables for differentiating the phenomena under investigation. Since organizations are highly complex entities, classificatory schemes must represent this complexity. An adequate overall classification would have to take into account *the array of external conditions, the total spectrum of actions and interactions within an organization, and the outcome of organizational behaviors.* A review of some of the efforts made to classify organizations will indicate the diversity of variables that have been considered, the relative fruitlessness of the schemes, and some possible future directions for taxonomic efforts.

2 Charles Perrow, "A Framework for the Comparative Analysis of Organizations," *American Sociological Review,* Vol. 32, No. 2 (April 1967), 203.

3 Daniel Katz and Robert L. Kahn, *The Social Psychology of Organizations* (New York: John Wiley & Sons, Inc., 1966), p. 111.

4 Burns, "Comparative Study of Organizations," p. 119.

5 See *Ibid.,* p. 123.

SOME TYPOLOGIES

By Goal or Function

This review will move from some relatively simple schemes to more elaborate formulations. Typical of the simple schemes is that of Talcott Parsons,[6] based on the type of function or goal served by the organization. In this analysis, Parsons is concerned with the linkages between organizations and the wider society. He distinguishes four types of organizations, according to what they contribute to the society.

The first is the *production organization*. As the name implies, this type of organization makes things that are consumed by the society. The second type is that oriented toward *political goals*. It seeks to insure that society attains its valued goals; it generates and allocates power within the society. The third type is the *integrative* organization, whose purposes are settling conflict, directing motivations toward the fulfillment of institutionalized expectations, and ensuring that the parts of society work together. The final form is the *pattern maintenance* organization, which attempts to provide societal continuity through educational, cultural, and expressive activities.

While each of these functions is clearly important for society (other societal goals could be identified), this type of classificatory scheme does not really say much about the organizations involved. In the first place, some organizations can be placed in more than one category. A large corporation, such as General Motors, is clearly a production organization. But it is also important in the allocation of power. Through public relations, corporate contributions to foundations and colleges, and attempts at working with disadvantaged youths, the same corporation falls into the other categories. Its prime effort is undoubtedly production, but these subsidiary concerns make such a classificatory scheme less than totally useful. Even more important, such a typology does not differentiate between the characteristics of organizations themselves. As Perrow noted, there can be as much—or more—organizational variation within such categories as between them.

Katz and Kahn

An elaboration of this same type of approach is provided by Katz

6 Talcott Parsons, *Structure and Process in Modern Society* (New York: The Free Press, 1960), pp. 45–46.

and Kahn.[7] Their first type of organization is the *production* or *economic* organization, which is concerned with "the creation of wealth, the manufacture of goods, and the providing of services for the general public or for specific segments of it." These production organizations can then be subdivided into primary, secondary, and tertiary forms. They provide instrumental integration for the society as a whole through their production of an output that is consumed, often as a basic survival need, by members of the society. The rewards these organizations offer serve as inducements "to keep the collective order working."

The second type is the *maintenance* organization, which is "devoted to the socialization of people for their roles in other organizations and in the larger society." This type can be subdivided into those organizations directly involved in maintenance, such as the church and school, and those concerned with restoration, either through health and welfare activities or rehabilitation and reform. These organizations provide normative integration for the society.

The third type, *adaptive* organizations, "create knowledge, develop and test theories, and, to some extent, apply information to existing problems." The most obvious examples here are universities, through their research functions, and other research organizations. Some artistic organizations would also qualify for this category because of their extension of human understanding and experience. These organizations provide a part of the informational integration that exists in a society.

The final type is the *managerial* or *political* organization. The concern here is with the "adjudication, coordination, and control of resources, people, and subsystems." The state is obviously the most central and visible such organization. Through its power to use and control force, the state is the central power source. Other organizations in this type would be government subsystems, pressure groups, labor unions, and special-interest organizations that represent such diverse groups as doctors, educators, and farmers. When penal institutions are viewed as law-enforcement agencies, they too would be political organizations.

This last point illustrates a difficulty with this formulation. Penal institutions are also clearly maintenance organizations in many cases. Both law-enforcement and rehabilitation orientations can be found within the same organizations, suggesting that the differentiations are something less than clear-cut. Katz and Kahn recognize the likelihood that a single organization will engage in more than one major function, either as an explicit program, as in the case of universities with their split between teaching and research, or as an adjunct to their major

---

[7] Katz and Kahn, *Social Psychology*, pp. 111–28.

function, as in the case of oil companies seeking protective tax legislation (a political activity) so that they may more effectively engage in production.

Katz and Kahn go beyond classifying organizations according to their major functions. They look at organizational characteristics as they interact with these major functions. Noting the seemingly limitless dimensions along which organizations can vary, they select four characteristics that seem to them basic for organizational operations. The first of these is the nature of the "through-put." Here the differentiation is between organizations that transform *objects* and those that transform *people*. A basic distinction here involves the fact that the people being transformed, even in prison-like situations, must be motivated to participate in the organization. The organization's staff must be able to react to an acting object. A second major difference is that people-processing organizations do not sell their outputs directly in the marketplace. Support comes indirectly, through taxes, subsidies, or gifts; and the output is consumed indirectly, through hiring practices or the return of well patients to the community. Here again, the distinction is not absolute, since production organizations must also deal with the human element.

The second organizational differentiation is between *expressive* and *instrumental orientations* on the part of organization members. Expressive orientations are characteristic of organizations in which members participate for some intrinsic satisfaction gained from their participation, while an instrumental orientation is one in which participation is for the purpose of receiving some reward that will then allow intrinsic satisfactions to be sought outside the organization. The expressive end of the continuum can be represented by organizations whose members come together for the sole purpose of engaging in a commonly enjoyed activity, such as model railroading or weightlifting, while the extreme of the instrumental orientation is characterized by a simple desire to receive a paycheck at the end of the week. Here again, there are relatively few pure types, since more instrumental orientations can enter almost any type of expressive activity (note the wide variety of motivations that people express for attending religious services), and people can come to enjoy even the most repetitious of assembly-line tasks.[8]

The third basis of differentiation concerns the *organizational structure* itself. Katz and Kahn suggests that organizations vary according to the degree to which their boundaries are open and permeable; the degree to which the structure is elaborated, both horizontally and vertically, into subunits and hierarchical levels; and the nature of the allocation

---

[8] See Charles R. Walker and Robert Guest, *The Man on the Assembly Line* (Cambridge, Mass.: Harvard University Press, 1952), p. 77.

system within the organization. This last differentiation refers to the extent to which rewards are distributed equally to organization members; the cooperative would lie at one end of the continuum, while the private organization that operates solely for the benefit of owners would lie at the other. Most organizations, again, fit in somewhere between these extremes. The allocation process is, of course, a source of conflict within the organization, and the presence of conflicting groups (management–labor) is another aspect of structural differentiation.

The final basis of differentiation is the manner in which organizations attempt to *utilize the energy or resources at their disposal*. This ranges from those organizations seeking to maintain an equilibrium, in terms of not expanding or contracting the amount of input or output, to those that seek to maximize the utilization of input so that more resources are retained in the organization than are expended. An example of the former extreme would be a corporation with an unchanging supply and market situation, which attempts to return a consistent profit to the owners over time. The latter extreme is represented by organizations that attempt to capture larger and larger shares of their market at increasingly lower costs. In a rapidly changing social environment, there would be a strong tendency for organizations to fall at the nonequilibrium end of the continuum.

Katz and Kahn then discuss the interplay between these organizational dimensions and the categorization based on societal functions performed. They argue that the societal functions have an impact on the way the organizational factors form configurations. While the relationships between the larger society and organizations are certainly important, the overlap and ambiguities present in the classification by major functions are so great that the distinction itself becomes practically meaningless. Later in this chapter, we will turn to a consideration of factors that appear to make more of a difference than those in the approach of Parsons and Katz and Kahn. Although the organizational characteristics that Katz and Kahn discuss are quite relevant dimensions along which organizations vary, the goals-and-functions approach does not seem to be a sufficiently discriminating classificatory basis.

Etzioni and Blau-Scott

The next set of typology schemes moves away from the reliance on an a priori differentiation between major societal functions. These schemes, two of which will be considered here utilize different sets of classificatory bases, each, however, also involving a single principle.

Etzioni and Blau and Scott made almost simultaneous attempts to provide classification systems for organizations using very different bases. The Etzioni classification uses *compliance* as the major source of differentiation between organizations.[9] Compliance is the manner in which lower participants in an organization respond to the authority system of the organization. The compliance is expressed through the nature of the lower participant's involvement in the organization. When coercion is the basis of authority, compliance is alienative; when remuneration is the basis of authority, compliance takes the form of a utilitarian (instrumental or calculative) orientation toward the organization; and when the authority basis is moral or normative and expressed through persuasion, compliance is moral. The three types of authority and three types of compliance are combined in a three-by-three classificatory scheme. Most organizations would fall into "congruent" types, in that they would be *coercive–alienative, remunerative–utilitarian,* or *normative–moral.* The incongruent types (e.g., coercive–utilitarian) would tend to move toward congruency, according to Etzioni.

The Blau-Scott formulation is based on a different principle.[10] The major criterion here is the prime beneficiary of the organization's actions. This is related to, but not the same as, the functions approach discussed above. In this case, the output of the organization as it is directly consumed by some segment of society is the basis of differentiation. The nature of the output is not the important thing, but who benefits, or *cui bono.* The nature of the beneficiaries helps determine the nature of member participation and the central problems faced by each organization type.

Blau and Scott derive four basic organization types. The first is the *mutual-benefit association,* in which the members themselves are the prime beneficiaries of the organization's actions. The second type is the *business concern,* with the owners as prime beneficiaries. The *service organization* is the third type, with the clients that are served as the prime consideration. The final type is the *commonweal organization,* in which the public at large receives the major benefits. Blau and Scott also recognized the possibility of mixed types, but their major emphasis is on the pure types.

Analysis of the Etzioni and Blau–Scott Systems

At first glance, both these typologies seem quite intrinsically satisfying. They utilize variables that are important in organizations. The question

[9] Amitai Etzioni, *A Comparative Analysis of Complex Organizations* (New York: The Free Press, 1961), pp. 23–67.

[10] Peter M. Blau and W. Richard Scott, *Formal Organizations* (San Francisco: Chandler Publishing Co., 1962), pp. 40–58.

is, however, are they adequate typologies? Two critiques suggest that they are not. (The critiques themselves, coincidentally, also appeared almost simultaneously.) Burns, in an analysis of the Etzioni system, notes that insofar as the environment allows, Etzioni believes that organizations will tend to shift their compliance structure toward the congruent types and congruent-type organizations will resist factors that push them toward incongruent compliance structures, since congruent types are more effective than incongruent types and organizations are under pressure to be effective. Burns then asks, "First, if there is so much pressure towards congruence, how do organizations get to be 'incongruent' in the first place? Second, what is the 'environment' doing in there if it is not to afford blanket cover for all contingencies which might weaken or wreck the hypothesis? And, third, for whom and for what are organizations reckoned to be 'effective'?" [11]

Burns is essentially saying that the Etzioni typology leaves too many things unexplained and utilizes some unwarranted assumptions. His criticisms of the Blau–Scott formulation take a different tack. He notes first of all that in many large businesses the managers actually control the organization, with the stockholders receiving benefits based on the discretion of the real controllers. He also notes that the hospital "operated as a business enterprise by a consortium of medical practitioners [may not be] fundamentally different from a hospital [that is] publicly maintained or privately endowed.[12] Burns makes a more fundamental criticism of the prime-beneficiary approach when he states that it is extremely difficult to isolate an explicit, stable, and coherent group served by any organization. The beneficiaries themselves have factions, disagree, and engage in power struggles. This is closely related to the issue of organizational goals, which is similarly fraught with the lack of explicitness, stability, and coherence. Burns concludes that neither of these typologies, based as they are on single principles, sufficiently deals with the complexities of organizational existence.

A quite different but equally critical approach to these typologies is taken by Hall, Haas, and Johnson.[13] This analysis is empirically based, and it is at the empirical level that the first problems with the typologies are evident. This study used 75 organizations as the basis for examining the utility of the typologies. In most cases, placement of the organizations into the suggested classifications was relatively easy. Business organizations generally fell into the "utilitarian" or "business" categories,

[11] Burns, "Comparative Study of Organizations," p. 121.

[12] *Ibid.*, p. 122.

[13] Richard H. Hall, J. Eugene Haas, and Norman J. Johnson, "An Examination of the Blau-Scott and Etzioni Typologies," *Administrative Science Quarterly*, Vol. 12, No. 1 (June 1967), 118–39.

prisons were classified as "coercive" and "commonweal," and so on. Problems in each typology arose, however. Public school systems, for example, are suggested by Etzioni to be primarily "normative" organizations, with the likelihood of "coercive" overtones. Since students must attend by law and can be adjudged delinquent if they do not, coercion is a strong basis for attendance in many cases. At the same time, the student who utilizes the school system as a means for social mobility or for vocational training is rather clearly treating it as an instrumental entity. He uses grades and knowledge as a means to an end. The diversity of the involvement on the part of the organization members makes placement in the three major types extremely difficult in many cases.

Similar difficulties were encountered with the Blau–Scott system. A basic issue was whether to use short-run or long-run benefits. Using schools again as the example, the client group—students—receives both short-run and long-run benefits. The society at large also receives important benefits from the operation of schools. A similar case exists with mass-media organizations, such as newspapers or television stations. While the owners are a major beneficiary, assuming a profitable operation, the public at large also benefits. In the case of welfare agencies, the client groups receive benefits, but so again does the public. A basic difficulty with both classificatory systems is, therefore, the fact that real organizations just do not fit into the categories suggested with the ease that would be desirable in a truly definitive typology. The final placement of the 75 organizations in the two systems is indicated in Table 2–1.

Mere placement of the organizations into the classifications does not really test the typologies. The critical function of a typology is to "allow us to combine a number of variables into a single construct, and thus allow us to deal with extremely complex phenomena in a relatively simple fashion." [14] In order to determine whether these typologies do in fact provide some ordering of organizational phenomena, a series of organizational characteristics were cross-tabulated with the classification schemes.

Complexity was the first characteristic considered. A series of indicators of complexity, such as the number of major divisions (horizontal differentiation), number of hierarchical levels (vertical differentiation), and the number of major activities performed by the organization were weakly related to the typologies. On each of the complexity variables considered, there was a rather considerable distribution of organizations within major types on both typologies. That is, no type of organization was clearly more or less complex. Even where statistically significant dif-

---

[14] David Mechanic, "Methodology of Organizational Studies," in Harold J. Leavitt, ed., *The Social Science of Organizations* (Englewood Cliffs, N.J.: Prentice-Hall, Inc., 1963), p. 158.

TABLE 2–1 TYPOLOGICAL PROBLEMS

BLAU-SCOTT

Mutual benefit
County medical association
County political party
Farm cooperative
Farmers' federation
Labor union organization
Private country club
Religious–fraternal organization
State church organization
Trade asosciation

Service
Civil rights organization
Delinquent reformatory
Insurance company
Juvenile detention center
Parochial school system
Private hospital
Private school
Private welfare agency
Public school system
Religious service organization
State psychiatric hospital
State school
University

Business
Bank
Hotel–motel
Manufacturing plant
Marketing organization
Newspaper
Private television station
Public transit firm
Public utility
Quarry
Railroad
Restaurant
Retail store
Trucking firm

Commonweal
City recreation department
Educational television station
Fund-raising agency
Governmental regulative agency
Law-enforcement agency
Military supply command
Municipal airport
Post office
State hospital
State penal institution

ETZIONI

Coercive
Juvenile detention center
Law-enforcement agency
State hospital
State penal institution
State school

Utilitarian
Bank
Farm cooperative
Governmental regulative agency
Hotel–motel
Insurance company
Labor union organization
Manufacturing plant
Marketing organization
Medical association
Municipal airport
Post office
Public transit firm
Public utility
Quarry
Railroad
Restaurant
Retail store
Trade association
Trucking firm

Normative
Church
City recreation department
Civil rights organization
County political party
Delinquent reformatory
Educational television station
Farmers' federation
Fund-raising agency
Local religious organization
Military supply command
Newspaper
Parochial school system
Private country club
Private hospital
Private school
Private television station
Private welfare agency
Public school system
Religious–fraternal organization
Religious service organization
State church organization
State psychiatric hospital
University

Source: Richard H. Hall, J. Eugene Haas, and Norman J. Johnson, "An Examination of the Blau-Scott and Etzioni Typologies," Administrative Science Quarterly, Vol. 12, No. 1 (June 1967), 120–21.

ferences emerged, enough deviant cases existed to prevent a conclusion that one type of organization is categorically different from another in terms of complexity. A further difficulty is that a type of organization that is high on one indicator of complexity is often low on another. The typologies offer few useful insights into the nature and degree of organizational complexity.

The next characteristic considered was the degree of formalization. Here again a series of indicators were utilized. Coercive and commonweal organizations are highly formalized in terms of the extent to which there are concrete job descriptions. These categories contain a number of penal institutions that can rely upon universalistic procedures and codified rules, as well as highly formalized authority systems. Normative and mutual-benefit organizations are found to be rather low in their degree of formalization. Both are concerned with obtaining and maintaining member support and loyalty. The two typologies predict rather well in the area of formalization. The penal institutions included in this study might make the results somewhat specious in that they are highly formalized and perhaps are overrepresented in the coercive and commonweal categories. This is part of a major methodological problem in the analysis of organizations: There is no clearly defined universe from which a sample can be selected. The six penal institutions in these categories may or may not be an overrepresentation. Since there is no real basis for determining the representativeness of the sample, the conclusion that coercive and commonweal organizations are more formalized will have to be taken as tentative.

The next organizational characteristic considered was the specificity of the organizations' goals. The official goals of the organizations in the study were categorized in terms of the ease of determining goal achievement. Not surprisingly, the business–utilitarian organizations are characterized by goals (profit) that can be translated into quantifiable and hence determinable terms. The typologies predict quite well here, but at a common-sense level.

The typologies do a fairly good job of predicting the form and extent of interdependency among the parts of the organizations. The business–utilitarian organizations have highly interdependent subunits because they must ensure that the component parts are coordinated (their central concerns lead to this). The normative and service organizations utilize committees as a coordination mechanism and also as a means of maintaining morale.

On measures of the nature of the organizations' external relationships and the kinds of changes that have occurred in recent years, no definitive patterns emerge, beyond those that could be predicted at a common-sense level. Business–utilitarian organizations engage in economic competition with other organizations; they also experienced the least amount of change among the organizations studied. There is almost no difference among the types in terms of general dependence on other organizations, and there was little differentiation among the types regarding other external relationships and change patterns.

On the basis of the analysis of these data, we conclude that the two typologies, aside from the rather simple differentiation concerning the compliance system and the nature of the prime beneficiary, have only a limited application insofar as total organizational analysis is concerned. Neither typology "differentiates clearly between organizations in terms of the variables considered important structural characteristics; e.g., complexity, activities, and formalization. Furthermore, there is no clear differentiation in terms of the factors related to change." [15]

An Empirically Derived Taxonomy

The taxonomic efforts discussed thus far have been deductive, in that the authors begin with one or more characteristics that appear to be crucial and then develop a system around these major variables. A drastically different approach has been taken by Haas, Hall, and Johnson in their attempt to construct an empirically derived taxonomy of organizations. [16] In this study, the basis for classifications was organizational characteristics as they existed in the same 75 organizations utilized in the evaluation of the Blau–Scott and Etzioni typologies.

Data regarding some 99 variables were collected from these organizations and then analyzed through the use of a computer program that matched organizations according to the characteristics they shared. Ten basic classes of organizations were identified. These classes and the organizational attributes they have in common are shown in Table 2–2.

Two things are immediately obvious from this table. The first is the seemingly strange combination of organizations in some of the classes. The second is that characteristics that appear to be quite trivial serve as the basis of differentiation in a number of cases. The organizations in each class share a combination of characteristics that are not found in the same pattern among the rest of the organizations included in the study. While organizations in different classes may have many other characteristics in common, these characteristics are not common in a

---

15 Hall et al., "Examination of Typologies," pp. 137–38.

16 J. Eugene Haas, Richard H. Hall, and Norman J. Johnson, "Toward an Empirically Derived Taxonomy of Organizations," in Raymond V. Bowers, ed., *Studies on Behavior in Organizations* (Athens, Ga.: University of Georgia Press, 1966), pp. 157–80.

TABLE 2–2   AN EMPIRICALLY DERIVED TAXONOMY

	Organizations	*Common Characteristics*

Class I	Restaurant (2)
	Governmental regulative
	  agency
	Motel
	Bank
	Insurance company
	Manufacturing plant
	Parochial school system
	Private television station
		Members enter the organization by
		  simple sign-up
		Members are primary/affiliate
		No racial restrictions on member-
		  ship
		No religious restrictions on member-
		  ship
		No physical requirements
		Geographical factors no bar to or-
		  ganizational success
		No shifts in organizational activity
		  over time

Class II	Manufacturing plant (7)
	Religious service organization
	State school
	Public school system
	Farmers' federation
	Post office
	State penal institution (3)
	Newspaper (2)
	Marketing organization (2)
	Retail organization (3)
	Farm cooperative (2)
	Labor union organization
	Public utility
	Hotel
	Bank
	Public transit firm
	Quarry
		Members enter organization by
		  simple sign-up
		No religious restrictions on member-
		  ship
		Compared to other organizations,
		  the organization faces average
		  geographic situations
		No departments engaged in produc-
		  tion of goods for internal use

Class III	Delinquent reformatory
	State penal institution
		Nonprofit, governmental organiza-
		  tions
		Provide a service for nonmembers
		Strong flexibility and change orien-
		  tation
		No departments engaged in sale of
		  product or service
		Overall complexity is .020–.029
		Low concreteness of positional de-
		  scriptions
		Written job descriptions at all levels
		No intradepartmental committees
		Three interdepartmental commit-
		  tees
		Three committees in total organiza-
		  tion

TABLE 2–2 (Cont.)

Organizations	*Common Characteristics*
	Source of major policy decisions is another organization
	Authority is not formalized in writing
	Medium emphasis on status distinctions
	Some members enter organization voluntarily and others by prescription—i.e., by law
	Primary members only
	Some primary members nonvoluntary
	Upper level turnover is 0–5%
	Limit to overall size of organization
	Limit to size of particular departments
	No racial restrictions on membership
	No religious restrictions on membership
	No physical requirements
	No citizenship requirement for membership
	Being on a blacklist is not a bar to membership
	Part of a larger organization
	No subsidiary organizations
	Tax supported
	Geographic factors no bar to organizational success
	Primary source of income is public tax
	Compared to other similar organizations, the organization faces average geographic situations
	Financial condition is satisfactory
	One or more shifts in activities in last three years
	Greater emphasis on some activities previously present
Class IV	Municipal airport	Commonweal organizations
	Educational television station	Nonprofit, governmental organizations
	Governmental regulative agency	Provide a service to nonmembers
		No departments engaged in production of goods for internal use
		No departments engaged in production of goods for external use

TABLE 2–2   (Cont.)

Organizations	*Common Characteristics*
	One department engaged in internal service or supportive activity
	No departments engaged in providing services for internal use
	One department engaged in the sale of products or services
	Mean number of hierarchical levels is three
	Concreteness of positional descriptions is medium
	No intradepartmental committees
	No interdepartmental committees
	No committees in the organization as a whole
	Source of major policy decisions is another organization
	Members enter the organization voluntarily
	Members enter the organization by simple sign-up
	Informal orientation program required of all members
	Members are primary/affiliate
	Primary members are all voluntary and paid
	The number of paid members is 1–99
	Total organizational members are 1–99
	Upper level turnover 0–5%
	No racial restrictions on membership
	No religious restrictions on membership
	No citizenship requirement for membership
	No physical requirements
	No subsidiary organizations
	Tax-supported
	Geographic factors no bar to organizational success
Class V Private hospital Trade association Private school Church	No departments engaged in production of goods for internal use No departments engaged in production of goods for external use

TABLE 2–2 (Cont.)

Organizations	*Common Characteristics*
Civil rights organization Private country club University Trucking firm	Penalties for rule violation not clearly stipulated Members enter the organization voluntarily
Class VI State hospital Delinquent reformatory	Nonprofit, governmental organizations Strong emphasis on internal efficiency Average emphasis on service to the public Five levels of workers No departments—internal No departments—external Provide a service to nonmembers Two departments engaged in internal service or supportive activities One department engaged in providing a service externally No departments engaged in sale of product or service Departments located entirely at one location Personnel located entirely at one location Written job descriptions at all levels Source of major policy decisions is another organization High centralization of authority High formalization of authority Medium emphasis on written communications Many rules Rules and policies reviewed often Penalties for rule violation clearly stipulated Penalties for rule violation stipulated in writing Some persons enter the organization voluntarily, others by prescription—i.e., by law Members enter the organization by simple sign-up Loosely structured orientation program for all members Members are primary only

TABLE 2–2   (Cont.)

Organizations	*Common Characteristics*
	Percentage difference between the largest department and the smallest department is .40–.49
	Planned limit on size of organization
	Planned limit on size of particular departments
	No racial restrictions on membership
	No religious restrictions on membership
	No age restrictions on membership
	Being on a blacklist is not a bar to membership
	No physical requirements for membership
	Citizenship is a requirement for membership
	Part of a larger organization
	No subsidiary organizations
	Tax-supported
	Primary source of income is public tax
	Organizational age is 46 years or more
	There has been a shift of emphasis in organizational activities: some emphasized more and others less
Class VII Private welfare agency Religious–fraternal organization	Presence of three goals
	Nonprofit, nongovernmental
	Provide service to members primarily
	Average emphasis on internal efficiency
	No departments engaged in production of goods for internal use
	No departments engaged in sale of product or service
	Departments located mostly in field
	Personnel located primarily in field
	High formalization of authority
	Medium emphasis on written communication
	Many rules
	Penalties for rule violation clearly stipulated

TABLE 2–2   (Cont.)

Organizations	*Common Characteristics*
	Penalties are moderate
	Members enter the organization by public ceremony
	Highly formalized orientation program
	Primary members are all voluntary, minority paid
	The number of paid members is 1–99
	No limit on total organizational size
	No limit on size of particular departments
	No racial restrictions on membership
	No citizenship requirements on membership
	No physical requirements for membership
	Being on a blacklist is not a bar to membership
	Being an ex-convict is not a bar to membership
	Not dependent on other organizations in general
	Faced with other than economic competition
	Government has slight control
	Geographic factors no bar to organizational success
	Compared to other similar organizations, the organization faces average geographic situations
	Organizational age is 46 years or more
	No shifts in major organizational activities over time
	Recent patterns are similar to long-range patterns in terms of personnel
Class VIII Juvenile detention center (2) Fund-raising agency Law-enforcement agency City recreation department State penal institution Local religious organization Private welfare agency	No departments engaged in production for internal use No departments engaged in production for external use No departments engaged in sale of product or service

TABLE 2–2   (Cont.)

	Organizations	*Common Characteristics*
	State church organization	
	Military supply command	
	Public school system	
	Labor union organization	
	University	
	State psychiatric hospital	
Class IX	State church organization	Two goals
	County political party	Cultural goals
		Mutual benefit associations
		Nonprofit, nongovernmental
		Strong growth orientation
		No departments engaged in production for internal use
		No departments engaged in production for external use
		No departments engaged in internal service
		All deparments in the field are within local county
		Personnel located primarily in field
		Personnel in field within local county
		Deepest single division has three levels
		Mean number of hierarchical levels is three
		Overall complexity is .000–.009
		Low concreteness of positional descriptions
		Rules and policies seldom reviewed
		Penalties for rule violation clearly stipulated
		Penalties for rule violation stipulated in writing
		Members enter the organization voluntarily
		Informal orientation program for all members
		Primary members are all voluntary, minority paid
		No limit on total organizational size
		No age restrictions on membership
		No racial restrictions on membership
		Presence of subsidiary organizations
		Faced with other than economic competition

TABLE 2–2   (Cont.)

	Organizations	Common Characteristics
		Slight governmental control
		Supply of potential members is average
		Geographic factors no bar to organizational success
		Compared to other similar organizations, the organization faces average geographic situations
		Primary source of income is contributions
		Organizational age is 46 years or more
		No shifts in major organizational activities over time
Class X	County medical association Railroad	Economic goals
		Provide service to nonmembers
		No departments engaged in production for internal use
		No departments engaged in production for external use
		Two departments engaged in internal service or supportive activities
		Personnel mostly in the field
		Mean number of hierarchical levels is three
		Ratio of number of committees divided by number of members is .000–.004
		Source of major policy decisions is board of trustees
		Low centralization of authority
		High formalization of authority
		High emphasis on going through channels
		Many rules
		Rules and policies occasionally reviewed
		Penalties for rule violation clearly stipulated
		Penalties for rule violation stipulated in writing
		Penalties are light
		Medium emphasis on status distinctions
		Members enter the organization voluntarily

TABLE 2–2   (Cont.)

Organizations	Common Characteristics
	Members are primary/secondary/ affiliate
	Upper level turnover 0–5%
	No limit on size of particular departments
	No racial restrictions on membership
	No religious restrictions on membership
	Excellent financial condition
	Organizational age is 46 years or more
	No shifts in major organizational activities over time

Source: Norman J. Johnson, "Toward a Taxonomy of Organization" (unpublished Ph.D. dissertation, The Ohio State University, 1966), pp. 186–234. [Note: Numbers in parentheses refer to the number of organizations involved.]

common configuration.[17] Each class contains organizations with a homogeneous set of characteristics that are found only in the specific configuration among the organizations in each class. The result is a taxonomic system not unlike that found in zoology. The "adding-on" of an additional characteristic from one class to another may completely differentiate mammals from amphibious creatures. The same thing *may* be true for organizations. The particular variables that serve as the basis for each class, not having been selected on an a priori basis, do not reflect the characteristics that most writers have considered to be important for organizational analysis. However, the fact that they are common to the organizations means that the organizations within each class must face the same kinds of issues, regardless of whether or not they appear to be similar organizations. Another parallel to zoological taxonomies is the fact that the major classes can be broken down into subclasses (species) that have similarly exclusive characteristics. These subclasses are characterized by the possession of more characteristics in common than the major classes.

The utility of this particular effort at developing a taxonomy is weakened by three major factors. The first is that the variables selected for inclusion might not be those that are most crucial for organizations. Although the attempt was made to include every organizational char-

---

[17] The characteristics listed for each class are stated in the terminology used in the original study. Some meanings may not be apparent without the original study.

acteristic thought to be important, work that has been done since this taxonomic effort has suggested several additional factors that might be central in any taxonomic effort. It is the characteristics of the variables included in this study that are its strengths and weaknesses. If it were to be done again, a modified selection of variables would be crucial. The second weakness of this taxonomy is the type of measurement of the variables. The data were gathered by means of tape-recorded interviews with executives in each organization, supplemented with records, tables of organization, and other printed matter. While the interviewees were very cooperative, their knowledge and perspectives about their organizations varied rather widely. On some apparently important variables, such as the distribution of status and power or the nature of changes in the organization, the information appears to be weaker than that on the number of divisions or the geographical dispersion of the organizations. Thus the data vary in terms of their completeness and depth. They also lack the strength that would have been achieved if the organizational characteristics had been determined by observations and interviews throughout the organization.

The third weakness of this taxonomy is essentially unavoidable. The nature of each class is limited by whether or not an organization was included in the study. There is no sampling universe from which the organizations to be included could have been selected. The taxonomy is thus a classification of only these 75 organizations, not of all organizations. Ideally, information about more organizations would be continually added to the analysis, thus allowing greater confidence in the generalizability of the classes and their bases. Unfortunately, this has not been done.

These evident weaknesses should not be taken as a reason for complete rejection of this approach. The empirical demonstration of relationships between organizational characteristics and factors affecting and affected by such characteristics will serve as the major basis for the approach to classification that will be proposed below. The major functions of organizations, their compliance structures, or the nature of the prime beneficiaries may turn out to be important classificatory bases. This must be demonstrated rather than simply suggested if adequate classificatory schemes are to develop.

THE COMPONENTS OF A CLASSIFICATORY SCHEME

The discussion thus far has been centered around several classificatory systems that have been proposed. Most of these have been based on factors that are thought to be, but that turn out not to be, crucial in differentiating organizations from each other on a meaningful basis. These schemes simply do not place organizations into categories that are sufficiently differentiated from each other in terms of important organizational characteristics. The empirically derived taxonomy suffers from the problems of the variables considered and the possible meaninglessness of the derived classes. In this section, some recent research will be reviewed with the intent of isolating variables that are thought to be and that have been found to be critical factors in differentiating types of organizations from each other.

Technology

A great deal of current interest has been focused on the nature of the organization's technology. This technology is affected by the "raw material" being manipulated by the organization. Perrow notes that this raw material

> . . . may be a living being, human or otherwise, a symbol or an inanimate object. People are raw materials in people-changing or people-processing organizations; symbols are materials in banks, advertising agencies and some research organizations; the interactions of people are raw materials to be manipulated by administrators in organizations; boards of directors, committees and councils are usually involved with the changing or processing of symbols and human interactions, and so on.[18]

The nature of the raw material makes a difference in terms of how the organization is structured and operated. According to Perrow, the critical factors in the nature of the raw material, and hence the nature of the technology employed to work on it, are the number of "exceptional cases encountered in the work" and the nature of the "search process" that is utilized when exceptional cases are found.[19] Few exceptional cases are found when the raw material is some object or objects that do not vary in their consistency or malleability over time. Many exceptions are found in the obvious cases of human beings and their interactions, or the less obvious cases of many craft specialties or frontier areas within the physical sciences. Search processes range from those that are logical and analytical to those that must rely upon intuition,

---

[18] Perrow, "A Framework for Comparative Analysis," p. 195. See also Williams A. Rushing, "Hardness of Material as Related to Division of Labor in Manufacturing Industries," *Administrative Science Quarterly*, Vol. 13, No. 2 (September 1968), 229–45, for data on the relationship between raw materials and organizational forms.

[19] *Ibid.*, pp. 195–96.

inspiration, chance, guesswork, or some other such unstandardized procedure. Examples of the first form of search would be the engineering process in many industries and computer programming in most instances. The second form of search would involve such diverse activities as advertising campaigns, some biomedical research, or many activities of the aerospace industry. The examples in both cases have been chosen to suggest the manner in which both the nature of the exceptions and the search process can vary across traditional organizational types.

Both the variables discussed take the form of continua along which organizations vary. These continua interact.

> On the one hand, increased knowledge of the nature of the material may lead to the perception of more varieties of possible outcomes or products, which in turn increases the need for more intimate knowledge of the nature of the material. Or the organization, with increased knowledge of one type of material, may begin to work with a variety of related materials about which more needs to be known, as when a social service agency or employment agency relaxes its admission criteria as it gains confidence, but in the process sets off more search behavior, or when a manufacturing organization starts producing new but unrelated products. On the other hand, if increased knowledge of the material is gained but no expansion of the variety of output occurs, this permits easier analysis of the sources of problems that may arise in the transformation process. It may also allow one to prevent the rise of such problems by the design of the production process.[20]

The variations along these continua affect both the task and social structures of organizations. The impact of variations in the technology of organizations is perhaps most graphically seen in Joan Woodward's analysis of 100 British manufacturing firms.[21] Woodward was concerned with the effects of different technologies on the management structure of the firms. She identified three types of technologies. The first is the small-batch or unit-production system, as exemplified by a ship-building or aircraft-manufacturing firm. The second type is the large-batch or mass-production organization, and the third is the organization that utilizes continuous production, as in the case of chemical or petroleum manufacturers.

Woodward's finding show that the nature of the technology vitally affected the management structures of the firms studied. The number of levels in the management hierarchy, the span of control of first-line supervisors, and the ratio of managers and supervisors to other personnel were all affected by the nature of the technology employed. This evidence, plus that of Perrow in support of his argument, leads to the

20 *Ibid.*, p. 197.
21 Joan Woodward, *Industrial Organizations* (London: Oxford University Press, 1962).

conclusion that the nature of the technology utilized in an organization is indeed a major basis of differentiation between organizations.

Environment

Before we turn to the consideration of the impact of varying technologies on organizations, an extension of the concept of technology is necessary. An organization's technology does not develop in a vacuum. The nature of the raw material, stressed by Perrow, is modified by the general environmental system in which the organization operates. Small private colleges work on the same raw materials as the huge state university. Firms utilizing steel in their production process can vary widely in the technology used. The technological systems are vastly different, as are the characteristics of the organizations involved. The crucial factor here appears to be the technological *environment* in which the organizations operate. Some organizations must face a rapidly changing technological environment, while others exist in a state of relative constancy over time. The effect of this difference can perhaps be seen in the case of office-equipment manufacturing firms. Before the advent of computers and other electronic equipment, these firms operated in a relatively constant technological environment. Their research and development, production, sales, and marketing were relatively standardized and unchanged over time. (The time period of stability is much less than that of other industries, but compared to the contemporary situation, it seems like a stable period.) The computer age ushered in a period of rapid change for the organizations involved, as well as for the more evident impact of their products. Research and development became paramount concerns. New organizations sprang up with new ideas to challenge the traditional leaders in the field. Thus, while the technology within the organization remains a critical factor, the general technological environment is the factor that sets the climate for the internal state of the organization.

The technological environment is but one aspect of an organization's environment. Political, economic, legal, and demographic conditions are all important for organizations. For example, churches and universities in the 1970s are facing situations that were not even seriously imagined a decade earlier. These changing conditions alter the operations of the organization, making practices anachronistic that were once sacred. These general environmental conditions and their impact on organizations are not only important for the sake of analysis, but also for a thorough and useful typology.

Additional insights into the importance of these factors can be seen in the research of Lawrence and Lorsch.[22] The organizations they studied were business firms in the plastics, processed foods, and container industries. The plastics firms faced an environment with a rapidly changing technology. The container industry, on the other hand, dealt with a constant environment in terms of customers and the technology used in producing the product, and the food-processing firms occupied an intermediate position. The plastics firms were much more internally differentiated than the container firms. Their whole organizational structure and operations were affected by the kind of environment confronted and the nature of the technology employed. Lawrence and Lorsch conclude:

> In this study we have found an important relationship among external variables (the certainty and diversity of the environment, and the strategic environmental issue), internal states of differentiation and integration, and the process of conflict resolution. If an organization's internal states and processes are consistent with external demands, the findings of this study suggest that it will be effective in dealing with its environment.[23]

While again our present concern is not with effectiveness, Lawrence and Lorsch's conclusion strongly suggests that the way an organization is organized is affected by the environmental and technological factors under discussion. We cannot assume that organizations always try to maximize effectiveness, but we can say that most organizations most of the time will try to operate in this manner. Therefore environmental and technological variations affect the internal characteristics of organizations.

Using a similar perspective, Derek Pugh and his colleagues found several "contextual variables" that were strongly associated with aspects of the internal structuring of organizations.[24] Using data from 46 English organizations, these researchers found that size, the nature of the technology, dependence on other organizations, and the number of operating sites were strong predictors of the manner in which activities were structured, authority concentrated, and work flow controlled. These relationships, while not necessarily causal nor inclusive of all the elements central to organizational analysis, do indicate the linkages between external and organizational characteristics.

[22] Paul R. Lawrence and Jay W. Lorsch, *Organization and Environment: Managing Differentiation and Integration* (Cambridge: Harvard Graduate School of Business Administration, 1967).

[23] *Ibid.*, p. 157.

[24] Derek S. Pugh, J. D. Hickson, C. R. Hinings, and C. Turner, "The Context of Organization Structures," *Administrative Science Quarterly*, Vol. 14, No. 1 (March 1969), 91–114.

Personnel

A final external factor that should be mentioned is the nature of the personnel coming into the organization. Studies of professionals in organizations show rather conclusively that the organization, if it wants to make optimal use of its professionals, must structure itself differently in those organizational segments where the professionals are present.[25] (Of course, an organization that is predominantly professional will be affected by their presence.) Other occupational groupings, such as craftsmen, have similar effects on organizations. This point raises another side issue. *Organizations exhibit intraorganizational variations.*[26] However, these variations, while important, will not concern us for the moment. Our concern is with those variables that are important for classifying organizations as a whole.

Variations in Structure and Process

We have looked at the external factors that affect organizations. It is time now to turn to what is affected. Organizations vary in terms of their structure and processes. Some structural elements have already been identified, such as formalization, complexity, and centralization. These elements are refinements of the concept of *bureaucracy,* a term that has been used in many ways. Common usage associates the word with governmental red tape and inefficiency, or any state of "overorganization." This usage has diminished the utility of the concept as it has developed in organizational literature, because of its connotations. But despite this, an examination of the concept will help identify some of the organizational characteristics that are important for classificatory purposes.

The concept is linked most closely to the work of Max Weber.[27] Weber discussed the elements of bureaucracy in terms of their combina-

25 See Peter M. Blau, "The Hierarchy of Authority in Organizations," *American Journal of Sociology,* Vol. 73, No. 4, (January 1968); William Kornhauser, *Scientists in Industry* (Berkeley: University of California Press, 1963); and Richard H. Hall, "Professionalization and Bureaucratization," *American Sociological Review,* Vol. 33, No. 1 (February 1968), 92–104.

26 See Richard H. Hall, "Intraorganizational Structural Variation: Application of the Bureaucratic Model," *Administrative Science Quarterly,* Vol. 7, No. 3 (December 1962), 295–308; Eugene Litwak, "Models of Organizations Which Permit Conflict," *American Journal of Sociology,* Vol. 67, No. 2 (September 1961), 177–84; and Lawrence and Lorsch, *Organization and Environment.*

27 Max Weber, *The Theory of Social and Economic Organization,* trans. A. M. Henderson and Talcott Parson (New York: The Free Press, 1947).

tion into an "ideal type"—that is, the set of characteristics that, if present in an organization, would cause the organization to be characterized as a true bureaucracy. This formulation allows the analyst to determine the degree to which an organization is bureaucratized. It is thus a continuous variable. It is also a multidimensional variable, according to Weber. He identified multiple attributes comprising the bureaucratic ideal type. Table 2–3 indicates the dimensions that Weber and others have suggested as central to the concept. As we can see from the table, later writers have been in general agreement with Weber about the characteristics crucial to the concept.

Since the general concept itself is a continuous variable, the attributes must therefore be treated as a set of dimensions. Unfortunately, this has not always been the case. All too often the concept has been treated in a unitary fashion and as a present–absent phenomenon. That is, the components of bureaucracy have been assumed to vary together, with organizations being either bureaucratic or nonbureaucratic. A "bureaucratic" organization would have to have all the dimensions present to a high degree, while a "nonbureaucratic" organization would be characterized by an absence of these dimensions. This was clearly not Weber's meaning in his development of the concept, nor does it correspond to reality. The more realistic approach would be to treat organizations as possessing characteristics of the bureaucratic model in *varying degrees along the several dimensions of bureaucracy.*

This is in fact what empirical evidence suggests. In a study that utilized this approach, I found that the ten organizations studied did not possess the bureaucratic attributes to the same degree across attributes.[28] That is, an organization can be highly bureaucratized in terms of having a well-developed set of procedural specifications, but at the same time be minimally bureaucratized in terms of its division of labor. Table 2–4 indicates how six bureaucratic attributes are related to each other (based on data from ten organizations). The important thing to note in this table is the independent variation among the attributes. None of the correlation coefficients is sufficiently high to permit the assumption that if an organization is highly bureaucratized in terms of one dimension, it is high on all dimensions. The dimensions vary independently in real organizations and the concept of bureaucracy itself cannot be treated as a unitary concept.

In a later study, it was found that five of the six dimensions of bureaucracy could be combined into a single scale of bureaucratization.[29]

[28] Richard H. Hall, "The Concept of Bureaucracy: An Empirical Assessment," *American Jorunal of Sociology*, Vol. 69, No. 1 (July 1963), 32–40.

[29] Richard H. Hall and Charles R. Tittle, "Bureaucracy and Its Correlates," *American Journal of Sociology*, Vol. 72, No. 3 (November 1966), 267–72.

TABLE 2–3   CHARACTERISTICS OF BUREAUCRACY AS LISTED BY MAJOR AUTHORS

Dimensions of Bureaucracy	Weber	Friedrich	Merton	Udy	Heady	Parsons	Berger	Michels	Dimock
Hierarchy of authority	*	*	*	*	*	*	*	*	*
Division of labor	*	*	*	*	*	*	—	*	*
Technically competent participants	*	*	*	*	—	*	*	—	—
Procedural devices for work situations	*	*	*	—	*	—	*	—	*
Rules governing behavior of positional incumbents	*	*	*	—	—	—	*	*	—
Limited authority of office	*	—	*	—	*	*	—	—	—
Differential rewards by office	*	—	—	*	—	—	—	—	—
Impersonality of personal contact	—	—	*	—	—	—	—	—	—
Administration separate from ownership	*	—	—	—	—	—	—	—	—
Emphasis on written communication	*	—	—	—	—	—	—	—	—
Rational discipline	*	—	—	—	—	—	—	—	—

Source: Richard H. Hall,"The Concept of Bureaucracy: An Empirical Assessment," The American Journal of Sociology, Vol. 69, No. 1 (July 1963), 34.

TABLE 2–4   RANK–ORDER INTERCORRELATION COEFFICIENTS
BETWEEN DIMENSIONS (N = Organizations)

	Hierarchy of Authority	Division of Labor	Rules	Procedures	Impersonality
Division of labor	.419				
Rules	.594	.134			
Procedures	.660	.678	.167		
Impersonality	.678	.266	.194	.624	
Technical qualifications	−.032	−.300	.627	−.303	.170

Note: The ranking of each organization was from most bureaucratic to least bureaucratic on each dimension.
Source: Richard H. Hall, "The Concept of Bureaucracy: An Empirical Assessment," The American Journal of Sociology, Vol. 69, No. 1 (July 1963), 37.

The technical competence dimension, which is inversely related in many cases to the other dimensions, is difficult to include in an overall bureaucratization scale. The impersonality dimension is the primary basis of differentiation in the scale. The other dimensions are present or absent (in the development of this scale it was necessary to treat the dimensions in a dichotomous fashion) largely in relationship to this dimension. While the technicalities of the procedures used are not of interest here, it is important to note that the general concept of bureaucracy has a basis in reality. The attributes that Weber and others have proposed are components of actual organizations and vary in their presence across organizations. These components and those derived from them appear to be central for the analysis of organizational structures; therefore, they are also central to the development of any adequate typology.

In the same study, some of the aspects of the technological system of the organization were also examined. In this examination, it became clear that the role of technology is important to the organizational structures, but that there are difficulties in the operationalization of some of the ideas expressed by Perrow and others. The organizations were ranked according to the degree to which they manipulate objects as opposed to ideas and the extent to which they work on "people" as opposed to "nonpeople." A panel of expert judges was asked to rank the organizations on these two dimensions and found the task very difficult. Every organization must be concerned with ideas and people as part of its technology. At the same time, ideas and people are of greater centrality to some organizations than others. A social work agency, for example, is generally more concerned with people than a trucking firm, but probably less concerned with ideas than a university. These are matters of degree rather than of kind.

Once the organizations were ranked, it was found that those primarily concerned with objects were more bureaucratic than those concerned with ideas. Similarly, people-oriented organizations were less bureaucratized than the nonpeople organizations. While the relatively small sample size (25) and the difficulties in operationalizing the two technology concepts preclude attaching too much certainty to the findings, the results are consistent with the argument presented earlier. The nature of an organization's technology does have an impact on the way it is structured.

Pugh, Hickson, and Hinings, approaching bureaucracy from a somewhat different standpoint, have further shown how organizations can be classified according to structural characteristics.[30] The dimensions of bureaucracy used are (1) the *structuring of activities,* or the degree of standardization of routines, formalization of procedures, specialization of roles, and extent to which behavior is specified by the organization; (2) the *concentration of authority,* or the centralization of authority at the upper levels of the hierarchy and in controlling units outside the organization; and (3) the *line control of workflow,* or the degree to which control is exercised by line personnel as opposed to control through impersonal procedures. Using a sample of 52 English organizations and the three bases of classification, they suggest the following types:

1. Full Bureaucracy: ". . . relatively high scores on both structuring of activities and concentration of authority, a high dependence score . . . , and a relatively low score on workflow integration of technology. . . . It has high scores on both standardization of procedures for selection and advancement, etc., and formalization of role definition. . . ."

2. Nascent Full Bureaucracy: Possesses the same characteristics, but not to such a pronounced degree.

3. Workflow Bureaucracy: "High scores on structuring of activities combined with relatively low scores on the remaining two structural factors. Their use of impersonal control mechanisms is shown by the high scores on formalization of recording of role performance as well as a high percentage of nonworkflow personnel and clerks . . . high scores of workflow integration."

4. Nascent Workflow Bureaucracy: ". . . show the same characteristics to a less pronounced degree, and are considerably smaller."

5. Preworkflow Bureaucracy: ". . . are considerably lower on scores of structuring of activities, but have the typical workflow–bureaucracy pattern of dispersed authority and impersonal line control."

30 D. S. Pugh, D. J. Hickson, and C. R. Hinings, "An Empirical Taxonomy of Work Organizations," *Administrative Science Quarterly,* Vol. 14, No. 1 (March 1969), 115–26.

6. Implicitly Structured Organizations: ". . . have low structuring of activities, dispersed authority, and high line control."
7. Personnel Bureaucracy: ". . . low scores on structuring and high scores on line control . . . high scores on concentration of authority." [31]

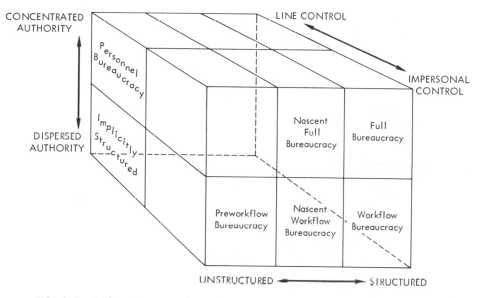

FIG. 2–1   A Three-Dimensional Typology

Source: D. S. Pugh, D. J. Hickson, and C. R. Hinings, "An Empirical Taxonomy of Work Organizations," Administrative Science Quarterly, Vol. 14, No. 1 (March 1969), 123.

This scheme is graphically shown in figure 2–1. The authors suggest that a developmental sequence occurs on two of their dimensions. More highly structured organizations develop as the organizations grow in size over time, and growth in size is in turn related to general economic development. The control dimension tends to move from line control —that is, control exercised by the workflow personnel themselves and their subordinates—to impersonal control. As technology develops, more and more of the control system is passed to "procedures dictated by standardization and the new specialists who devise the procedures." [32] No such developmental sequence is seen in the case of the concentration of authority; the patterns here are linked to historical factors and the auspices under which the organization operates. This line of reasoning

[31] *Ibid.*, pp. 121–23. Note that these are the same concepts used earlier by these authors.
[32] *Ibid.*, p. 124.

strengthens the argument that factors external to the organization (contextual variables) must be considered in the development of a totally adequate typology.

The components of bureaucracy are the structural attributes that are often used in organizational analyses. Other combinations of structural variables have been suggested. Pugh, Hickson, et al.[33] propose that six primary dimensions comprise the basis of organizational structure: (1) *specialization,* or the division of labor, (2) *standardization* of procedures and roles, (3) *formalization,* in terms of written specifications of how actions are to be performed, (4) *centralization* of authority, (5) *configuration,* or the shape of organizations in terms of their spans of control, segmentation of tasks, etc., and (6) *flexibility,* or the amount, speed, and acceleration of the rate of change. Other writers, such as Aiken and Hage, Blau, and Meyer, have concentrated on centralization of authority, complexity, and formalization.[34] Thus, while there is general consensus regarding the major structural components (the definitions of the components are only minimally different), the terminology is not yet common. The consensus is sufficient to permit some confidence that the major structural components have been identified. They have also been investigated empirically.

As important as the structural variables are those involving the processes within an organization. Factors such as the use of power, centralization and decentralization, decision making, communications, conflict, and interaction patterns vary in the same manner as the structural properties that have been discussed and must be included in any classification scheme.

Output

The discussion thus far has shown that an organization's technology and more general environment are linked to its structure and processes.

[33] D. S. Pugh, D. J. Hickson, C. R. Hinings, K. M. MacDonald, C. Turner, and T. Lupton, "A Conceptual Scheme for Organizational Analysis," *Administrative Science Quarterly,* Vol. 8, No. 3 (December 1963), 301–7.

[34] Michael Aiken and Jerald Hage, "Organizational Alienation: A Comparative Analysis," *American Sociological Review,* Vol. 31, No. 4 (August 1966), 497–507; Hage and Aiken, "Relationship of Centralization to Other Organizational Properties," *Administrative Science Quarterly,* Vol. 12, No. 1 (June 1967), 72–92; Hage and Aiken, "Program Change and Organizational Properties: A Comparative Analysis," *American Journal of Sociology,* Vol. 72, No. 5 (March 1967), 503–19; Blau "Hierarchy of Authority"; and Marshall W. Meyer, "Two Authority Structures of Bureaucratic Organization," *Administrative Science Quarterly,* Vol. 13, No. 2 (September 1968); 211–28; Meyer, "Automation and Bureaucratic Structure," *American Journal of Sociology,* Vol. 74, No. 3 (November 1968), 256–64; Meyer, "Expertness and the Span of Control," *American Sociological Review;* Vol. 33, No. 6 (December 1968), 944–51.

Differing types of technology and environment are seen to result in differing types of structure and process. The final component for an adequate typology is the nature and impact of an organization's output. Here Blau and Scott's idea of prime beneficiary may turn out to be highly relevant. Organizations do have outputs of varying sorts that are consumed or utilized by other segments of the society. The nature of the input (general environment and technology) is modified by the organization as it develops its output. All three aspects of the nature of organizations have to be considered in developing a typology with maximum utility.

The output component, of course, is a link back into the environment. An organization's output itself has an impact on future inputs, but can be analytically separated. Some important components in the analysis of outputs appear to be the organization's relative power in regard to the recipients of its actions; the presence of other organizations that produce the same output and are potential and real sources of conflict or cooperation; the general acceptance by customers, clients, and the wider society of the organization's product or service; and the congruence between the environment's demands and what the organization supplies. These output components, while important and the subject of a rather extensive body of writing, have not received much empirical investigation. Their importance can be seen, however, in a number of unrelated empirical investigations.

Burton Clark, in a study of an adult education organization,[35] found that the organization essentially had no power over the recipients of its actions (it also had no power over its inputs, nor over the students in the system). In contrast to the greater power held by other educational organizations, it could not tell the environment that what it was doing to and for the students should be willingly accepted and consumed. Educational organizations in general have less power over their environment than some other organizations, with school boards, PTA groups, alumni, trustees, and legislators forming potential and actual strong control groups. However, they can usually say, "We know what is best for the student in terms of curriculum, course content, etc." The adult education system studied by Clark could not do this. Many other organizations have significantly more power over their systems, as in the case of a toothpaste manufacturer's advertising that its new product will make teeth significantly less likely to fall out. The public, not presuming to have the knowledge about toothpaste that it does about the educational process, assumes that the advertising is correct and buys the toothpaste. This type of power is symbolized best by the statement

---

[35] Burton R. Clark, *Adult Education in Transition* (Berkeley: University of California Press, 1956).

of the former president of General Motors that "what is good for General Motors is good for the nation."

The presence or absence of other organizations in the same field is obviously important to the way output is consumed. A monopoly in an area that is in demand makes an organization operate differently from one that has stiff competition. In the former case, the organization has a great deal more control over what it does and how it operates. If it is in a competitive or even cooperative relationship with other organizations at the output end of its operations, it must devote some of its activities toward these relationships. The same is true, of course, at the input point.

Selznick's classic study of the Tennessee Valley Authority's early history[36] is a clear example of the impact on an organization of having its own outputs not accepted at first by its relevant environment. The TVA had to alter drastically what it did and how it was structured before local acceptance was realized. If an organization's product or service is not accepted by the environment, it either ceases to exist, continues its existence by subsidy from a parent organization or other donors, or modifies its output. In the case of subsidy, there is a strong tendency for changes to occur over time, since the economic and social costs of such subsidies are more than most benefactors are willing to bear. A major factor here appears to be the extent to which organizations are insulated from direct economic or social accounting.

An organization that is oriented toward profit and has direct evidence of an activity's unprofitability, as in the case of a subsidiary organization that continues to lose money, is very likely to attempt to make some direct changes in the operation. On the social side, the issue is somewhat more clouded. The social impact of most organizations is difficult to assess in almost all cases. A clear example of nonacceptance of a social program and the results on the organization can be seen in the recurring controversies over sex education in the public schools. Nonacceptance, in the form of open resistance to the programs on the part of some of the public, has led to the defeat of persons running for school board positions, with those elected having run on the basis of making changes in the sex education program. The organizational effects are a changed power structure and usually a sex education program that is altered. When the economic or social nonacceptance cannot be as readily assessed as in the examples discussed, the organizational effects of the nonacceptance are tempered. Organizational alterations will occur at both a slower and a less extensive rate.

36 Phillip Selznick, *TVA and the Grass Roots* (New York: Harper Torchbook Edition, 1966). Originally published 1949, University of California Press, Berkeley.

The discussion of nonacceptance has been based on organizations that are oriented toward the more general public. A very different picture emerges when we consider organizations that are directed toward serving their own members. These, which have been labeled voluntary or mutual-benefit organizations, are exceptional in many ways. In the matter under discussion, public acceptance remains an important matter but in quite a different way. Although these organizations serve their own members, many of them have values they would like to see accepted by the wider society. Political parties, religious organizations, and protest organizations are all voluntary and all have wider publics. The degree to which the more general public accepts their values varies. The organizations themselves differ widely in the importance they attach to public acceptance. For the Democratic or Republican political parties, such acceptance is vital, while for the Vegetarian Party it is not so crucial.

Even those voluntary organizations that are primarily inwardly oriented toward their own members must obtain some general public acceptance if they are to persist over time. Members who resign or die must be replaced. Since these organizations are typically based upon some set of values, either new members must be recruited from a population that holds these values, or the values must be learned by nonbelievers. In either case, marginal organizational values would be a threat to continued organizational existence. Some of the complexity in the relationship between values and voluntary organizations can be seen in Joseph Gusfield's study of the Women's Christian Temperance Union (WCTU).[37] This organization, which at its heyday had a large membership and a strong impact on the development of the Prohibition movement in the United States, was confronted with the question of whether or not to modify its own views in the light of the changed public attitude toward alcoholic beverages after the death of Prohibition. The organization chose to adhere to its belief in abstinence rather than shift to the more popular view of moderation in drinking. Its membership declined, recruitment became more and more difficult, its impact on the public has become minimal. At present, the WCTU is almost exclusively a "mutual-benefit" organization, in that its members talk largely to themselves, rather than to the wider public.

This excursion into the topic of voluntary organizations raises an important issue. In many ways it is difficult or impossible to include voluntary organizations in our general definition and classification system of organizations. The unclear boundaries, the varying involvement

[37] Joseph R. Gusfield, *Symbolic Crusade* (Urbana, Ill.: University of Illinois Press, 1963).

on the part of members, and the relationships with the environment all contribute to this assessment. Furthermore, many of the structural characteristics of other organizations are either not present at all or are present in such a different fashion that it seems impossible to discuss the voluntary organization from the same perspectives as other organizations. Since we are concerned with all organizations, however, voluntary organizations will be considered in the analysis, including typological efforts. Information and conclusions about the consequences of some variable, such as the distribution of power, will be assumed to be as relevant for voluntary organizations as for the nonvoluntary. The structural and processual characteristics we will be discussing are all variables, and so they vary in their degree of presence or absence in organizations. The voluntary organization can therefore be included in the analysis with the realization that some components of the analysis may not be relevant for the voluntary organization if the components are not present in it. This admittedly awkward conclusion avoids the pitfalls of total inclusion or exclusion and concentrates instead on the importance of the variables involved.

To return to ouput relationships as part of a system of organizational classification, another element of this category that has been identified is the specific nature of the relationships with clients and customers. Mark Lefton and William Rosengren [38] have suggested that two major dimensions of these relationships can be identified, based upon the scope of the organization's interactions with the client. The lateral dimension involves the amount of *social space* in the relationship, or the degree to which the client is viewed as a total person. A long-term therapeutic hospital exemplifies large social space, whereas the short-term general hospital is concerned with only a specified illness and not with other components of the individual. The second dimension is the longitudinal, or *social time* aspect. Using the medical example again, the emergency room of a hospital has a short-time interest in the client, while the tuberculosis hospital has a long-term involvement with its patients. According to Lefton and Rosengren, these dimensions vary somewhat independently.

These variations in client involvement are then related to a series of issues that organizations must resolve, including the conformity and commitment of the client to the organization, problems of achieving consensus among the staff, and the nature of interorganizational collaboration. The client in this case is considered as someone outside the organization, with the organization's activities as outputs affecting him.

---

38 Mark Lefton and William R. Rosengren, "Organizations and Clients: Lateral and Longitudinal Dimensions," *American Sociological Review*, Vol. 31, No. 6, (December 1966), 802–10.

For the long-term and extensive social space relationship, it is more difficult to exclude the client from membership in the organization and therefore to put him at the output end of the equation.

Nevertheless, the point made in the Lefton and Rosengren research is important for the present discussion. If the output of an organization requires consensus and commitment on the part of clients and customers, the organization will have to take actions toward this end. If, on the other hand, the organization does not have to be concerned about these issues, its energies need not to be invested in the maintenance of good client–customer relationships. An extremely practical example of this is in the case of defense contractors, who require consensus and commitment from the government for their continued operations, and who therefore frequently employ a large number of retired military personnel in the hope that their knowledge and contacts will ensure continued contracts for military purposes. They attempt thus to manipulate the customer as their relevant environment. Other organizations of similar size that are not so dependent on single customers also attempt to ensure continued survival and profit through advertising to the general public. The form and content of the organizations' efforts in these two settings are drastically different; so we see that client–customer relationships are another important consideration in organizational outputs.

The discussion in this section has not focused specifically on classificatory systems. *It has tried to identify some of the major elements necessary for organizational analysis.* It is these elements, plus those that are identified in future research, that should serve as the basis for an adequate taxonomy of organizations. This taxonomy should treat the organization as both a dependent and an independent variable. It is a dependent variable when we consider factors such as technology, the general environment, and the nature of the personnel coming into the organization—all independent variables that should be related to the nature of the organizations themselves in terms of their structures and processes. The organization becomes the independent variable in relation to the impact of its outputs, the compliance structure, employee morale and satisfaction, or patterns of internal conflict. The adequate typology should be empirically based. Relationships that have been demonstrated should serve as the basis for classification and the demonstration of further relationships.

Although a typology of organizations is not available, many empirical relationships have been demonstrated and others have been hypothesized and proposed. As these are tested, the typological effort will advance, and it may be possible at some future time to state that an organization with an x environmental configuration will have a y structural and processual system with a z set of output relationships. Most of the rest of the analysis in this book will be concerned with the further identification of the elements that are central for the understanding of organizations. Where they are known, the relationships among these elements will be discussed. While no typology per se will be presented, since this would be premature, elements that are important for such typologies will be examined. It will be suggested, for example, that organizations that are highly formalized have a series of other characteristics in common. It is from this type of approach that a useful typology can eventually be developed.

SUMMARY AND CONCLUSIONS

Classificatory schemes are needed in every facet of social life for thought and action. Despite the need for typologies, no adequate scheme for organizations is available. The "common-sense" divisions between profit and nonprofit or governmental and nongovernmental organizations yield more confusion than clarity. Typologies based upon a single basic principle, such as those of Parsons, Etzioni, and Blau and Scott, do not sufficiently differentiate between organizations and do not divide organizations on more than a single meaningful issue. The attempt to derive a taxonomy from a mass of empirical data suffered because of weaknesses in the data and limitations on the relevance of the variables measured. It was proposed that the development of an adequate typology must await further empirical investigations that demonstrate established relationships between central organizational elements. These elements are in the areas of the environmental factors that come into the organization, structural and processual factors within the organization itself, and the relationships between the organization and the utilizers and recipients of its performance. The demonstration of relationships among these major areas should permit the development of a usable classification system.

Thus far we have been basically presenting the conceptual model to be used in the analysis. In this chapter, the model was presented as a way in which a typology could be developed. But conceptual models and typologies are meaningless unless the subject matter means anything itself. It is time now to get into the issue of what organizations do and how well they do it.

GOALS
AND
EFFECTIVENESS

3

Most of the discussion thus far has made use of the concept of organizational goals either explicitly or implicitly. From the original definitions to the major models of organizations in the literature, the goal concept has ranged from the status of primary importance to that of whipping boy for those who believe that organizations are basically not goal-seeking entities. In either case, attention is paid to goals. And also, since organizations are engaged in activities of one sort or another and these activities accomplish something, the issue of goal attainment, or effectiveness (even those who deny the relevance of the goal concept are concerned with effectiveness), is an inseparable part of the discussion.

The plan of this chapter is to examine the nature of organizational goals, as abstractions and as practical and research issues, and then to consider varying approaches to effectiveness. Since effectiveness can be approached from more perspectives than just that of the organization itself, the discussion here will examine the other parties concerned with respect to how an organization accomplishes what it sets out to do and how it affects them. The analysis will be based on the ideas discussed in the previous chapter and should serve to make some of the abstractions more real as specific research and practical problems are discussed.

ORGANIZATIONAL GOALS

"An organizational goal is a desired state of affairs which the organization attempts to realize." [1] This desired state of affairs is by definition many things to many people. In a large organization, top executives may see the organization seeking one kind of state while those in the middle and lower echelons may have drastically different goals for the organization and for themselves personally. Even in an organization in which there is high participation in decision making and strong membership commitment, it is unlikely that there will be a totally unanimous consensus on what the organization should attempt to do, let alone on the means of achieving these ends.

The goal idea at first glance seems most simple in the case of profit-making organizations. Indeed, much of the research on effectiveness has used this type of organization because of goal clarity. The readily quantifiable profit goal is not such a simple matter, however. It is confounded by such issues as the time perspective (long-run or short-run profits); the rate of profit (in terms of return to investors); the important issue of survival and growth in a turbulent and unpredictable environment that might in the short run preclude profit making; the intrusion of other values, such as providing quality products or services, or benefiting mankind; and the firm's comparative position vis-à-vis others in the same industry. Leaving aside for the moment the question of *whose* goals these alternative values might represent, the difficulties apparent in the straightforward profit-making firm are indicative of the difficulties inherent in determining what the goals of an organization really are. When the situation is shifted to a consideration of the goals of a government agency, university, or church, the determination of the organization's goals becomes almost impossible.

Take, for example, the case of a governmental regulative agency charged with administering the public utilities laws and regulations of a state. A casual view suggests that this is a unitary goal, assuming that the laws and regulations are clearly stated. However, this assumption is seldom met, given the large number of lawyers and other technical experts employed by the agency for the purpose of developing and defending interpretations of the existing laws. Administration in such a case is not a simple matter either, since the choice between active and pas-

---

1 Amitai Etzioni, *Modern Organizations* (Englewood Cliffs, N.J.: Prentice-Hall, Inc., 1964), p. 6.

sive administration is a political and organizational football. The well-known distinction between the letter and the intent of the law becomes an issue for such agencies as they develop their operating procedures. What is the goal for the agency? If it is staffed by personnel who have values above and beyond simply administering the existing laws (every organization contains personnel with differing values), their own values toward social action or inaction can clearly modify the stated goals of the organization. In the case of the public utilities agency, beliefs in such diverse areas as air and water pollution, the nature of the publics served by the agency (the public, segments of the public, or the organizations involved), the desirability of maintaining certain public services despite their unprofitability (as in the case of railroad passenger service), and competition versus monopoly in public services—these merely exemplify the range of alternatives available as goals for this organization aside from those found in its formal charter.

The three commonly stated goals of colleges and universities—teaching, research, and public service—are almost by definition too vague to serve as much of a guide for organizational analysis or practice. In the light of contemporary reality, it can also be seen that they have become essentially incompatible in practice. Universities and colleges tend to concentrate on one of the three goals to the exclusion of the others. While emphases change, the basic issue of deciding among these goals remains. And also, since each contains vast uncertainties—exactly what is meant by good teaching, research, or service?—the use of the goal concept in this setting becomes excruciatingly difficult.

With an understanding of some of the difficulties in the utilization of the goal concept, let us examine the concept more systematically.

The Meaning of Organizational Goals

Organizational goals can be approached from a variety of perspectives. Parsons has cogently pointed out that organizational goals are intimately interwined with important and basic societal functions, such as integration, pattern maintenance, and so on.[2] From this point of view, organizational goals are really an extension of what the society needs for its own survival. At the other extreme is the position that organizational goals are nothing more than the goals of the individual members of the organization. Both positions disguise more than they illuminate. If the level of analysis is kept in the broad societal-function

[2] Talcott Parsons, *Structure and Process in Modern Societies* (New York: The Free Press, 1960), pp. 17–22 and 44–47.

framework, the variations in goals and activities among organizations performing the same basic functions are ignored. If the level of analysis focuses on just the variety of individual goals, the whole point of organizations is missed—if there were only individual goals, there would be no point in organizing. Clearly, many individuals may have the same goal, such as making a profit, furthering a cause, or destroying an enemy. Clearly also, however, when these people come together in the form of an organization, the profit, cause, or destruction becomes an abstraction toward which they work together.

Organizational goals by definition are creations of individuals, singly or collectively. At the same time, the determination of a goal for collective action becomes a standard by which the collective action is judged. As we will see, the collectively determined, commonly based goal seldom remains constant over time. New considerations imposed from without or within deflect the organization from its original goal, not only changing the activities of the organization, but also becoming part of the overall goal structure. The important point is that the goal of any organization is an abstraction distilled from the desires of members and pressures from the environment and internal system. While there is never 100 percent agreement among members as to what organizational goals are or should be, members can articulate a goal that is a desired state for the organization at some future point in time.

This approach is in some ways similar to that of Herbert Simon. Simon's major focus is on decision making within the organization. He notes that:

> When we are interested in the internal structure of an organization, however, the problem cannot be avoided. . . . Either we must explain organizational behavior in terms of the goals of the individual members of the organization, or we must postulate the existence of one or more organizational goals, over and above the goals of the individuals.[3]

Simon then goes on to differentiate between the goals or value premises that serve as inputs to decisions and motives, and the causes that lead individuals to select some goals over others as the basis for their decision making. He keeps the goal idea at the individual level, but offers the important notion that the goals of an organization at any point in time are the result of the interaction among the members of the organization.

To this we would add that external conditions also affect the nature of an organization's goals. An example is the case of many current military organizations. The official goal is typically to protect the state

[3] Herbert A. Simon, "On the Concept of Organizational Goal," *Administrative Science Quarterly*, Vol. 9, No. 1 (June 1964), 2.

and its people from external threats. The leaders of the military organization may come to believe, for any number of reasons, that the goal is to be victorious over a wide variety of enemies (this is not necessarily the same as protecting the state). This then becomes the goal until it is modified by interactions or conflicts with lower-level personnel, or with external forces in the form of some type of civilian control, with the goal again becoming altered to engagement in limited wars without winning or protecting the state. In this hypothetical and oversimplified example, the goals of individual organization members, particularly those in high positions, are crucial in goal setting. These goals are modified in the course of internal and external interactions.

In Simon's approach, goals become constraints on the decision-making process. The constraints are based on abstract values around which the organization operates. Decisions are made within the framework of a set of constraints (goals), and organizations attempt to make decisions that are optimal in terms of the sets of constraints they face. While the approach taken here is not based solely on the decision-making framework, the perspective is the same. Organizational actions are constrained not only by goals, but also by the external and internal factors that have been discussed. In probably the great majority of cases, goals are one, if not the only, relevant constraint.

Operative Goals

Treating goals as abstract values has the merit of showing that organizational actions are guided by more than the day-to-day whims of individual members. At the same time, abstract values are just that—abstract. They must be converted to specific guides for the actual operations of an organization. Perrow takes this position when he distinguishes between "official" and "operative" organizational goals.[4] Official goals are "the general purposes of the organization as put forth in the charter, annual reports, public statements by key executives and other authoritative pronouncements." Operative goals, on the other hand, "designate the ends sought through the actual operating policies of the organization; they tell us what the organization actually is trying to do, regardless of what the official goals say are the aims."

This distinction is grounded in reality. Two organizations, both with the official goal of profit making, may differ drastically in the amount of emphasis they place on making profits. Blau's examination of two em-

---

[4] Charles Perrow, "The Analysis of Goals in Complex Organizations," *American Sociological Review*, Vol. 26, No. 6 (December 1961), 855.

ployment agencies with the same official goals shows wide variations between the agencies in what they were actually trying to accomplish.[5] In his discussion of this point, Perrow states:

> Where operative goals provide the specific content of official goals, they reflect choices among competing values. They may be justified on the basis of an official goal, even though they may subvert another official goal. In one sense they are means to official goals, but since the latter are vague or of high abstraction, the "means" become ends in themselves when the organization is the object of analysis. For example, where profit making is the announced goal, operative goals will specify whether quality or quantity is to be emphasized, whether profits are to be short run and risky or long run and stable, and will indicate the relative priority of diverse and somewhat conflicting ends of customer service, employee morale, competitive pricing, diversification, or liquidity. Decisions on all these factors influence the nature of the organization, and distinguish it from another with an identical official goal.[6]

From this perspective, operative goals become the standards by which the organization's actions are judged and around which decisions are made. In many cases these operative goals reflect the official goals, in that they are abstractions made more concrete. However, operative goals can evolve that are basically unrelated to the official goals. In this regard, Perrow notes:

> Unofficial operative goals, on the other hand, are tied more directly to group interests, and while they may support, be irrelevant to, or subvert official goals, they bear no necessary connection with them. An interest in a major supplier may dictate the policies of a corporation executive. The prestige that attaches to utilizing elaborate high-speed computers may dictate the reorganization of inventory and accounting departments. Racial prejudice may influence the selection procedures of an employment agency. The personal ambition of a hospital administrator may lead to community alliances and activities which bind the organization without enhancing its goal achievement. On the other hand, while the use of interns and residents as "cheap labor" may subvert the official goal of medical education, it may substantially further the official goal of providing a high quality of patient care.[7]

Operative goals thus reflect the derivation and distillation of a set of goals from both official and unofficial sources. These operative goals are developed through interaction patterns within the organization, but persist after the interactions are completed. They reflect the "desired state of affairs," or abstract official goals, the modifications and subver-

---

5 Peter M. Blau, *The Dynamics of Bureaucracy* (Chicago: University of Chicago Press, 1955).
6 Perrow, "Analysis of Goals," pp. 855–56.
7 *Ibid.,* 6. 856.

sions of these by personnel in decision-making positions, and the force of pressures from the external environment. It is the combination of official goals with internal and external factors that leads to an existing set of operative goals.

If the use of unofficial goals is carried too far, of course, every organization could be viewed as having a huge, perhaps infinite, number of such goals. The distinction must be made, therefore, between goals and operating policies and procedures. The latter are the exact specifications, formally or informally stated, of what individual actors at all levels are to do in their daily activities. Goals, on the other hand, remain at the abstract level, serving as constraining or guiding principles from which policies and procedures can be derived. Operative goals are abstractions in the same way as official goals. They are a set of ideas about where the organization should be going, which are operationalized into specific plans and procedures.

The Determination of Organizational Goals

How does one find out exactly what the goals of an organization are? From the research point of view, this is a vital step if there is to be any concern with issues such as effectiveness, personnel and resource allocation, or optimal structuring. In a very real sense, organizational research must be concerned with goals if it is to be anything more than simply descriptive. For the member of the organization at any level, goal determination is similarly vital. If he misses what the goals really are, his own actions may not only not contribute to the organization, they may contribute to his own organizational demise. Members of organizations must know the "system" if they are to operate within it or to change it. From the discussion above, it should be clear that the "system" is much more than official statements.

The vital importance of understanding operative goals can perhaps best be exemplified by an actual case.[8] The case in point is the familiar one of the goals of a university. The University of Minnesota *Faculty Information* booklet contains the following statements:

TEACHING

The University emphasizes excellence in teaching. The first duty of every faculty member engaged in instruction is the communication of knowledge and values to students, and the stimulation of their intellectual ability, curiosity, and imagination.

[8] Cases and case studies are useful as examples, but they cannot be used as bases for generalizations concerning other organizations, even of a very similar type.

RESEARCH

Research is the second strong arm of the University. The faculty member is aided in obtaining funds and facilities for research, and is encouraged to contribute to the ever-expanding realms of human knowledge.

PUBLIC SERVICE AND PROFESSIONAL COMMITMENTS

. . . .

UNIVERSITY SERVICE

. . . .

COMMUNITY SERVICE

. . . .[9]

As everyone must know, these goals are not equally stressed, even though the official pronouncement would lead one to believe otherwise. If a new (or old) faculty member actually believed what he read, he would probably soon find himself at a distinct disadvantage. One of the questions asked of the faculty, in at least one department, when salary increases for the coming year were being considered was the number of offers from other universities that each had received. The larger number of offers, apparently, the greater the likelihood of receiving a substantial raise, and vice versa. But the vast majority of such offers are forthcoming to those who are active in the research side of the goal equation, since the other factors cannot be readily visible to other institutions. This is not an unusual case, nor is the meaning of it limited to colleges and universities. Knowledge of operative goals is imperative for effective functioning and for the effective implementation of one's own ideas. At the extreme, such knowledge is necessary for individual survival in organizations.

Operative-goal determination for the individual is obviously important. It is plainly part of the ongoing organizational system, also, and thus central to organizational functioning. It is equally important for the organizational analyst. The significance of operative goals forces the analyst to go beyond the more easily determined official goals. The key to finding out what the operative goals are lies in the actual decisions of the top decision-makers in the organization. The kinds of decisions they make about allocation of resources (money, personnel, equipment, etc.) are a major indicator. In a study of juvenile correctional organizations, Mayer Zald found that resources were consistently allocated to the custodial and traditional aspects of the institutions rather than to professional treatment personnel, despite official pronouncements that

[9] *Faculty Information* (Minneapolis: University of Minnesota, 1966), pp. 7–8.

rehabilitation was the goal.[10] Although lower-level personnel influence the decisions made in the organization, it is the people near or at the top who have the major and sometimes final say in organizational matters.

The determination of these operative goals is more easily said than done. Organizations may be reluctant to allow the researcher or member access to the kinds of records that show the nature of resource allocation. In interviews they may tend to repeat the official goal as a form of rhetoric. However, the analyst or member can determine operative goals through the use of multiple methods of data collection from a variety of goal indicators, such as the deployment of personnel, growth patterns among departments, examination of available records, and so on.

Since operative goals reflect what the major decision-makers believe to be the critical areas and issues for the organization, it follows that the operative goals will shift as internal and external conditions impinge upon the organization. It was argued in the last chapter that these conditions can deflect the organization from a pursuit of its goals. In a real sense, the operative goals are deflected by these threats or conditions during periods of severe stress. At the same time, *the operative goals will usually reflect some variation on the theme of the official goal.* That is, operative goals are generally based on the official goals, even though there is not perfect correspondence. Profit-making organizations vary in their emphases, colleges and universities pay more or less attention to teaching, research, and so on, and hospitals are concerned to varying degree with teaching, patient care, and research. If the official goals remain the same when pressures, conditions, and priorities change, the shift in operative goals will be mainly in emphasis.

Changes in Organizational Goals

Organizational goals change for three major reasons. The first is direct pressure from external forces, which leads to a deflection from the original goals. Second is pressure from internal sources. This may lead the organization to emphasize quite different activities than those originally intended. The third factor is changed environmental and technological demands that lead the organization to redefine its goals. While this is similar to the first reason, the factors here occur in *indirect*

---

[10] Mayer N. Zald, "Comparative Analysis and Measurement of Organizational Goals: The Case of Correctional Institutions for Delinquents," *The Sociological Quarterly*, Vol. 4, No. 2 (Spring 1963), 206–30.

interaction with the organization, whereas in the first case the organization is in *direct* interaction with the relevant environmental factors.

The impact of external relationships on goals is best seen in Thompson and McEwen's analysis of organization–environmental interactions.[11] They note that organizational goal setting is affected by competitive, bargaining, co-optative, and coalitional relationships with the environment. In the competitive situation—"that form of rivalry between two or more organizations which is mediated by a third party"—organizations must devote their efforts toward gaining support for their continued existence. Competition is most easily seem among business firms that compete for the customer's dollar, but it is also very evident among government agencies as they compete for a share of the tax dollar or among religious organizations as they compete for members and their support. (Religious and other voluntary organizations must also compete with alternative organizations for membership and money.) Competition partially controls the organization's "choice of goals" in that its energies must be turned to the competitive activity. Continuous support is vital for continued survival as an organization.

Bargaining also involves resources, but in this case the organization is in direct interaction with supplier, consumer, and other organizations. In the bargaining situation, the organization must "give" a little to get what it desires. Bargaining takes place in standard relationships between two organizations, as in the case where a routine supplier is asked to alter its goods for the organization. This "custom" order will cost the supplier more money and hence he bargains for a better price, with the organization bargaining to get its custom equipment at the old price. Thompson and McEwen note that universities will often bargain away the name of a building for a substantial gift. Government agencies may bargain by not enforcing certain regulations in order to maintain support for the seeking of other goals. The impact of bargaining is more subtle than that of competition, but it has a similar impact on goal setting.

Co-optation is "the process of absorbing new elements into the leadership or policy-determining structure of an organization as a means of averting threats to its stability or existence." [12] The classic study of co-optation is Selznick's *TVA and the Grass Roots,* in which he documents the impact of bringing new societal elements into the governing structure of the TVA.[13] The organization shifted its emphases partially as a

11 James D. Thompson and William J. McEwen, "Organizational Goals and Environment: Goal Setting as an Interaction Process," *Administrative Science Quarterly,* Vol. 23, No. 1 (February 1958).

12 *Ibid.,* p. 27.

13 Phillip Selznick, *TVA and the Grass Roots* (New York: Harper Torchbook Edition, 1966).

result of the new pressures brought to bear in the decision-making system. It is no accident that boards of directors or trustees contain members from pressure groups important to the organizations involved. If a member of a group that is antipathetic to the organization can be brought into the organization, the antipathy can be minimized. At the same time, the presence of person on a controlling board has an influence on decisions made, even though the hostility rate may be down. The recent movement toward "student power" among high school and college students is interesting to observe in this regard. It is predicted that student members of college and university governing bodies and boards of trustees will be co-opted—that is, the students will become part of the power structure and take its view—but also that the organizations involved will find their goal setting at least minimally influenced by the presence of the students. Co-optation is thus a two-way street. Both those co-opted and those doing the co-opting are influenced.

The final type of external relationship is coalition, or the "combination of two or more organizations for a common purpose. Coalition appears to be the ultimate or extreme form of environmental conditioning of organizational goals." [14] While seeking common purposes, coalitions place strong constraints on the organizations involved, since they cannot set goals in a unilateral fashion.

Although it is clear that other environmental factors also affect the nature of organizational goals, Thompson and McEwen's analysis centers around transactions with other organizations. They suggest a very important consideration in the determination of the operative goals of an organization: Organizations operate in a "field" of other organizations, [15] and these affect what the focal organization does. While this has been amply demonstrated in economic analysis of market competition, the impact goes beyond this type of relationship. The interactions we have described are direct evidence that the use of official-goal statements would be misleading, since the transactions with other organizations by definition would deflect an organization from its official goal.

Operative goals are also affected by what goes on inside an organization. A given set of goals may be altered drastically by changes in the power system of the organization, new types of personnel, as in the case of a sudden influx of professionals, and the development of new standards that supersede those of the past. Etzioni has called this phenomenon "goal displacement." [16]

14 Thompson and McEwen, "Organizational Goals and Environment," p. 28.
15 For a further discussion of this point, see Roland L. Warren, "The Interorganizational Field as a Focus for Investigation," *Administrative Science Quarterly*, Vol. 12, No. 3 (December 1967), 396–419.
16 Etzioni, *Modern Organizations*, p. 10.

Goal displacement is clearly evident in Robert Michels' analysis of Socialist parties and labor unions in Europe in the early twentieth century.[17] In this study he developed the idea of the "iron law of oligarchy." Michels pointed out that these revolutionary groups began as democratic organizations. The need for organization to accomplish the revolutionary purposes (operative goals) led to the establishment of leaders of the organizations. The leaders, tasting power, did not want to relinquish it, and therefore devoted much of their energies to maintain their positions. Since members of most voluntary organizations, even revolutionary parties, are politically indifferent, and since the skills necessary for leading the parties are not universally distributed, the leaders could rather easily perpetuate themselves in power—in part by co-opting or purging the young potential leaders. The emphasis in the parties shifted to organizational maintenance, at the expense of militancy and revolutionary zeal. Close parallels to this situation exist in contemporary revolutionary and militant movements of every political and social persuasion.

A different form of goal displacement can be seen in Robert Scott's analysis of the "sheltered workshop for the blind." [18] When these workshops were formed in the early twentieth century, the overall goal was to integrate the blind into the industrial community. However, it was recognized that many blind people could not work in regular factories, and so the sheltered workshops were developed to provide the blind with work (making brooms and mops, weaving, chair caning, etc.) as a social service. Owing to a series of events, the workshops began to define themselves as factories in competition with nonblind producers of goods. The emphasis shifted from helping the blind to employing competent workers (not necessarily mutually exclusive categories), and the social-service function largely fell by the wayside. Part of the reason for the shift in emphasis lay in changed environmental conditions, with an increased demand for the workshops' products. But it appears that these demands could have been resisted and the original intent of the workshops maintained intact. The internal decision-making process led to the development of clearly different goals from those professed at the outset.

Still another type of displacement can be seen in what Etzioni calls "over-measurement" and Bertram Gross labels "number magic." [19] Both refer to the tendency for organizations of all types to organize their energies (goals) around activities that are easily quantified. Easy quan-

17 Robert Michels, *Political Parties* (New York: The Free Press, 1949).

18 Robert A. Scott, "The Factory as a Social Service Organization: Goal Displacement in Workshops for the Blind," *Social Problems,* Vol. 15, No. 2 (Fall 1967), 160–75.

19 Etzioni, *Modern Organizations,* pp. 8–10; and Bertram M. Gross, *Organizations and Their Managing* (New York: The Free Press, 1968), p. 293.

tification leads to counting publications of university faculty rather than evaluating classroom performance, looking at output per worker rather than "diligence, cooperation, punctuality, loyalty, and responsibility,"[20] and counting parishioners in a church rather than assessing the spiritual guidance of the parishioners.[21] These examples could be multiplied many times for many organizations. The obvious solution to this problem is to use multiple indicators for determining the extent to which organizations are achieving their goals. When this is not done and the easily quantifiable measure is stressed, organizational goals become deflected toward the achievement of the easily measured aspect.[22] This may in turn actually defeat the purpose for which the organization was designed. These internal sources of goals change can be found in any organization and are a basic part of the determination of the operative goals. In the extreme cases discussed here, the changes are rather clearly dysfunctional in terms of the official and original operative goals; but the processes inherent in these changes are a normal part of the goal-setting process.

The final source of goal change is a more generalized environmental pressure—generalized, that is, in terms of falling within abstract categories such as technological development, cultural changes, and economic conditions; however, the impact on the organization is direct. Several studies are available that provide direct evidence for this basis of goal change. Perhaps the most dramatic evidence comes from David L. Sills' analysis of the national Foundation for Infantile Paralysis.[23] Although the study was completed before the transition to be discussed was accomplished, the change in operative goals is very evident. The foundation was formed to assist in the prevention and treatment of polio through research, coordinating, and fund-raising activities. At the time the foundation was organized, polio was a major health problem, highlighted by Franklin D. Roosevelt's crippled condition as a result of the disease. Roosevelt himself founded the organization in 1938 at the height of his own popularity and the seriousness of the polio problem. The organization grew rapidly, and its March of Dimes became a very successful volunteer fund-raising effort.

In less than two decades, the organization accomplished its primary goal. Through the development of the Salk and Sabine vaccines, polio has largely been eliminated as a serious health hazard. Rehabilitation

[20] Gross, *Organizations and Their Managing*, p. 295.

[21] Etzioni, *Modern Organizations*, p. 10.

[22] For an extended discussion of this point, see W. Keith Warner and A. Eugene Havens, "Goal Displacement and the Intangibility of Organizational Goals," *Administrative Science Quarterly*, Vol. 12, No. 4 (March 1968), 539–55.

[23] David L. Sills, *The Volunteers* (New York: The Free Press, 1957).

facilities have been consistently improved to assist those who suffer from the effects of polio contracted in the past (the number of new cases at present is insignificant). For the organization, these events presented a clear dilemma. The choice was between going out of business and developing a new goal. The latter alternative was chosen, as the organization decided to concentrate on "other crippling diseases," with particular emphasis on birth defects. Sills suggests that the presence of a strong national headquarters together with committed volunteers should maintain the organization over time. The historical evidence seems to confirm this, although the organization does not appear to be as strong as it was during the polio epidemics.

The volunteer and nonvolunteer members of this organization had a vested interest in its maintenance. At the same time, technological developments outside the organization made its continuation questionable because of its operative goals at that time. The focus of the organization shifted to adapt to the changed technology. While some of the operative goals remained the same, others shifted to meet the new concerns.

The impact of technological shifts can also be seen in Lawrence and Lorsch's analysis of firms in the plastics industry. In this case, technological change, in the form of a rapidly changing "state of the art," is an ever-present and pressing factor of the environment. In discussing the performance of organizations in this industry, Lawrence and Lorsch comment:

> The low-performing organizations were both characterized by their top administrators as having serious difficulty in dealing with this environment. They had not been successful in introducing and marketing new products. In fact, their attempts to do so had met with repeated failures. This record, plus other measures of performance available to top management, left them with a feeling of disquiet and a sense of urgency to find ways of improving their performance.[24]

This sense of urgency would be translated into altered operative goals for the organization as it seeks to cope more effectively with the rapidly changing technological system.

Technology is not the only environmental factor impinging upon the organization, despite its apparent centrality. The general values in the environment surrounding an organization also affect its operation. Burton Clark's analysis of the adult education system in California indicates clearly that an organization is vitally affected by the values of those whom it serves and whose support it seeks.[25]

[24] Paul R. Lawrence and Jay W. Lorsch, *Organization and Environment: Managing Differentiation and Integration* (Cambridge: Harvard Graduate School of Bussiess Administration, 1967), p. 42.

[25] Burton R. Clark, "Organizational Adaptation and Precarious Values," *American Sociological Review*, Vol. 21, No. 3 (June 1956), 327–36.

The adult education system's official goals are concerned with relatively lofty matters, such as awareness of civic responsibilities, economic uplift, personal adjustment in the family, health and physical fitness, cultural development, broadened educational background, and the development of avocational interests. This educational system suffers from a number of handicaps. It is part of the public educational system but not part of the normal sequence. It is a "peripheral, non-mandatory" part; and this marginality is heightened by the fact that the system operates on an "enrollment economy." That is, school income is determined largely by attendance (paid) in classes. If attendance declines, support for the program from tax revenues is likely also to decline. Course enrollments become *"the* criterion by which courses are initiated and continued." [26]

Courses are offered only if they are popular. It is not surprising, therefore, to find classes in cake decorating, rug making, and square dancing. While these are legitimate avocational activities, the pressure for courses such as these precludes much attention being paid to the other official goals and increases the criticisms of the adult education program from other segments of the educational enterprise. The adult education administrators are thus caught in the bind of trying to maintain attendance in the face of competing demands for the potential student's time and trying to satisfy the pertinent criticism of other educators and members of the legislature. The values of the clientele are inconsistent with those of the system itself. The organization adapts to their demands, but then finds itself out of phase with another part of its relevant environment.

Organizations in the service area are constantly confronted with changed values that make their services in greater or lesser demands. Colleges and universities were unprepared for the rise in enrollments caused by the increased valuation placed on education during most of the 1960s. While demographic conditions would have led to a prediction of some increase, more than the expected proportions of high school graduates opted for college as opposed to other endeavors (for whatever reason). These changed values have obviously affected the goals of the organizations as they are forced to "process" students at the expense of some of the traditional goals. [27]

Shifts in cultural values and their impact on the goals of organizations are obvious in the profit-making sector also. While the goals of profit may remain, the operative goals shift as more energies are put into market research and as organizations redefine themselves as "young" organizations for the "now" generation. These are often more than

---

[26] *Ibid.,* p. 333.

[27] The case of the WCTU, discussed earlier, illustrates what happens when an organization *does not* adapt to changed values. The current shifts in college enrollment illustrate still another shift of values.

advertising slogans, in that internal transformations have occurred to refocus the organizations' activities.

Shifts in the economic and political systems surrounding an organization would have similar influences on the goals of the organization involved. While much more than goals are affected by these interactions with the environment, it should be clear that organizational goals, like the organizations for which they serve as constraints and guides for action, are not static. Internal and external factors affect them. The relative strength of the various factors affecting goals, which would include the decision-making and power processes within the organization, have not been determined. We do know that these factors are operative, but we cannot specify the conditions under which the importance of these factors varies.

The Utility of the Goal Concept

The factors that affect goals, and the fact that the meaningful goals for an organization are not those officially pronounced, might lead us to reject the goal concept altogether. But there is still the simple but basic fact that the organization would not exist if it were not for some common purpose. Except in the case of conscription, as in the military system or the public schools, members come to the organization willingly, if not enthusiastically. In all cases, the organization engages in some activity. This activity is not simply random behavior; it is based on some notion of what the purpose of the action is.

This purpose or goal is the basis for organizational activities. It is true that means can come to be emphasized more heavily than the goal itself, that members of the organization may have no idea of why they are doing what they are doing, and that ritualistic adherence to outmoded norms may become the norm; but these behaviors would be impossible without the presence of a goal. Even when forgotten or ignored, the goal is still the basis for the organization, since the means would not have developed without it in the first place.

From the discussion above, it is clear that most organizations have more than one goal. These multiple goals may be in conflict with one another; even then, they are still a basis for action. The action itself may or may not conflict with conflicting goals. The relative importance of the goals can be determined by the way the organization allocates its resources to them. Since both external and internal pressures affect goals, along with the more rational process of goal setting, goals cannot be viewed as static. They change, sometimes dramatically, over time. These changes, it should be stressed, can occur because of decision making within the organization. This decision making is almost by definition a consequence of internal or external forces. Goal alterations decided within the organization are a consequence of the interactions of members who participate in the goal-setting process. This can be done by an oligarchic elite or through democratic processes (in very few organizations would a total democracy prevail).

Shifts in goals can also occur without a conscious decision on the part of organization members—that is, as a reaction to the external or internal pressures without a conscious reference to an abstract model of where the organization is going. While this is not goal-related behavior, the persistence of such activities leads to their becoming operative goals for the organization, as where the organization focuses its efforts on achieving easily measured objectives at the expense of more central but less easily measured goals.

It is at this point, of course, that the goal concept is most fuzzy. If an organization is oriented toward some easily quantifiable objective for the sake of measuring its achievements, the analyst can stand back and say, "Aha, this organization isn't doing what it is supposed to do!" At the same time, the easily quantified goal is an abstraction despite its easy quantification, just as is the possibly more lofty objective that serves as the analyst's point of departure. The analyst can also point out the deflections that occur as a result of the external and internal pressures discussed. Concentration upon deflections from official goals, whether they are due to quantification or external and internal pressures, can lead to the decision that goals are really not relevant for organizational analysis. It is at this point that the work of Perrow and Simon is most pertinent. Perrow's emphasis on the operative goals, however they are developed, and Simon's notion that goals place constraints on decision making both suggest that goals are relevant, even central, for organizational analysis. It does not matter what the source of operative goals might be; what does matter is that they come into the decision-making and action processes of the organization. They are still abstractions around which the organization and its members behave.

The goal concept, with the modifications we have discussed, is vital in organizational analysis. The dynamics of goal setting and goal change do not alter the fact that goals still serve as guides for what happens in an organization. If the concept of goals is not used, organizational behavior becomes a random occurrence, subject to whatever pressures and forces exist at any point in time. Since organizations have continuity and do accomplish things, the notion of goals as abstractions around which behavior is organized remains viable.

The analysis of goals is a rather empty exercise until the second part of the equation is added. Since a goal is something that is sought, the seeking leads to the issue of goal accomplishment, or effectiveness. Since goals are seldom accomplished, except in rare cases such as that of the National Foundation for Infantile Paralysis, *effectiveness* is a more usable term than *accomplishment*. The discussion of effectiveness that follows is based on the goal notion that has been developed, and also on the perspective taken in the previous chapter—that organizations attempt to be rational and goal-seeking, but are deflected by the kinds of pressures and forces that have been described.

EFFECTIVENESS

Effectiveness has been defined as the "degree to which [an organization] realizes its goals." [28] From the discussion of goals, it should be clear that effectiveness is not a simple issue. The basic difficulty in analyzing it is the fact of multiple and often conflicting goals in many organizations. Effectiveness in one set of endeavors may lead to noneffectiveness in another, particularly in the case of multipurpose organizations.

Effectiveness is a difficult issue from another standpoint. *Efficiency* is often confused with effectiveness. Etzioni defines efficiency as the "amount of resources used to produce a unit of output." [29] Clearly, an organization can be efficient without being effective, and vice versa. Recent controversies regarding certain poverty programs illustrate this point. The costs (efficiency) of producing a well-trained and well-adjusted person who came from a disadvantaged background were higher than those of producing a college graduate at some elite universities. The programs may have been effective—although this was never directly confirmed—but they were not efficient, at least from the point of view of many legislators. Efficiency and effectiveness are often closely related, but it is dangerous to assume without careful investigation that they are identical.

Despite the difficulties with the concept of effectiveness, it is one that captures the attention of almost everyone concerned with organizations. For the organization member, the effectiveness issue really boils down to the question, "Is it worth it?" While not every member is concerned with the issue, certainly those in decision-making positions are. For the organizational analyst, the same question applies, since he also wants to know whether the relationships he is examining mean anything.

[28] Etzioni, *Modern Organizations,* p. 8.
[29] *Ibid.*

The Goal Approach

The interest in effectiveness has not led to a definitive set of studies or conceptual approaches to the issue. A good part of the difficulty in assessing effectiveness lies in the problems surrounding goals. Most analyses of effectiveness are built around some version of a goal model of organization. In a relatively early study of effectiveness, Basil Georgopoulos and Arnold Tannenbaum argued that measures of effectiveness must be based on organizational means and ends, rather than relying on externally derived criteria.[30] They found that productivity, flexibility, and absence of strain and conflict were both interrelated and associated with independent assessments of effectiveness. These indicators of effectiveness were closely related to the goals of the organizations studied.

In a major effort to make some sense of the effectiveness issue, James Price has recently compiled a set of propositions dealing with effectiveness.[31] The propositions are drawn from some fifty research monographs (not all concerned specifically with effectiveness) and deal with a variety of qualities assumed by Price to be indicators of effectiveness—including productivity, morale, conformity, adaptiveness, and institutionalization. Productivity is taken as the indicator most closely related to effectiveness. Unfortunately, as Price notes, the indicators themselves do not vary together in actual practice, and what might be related to morale might be unrelated to productivity. This problem illustrates a major issue in the analysis of organizational effectiveness: Since organizations generally pursue more than one goal, the degree of effectiveness in the attainment of one goal may be inversely related to the degree in the attainment of other goals. This sort of thing does occur quite often, apparently, and so organizations must choose between the goals they seek to attain, thus reinforcing the idea that the operative goals of the organization are the result of internal choice processes and external pressures. This point also raises the strong possibility that *organizations cannot be effective,* if the idea is accepted that almost every organization has multiple goals.

Despite these problems, which Price acknowledges in part, he then links organizational characteristics to effectiveness. He suggests, for example, that organizations are likely to be more effective when they have a high degree of division of labor, specialized departmentalization, and

[30] Basil S. Georgopoulos and Arnold S. Tannenbaum, "A Study of Organizational Effectiveness," *American Sociological Review,* Vol. 22, No. 5 (October 1957), 534–40.
[31] James L. Price, *Organizational Effectiveness: An Inventory of Propositions* (Homewood, Ill.: Richard D. Irwin, Inc., 1968).

continuous systems of assembling output. (These terms will be defined in more detail in later sections of this book.) Also related to effectiveness are such things as the acceptance of the legitimacy of the decision-making system, a high degree of organizational autonomy, and high rates of communication within the organization.[32] Although the propositions may be oversimplified, as William Starbuck has suggested,[33] they provide a starting point from which systematic examinations of effectiveness may begin. Rather than propositions, Price's work actually presents a series of hypotheses about effectiveness that are subject to empirical verification.

An additional problem with the Price inventory, and one that characterizes most effectiveness studies, is the use of productivity as the major indicator. This is misleading and/or inapplicable in service organizations and less than perfect in many production organizations. The positive role of conflict in certain circumstances is also typically ignored.

The Price analysis is based on the assumption that organizations are goal-seeking entities. It also recognizes that the attainment of one goal may operate against (be dysfunctional for) the attainment of another. The more complex the organization in terms of the operative goals on which it is based, the more difficult the effectiveness issue becomes. The problem becomes further compounded, of course, when an organization stresses the easily quantifiable measures of effectiveness when these are not true indicators of its total purposes.

The System-Resources Approach

Stanley Seashore and Ephraim Yuchtman [34] have attempted to avoid some of the pitfalls of the goal approach by essentially ignoring organizational goals in their analyses of effectiveness. They criticize those who use the goal approach on the ground that the determination of goals is extremely difficult, if not impossible. Their criticism is largely of those who advocate the use of the official, rather than operative goals. Where they do consider the operative goals, they note that the are often conflicting goals for the same organization. Instead of the goal model, Sea-

32 *Ibid.*, pp. 203–4.

33 William H. Starbuck, "Some Comments, Observations, and Objections Stimulated by 'Design of Proof in Organizational Research,'" *Administrative Science Quarterly*, Vol. 13, No. 1 (June 1968), 135–61.

34 Stanley E. Seashore and Ephraim Yuchtman, "Factorial Analysis of Organizational Performance," *Administrative Science Quarterly*, Vol. 12, No. 3 (December 1967), 377–95; and Yuchtman and Seashore, "A System Resource Approach to Organizational Effectiveness," *American Sociological Review*, Vol. 32, No. 6 (December 1967), 891–903.

shore and Yuchtman suggest the use of a "system-resources" model for the analysis of organizational effectiveness.

The system-resources approach is based on the idea of the organization as an open system. As such, it engages in exchange and competitive relationships with the environment. Effectiveness becomes the "ability of the organization, in either relative or absolute terms, to exploit its environment in the acquisition of scarce and valued resources." [35] These resources are acquired in the competitive and exchange relationships. An organization is most effective when it "maximizes its bargaining position and optimizes its resource procurement." This approach links the organization back into the society by noting that it is in interaction with the environment and thus must gain resources from that source.

In an empirical examination of this approach, Seashore and Yuchtman used data from 75 insurance sales agencies located in different communities throughout the United States. Data from these agencies were factor-analyzed. The analysis yielded ten factors that were stable over time. These were:

1. Business volume
2. Production cost
3. New member productivity
4. Youthfulness of members
5. Business mix
6. Manpower growth
7. Management emphasis
8. Maintenance cost
9. Member productivity
10. Market penetration [36]

These factors are not taken as indicators for all organizations. The factors of youthfulness of members, for example, while related to performance in this case, may be part of a phase or cycle in the life of these organizations. In interpreting the results of this analysis, Seashore and Yuchtman note that factors such as business volume and penetration of the market could be considered goals, but member productivity and youthfulness certainly cannot. They conclude that while not all the factors associated with performance can be considered as goals, they can be regarded as important resources gleaned from the environment.

This approach would essentially do away with goals as a component of the analysis of effectiveness. It also suggests that there is no universal standard by which effectiveness can be judged, making the effectiveness

---

[35] Yuchtman and Seashore, "A System Resource Approach," p. 898.
[36] Seashore and Yuchtman, "Factorial Analysis," p. 383.

issue one that would have to be handled organization by organization, or at least type of organization by type of organization.

Viewed from another perspective, the Seashore–Yuchtman approach does not differ markedly from the one that has already been discussed. The acquisition of resources from the environment is based upon the official goal of the organization (Seashore and Yuchtman use the term *ultimate criterion*[37]). Movement toward this goal or ultimate criterion is difficult if not impossible to measure. The next step is to specify the operative goals (*penultimate criteria* in the Seashore-Yuchtman approach) and other activities in which the organization engages. Performance or effectiveness according to these criteria is more easily assessed. Growth in business volume is an operative goal in this sense, while youthfulness in members is merely a cyclical factor associated with performance on the other factors. The issue of goals versus resource allocation is therefore in many ways an argument over semantics. The acquisition of resources does not just happen.[38] It is based on what the organization is trying to achieve—its goal—but is accomplished through the operative goals. The Seashore–Yuchtman perspective is very useful in its attention to environmental transactions and its use of organizationally based data. Although they argue against the goal model, their own work is not that much different from the perspective taken here. Their approach is an empirical verification of the importance of the operative-goal concept.

This discussion of organizational effectiveness leads to the conclusion that there is no single indicator of effectiveness, even a group of common indicators, that can be used across organizations. Instead, the approach must be that operative goals serve as the bases for assessments of effectiveness. These operative goals are built around acquiring and maintaining environmental support. To these external considerations must be added the internal factors that Price suggest—morale, adaptiveness, and so on.

The Multiple Criteria of Effectiveness

The relevance of the multiple-criteria approach to effectiveness is seen in practice when data from business managers is considered. Thomas

---

37 *Ibid*, p. 378.

38 Mayer N. Zald, in "Urban Differentiation, Characteristics of Boards of Directors, and Organizational Effectiveness," *American Journal of Sociology*, Vol. 73, No. 3 (November 1967), uses the acquisition of resources as the criterion for effectiveness. In this case, the presence of high-status members on the boards of directors of YMCA branches is related to effectiveness because of their success in bringing in resources.

Mahoney and William Weitzel examined the criteria that managers used in assessing the performance of subunits under their direction.[39]

> General business managers tend to use productivity and efficient performance. These high-order criteria refer to measures of output, whereas lower-order criteria tend to refer to characteristics of the organization climate, supervisory style, and organizational capacity for performance. The research and development managers, on the other hand, use cooperative behavior, staff development, and reliable performance as high-order criteria; and efficiency, productivity, and output behavior as lower-order criteria.[40]

These differences can be found within the same organization.

This research demonstrates the fact that effectiveness criteria as developed by the organization itself do not vary together. In a very real sense, the complex organization thus cannot be effective, if effectiveness is taken in a global or ultimate sense. It can be effective on one or several criteria, but must be less effective or ineffective on others. In fact, efforts to increase effectiveness on one criterion can provide an oppositional force to achieving effectiveness on another. The fact that choices among criteria must be made reinforces the utility of the goal concept, since these choices will be based at least partially on the operative goals of the moment.

Implicit in the discussions of effectiveness, regardless of perspective, is the assumption that the organization operates in a relatively free market and the customer or client is free to select an alternative organization if his needs are not being met. When he shifts to another organization, resources are not allocated to the original organization and effectiveness diminishes. In the goals perspective, profits or community support would decrease as this occurs. The free-market assumption is an important one and makes sense for many organizations. There are, however, many organizations that have an essentially captive market. This can be most easily seen in the case of some service organizations, such as schools or public welfare agencies, but it is also the case for the military and for many business organizations that enjoy a near monopoly in an area. In these cases, an important consideration in the effectiveness equation is typically ignored—the response of the customer or client to the organization.

If the client is not receiving the services he feels are important to him, the organization cannot be judged as being totally effective, regardless of what the organization members themselves think. For example, if

---

[39] Thomas A. Mahoney and William Weitzel, "Managerial Models of Organizational Effectiveness," *Administrative Science Quarterly*, Vol. 14, No. 3 (September 1969), 357–65.
[40] *Ibid.*, p. 362.

a particular form of public welfare makes the recipients feel degraded and does not help them move into a more meaningful life style, the welfare system in question is not as effective as it might be. In fact, it could be posited that the conditions under which the organization might judge itself to be effective, such as the number of cases handled or the amount of money disbursed, might be counter to the client perception of what the organization should be doing.

This consideration raises again the point that it is difficult for organizations to be effective. In this case the organization might be achieving its multiple goals as it sees it, but be ineffective in accomplishing what its clients see as being of primary importance. In issues like this, of course, it is difficult, if not impossible, to determine the extent to which the "experts" in the organization should be listened to as opposed to a concern with lay opinion. The potential for conflict must be recognized, however, and the organization should be aware of the values of its constituents.

Recent client and consumer movements should bring this issue into the open more clearly. At the present time, it is difficult to determine how the organizations involved will react, other than with resistance.

SUMMARY AND CONCLUSIONS

This chapter has been concerned with two central but controversial issues in organizational analysis. Perspectives on goals have ranged from seeing them as the key to understanding organizations to considering them of no use whatsoever. The approach taken here has been to acknowledge the fact that official goals do not tell us very much about the organization, and to adopt instead the operative-goal concept, as a means of focusing on what organizations actually do. The operative goals serve as abstract ideas around which behavior is organized. These ideas take the form of constraints on decision making in determining where the organization's resources will be placed. The operative goals can and usually do change as a result of internal and external factors. These changes can deflect the organization quite dramatically from its original (official) purposes, reflecting a response to reality in most cases. Changes in goals can also lead to the disintegration of an organization, if the new operative goals do not allow the organization to have sufficient resources brought in to ensure survival. Operative goals are translated into policies that guide the day-to-day activities of the organization.

Changes in policy reflect alterations in the pattern of the organization's goals.

Effectiveness was treated within the operative-goals framework. Since the very concept of operative goals suggests a complex goals structure, effectiveness cannot be viewed from an all-or-none perspective. Effectiveness is a relative phenomenon, with an absence of covariation among many of the criteria and possibly inverse relationships among others. The complexity of organizations, almost by definition, precludes effectiveness on all criteria. The specific type of effectiveness sought reflects the operative goals as they have evolved over time.

This first section has been designed as an introduction to the nature of organizations. We have been concerned with such matters as definitions, typologies, and perspectives on the subject matter. The next step in the analysis is to examine organizational structure in order to identify those structural characteristics that are most crucial for the behavior of the organization and its members.

part two

ORGANIZATIONAL STRUCTURE

Organizational structure is ubiquitous for anyone who has any contact with organizations. For the new employee, structure is an imposed condition as soon as he is told, "You report to Mr. Jones." Even in those cases where there is a relatively "loose" structure, as in the case of law firms or academic departments, there is a structure based on principles of seniority and expertise. The customer or client dealing with an organization similarly confronts structure as he selects merchandise or services from one segment of the organization, charges his purchases at another, and is billed by still a third. The hospital patient is treated and served by many different structural units during his stay.

The organizational analyst is faced with a similar situation. Structure is a fact in any organization and is the point from which analyses of most facets of organizational life must begin. While it is possible to study goals without much concern for structure, it would be fruitless to examine effectiveness without considering the various structural arrangements that might be related to different forms of effectiveness. As we will see in detail later, processes within the organization can significantly transform structure, but a structure remains at some point in time the starting point. The same is true for external factors and their impact on organizations.

The interpersonal relationships in an organization are vitally affected by structural considerations. The placement of a person in an organization after he is hired determines with whom he will interact. This can be most easily seen in the case of the man on the assembly line, who is limited in spatial mobility and temporal opportunity in terms of interaction possibilities. It is equally important for office workers, as the placement of their desks leads to interactions with those in close proximity. As important as the sheer physical placement of a person are the communication and authority patterns established by the organization. These determine the persons with whom he has official contact and thus also determine much of his interaction patterning.[1]

The determination of an organization's structure appears to be quite an easy task when the organization has a fully developed organizational chart showing line of authority and communication, and a manual of procedures and rules specifying the extent to which positions and tasks are predefined for the incumbents. This ease is only possible, however, when one can be sure that these officially described relationships are in fact followed in the day-to-day operations of the organization—and as everyone knows, this is not usually the case. Deviations of some magnitude almost inevitably occur in any type of organization. This means that for the member of the organization, experience must supplement official statement; while for the analyst, supplementary data must be added to official statements.

Since most organizations do not have such highly developed charts and procedural manuals, the determination of structure requires more sophisticated techniques. Researchers have developed a series of these, which will be presented in the chapters that follow. While

---

[1] For a discussion of relationships between structural characteristics and job attitudes and behavior, see Lyman W. Porter and Edward E. Lawler III, "Properties of Organization Structure in Relation to Job Attitudes and Behavior," *Psychological Bulletin*, Vol. 64, No. 1 (January 1965), 23–51.

they cannot be called "perfect" in the sense that they have demonstrated validity and comparability for all types of organizations, the measures of structure do appear to be sufficient to allow generalizations about structure to be made. It is evident that the development of structural measures has come a long way in recent years—indeed, that it has proceeded beyond some other important components in organizational analysis. And the development of relatively sound measures in this area provides a starting point for more sophisticated research into other aspects of organizational operations.

While the measurement and description of structure is an interesting process and exercise in its own right, it means little unless it is related to something. The intent of the chapters in this section is to demonstrate the "correlates" of various structural arrangements in organizations. These correlates will range from such internal factors as morale and decision making to the impact of structure on external relationships. We will also be concerned with the interrelationships of structural characteristics themselves. The purpose of these chapters is thus to indicate what difference different structural arrangements make for the behavior of organizations and their members.

As is the case in any such endeavor, a choice had to be made among topics to be taken up. A review of recent research and writing on structure suggests a wide array of possible topics. ("Recent" is not intended to demean the contributions of earlier writers, but to indicate where the contemporary action is.) Pugh, Hickson, et al. have been concerned with specialization, standardization, formalization, centralization, configuration, and flexibility.[2] Blau and his associates have dealt with hierarchical patterns such as span of control and the number of levels of hierarchy, together with organizational size.[3] The size issue has concerned many other writers as well. Aiken and

---

[2] D. S. Pugh, D. J. Hickson, et al., "A Conceptual Scheme for Organizational Analysis," *Administrative Science Quarterly*, Vol. 8, No. 3 (December 1963), 301–7; and D. S. Pugh, D. J. Hickson, C. R. Hinings, and C. Turner, "Dimensions of Organizational Structure," *Administrative Science Quarterly*, Vol. 13, No. 1 (June 1968), 65–105.

[3] Peter M. Blau, "The Hierarchy of Authority in Organizations," *American Journal of Sociology*, Vol. 73, No. 4 (January 1968); Peter M. Blau, Wolf V. Heydebrand, and Robert E. Stauffer, "The Structure of Small Bureaucracies," *American Sociological Review*, Vol. 31, No. 2 (April 1966), 179–91; and Marshall W. Meyer, "Two Authority Structures of Bureaucratic Organizations," *Administrative Science Quarterly*, Vol. 13, No. 2 (September 1968), 211–28.

Hage have concerned themselves with centralization, formalization, and complexity.[4]

Any choice made in these circumstances is somewhat arbitrary. In this case, the choice of topics reflects some of the common interests noted above and in the other references. The specific topics to be covered in this section will be *size, complexity,* and *formalization.* Most of the other components of structure can be arranged in these categories.

[4] Michael Aiken and Jerald Hage, "Organizational Alienation: A Comparative Analysis," *American Sociological Review,* Vol. 31, No. 4 (August 1966), 497–507. Hage and Aiken, "Relationship of Centralization to Other Organizational Properties," *Administrative Science Quarterly,* Vol. 12, No. 1 (June 1967), 72–92; and Hage and Aiken, "Program Change and Organizational Properties: A Comparative Analysis," *American Journal of Sociology,* Vol. 72, No. 5 (March 1967), 503–19.

ORGANIZATIONAL SIZE

4

Is the size of an organization the key to understanding what happens to the organization and its members? Or is size just an insignificant variable that only seems to be important, when in reality it is other factors that account for organizational characteristics? These are the basic questions this chapter seeks to answer.

The issue of size has been a compelling one in organizational analysis. At times, some investigators seem to have looked upon size as a sort of mathematical answer to the puzzle of the organizational universe. Others have hardly considered size at all, suggesting by this omission that it is irrelevant. This chapter will examine the research available on the subject to determine what, in fact, size is related to and where it is or is not important.

THE NATURE OF SIZE

Size is obviously the number of employees in an organization. Or is it? This is an adequate definition only in those cases where the organization is composed solely of full-time paid employees.[1] The issue is much more complex, however, when volunteer and/or part-time personnel comprise a major part of the organization. For example, a county political party organization may have five or six paid employees between elections. During the heat of an intense political campaign, the number might be multiplied by a thousand or more volunteer and unpaid people, with these people working varying numbers of hours. Similarly, a grocery-store chain may have several thousand full-time employees, but its effective size is much larger because of the great number of part-time workers. In both cases, using just the number of full-time paid employees would be extremely misleading in any kind of comparative research.

The Conceptual Issue

The problem of numbers can be resolved, as we will see shortly. A more basic issue in regard to size is the conceptual one, in terms of who is counted as an organization member in the first place. Again, in the case of organizations with paid employees, the issue is a rather simple one, although even here, customers, clients, and stockholders could be included within the organization. Since it has been amply demonstrated that these "outsiders" can have an important impact on the organization, they could legitimately be included in analyses. However, their primary interests lie outside the organization, and so they can be excluded for the present purposes. The issue is more difficult when some nonemployees are included within the organization.

A striking example of the difficulties inherent in this situation can be seen in the case of many prisons. Prisoners, unlike the other members of such an organization, are in the organization all the time. For them it is a "total institution," in Goffman's terms.[2] Prisoners also work in the laundry, kitchen, shops, and so on. Further complicating the issue is the fact that the number of paid employees per prisoner can vary,

---

[1] Several authors prefer to deal with size in terms of "scale of operation," noting that an organization with a small number of members may have huge assets or sales or add a great deal to the number of employees through capital investment. While this is undoubtedly the case, few studies have utilized such an approach and, in general, the scale of operations will be closely related to size as defined here. Seymour Melman, "The Rise of Administrative Overhead in the Manufacturing Industries of the United States, 1899–1947," *Oxford Economic Papers (New Series)*, 3, January 1951, pp. 62–112, uses several measures of scale of operation. Oscar Grusky, "Corporate Size, Bureaucratization, and Managerial Succession," *American Journal of Sociology*, Vol. 67, No. 3 (November 1961), also uses scale of operation.

[2] Erving Goffman, "On the Characteristics of Total Institutions," in *The Prison*, ed. Donald R. Cressey (New York: Holt, Rinehart & Winston, Inc., 1961).

given differing emphases on custody, rehabilitation, and level of security. The same issue, with perhaps the exceptions of security, custody, and rehabilitation, is seen in colleges and universities, where the clients served are an integral part of the organization and also work in the organization, as research assistants, secretaries, janitors, and so forth.

The Methodological Issue

These conceptual difficulties are eased when research on size is examined. While various research efforts have utilized different measures of organizational size in these settings containing clients, inmates, or students, there is a high correlation among the different possible measures. Theodore Anderson and Seymour Warkov, in an examination of general and tuberculosis hospitals, found correlations of .966 and .977 between average daily patient load and the total hospital labor force.[3] In a study of colleges and universities, Amos Hawley, Walter Boland, and Margaret Boland found a correlation coefficient of .943 between student enrollment and the number of full- and part-time faculty.[4] While the conceptual issue is not resolved because of these data, measures of size do appear to be largely interchangeable for research and operational purposes.

Hall, Haas, and Johnson resolved the difficulty with part-time and volunteer workers by computing the number of full-time equivalent workers in the total labor force of an organization. This involves determining the number of hours per year contributed to the organization by such workers, divided by the number of hours a full-time employee normally works in a year.[5] The use of the full-time equivalent size permits comparisons to be made among organizations engaging in widely different activities.

There is one additional component of the size factor that should be noted. In an analysis of 46 English organizations, Pugh et al., utilizing the number of employees in a standard fashion, also looked at the net assets of the organizations. As in the relations between numbers of employees and total number of members, a high correlation (.78) was found

[3] Theodore Anderson and Seymour Warkov, "Organizational Size and Functional Complexity," *American Sociological Review*, Vol. 26, No. 1 (February 1961), 25.

[4] Amos Hawley, Walter Boland, and Margaret Boland, "Population Size and Administration in Institutions of Higher Education," *American Sociological Review*, Vol. 30, No. 2 (April 1965), 253.

[5] Richard H. Hall, J. Eugene Haas, and Norman J. Johnson, "Organizational Size, Complexity, and Formalization," *American Sociological Review*, Vol. 32, No. 6 (December 1967), 905.

between number of employees and net assets.[6] Thus, we may conclude that an organization's membership size is also closely related to its financial size. Large organizations are large in terms of both their membership and their resources.

In the discussion that follows, the size factor will be referred to as "organizational members" rather than "number of employees," because of the relationships we have mentioned. Since the purpose of the total analysis is a better understanding of organizations of all types, the use of members as the basis for discussion allows more kinds of organizations to be included. As we shall see, the findings in regard to size appear to be quite consistent across a wide spectrum of "types" of organizations.

CORRELATES (AND NONCORRELATES) OF SIZE

Investigations of the size factor have led to rather contradictory conclusions. Writers such as Theodore Caplow and Oscar Grusky have suggested that large organizations are by definition more complex and formalized than small ones.[7] F. Stuart Chapin and John Tsouderos concluded that large organizations are more bureaucratized than smaller units.[8] Pugh and his associates maintain that size *causes* (emphasis added) structuring of organizations through "its effect on intervening variables such as frequency of decisions and social control." [9] Blau and Schoenherr suggest that size is the major factor in determining the "shape" of an organization.[10] Other writers, such as Blau and Scott, Zelditch and Hopkins, and Hall, Haas, and Johnson, have argued that size is not the critical factor in the determination of the form of an

6 D. S. Pugh, D. J. Hickson, C. R. Hinings, and C. Turner, "The Context of Organizational Structures," *Administrative Science Quarterly*, Vol. 14, No. 1 (March 1969), 98. These organizations are heavily concentrated in batch and mass-production industries. Where the work process requires expensive equipment (automation) and fewer personnel, this relationship would probably not be as high.

7 Theodore Caplow, "Organizational Size," *Administrative Science Quarterly*, Vol. 1, No. 4 (March 1957), 484–505; Theodore Caplow, *Principles of Organization* (New York: Harcourt Brace Jovanovich, Inc., 1965), pp. 25–28; and Oscar Grusky, "Corporate Size," *op. cit.*

8 F. Stuart Chapin, "The Growth of Bureaucracy: An Hypothesis," *American Sociological Review*, Vol. 16, No. 6 (December 1951), 835–56; and John E. Tsouderos, "Organizational Change in Terms of a Series of Selected Variables," *American Sociological Review*, Vol. 20, No. 2 (April 1955), 206–10.

9 Pugh et al., "The Context of Organization Structures," p. 112.

10 Peter M. Blau and Richard A. Schoenherr, *The Structure of Organizations* (New York: Basic Books, Inc., Publishers, 1971).

organization.[11] In this section, empirical findings in regard to size will be reviewed and the exact relevance of size will be discussed. The contradictions in the literature will be resolved by assessing the salience of the size factor in relationship to other organizational characteristics.

Size and Structure

The arguments "in favor" of size are quite compelling. Marshall Meyer found that size is positively correlated with both number of levels (hierarchical differentiation) and number of division (horizontal or functional differentiation).[12] Large organizations are thus more structurally complex than smaller ones. Hall and Tittle found a modest relationship between size and the perceived degree of bureaucratization in a series of organizations.[13] In their study of 46 English organizations, Pugh and his associates used size as a "contextual variable," relating it to various aspects of organizational structure. Their findings indicate the reason that size is given such an important place in the analysis of organizations. They conclude:

> The correlations between the logarithm of size and structuring of activities ($r = 0.69$) lends strong support to descriptive studies of the effects of size on bureaucratization. . . . Larger organizations tend to have more specialization, more standardization and more formalization than smaller organizations. The *lack* of relationship between size and the remaining structural dimensions, i.e., concentration of authority and line control of workflow . . . was equally striking.[14]

The last statement symbolizes the difficulties with the size variable. Size may not be the most significant factor in understanding organizations, even though it is related to some important organizational characteristics. This conclusion is supported by the work of Hall, Haas, and

---

11 Peter M. Blau and W. Richard Scott, *Formal Organizations* (San Francisco: Chandler Publishing Co., 1962), p. 7; Morris Zelditch, Jr., and Terrence K. Hopkins, "Laboratory Experiments with Organizations," in Amitai Etzioni, *Complex Organizations* (New York: Holt, Rinehart & Winston, Inc., 1961), p. 470; and Hall et al., "Organizational Size."

12 Marshall W. Meyer, "Two Authority Structures of Bureaucratic Organization," *Administrative Science Quarterly*, Vol. 13, No. 2 (September 1968). Meyer does *not* find that these two forms of differentiation occur together.

13 Richard H. Hall and Charles R. Tittle, "Bureaucracy and Its Correlates," *American Journal of Sociology*, Vol. 72, No. 3 (November 1966), 267–72.

14 Pugh, et al. "Context of Organizational Structures," p. 98. ("Workflow" here refers to the major activity of the organization.)

Johnson. Using data from the same 75 organizations discussed above, they conclude:

> In general, the findings of this study in regard to size are similar to those of previous research which utilized size as a major variable; that is, the relationships between size and other structural components are inconsistent. As Tables [4–1 and 4–2] indicate, there is a slight tendency for larger organizations to be both more complex and more formalized, but only on a few variables does this relationship prove to be strong. On others, there is little, if any, established relationship.
>
> The complexity indicators related to size fall within three major categories. The first of these is spatial dispersion. This conclusion, in which both physical facilities and personnel are considered, is congruent with the suggestion of Anderson and Warkov that the relative size of the supportive component is also related to spatial dispersion. On a common-sense basis, such dispersion is possible only for sufficiently large organizations. A decision to add dispersed facilities may require a secondary decision to add more personnel, rather than the reverse. It also appears that a very large or extensive market is more easily or economically reached through physical dispersion. Thus, it could be argued that both size and complexity are dependent upon available economic "input," and to the extent to which such potential "input" is dispersed, large organizations will also be more complex in regard to physical dispersion.
>
> A second set of significant relationships is found in regard to the hierarchical differentiation. Although Woodward has noted differences in the "width" of the span of control according to the technological stages of industry, the generally accepted principle of limiting the number of subordinates supervised by one person seems to be operative here. More hierarchical levels are found in larger organizations.
>
> The third set of significant relationships is in the area of intradepartmental specialization or the specific division of labor. While the number of divisions is not related to size, this form of internal differentiation is. Performance of the major organizational activities plus such prerequisites as accounting and personnel management apparently are accomplished by departmentalization regardless of organizational size. Further specialization may take place within the existing departmental structure as the organization grows in size.
>
> In general, the relationships between size and the complexity indicators appear to be limited to a few factors. Even in those relationships found to be statistically significant, enough deviant cases exist to cast serious doubts on the assumption that large organizations are necessarily more complex than small organizations.
>
> The same general conclusion can be reached in regard to the formalization indicators. . . . Relatively strong relationships exist between size and the formalization of the authority structure (B-1), the stipulation of penalties for rule violation in writing (D-3), and the orientation and in-service training procedures (E-1 and E-2). A general association does exist to the extent that larger organizations tend to be more formalized on the other indicators, even though the relationship is quite weak.
>
> The most immediate implication of these findings is that neither complexity nor formalization can be implied from organizational size. A social

TABLE 4–1 COMPLEXITY INDICATORS BY ORGANIZATIONAL SIZE

	Less than 100 (N = 20) (in percent- ages)	Size 100–999 (N = 35) (in percent- ages)	1,000 or more (N = 20) (in percent- ages)
A. Division of Labor—General			
1. Number of Goals			
1	30	29	20
2	45	46	45
3 or more	25	25	35
Kendall's Tau C = .08			
2. Presence of Second Major			
Activity	65	69	70
No second activity	35	31	30
Second activity present			
Kendall's Tau C = .04			
B. Division of Labor—Specific			
1. Number of Major Divisions (Horizontal Differentiation)			
1–4	30	20	25
5–6	20	37	25
7 or more	50	43	50
Kendall's Tau C = .02			
2. Divisions within Most Special- ized Single Department			
1–3 subdivisions	55	23	5
4–6 subdivisions	20	26	45
7 or more subdivisions	25	51	50
Kendall's Tau C = .27			
3. Mean Number of Subdivisions per Department			
1 or 2 subdivisions	70	29	20
3 subdivisions	20	29	25
4 or more subdivisions	10	42	55
Kendall's Tau C = .35			
C. Hierarchical Differentiation			
1. Number of Levels in Deepest Single Division			
2 or 3 levels	55	14	10
4 levels	35	43	40
5 or more levels	10	43	50
Kendall's Tau C = .35			
2. Mean Number of Levels for Organization as a Whole (Vertical Differentiation)			
2 or 3	90	60	50
4 or more	10	40	50
Kendall's Tau C = .31			

TABLE 4–1   (Cont.)

	Less than 100 (N = 20) (in percent- ages)	Size 100–999 (N = 35) (in percent- ages)	1,000 or more (N = 20) (in percent- ages)
D. Spatial Dispersion			
1. Dispersion of Physical Facilities			
all in one location	45	46	25
mostly in one location, some in field	30	37	35
mostly in field (dispersed)	25	17	40
Kendall's Tau C = .14			
2. Location of Physical Facilities			
one location	45	46	20
within city or county	35	17	20
state–national–international	20	37	60
Kendall's Tau C = .23			
3. Degree of Dispersion of Personnel			
All in one location	35	34	16
Mostly at one location, some in field	25	34	47
Mostly in field (dispersed)	40	32	37
Kendall's Tau C = .06			
4. Location of Personnel one location			
within city or county	35	34	15
state–national–international	40	20	15
Kendall's Tau C = .24	25	46	70

Source: Richard H. Hall, J. Eugene Haas, and Norman J. Johnson, "Organizational Size, Complexity, and Formalization," American Sociological Review, Vol. 32, No. 6 (December 1967), pp. 908–9.

scientist conducting research in a large organization would do well to question the frequent assumption that the organization under study is necessarily highly complex and formalized. If these two general factors are relevant to the focus of his research, he will need to examine empirically, for each organization, the level of complexity and formalization extant at that time. The ideal research procedure would be to have standardized measures of these phenomena to allow comparative research. At the minimum, the degrees to which these phenomena are present should be specified, at least nominally.

A second implication of these findings lies in the area of social control. Increased organizational formalization is a means of controlling the behavior

TABLE 4–2   FORMALIZATION INDICATORS BY ORGANIZATIONAL SIZE

	Less than 100 (N = 20) (in percentages)	*Size 100–999 (N = 35) (in percentages)*	*1,000 or more (N = 20) (in percentages)*
A. Roles			
1. Concreteness of Positional Descriptions			
Low	45	17	20
Medium	35	46	55
High	20	37	25
Kendall's Tau C = .12			
2. Presence of Written Job Descriptions			
None	35	26	20
Present only at some levels	40	23	50
Present throughout organization	25	51	30
Kendall's Tau C = .01			
B. Authority Relations			
1. Degree of Formalization of Authority Structure			
Low or medium	58	32	26
High	42	68	74
Kendall's Tau C = .25			
2. Codification of Authority Structure in Writing			
Not codified	58	26	47
Codified	42	74	53
Kendall's Tau C = .08			
C. Communications			
1. Degree of Emphasis on Written Communications			
Low	35	17	30
Medium	55	57	55
High	10	26	15
Kendall's Tau C = .05			
2. Emphasis on Using Established Communications Channels			
Low	35	23	15
Medium	25	37	30
High	40	40	55
Kendall's Tau C = .13			

TABLE 4–2   (Cont.)

	Size		
	Less than 100 (N = 20) (in percent-ages)	*100–999 (N = 35) (in percent-ages)*	*1,000 or more (N = 20) (in percent-ages)*
D. Norms and Sanctions			
1. Number of Written Rules and Policies			
Less than 12	32	17	21
More than 12	68	83	79
Kendall's Tau C = .08			
2. Penalties for Rule Violation Clearly Stipulated			
No	65	44	47
Yes (for at least some members)	35	56	53
Kendall's Tau C = .14			
3. Stipulation of Penalties for Rule Violation in Writing			
No	70	50	42
Yes (for at least some members)	30	50	58
Kendall's Tau C = .22			
E. Procedures			
1. Formalization of Orientation Program for New Members (Only Programs for All New Members Included; N = 57)			
No Program or Low Formalization	83	63	50
High Formalization	17	37	50
Kendall's Tau C = .26			
2. Formalization of In-service Training Program for New Members (Only Programs for All New Members Included; N = 36)			
No program or low formalization	77	47	50
High formalization	23	53	50
Kendall's Tau C = .26			

Source: Richard H. Hall, J. Eugene Haas, and Norman J. Johnson, "Organizational Size, Complexity, and Formalization," American Sociological Review, *Vol. 32, No. 6 (December 1967), 910–11.*

of members of the organization by limiting individual discretion. At least one aspect of complexity, hierarchical differentiation, also is related to social control in that multiple organizational levels serve as a means of maintaining close supervision of subordinates. It seems rather clear, on the basis of this evidence, that a large organization does not necessarily have to rely upon impersonal, formalized control mechanisms. At the same time, the fact that an organization is small cannot be taken as evidence that a *gemeinschaft* sort of social system is operating. An organization need not turn to formalization if other control mechanisms are present. One such control mechanism is the level of professionalization as Hage and Blau et al. have suggested. The organizations with more professionalized staffs probably exhibit less formalization.

These findings suggest that size may be rather irrelevant as a factor in determining organizational structure. Blau et al. have indicated that structural differentiation is a *consequence* of expanding size. Our study suggests that it is relatively rare that the two factors are even associated and thus the temporal sequence or causality (expanding size produces greater differentiation) posited by Blau and colleagues is open to question. In these cases where size and complexity are associated, the sequence may well be the reverse. If a decision is made to enlarge the number of functions or activities carried out in an organization, it then becomes necessary to add more members to staff and new functional areas.[15]

Size and Technology

There are evident inconsistencies between these findings and those of Pugh et al. and Meyer that were reported above. Some of Blau's research also suggests that the number of hierarchical levels increases with increased size. When these various findings and the organizations included for analysis are examined more closely, however, the inconsistency in the findings can be resolved. The major factor that should be introduced into the relationship is the nature of the organization's technology. If the technology involves a rather routinized product or service, formalization and complexity would tend to increase with increased size. If, on the other hand, the technology is built around nonstandard products and services, the relationship will not hold.

This interpretation is reinforced by the recent analysis of Hickson et al.[16] These authors break down the general concept of technology into three components: *Operations technology* refers to the techniques used in the workflow activities of the organization. *Materials technology* refers

15 Hall et al., "Organizational Size," pp. 111–12.

16 D. J. Hickson, D. S. Pugh, and Diana C. Pheysey, "Operations Technology and Organizational Structure: An Empirical Reappraisal," *Administrative Science Quarterly,* Vol. 14, No. 3 (September 1969), 378–97.

to the materials used in the workflow; it is conceivable to have a highly sophisticated technique applied to relative simple materials. The final form of technology is concerned with *knowledge*. This involves the varying complexities in the knowledge system used in the workflow. In their own research, these authors have been concerned with operations technology.

In the English organizations they studied, operations technology had a secondary effect in relationship to size. They conclude:

> *Structural variables will be associated with operations technology only where they are centered on the workflow. The smaller the organization, the more its structure will be pervaded by such technological effects; the larger the organization, the more these effects will be confined to variables such as job-counts of employees on activities linked with the workflow itself, and will not be detectable in variables of the more remote administrative and hierarchical structure.*[17]

These findings mean that operations technology will intervene before the effects of size in these work organizations. They also imply that the administrative element in large organizations will be relatively unaffected by the operations technology. It is here that the form of the knowledge technology, which was not examined, becomes important. Marshall Meyer has found that the introduction of automated procedures into the administrative structures of state and local departments of finance results in more levels of hierarchy, a wider span of control for first-line supervisors, fewer employees under the direction of higher supervisors, and fewer responsibilities—with more communications responsibilities—for members who are nominally in supervisory positions.[18] In these particular organizations, the introduction of automation would be found in relatively simple knowledge technologies.

If the converse of the Meyer findings is considered, a very different picture emerges. If administrative and organizational procedures are highly nonroutine and are laden with problems and new issues, a less complex, less formalized system would be expected.[19] It is thus very possible, as has been previously suggested, that the various segments of an organization can have quite different structures. The operations of an organization could be highly formalized and complex, while other units take an entirely different form. Empirical verification for this position is

---

[17] *Ibid.*, pp. 394–95. (Italics in original.)

[18] Marshall W. Meyer, "Automation and Bureaucratic Structure," *American Journal of Sociology*, Vol. 74, No. 3 (November 1968).

[19] This argument follows that of Charles Perrow in "A Framework for the Comparative Analysis of Organizations," *American Sociological Review*, Vol. 32, No. 2 (April 1967).

supplied by Hall's analysis of intraorganizational structural variations.[20] The findings from this study do indicate structural differences between operating and administrative and research units.

Hickson and his associates have correctly concluded from their data that size is more important than technology in determining structure. Their data are based on work organizations that essentially have quite standardized materials and operations. They are most confident of their results on manufacturing organizations only after they have reconstructed their sample to exclude service and administrative units.[21] In the case of a limited variation in technology, size is probably a major factor.

Professionalization

A related consideration is the nature of the employees in the organization. A major dimension appears to be the level of professionalization of the labor force. This is usually strongly related to, but not identical with, the routinization issue discussed above. Studies of professionals in organizations have come up with quite consistent findings: The organizations involved are *less* formalized than organizations without professionals.[22] As the level of professionalization of the employees increases, the level of formalization decreases. (The data for this statement are based upon comparisons between professional groups, rather than on longitudinal studies of occupational groups going through the process of professionalization.) The presence of professionals appears to cause a diminished need for formalized rules and procedures. Since professionals have internalized norms and standards, the imposition of organizational requirements is not only unnecessary; it is likely to lead to professional–organizational conflict.

Complexity is also related to the degree of professionalization of the labor force, but in a different way. Blau and his associates have found that professionalization is likely to be accompanied by an increase in the number of levels in the hierarchy.[23] They attribute this to increased

---

[20] Richard H. Hall, "Intraorganizational Structural Variation: Application of the Bureaucratic Model," *Administrative Science Quarterly*, Vol. 7, No. 3 (December 1962), 295–308.

[21] Correspondence from D. J. Hickson, November 25, 1969.

[22] See William Kornhauser, *Scientists in Industry* (Berkeley: University of California Press, 1963); and Richard H. Hall, "Professionalization and Bureaucratization," *American Sociological Review*, Vol. 33, No. 1 (February 1968), 92–104.

[23] Peter M. Blau, "The Hierarchy of Authority in Organizations," *American Journal of Sociology* Vol. 73, No. 4 (January 1968); and Blau, Heydebrand and Stauffer, "The Structure of Small Bureaucracies," *American Sociological Review*, Vol. 31, No. 2 (April 1966).

communications needs, as information is generated and utilized by the professionals for use by the larger organization. At the same time, the organization of the professional departments tends to be rather "flat." That is, the concept of equality among professionals (lawyers should be given equal formal status within a legal department) leads to little differentiation within a department. The model followed is the collegial, which is characterized by few formal distinctions or norms and by little in the way of formalized vertical or horizontal differentiation.

It is interesting to note that departments composed of professionals exhibit little structural differentiation from professional firms or organizations. Legal or research departments tend to be organized like law firms or research organizations.[24] The work of the professional is likely to be highly complex. Within a research division, university department, law firm, or hospital, there can be extreme diversity in the activities being performed. There is an intense division of labor. This complexity is not organizationally imposed, however. It is a consequence of the differentiation of activities among the professionals and is thus not a formal organizational characteristic.

The diversity of activities further enhances the need for vertical communications, confirming the requirement of a long hierarchy as suggested by Blau et al. The need for a longer hierarchy is further supported by the need for coordination of the activities of professionals with that of the rest of the organization. Lawrence and Lorsch have found that heavy engagement in research and development, a professional activity, increases strains in the organization and thus the need for coordination.[25]

The role of technology and the related aspect of the professionalization of the labor force have been introduced at this time to indicate some factors that appear to interact with size in determining organizational structure. It is premature to assign primacy to any one factor in the development of particular organizational configurations. The recent works of both Blau et al. and Pugh, Hickson, et al. have emphasized size as being more important than technology or other factors in influencing organizational structure. The findings of Hall et al., based on a wider but unsystematic sample of organizations, suggest that size cannot be taken as the determining factor. Although further research is needed for a real resolution of these differences, the interaction of size and tech-

24 Richard H. Hall, "Some Organizational Considerations in the Professional–Organizational Relationship," *Administrative Science Quarterly*, Vol. 12, No. 3 (December 1967), 461–78.

25 Paul R. Lawrence and Jay W. Lorsch, *Organization and Environment: Managing Differentiation and Integration* (Cambridge: Harvard Graduate School of Busiess Administration, 1967).

nology (including level of professionalization) would appear to be the most promising approach.[26]

Size and Workflow

The nature of the intricate relationship between these variables is at least partially illuminated by the conclusions of Hickson et al. that *"variables of operations technology will be related only to those structural variables that are centered on the workflow."* [27] They go on to state that the larger the organization, the less the impact of workflow-related activities on the rest of the organization.

Two additional points must be made before these findings can be integrated into an overall conclusion. The concept of workflow is based on the major activity of an organization. In a factory, the major activity is producing and distributing the output. A bus company has "equipment (buses) and a sequence of operations (bus routes)." [28] A university has students and teachers and teaching and research. The technology centered on the workflow is thus highly varied, as are the structures involved.

At the same time, in larger organizations there is a great deal of activity that has little or nothing to do with the workflow itself. This is the administrative component of the organization. Hickson and his colleagues note that in smaller organizations, the workflow more strongly influences the nature of the administrative arrangements, while in larger organizations this effect is dampened. This is in keeping with the suggestion made earlier that internal structural variations must be analyzed along with total organizational structure. Technology affects structure at the workflow level. The administrative component of larger organizations, while not affected by the workflow or operations technology, has a technology of its own. Meyer's findings in regard to the impact of automation suggest that while in standard administrative systems, increased size is related to increased formalization and complexity, variations in administrative technology have significant impacts on administrative structure. Thus, here as well as at the workflow level, technology remains important. Administrative technology probably does not change as fast as operations technology, and so the size factor remains an important determinant of structure at this level.

---

26 See the data presented by Pugh et al., "Context of Organizational Structures," pp. 109–10, for partial confirmation of this point.

27 Hickson et al., "Operations Technology," p. 395. (Italics in original.)

28 *Ibid.*, p. 380.

Before we turn to a consideration of size and the administrative component of organizations, one further point should be made about size and general organizational structure. While size and technology have been shown to be closely related to the nature of an organization's structure, it would be wrong to attribute direct causality to either factor (assuming, of course, that strong relationships can be interpolated into causal statements). As noted above in the citation by Hall et al., it is the *decision* to increase the number of activities or scope of operations that leads to changes in size and thus to structural alterations. These decisions would be greatly influenced by the size and nature of the *environment* into which the organization's output flows. If the organization perceives additional markets for its products or services, it will expand. If it is operating in a system of rapid technological change, it will adapt to, incorporate, and participate in those changes.

SIZE AND THE ADMINISTRATIVE COMPONENT

The relative size of the administrative component of an organization is in many ways an indicator of the organization's efficiency. The smaller the proportion of resources spent on administration, the greater the amount left for the major organizational activities. Despite the interest in this subject by students of organizations, evidence concerning the relationships between size and the administrative component has been, until recently, scanty and contradictory.

Early research and speculation tended to suggest that as organizations increased in size, the relative size of the administrative component increased disproportionately.[29] Later research has tended to contravene this, suggesting that the relationship is in the opposite direction, or curvilinear.[30] Some of the confusion in the information on this subject is linked to definitional problems. A commonly used definition for these purposes is "staff versus line," with the staff composing the administrative component. Unfortunately, these terms are not used consistently

---

[29] The speculative efforts are typified by the semiserious work of C. Northcote Parkinson, *Parkinson's Law* (Boston: Houghton Mifflin Company, 1957), pp. 2–13. Research in this area is exemplified by Fred C. Terrien and Donald C. Mills, "The Effect of Changing Size upon the Internal Structure of an Organization," *American Sociological Review*, Vol. 20, No. 1 (February 1955), 11–14.

[30] See Anderson and Warkov, "Organizational Size"; Hawley et al., "Population Size"; J. Eugene Haas, Richard Hall, and Norman Johnson, "The Size of the Supportive Component in Organizations: A Multi-organizational Analysis," *Social Forces*, Vol. 42, No. 1 (October 1963), 9–17.

even in industrial practice, let alone in organizations where line (production) activities are less clear. Other research has utilized occupational titles derived from the Bureau of the Census.[31] The use of occupational titles in this way has been restricted to examinations of the size of the administrative component by broad industrial classifications, and can lead only to generalizations about the overall proportion of personnel devoted to administration within broad industry categories, since information about specific organizations is not available. A further difficulty with the use of census-based data is that they have been limited to production organizations. Since much, if not a majority, of the organizational "action" occurs outside private industry, this is a severely limited perspective.

In their analysis of hospitals, Anderson and Warkov used the "percent of all employees classified in the category, 'General Hospital Administration.'"[32] This is a sound measure for hospitals, but it obviously cannot be used in other settings. Furthermore, other kinds of organizations may define their administrative component differently. This would lead to extreme difficulties in generalization. Since the important issue here for practical and research purposes is really administrative overhead, in terms of costs and energies expended, a preferable approach would be to have a more generally applicable definition. Haas, Hall, and Johnson have proposed that the definitional and conceptual problem can be resolved by taking account of all the personnel in an organization who engage in "supportive" activities.[33] Thus, custodial workers, some drivers, cafeteria employees, clerical help, and so on, are included in the administrative component, regardless of whether they are directly employed in "staff" or "general administrative" divisions.

The use of this kind of approach is based on the idea that the crucial factor is really the number of workers engaged in activities centered around the organization's major activities. That is, organizational personnel can be divided into those who contribute directly to the attainment of the organization's goals and those who do not. As we have said, not *all* of anyone's activities are directly goal-related, but most personnel can be easily placed into the direct or indirect (administrative component) categories. This type of definition has the advantage of being applicable in all types of organizations, and this is particularly

31 See William A. Rushing, "The Effects of Industry Size and Division of Labor on Administration," *Administrative Science Quarterly*, Vol. 12, No. 2 (September 1967), 273–95; and Louis R. Pondy, "Effects of Size, Complexity, and Ownership on Administrative Intensity," *Administrative Science Quarterly*, Vol. 14, No. 1 (March 1969), 47–60. This approach is based on and extends the earlier work of Melman, "Rise of Administrative Overhead."

32 Anderson and Warkov, "Organizational Size," p. 25.

33 Haas, Hall, and Johnson, "Size of the Supportive Component," p. 12.

important when we consider administrative types of organizations. Government bureaus, for example, can thus be compared with manufacturing organizations or hospitals in a reasonable way. The "administrator" in a government agency is equivalent to the "production manager" in industry, as are some clerical workers to assembly-line workers.

Findings from research that uses this approach to the administrative component indicate that the relationship under discussion is curvilinear. That is, the size of the administrative component is *"greater* for the smaller (0–700 employees) and larger (over 1,400 employees) organizations than for those of moderate size." [34] Since the number of organizations used in this study was quite small, these finding cannot be taken as conclusive. However, the same general findings were reported by Hawley et al. in their study of colleges and universities, so that the curvilinear relationship suggested may be the true one.

The studies by Haas et al. and Hawley et al. also suggest that the relative size of the administrative component decreases as organizational size increases. The tendency toward curvilinearity is slight, and the increase among the large organizations does not reach the level found in the smaller organizations. The fact that there is a strong tendency for the administrative component to decrease in size is consistent with the findings of Anderson and Warkov and of Reinhard Bendix.[35] Organizations do apparently achieve an economy of scale, in that the number of persons engaged in administration is lessened as the organization increases in size.

There are a number of explanations for such economies. It is clear that certain tasks are required for organizational existence in contemporary society. Personnel administration, accounting, janitorial services, and so on, must be performed regardless of organizational size. In the extremely small organization, these may all be performed by the same person, but in organizations of even moderate size (the exact numbers are not known), separate personnel are needed for each of these functions. In the smaller organizations, "the personnel engaged in such activities may be 'underused' in the sense that full use is not made of their efforts in their particular areas of specialization. As organizations become larger, these same persons can perhaps continue to handle the supportive work load without the addition of other personnel. In other words, more complete use is made of such persons, thus reducing the proportion of the total personnel needed to maintain supportive activities." [36] Larger organizations would also be the most likely, from a

---

34 *Ibid.,* p. 14.

35 Anderson and Warkov, "Organizational Size"; and Reinhard Bendix, *Work and Authority in Industry* (New York: John Wiley & Sons, Inc., 1956), p. 222, Table 7.

36 Haas et al., "Size of the Supportive Component," p. 16.

financial point of view, to install computers and other labor-saving devices and thus reduce the size of the administrative component.

The size of the administrative component is influenced by factors other than the size of the organization. In fact, according to some analysts, organizational size is not the critical factor in understanding the size of the administrative component. Louis Pondy, in reviewing the literature on this issue, concludes that technology is a major contributor to the administrative configuration. He notes that task complexity and an intensive division of labor require administrative personnel for coordination purposes.[37] Anderson and Warkov's findings that spatial dispersion and multiple departments of the same organization increase the size of the administrative component is also taken as an indicator of the effects of heightened technological development. In addition, it would appear that organizations whose activities require technological innovations through research and development would almost by definition have proportionately more personnel involved in the administrative (supporting-activities) component.

Pondy's own research confirms the importance of technological factors, but adds into the equation the additional factor of the form of organizational control. Pondy's data are taken from census information by industry, and are thus subject to the limitation that they are not based on data from organizations per se. However, his research yields useful insights into the processes leading to differential patterning of the administrative component. He finds, consistent with the argument presented here, that the administrative-component size decreases with increased organizational size. He then adds in, as an additional variable, the form of ownership of the organization. The data suggest that owner-managers and partnerships are less likely to add professional and administrative personnel, probably owing to their unwillingness to dilute their personal power.[38] Although this might lead to less profitability, it maintains the existing organizational stability. But in incorporated firms, the addition of professionals and administrators, while increasing costs, also appears to increase profits.

These findings and the interpretations given them suggest that in nonprofit organizations, the same processes would probably operate. Organizations controlled by a "strong" administrator (college president, hospital administrator, government agency chief, etc.) would be expected to have a lower proportion of personnel engaged in administrative tasks. It also appears that administrative costs, if they are incurred by the utilization of skilled personnel, would actually lead to increased organizational effectiveness, since profits in industry are an indicator of effectiveness.

[37] Pondy, "Effects of Size," p. 47.
[38] *Ibid.*, p. 57.

The power distribution in the organization also affects the size and nature of the administrative component, as do the technological system of the organization and the general and specific environments in which the organization operates. From these standpoints, the impact of organizational size assumes secondary importance. In fact, size may be a reflection of the very kinds of ownership and technological–environmental conditions that have been discussed throughout this book. Even as an indicator, size must be combined with other factors to yield any composite picture of an organization. One would need to know quite a bit about an organization's technology and environment before one would be able to predict intelligently its structural characteristics. Size would be included in any predictive equation, but as a secondary factor.

The discussion of size thus far has had rather negative overtones, in that its importance has been largely discounted, or at least greatly modified. At the same time, size as a structural condition has some important relationships with other facets of organizational existence.

THE IMPACT OF SIZE

For anyone who has any contact with organizations as an employee, client, or customer, the size factor has an immediate reality. A large organization confronts these individuals with many unknowns, and size is probably the first thing that they notice. There are sheer numbers of people doing things that are at first beyond comprehension. Unfortunately, the impact of organizational size on the individual has not been systematically investigated. A subjective impression is that the size factor has an immediate impact that then diminishes the longer a person is in the organization.

This impression comes from two indirectly related sorts of studies. The first type of evidence is from the investigations of the "informal work group," a phenomenon that has been universally found in all types of organizations and at all levels within them. It involves the interaction patterns that develop on the job among co-workers. These interaction patterns may or may not represent deviations from official expectations— for the present analysis, this issue is unimportant. What is important is the fact that members of organizations, large and small, are found in such groups. These groups become a meaningful part of the organization for their members. The impact of size is therefore probably strongly moderated by such groups. The person who is an isolate for whatever reason would not have the effect of size moderated and would probably face the impact continually. The impact in this case cannot be categorically considered either positive or negative in terms of the mental health of the individual.

The second source of indirect evidence about the impact of size on the individual comes from studies in the community. Here the evidence suggests that although in a large community an individual does not know or interact with the majority of those with whom he comes in contact, he still maintains primary relationships with many persons in and out of his own family.[39] A smaller proportion of his relationships are warm and open, but the total number is probably not too different in a large community from that in a small one. This same point would appear to be true in organizations. Without the research that is needed for verification of these ideas, it seems clear that the immediate effects of size on the individual are moderated by the processes discussed. Studies of membership participation in voluntary organizations of varying sizes usually conclude that there is less participation in larger organizations. Paul Wilken, on the other hand, in a study of church congregations, found that size was less important in predicting participation than other factors, such as the age composition of the congregation, growth rate, and location in urban or rural areas.[40] Here again, additional research is needed.

Impact on the Individual

Research evidence regarding the relationships between size and individual performance and reactions to the work situation is inconclusive. Leo Meltzer and James Salter report that among the physiological scientists they studied, no relationship was found between size of the employing organization and scientific productivity as measured by number of publications. On the other hand, there is a curvilinear relationship between size and job satisfaction. Satisfaction is greater in medium-sized (21 to 50 employees) than in either large or small organizations.[41] While other research has pointed to negative relations between size and morale, the absence of good comparative data on this subject makes any conclusion reached tenuous at best. Meltzer and Salter suggest that

[39] For a discussion of this issue, see Joel I. Nelson, "Clique Contacts and Family Orientations," *American Sociological Review*, Vol. 31, No. 5 (October 1966), 663–72.

[40] Paul H. Wilken, "Organizational Size and Member Participation: A Study of Lutheran Church Organizations" (unpublished manuscript, Department of Sociology, University of North Carolina, 1970).

[41] Leo Meltzer and James Salter, "Organizational Structure and the Performance and Job Satisfaction of Physiologists," *American Sociological Review*, Vol. 27, No. 3 (June 1962), 351–62.

variables other than size are probably more important in accounting for morale and satisfaction.[42]

Approaching the issue from the standpoint of *stress* felt by the individual in the organization, the comprehensive research of Kahn et al. comes to the same conclusion. They note:

> Americans are accustomed to thinking of growth as synonymous with organizational life, and of large size as a condition for maximum efficiency. Against these assertions must be placed the finding that stress and organizational size are substantially related. The curve of stress begins to rise as we turn from tiny organizations to those of 50 or 100 persons, and the rising curve continues until we encounter the organizational giants. Only for organizations of more than 5,000 persons does the curve of stress level off—perhaps because an organization so large represents some kind of psychological infinity and further increases are unfelt.[43]

The authors then go on to suggest that the eradication of stress cannot realistically be accomplished by shrinking organizations down to small size, since the economic consequences of such a move would be "tragic." They suggest that the reason for stress in large organizations is the need for coordination among the many members, and that the way to reduce stress is by reduction of coordination requirements. This can be done, in their opinion, by giving subunits more autonomy.

The research findings discussed suggest that size is related to morale factors. Larger organizations do present their members with situations that lead to stress and lowered morale. The effects of size are undoubtedly different on different types of members.[44] A subjective impression, for example, is that students who come to a large university from a small town with a small high school face a much more stressful situation than those from large urban schools. The same would appear to be true for other kinds of members in other kinds of organizations. The kinds of expectations and general background a person brings to the organization will be a major factor in determining how he reacts to the organization.

The issues being discussed here are obviously important in any broad conception of human values. Some of the student unrest of the late 1960s can be attributed to the size of the organizations involved. Charges of depersonalization, being treated like an IBM card, regimented learning, and so on, are essentially true. The nature of large organizations is such

---

[42] *Ibid.*, pp. 360–62.

[43] Robert L. Kahn, Donald M. Wolfe, Robert P. Quinn, J. Diedrick Snoek, and Robert A. Rosenthal, *Organizational Stress: Studies in Role Conflict and Ambiguity* (New York: John Wiley & Sons, Inc., 1964), p. 394.

[44] For some suggestions regarding alternative reaction patterns, see Robert Presthus, *The Organizational Society* (New York: Alfred A. Knopf, Inc., 1962).

that members must to some degree be treated as members of categories, rather than as separate individuals. At the same time, large organizations can and do vary in structure and performance. The negative effects of size can be minimized, if not eliminated, through such devices as granting more subunits autonomy and decentralization. Except for some attempts at communal living among those who choose to "drop out" of society, a return to the "good old days" of small, intimate organizations is impossible. It is impossible for two major reasons. The first is that contemporary technology for all kinds of organizations is such that it is probably impossible to keep an organization at a small size. (It is hardly conceivable that a moratorium would be called on technological development and that a society would be forced to go back to an earlier technological state.) The second reason is that human values themselves have undoubtedly shifted. Whether for better or worse, most members of the contemporary large organization are probably more satisfied there than they would be in a smaller, more intimate setting. While no claim is made that this is inherently good, it does seem to be the real condition.

Impact on the Society

When the focus is shifted from the impact of size of organization on the individual to the impact on the society at large, the overall picture is the same. However, the evidence is extremely weak because of the fact that discussions of the impact of larger organizations on the society have been politicized and moralized, rather than systematically researched.

The evidence is overwhelming that organizations of all types are growing larger and that consolidations, mergers, informal cooperation, and the growth of the conglomerate are further limiting the power and discretion of individual organizations. There are those who think that the growth of large organizations is dangerous for the society in terms of limitations of competition, concentration of power, reduced freedom for the individual, and even national security. On the other hand, there are whose who view this development without such fears, and with a positive anticipation that this will lead to a better life for individuals and the total society. Not only, they feel, will larger organizations be better able to provide the goods and services needed; rationality will prevail in them, with patterns of racial and sexual discrimination, promotion of the incompetent, and so on, eliminated, and they will provide the framework for the technological and social advances that the society so evidently needs. A balanced perspective on the impact of large organizations on the society would probably indicate that the truth falls somewhere in between these extremes.

This issue will be examined in detail in the last chapters of this book. For the present, let us note only that large organizations seem to have a mixed impact on the society, basically along the lines briefly traced above. Regardless of the political and moral consequences of the increased scale of organizations, it appears that they are here to stay. The complexities of modern technology and the demand for coordinated delivery of goods and services really mean that the society must adjust to the organizations it has created—and to control them, if this is desired.

Impact on the Organization

The last type of impact of size that we shall mention is that on the organization itself. While most of this chapter has been concerned with relationships between size and other structural characteristics, there has been little attention to the processes that occur within organizations. Research has concentrated largely on structural relationships, but there are strong indications that processual changes also take place among large organizations. Anthony Downs has suggested that large organizations have quite different control systems from their smaller counterparts. Control is impossible for any one man or set of men at the top. Downs attributes this to the limitations on the mental capacity of those at the top.[45] This is not to say that large organizations are run by incompetents (regardless of the implications of the Peter Principle [46]), but rather that events and conditions are too complex for anyone to comprehend totally. At the same time that control becomes difficult, coordination also becomes a problem. The subunits of large organizations apparently begin to engage in activities that are out of the control and coordinative power of those at the top of the organization, since the subunits are large organizations in and of themselves.

While size increases problems of this sort, it also permits the accumulation of resources that can be used to attempt to bring more rationality into the system. J. K. Galbraith has suggested that large size facilitates planning, a vital function in a complex and changing society.[47] Boland, in a study of colleges and universities, found that large size was associated with the development of "centers," or organizational personnel

[45] Anthony Downs, *Inside Bureaucracy* (Boston: Little, Brown and Company, 1967), p. 143.

[46] Laurence J. Peter and Raymond Hull, *The Peter Principle* (New York: William Morrow & Co., Inc. 1969).

[47] John Kenneth Galbraith, *The New Industrial State* (Boston: Houghton Mifflin Company, 1967), pp. 31–33.

specifically concerned with public relations. These centers allow mediation with the external environment, which further allows more control over that environment. At the same time that control over external relations is centered at the top of the organization, power increases for the faculty (lower-level employees).[48] This is consistent with the argument of Downs. In large organizations, the division of labor and power develops in such a way that lower-level individuals and units gain in power. Higher-level personnel and units, while losing some power in terms of internal control, gain in terms of interactions with the environment through planning and direct interactions. The lower-level personnel are thus still dependent upon those in higher positions, but on a different basis.

Another important aspect of the impact of size on the organization is that larger size apparently minimizes the role that any single individual plays in the organization. Evidence from studies by Oscar Grusky and Louis Kriesberg suggests that succession or turnover among top management has less influence on large organizations than on small ones.[49] This is probably a consequence of the diffusion of control and decision-making processes in such organizations. William Faunce reports that the presence of large locals in a national union enhances the democratic process at the national level, suggesting that power is indeed diffused to larger subunits.[50]

A further implication of these findings is that while large organizations probably cannot operate as true democracies, or as entities in which power is totally diffused to lower participants because of their expertise, the power of those at the top of the organization would be increasingly limited with increased size. This would then imply that the idea of a "power elite" composed of the leaders of large organizations in a society may be less threatening to the society than was originally believed. That is, even if such an "elite" did exist through formal or informal communication and social networks, it appears that its impact would be minimized by its members themselves not having any kind of ultimate power within their own organizations. Only in those cases where subordinates in the organizations totally accepted the directions given by their superiors, and where their own expertise led them to the same con-

[48] Walter R. Boland, "Size, Organization and Environmental Mediation: A Study of Colleges and Universities" in J. Victor Baldridge, ed., *Academic Governance in the Administration of Higher Education* (Berkeley, Calif.: McCutchan Publishing Corp., 1971).

[49] Oscar Grusky, "Corporate Size, Bureaucratization, and Managerial Succession," *American Journal of Sociology*, Vol. 67, No. 3 (November 1961), 261–69; and Louis Kriesberg, "Careers, Organizational Size and Succession," *American Journal of Sociology*, Vol. 68, No. 3 (November 1962), 355–59.

[50] William A. Faunce, "Size of Locals and Union Democracy," *American Journal of Sociology*, Vol. 68, No. 3 (November 1962), 291–98.

clusions, would we find unified organizations moving in consistent directions for the benefit of the organization alone. Reality, as expressed in the available data, suggests that this would not be the case. Instead, a good deal of opposition and contradictory information and advice within a large organization would seem to be a more realistic picture. The role of the elite would thus be minimized.

The discussion thus far has treated size in a rather static way, as though each organization were of a certain size and that was it. This is obviously not the case. Organizations grow (or decline, but declines are an exception) to their particular size. The final section in this chapter will be concerned with the issue of growth.

ORGANIZATION GROWTH

There has been very little research on the growth of organizations.[51] Most discussions of growth are based upon cross-sectional data, which allow inferences to be made, but not an examination of the processes involved in growth. The most comprehensive overview of the growth process is William Starbuck's. He suggests that the following motivations for growth are important. (These are managerial motivations. They reflect reactions to rational considerations and external and internal pressures.)

1. Organizational self-realization (trying to accomplish better what the organization is attempting to do)
2. Adventure and risk (the desire for new experiences)
3. Prestige, power, and job security
4. Executive salaries (salaries rise exponentially as organizational size increases)
5. Profit
6. Costs
7. Revenue
8. Monopolistic power
9. Stability
10. Survival [52]

---

[51] An exception is Mason Haire, "Biological Models and Empirical Histories of the Growth of Organizations," in Mason Haire, ed., *Modern Organization Theory* (New York: John Wiley & Sons, Inc., 1959), pp. 287–93.

[52] William H. Starbuck, "Organizational Growth and Development," in James G. March, ed., *Handbook of Organizations* (Chicago: Rand McNally & Co., 1965), p. 454.

The relative importance of these sometimes opposing motivations is unfortunately not specified; but they do represent at least some of the factors that go into the growth process. Growth occurs as both organizations and their members seek to enhance their positions both absolutely and relatively. Starbuck states, "By far the most widely accepted approach to growth has been that growth is either a means of attaining other goals or a side effect of such attainment, rather than an end in itself." [53] This is consistent with the argument made earlier that size should not be taken as the causal factor in structural differentiation in organizations.

Starbuck suggests that there is no one pattern of organizational growth, even though some have appeared in the literature. When growth takes place, the processes of formalization, greater complexity, and redistribution of power occur as the organization seeks to handle its increased size. If all organizations utilized the same technology or were confronted with the same external and internal pressures, patterns of growth could probably be discerned. Since this is not the case, growth must be viewed as a process with multiple causes and consequences. The "state of the art" is such that we cannot yet move from causes to predictions of consequences; the causal factors have been insufficiently developed for such predictions to be made. From the discussion of size presented above, it can be seen that growth has some effects, strongly modified by technological and environmental factors, on both structure and process within the organization.

Consequences of Growth

On a more subjective level, growth appears to have some important consequences for the organization and interaction patterns among its members. Growth brings new members into the organization. They come in at all levels and with a variety of experience, expertise, motivations, and desires for the organization and themselves. An immediate consequence of their arrival is that they upset existing patterns of interaction and communication. Existing social relationships are altered as the new members find their niches in the social structure. For the veteran members of the organization this is somewhat threatening, since the former power arrangements are now distorted and new alignments emerge. The same factors would exist, of course, under conditions of rapid turnover; but then the presence of new members would be expected, and the fact of rapid turnover would tend to preclude the development of extremely

[53] *Ibid.*

solid relationships. In the case of growth, the new members are super-imposed on the existing system and penetrate into it, with the frequent result of setting the "new guard" versus the "old guard."

Communication patterns between the groups are often blocked or nonexistent; within groups, heightened solidarity can develop, which further decreases between-group interactions.[54] If the organizational arrangements are such that communication and cooperation are expected and necessary, such a development is clearly dysfunctional for the organization. When new members are absorbed into the existing system, disruption occurs as the previously existing system becomes no longer operative. The total membership has to learn what the new pattern is and react accordingly. In any case, the social system is disrupted.

From the evidence on size, it is clear that some increases in formalization will occur with growth. Coordination becomes more difficult. For the individual who has been in the organization, these developments are probably the most disturbing. He is used to an older system that has been replaced owing to forces beyond his control. It appears that much of the discontent and protest at universities is due to the growth factor. Joseph Scott and Mohamed El-Assal suggest that:

> In becoming large, high quality, and heterogeneous, many schools had to expand and to formalize their administrative structures in order to coordinate large diverse numbers of communication activities and people in the massive educational enterprises of teaching, research, and public service. Accordingly, they expanded their administrative staff personnel—such as vice-presidents, deans, associate deans, department chairmen, associate department chairmen, administrative assistants, secretaries, executive secretaries, clerks, clerical helpers, and consultants. Simultaneously, they formalized and routinized their administrative procedures in order to coordinate and to regulate the granting of examinations, of degrees, of stipends, of scholarships, research on human subjects, teaching and research facilities, housing, extracurricular organizations, teaching schedules, speakers, sports activities, and hiring, termination, promotion and evaluation of personnel.[55]

While these staff functions have not increased as rapidly as the growth of the total organization,[56] the growth has been there. One result, as Scott and El-Assal note, has been the impersonalization of the educational process. They suggest that this is the major factor leading to student protest. It certainly is a fact that this is a primary component of such protests.

[54] This is essentially one of Lewis Coser's arguments in Coser, *The Functions of Social Conflict* (New York: The Free Press, 1956), p. 95.

[55] Joseph W. Scott and Mohamed El-Assal, "Multiversity, University Size, University Quality and Student Protest: An Empirical Study," *American Sociological Review*, Vol. 34, No. 5 (October 1969), 708.

[56] See Hawley et al., "Population Size."

Another factor related to growth is that faculty and administrators themselves, as the permanent members of the organization, must react to the growth in numbers of faculty, staff, and students. Universities tend to be conservative, and the reaction is often to proceed according to past prescriptions of success. That is, things are done the way they have been done in the past, where tenure and seniority play a dominant role in the advancement process. The same would probably be true of other organizations that deal with people as their primary "through-put" (social-work agencies, schools, hospitals, etc.).

As a result, these organizations do not really seem to change with growth, except by additional routinization and formalization; and when this is added to the fact the "through-put" itself has changed in most instances, we find a situation that is ripe for discontent and protest. Boland suggests that additional energies be put into public relations and financial affairs; this would lead to a further tendency to detract from concerns with internal affairs.[57]

Universities at the present time are probably the most conspicuous example of some of the consequences of growth. Growth does make a difference to the organizations and individuals involved, and the response to it must be appropriate to the conditions under which the growth occurs. The absorption of new members into an organization is not easy, but it is something that almost every organization must face. Because of the dearth of appropriate models to follow, organizations tend to bring their own past experiences to bear in this situation, rather than borrowing from other organizations or trying new approaches. As industry has increased its use of professional personnel, it is clear that problems could have been avoided by seeking effective models outside the industrial setting for the utilization of professionals. Colleges and universities, as well as other kinds of organizations, should perhaps look outside their own ranks for appropriate models, or attempt to develop new ones, as they too face the problems associated with growth.

SUMMARY AND CONCLUSIONS

The basic theme of this chapter has been that size has a variable impact on the organization and that it cannot be taken as a simple predictor, as it often is. It was first pointed out that the various indicators of size, such as number of employees, number of total members, and

---

[57] Boland, "Size, Organization and Environmental Mediation."

financial scope, are closely related. Organizations that are large on one of these factors are very likely to be large on the others. It is clear that organizations are growing larger for a combination of reasons, so the size factor is an important consideration in understanding the conditions of contemporary society.

Research findings have indicated that large size is related to increased complexity in terms of specialization and horizontal and vertical differentiation. These findings are not strong enough, however, to permit the assumption that all large organizations are more complex in these ways and vice versa. Size is also moderately related to increased formalization, according to the studies examined.

The size factor is greatly modified by the technology or technologies employed by the organization. Size and technology combine to yield particular structural configurations. Further modifications of the impact of size are caused by environmental factors and the presence of particular kinds of personnel, such as professionals. As an explanatory tool, size must be utilized in conjunction with these other characteristics.

The extensive studies of the size of the administrative component in organizations relative to their overall size yield the conclusion that there is a tendency toward a curvilinear relationship, in that the administrative component tends to decrease in size as organizational size increases, but in very large organizations, the relative size of the administrative component again increases—although not up to the level that it assumes in small organizations. The overall size of an organization is important in terms of the number of personnel needed for control, communications, and coordination. In extremely large organizations, therefore, one would expect that the administrative component would enlarge as the demands of size are more strongly felt.

Large size has an impact on the individuals in the organization. There is more stress, and the depersonalization process can lead to a great deal of discomfort for many members. These negative consequences are at least partially alleviated by the presence of informal friendship groups found in all organizations. It was suggested that the impact of large organizations on the society as a whole is mixed, in that although social and technological advances can probably more easily be accomplished through large organizations, the concentration of power in large organizations may very well concentrate power in the society, and if unchecked, this situation is a threat to democratic processes. For the organization, large size creates the aforementioned problems of difficulties in control, coordination, and communications. At the same time, it gives the organization more power over its environment, more resources for planning, and less dependence on particular individuals.

When the analysis shifted from size as a static condition to growth as a dynamic process, it was seen that growth tends to upset any existing organizational equilibrium. Both the organization and its members must respond to the presence of the new members and increased size. The response of the organization tends to be in traditional ways, in that it does more of what it has been doing. But growth appears to require new organizational responses, especially when it is coupled with changed technological and environmental conditions.

This chapter has indicated that there are no "laws" regarding size and other organizational characteristics. The basic theme has been that size, while related to some important characteristics, is not as important as other factors in understanding the form organizations take. When size (and growth) is taken in conjunction with technological and environmental factors, predictions regarding organizational structures and processes can be made.

The next chapter will examine the nature of organizational complexity and its consequences for the organization, in the same basic format that has been followed here.

COMPLEXITY

5

Complex organizations. The term describes the subject matter of this entire book—and indeed is the title of several important works dealing with the same basic subject matter. In this chapter we will look at the concept of complexity carefully, noting what it is, its sources, and its consequences. From this examination it should become clear that the complexity of an organization makes an important difference in the behavior of its members, other structural conditions, processes within the organization, and relationships between the organization and its environment. The premise will again be that external conditions and internal processes are the dominant factors determining the form of an organization.

Like size, complexity is one of the first things that hits a person entering an organization of any degree of complexity beyond the simplest form. A division of labor, job titles, multiple divisions, and hierarchical levels are usually immediately evident. Any familiarity with large corporations (and many small ones), the government, the military, or a school system verifies this. Organizations that seem very simple at first glance may exhibit interesting forms of complexity. Local voluntary organizations, such as the Rotary Club, labor union locals, and garden clubs usually have program, publicity, membership, community service, education, finance, and other committees with their attendant structure. While they are not as complex as some others, these kinds of organizations must make provisions for the control and coordination of activities just like their more complex counterparts.

The complexity issue is itself complex, because the individual parts of an organization can vary in their degree of complexity. In a study of the regional office of a major oil company, for example, it was found that there were six divisions, as shown on the organization chart, figure 5–1. The heads of the divisions had equal rank in the organization,

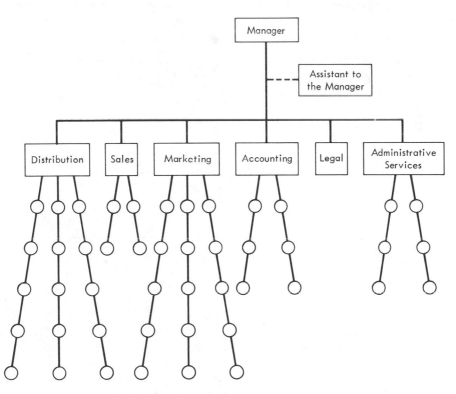

FIG. 5–1   Regional Office Organization

and each was thought to be equally important to the overall success of the organization. When the divisions themselves were examined, it was found that they varied not only in size—from three to 100 members— but also in complexity. The largest division, distribution, had five separate hierarchical levels with three important subdivisions, each of which was further specialized by tasks performed by specific work groups.

The smallest division, which performed legal services associated with land acquisition and other problems of service-station development, was composed of a lawyer and two secretaries.

Another example of the intraorganizational variations in complexity can be seen in manufacturing firms with research and development departments. These departments are likely to be characterized by a shallow hierarchy when compared with other divisions of the organization. While there may be several levels above the actual research and development workers, these personnel will be rather loosely supervised, with a wide span of control. In manufacturing departments, the span of control for each supervisor is shorter and the whole unit will look more like a pyramid. (See figure 5–2.)

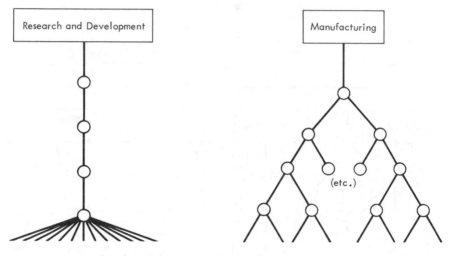

FIG. 5–2   The Shape of Two Departments
in the Same Organization

These examples have been brought up to indicate the obvious—complexity is not a simple issue. The concept contains several components, which do not necessarily vary together. At the same time, the concept itself conveys a meaning in organizational literature. The meaning is basically that complex organizations contain many subparts requiring coordination and control, and the more complex an organization is, the more serious these issues become. Since organizations vary widely in their degree of complexity, regardless of the specific component of complexity used, and since wide variations are found within specific organizations, the issue is an important one for the overall understanding of organizations.

Before we can make sense out of the various research studies on complexity, we must examine the components of the concept.

COMPLEXITY AS A VARIABLE

The three elements of complexity most commonly identified are horizontal differentiation, vertical or hierarchical differentiation, and spatial dispersion.

Horizontal Differentiation

Horizontal differentiation is the way the tasks performed by the organization are subdivided among its members. Unfortunately for conceptual clarity, there are two basic ways in which such tasks can be broken down and assigned. The first way is to give highly trained specialists a rather comprehensive range of activities to perform, and the second is to minutely subdivide the tasks so that nonspecialists can perform them. The first approach is exemplified by the professional or craftsman in the organizational setting who is responsible for complete operations on his own.[1] He is given the responsibility and the authority to carry out the task to its completion. The second form of horizontal differentiation is most plainly seen on the assembly line, where each worker performs only one or a few repetitive tasks. The nature of the task itself is important here, since it is the routine and uniform task that is most amenable to the second type of differentiation; nonroutine and quite varied tasks are more commonly subdivided according to the first type.

Several writers have developed specific definitions for these forms of horizontal complexity. Jerald Hage, in his "axiomatic" theory, defines complexity as the "specialization in an organization . . . measured by the number of occupational specialties and the length of training required by each. The greater the number of occupations and the longer the period of training required, the more complex the organization." [2]

---

[1] For a discussion of craft-organized work, see Arthur L. Stinchcombe, "Bureaucratic and Craft Administration of Production," *Administrative Science Quarterly,* Vol. 4, No. 2 (September 1959), 168–87. For a comprehensive discussion of the nature of professionally controlled work, see Howard M. Vollmer and Donald L. Mills, *Professionalization* (Englewood Cliffs, N.J.: Prentice-Hall, Inc., 1966); Richard H. Hall, *Occupations and the Social Structure* (Englewood Cliffs, N.J.: Prentice-Hall, Inc., 1969), Chapter 4.

[2] Jerald Hage, "An Axiomatic Theory of Organizations," *Administrative Science Quarterly,* Vol. 10, No. 3 (December 1965), 294.

The assumption here is that the more training a person has, the more he is differentiated from another person who might have a similar amount of training but in a different specialty. This definition is almost identical in its implications to that of James Price, who states, *"Complexity* may be defined as the degree of knowledge required to produce the output of a system. The degree of complexity of an organization can be measured by the degree of education of its members. The higher the education, the higher the complexity."[3]

In some later research, Hage and Aiken develop this approach further:

> We interpret complexity to mean at least three things: the number of occupational specialties, the professional activity, and the professional training. Organizations vary in the number of occupational specialties that they utilize in achieving their goals. This variable was measured by asking respondents to report their major duties; each respondent was then classified according to the type of occupational specialty, e. g., psychiatrist, rehabilitation counselor, teacher, nurse, social worker, and so on. The variable, degree of professional activity, reflects the number of professional associations in which the respondents were involved, the number of meetings attended, and the number of offices held or number of papers given at professional meetings. The amount of professional training was based on the amount of college training as well as other professional training.[4]

Hage and Aiken's research was carried out in health and welfare organizations, where the emphasis on professional backgrounds was very appropriate. While this emphasis is not universally applicable in all types of organizations, the point regarding extent of training and depth of experience would hold across organizations.

This form of horizontal differentiation introduces additional complexities into the organization, in that a high level of specialization requires coordination of the specialists. In many cases, personnel specifically designated as coordinating personnel have to be assigned to ensure that the various efforts do not work at cross-purposes and that the overall organizational tasks are accomplished.

A different approach to horizontal differentiation can be seen in the work of Peter Blau and Richard Schoenherr. The definition here is the "number of different positions and different subunits in the organization,"[5] and the emphasis is on the formal structure as defined by the

3 James L. Price, *Organizational Effectiveness: An Inventory of Propositions* (Homewood, Ill.: Richard D. Irwin, Inc., 1968), p. 26.

4 Jerald Hage and Michael Aiken, "Relationship of Centralization to Other Structural Properties," *Administrative Science Quarterly,* Vol. 12, No. 1 (June 1967), 79–80.

5 Peter M. Blau and Richard A. Schoenherr, *The Structure of Organizations* (New York: Basic Books, Inc., Publishers, 1971), p. 16.

organization.[6] An organization is more complex if it has more such positions and subunits. Organizations spread out horizontally as work is subdivided for task accomplishment. This definition is similar to the indicators of complexity used by Hall and his associates, as reported in Chapter 4 (pp. 114–16). They used the number of divisions within an organization and the number of specialties within the divisions as complexity indicators. Pugh and his associates approach the issue in a closely related way, although they use the term "specialization" in their discussion of this phenomenon. They also introduce the concept of "configuration" as an overall indicator of the "shape" of the organization. This latter concept contains the vertical as well as the horizontal factor of the way work is subdivided by task.

These two approaches to horizontal differentiation appear to have very similar roots, in that both are concerned with the division of labor within the organization. These are actually alternative ways by which work can be subdivided. Both forms of differentiation may exist within the same organization, but not in regard to the same task assignment.

Vertical Differentiation

Vertical or hierarchical differentiation is a less complicated matter. Research into this vertical dimension has used straightforward indicators of the depth of the hierarchy. Meyer uses the "proliferation of supervisory levels" as his measures of the depth of an organization.[8] Pugh et al. suggest that the vertical dimension can be measured by a "count of the number of job positions between the chief executive and the employees working on the output."[9] Hall et al. used the "number of levels in the deepest single division" and the "mean number of levels for the organization as a whole" (total number of levels in all divisions/number of divisions) as their indicators.[10]

These direct indicators of vertical differentiation involve an important

---

6 We shall disregard for the present the common distinction between "formal" and "informal" aspects of organizational structure. While deviations from formal organizational arrangements are the rule rather than the exception, the fact is that the formal structure, as used by several of the studies to be discussed, is the framework within which informal patterns are operative. A more extensive examination of this issue will be presented in the next section of the book.

7 D. S. Pugh et al., "Dimensions of Organizational Structure," *Administration Science Quarterly*, Vol. 13, No. 1 (June 1968), 72–74 and 78–79.

8 Marshall W. Meyer, "Two Authority Structures of Bureaucratic Organization," *Administrative Science Quarterly*, Vol. 13, No. 2 (September 1968), 216.

9 Pugh et al., "Dimensions," p. 78.

10 Richard H. Hall et al., "Organizational Size, Complexity, and Formalization," *American Sociological Review*, Vol. 32, No. 6 (December 1967), 906.

assumption that should be made explicit. They assume that authority is distributed in accordance with the level in the hierarchy; that is, the higher the level, the greater the authority. In the vast majority of cases, this would be a valid assumption. It is possible, however, that the proliferation of levels represents phenomena other than the distribution of authority. For example, in organizations that utilize professional personnel, arrangements may not have been made to allow advancement within the same job title. A physicist may be hired as a physicist, but if the organization's policies do not allow much of a salary range for that job title, the person in question may be "promoted" to a higher position without an actual change in his work. In this example, the organization would not be as deep as it appears. Many organizations facing this issue have removed salary restrictions for their professional personnel, allowing the person to retain his job title, but providing a wider range of pay within a particular job title. The possibility remains that an essentially false hierarchy can be observed through the exclusive use of number of levels as defined by the organization.

Another difficulty, similar to this issue, is the question of whether authority is actually distributed throughout the hierarchy. This issue will be taken up in detail in a later chapter, but it should be noted at this point that it is possible for a relatively deep hierarchy to have the power retained at the top of the organization, with those in intermediate positions having little to do other than routine administrative work. In both these exceptions to the rule that says authority is distributed according to the rank in the hierarchy, an extremely detailed knowledge of the organization is necessary before these conclusions may be drawn. In the great majority of cases, the simple measures of vertical differentiation that have been used are realistic indicators of the distribution of authority.

Both horizontal and vertical differentiation present organizations with control, communication, and coordination problems. Subunits along either axis (this would include both aspects of horizontal differentiation) are nuclei that are differentiated from adjacent units and the total organization according to horizontal or vertical factors. The greater the differentiation, the greater the potentiality for difficulties in control, coordination, and communications.

Spatial Dispersion

The final element in complexity, spatial dispersion, can actually be a form of horizontal or vertical differentiation. That is, activities and personnel can be dispersed in space according to either horizontal or vertical functions by the separation of power centers or tasks. The former case is represented by field offices of sales or welfare organizations, in which the tasks performed by the various field offices are essentially identical (low complexity on the horizontal axis) and the power in the organization is differentiated between the central office and the field offices. The latter case is exemplified by local plants of a manufacturing concern, each of which is specialized by product and technology.

Spatial dispersion becomes a separate element in the complexity concept when it is realized that an organization can perform the same functions with the same division of labor and hierarchical arrangements in multiple locations. A business firm, for example, can have a complex set of sales procedures requiring highly specialized salesmen in the field. These salesmen can be dispersed from a central office or through regional or state or local offices, with essentially the same hierarchical arrangements. Complexity is thus increased with the development of spatially dispersed activities, even if the horizontal and vertical differentiation remains the same across the spatially separated units.

Operationalization of the spatial-dispersion concept is relatively simple. In a study of labor union locals, Edna Raphael notes, "The spatial dispersion of members refers to the number of spatially separated places in which the members of a local union are employed. This . . . is a continuous quantitative variable. At one extreme of the continuum, organizations have memberships concentrated in one-plant settings. At the opposite end of the continuum, the members are so extremely dispersed spatially that they even rotate continuously among numerous shops, jobs, and employers within a geographical space of at least several square miles." [11] Hall, Haas, and Johnson used the following indicators in their study: (1) the degree to which physical facilities are spatially dispersed, (2) the location (distance from the organizational headquarters) of the spatially dispersed facilities, (3) the degree to which personnel are spatially dispersed, and (4) the location of spatially dispersed personnel.[12] These various indicators were highly intercorrelated on the basis of the data from this study.

Variance of Complexity Elements

The discussion thus far has suggested that the three major elements of complexity vary, often independently of each other. Before turning to a further discussion of such independent variance, it should be stressed that these elements can obviously vary together. Noncomplex organizations with little horizontal, vertical, or spatial complexity can easily be

---

[11] Edna Raphael, "The Anderson-Warkov Hypothesis in Local Unions: A Comparative Study," *American Sociological Review*, Vol. 32, No. 5 (October 1967), 770.
[12] Hall et al., "Organizational Size," p. 906.

identified. The small business is the example that comes most readily to mind. The same phenomenon can occur, however, in large organizations. Michel Crozier's analysis of two separate governmental organizations in France graphically demonstrates this.[13] The first organization, a clerical agency, was characterized by a very simple division of labor: While tasks were highly routine and repetitious, there was little differentiation among them. There was also a very shallow hierarchy, considering the size of the organization. The organization is not complex on the horizontal and vertical axes.

The third axis of spatial dispersion is added when the French tobacco company (the "Industrial Monopoly") in Crozier's analysis is considered. There are thirty spatially dispersed plants comprising the system. The plants are fairly large, with 350 to 400 employees on the average, but there are only six categories of workers in each plant. Production workers, who are paid equal wages throughout the system, comprise the bulk of the labor force, and there is little differentiation among their tasks. Maintenance workers are more specialized, with electricians, boilermakers, and metal workers in this group. The third group is the shop foremen, who hold supervisory positions in both plant and white-collar office operations. Even here, the tasks performed are quite similar. Administrative jobs, such as personnel, purchasing, or accounting, are few in number and minimally professionalized. There is one technical engineer per plant. The final position is that of the plant director, who usually has an assistant.

This relatively large dispersed organization is structurally very simple. The simplicity does not mean that it does not face severe problems—Crozier documents these in great details—but that the problems are based on external and internal conditions that are not related to its structure. The imposition of civil service personnel regulations, the power of the maintenance personnel—who can actually control the output of the plants by the speed at which they maintain the equipment—and certain characteristics of the French society of which they are a part combine to make these organizations much less efficient and effective than they might be. It seems clear that increased complexity on the vertical and horizontal axes would do little to improve the performance of these plants. In both the tobacco monopoly and the clerical agency (which was also characterized by a poor performance record), the structural characteristics are based upon the tasks to be performed and the technology available, rather than being a simple function of size. These noncomplex organizations are massive systems designed to perform simple and unchanging tasks. It can be hypothesized that if the tasks and technology

13 Michel Crozier, *The Bureaucratic Phenomenon* (Chicago: University of Chicago Press, 1964).

were altered to develop a more effective system, the organizations would become more complex.

In direct contrast to the simple organizations just described, the diversified industrial or government organization serves as an example of the organization that is complex on all three axes. Huge industrial concerns, such as Standard Oil of New Jersey or du Pont, are characterized by extreme complexity. The same would be true for operations of national, state, and some local governments, as well as such diverse organizations as the Catholic Church, the New York City school system, and the University of California.

These extreme cases serve as a reminder that organizations can be highly or minimally complex in all facets of the complexity concept. Other common-sense examples suggest that such covariance is not the necessary pattern A college, for example, usually has a low degree of vertical differentiation and usually no spatial dispersion, but a high degree of horizontal differentiation. Most manufacturing plants would have a greater division of labor along the horizontal axis than those studied by Crozier, although the hierarchical levels may be the same. The offensive unit of a football team is highly specialized but essentially has only two ranks. High vertical differentiation with little horizontal differentiation is exemplified by the army batallion.

This multifaceted approach to complexity would suggest that the determinants of different structural arrangements must be approached empirically, rather than from some a priori assumption such as size. Although size is related to complexity, as was indicated in the previous chapter, factors other than size appear to be of greater importance in determining complexity. Since the various axes of complexity themselves do not always vary together, and the factors associated with horizontal differentiation may not be the same as and may even conflict with those associated with vertical differentiation, the issue becomes even more difficult.

In the next section, examining the factors that have been found to be related to the various aspects of complexity, the relationships to be discussed will be in two directions—those factors that appear to contribute to varying degrees of complexity and those that lead from such degrees.

COMPLEXITY RELATIONSHIPS

Our organization of the evidence regarding complexity will be around the findings of several important research projects that have dealt with that subject. This mode of presentation will lead to some overlap as specific findings are discussed, but it will demonstrate the extent of agreement resulting from studies of a wide variety of organizations approached by similar but not identical methodologies. These research findings will also indicate the importance of complexity as a variable in understanding organizations.

It should be stressed at the outset that size is related to complexity in the manner discussed in the previous chapter. The position taken here is that size is not the major determinant of complexity. At the same time, the fact is that size is related to complexity on all three axes. Larger organizations are generally more complex than smaller ones. As the research will indicate, however, this relationship is based on more than size, since various configurations of complexity come about because of factors other than size.

AIKEN AND HAGE.   The first set of research findings are those of Michael Aiken and Jerald Hage. Their data are based on "sixteen social welfare and health agencies located in a large midwestern metropolis. . . . Ten agencies were private; six were either public or branches of public agencies. These agencies were all welfare organizations that provide rehabilitation and psychiatric services, or services for the mentally retarded (as defined by the directory of the community chest). The agencies vary in size from twelve to several hundred full-time staff." [14]

Hage and Aiken use the number of occupational specialties and the professionalization of the labor force as their indicators of horizontal differentiation, it will be remembered. The first finding from this study is that a high degree of complexity is associated with a low degree of centralization. If an organization is complex, decision making is likely to be distributed to the occupants of the diversified positions within the organization. Since these data are based on employees that are moderately professionalized, and since one of the hallmarks of professionalization is the ability and desire to make decisions autonomously, this finding is not surprising. Hage and Aiken note that "The decentralized arrangement relies upon the skills and expertise of its members. . . ." [15] When complexity involves differentiation along the horizontal axis in this way, decentralization of decisions ensues when the members of the organization are qualified to make decisions on their own and the organization's behalf. There is no suggestion that this form of decentralization would occur in the other form of horizontal differentiation.

In a second study, these authors examined the rate of program

[14] Hage and Aiken, "Relationship of Centralization," pp. 74–75.

[15] *Ibid.*, p. 90. For a further discussion of these relationships, see Richard H. Hall, "Professionalization and Bureaucratization," *American Sociological Review*, Vol. 3, No. 1 (February 1968), 92–104.

change of the sixteen agencies.[16] Program change in these agencies involves the adoption of new services and techniques. The implication is that program change is associated with attempts at increasing the quality of the services rendered. Whether this is in fact the case is not specified, but it can be hypothesized that in a period of rapid change in the total social system and rapid developments in treatment technologies, program change would at least be related to efforts to upgrade the services performed.

The findings from this study suggest that complexity is related to the rate of program change. The more occupational specialties represented in an agency, the greater the likelihood of program change. However, the effect of this form of complexity is minimized when other organizational characteristics are examined. The function (or task) of the organization, as defined by the amount of time a client spends with the agency (the more time the client spends with the agency, the more complete its service), is highly correlated with the number of occupational specialties. When organizational size and auspices are controlled, the relationship between the number of occupational specialties and rate of program change disappears. This is explained by the sequence of the development of these characteristics. The function, size, and auspices affect the number of occupational specialties found in an organization, and this is in turn related to the rate of program change. Since function is the strongest of the predictors, the line of reasoning presented previously is again confirmed. What an organization does affects its structure, in terms of both size and occupational specialization.

Evidence from the same study in regard to vertical differentiation suggests that when authority is concentrated at the top of the organization, the rate of program change decreases. Although Hage and Aiken do not have direct information on the number of hierarchical levels, the implication from their data is that a low numbers of levels is negatively associated with this form of change. In this case, the lower-level organizational members—professionals—are not used in the decision-making process and are thus underutilized. Another finding in the same study bears directly on this, in that the rate of participation in decision making is strongly and positively related to high rates of program change. The effective utilization of professional personnel involves their being allowed to enter the decision-making process through some power in the hierarchy. If they are without power, their contributions are minimized. These findings and the derived interpretations are consistent with the general literature on professionals in organizations.

Both vertical and horizontal differentiation are related to higher rates

[16] Jerald Hage and Michael Aiken, "Program Change and Organizational Properties," *American Journal of Sociology*, Vol. 72, No. 5 (March 1967).

of program change. This finding suggests that when such forms of differentiation are present, there will be a lot of information flowing in the system—information that will contain conflicting ideas and proposals. Organizations that are complex in this way face the problem of integrating the diverse occupations and ideas deriving from the different organizational members. Later studies confirm that such conflict is present and must be dealt with by the organization. The proper method of handling such conflict is *not* by suppression; we have seen that this would represent the exact opposite of the effective utilization of highly trained personnel. We will see later that such conflicts actually work to the organization's advantage.

Aiken and Hage continued their investigation of these sixteen agencies three years later, following up some of the leads from the previous research. The dependent variable in the most recent study was organizational interdependence, as indicated by the number of joint programs in which the agencies participate. The findings from this analysis are not surprising in light of the earlier findings and discussion. *"Organizations with many joint programs are more complex organizations, that is they are more highly professionalized and have more diverse occupational structures."* [17] The interpretation given to these findings is that a decision to engage in joint programs leads to the importation of new specialties into the organization, since joint programs are likely to be highly specialized and the personnel in the agency would not have the skills necessary for participation.

These findings have interesting implications for organizations and for the society of which they are a part. Aiken and Hage state:

> Our assumptions help to explain the increasing frequency of organizational interdependency, especially that involving joint programs. As education level increases, the division of labor proceeds (stimulated by research and technology), and organizations become more complex. As they do, they also become more innovative. The search for resources needed to support such innovations requires interdependent relations with other organizations. At first, these interdependencies may be established with different goals and in areas that are more tangential to the organization. Over time, however, it may be that cooperation among organizations will multiply, involving interdependencies in more critical areas, and involve organizations having more similar goals. It is scarcity of resources that forces organizations to enter into more cooperative activities with other organizations, thus creating more integration of organizations into a community structure. The long-range consequence of this process will probably be a gradually heightened coordination in communities.[18]

[17] Michael Aiken and Jerald Hage, "Organizational Interdependence and Intraorganizational Structure," *American Sociological Review*, Vol. 33, No. 6 (December 1968), 920.

[18] *Ibid.*, pp. 928–29.

If there is a tendency for organizations to become more complex because of internal and external pressures, the implication of these findings is that joint programs and other interorganizational relationships will continue to develop, probably at an increasing rate. This would in the long run lead to a society in which the web of interrelationships between organizations would become extremely intricate and the total society more organizationally "dense." This in turn implies a condition in which both individuals and the society as a whole are dependent upon fewer and more complex organizations. The nature of these organizations and their orientation toward the good of the few or the many present the society with the dilemma of the source of control of the organizations. If this trend is realized, decisions regarding organizational futures become decisions about society.

The short-run implications of these findings would seem to be that the more complex an organization is, the more complex it will become, since the development of new programs and interorganizational relationships both lead to additional complexity. The Aiken Hage approach to complexity has been organized around the utilization of professionals to accomplish and advance the tasks of the organizations studied. Since not all organizational members are professionalized and horizontal differentiation involves more than this variable, our focus will now shift to alternative modes of differentiation and their relationships with other variables.

BLAU AND ASSOCIATES.   Peter Blau and his associates have been engaged in a systematic investigation of several kinds of organizations in a wide variety of settings. Although Blau attributes many of the findings from his studies to sheer impact of size in contrast to the argument presented here, the findings in regard to complexity are extremely important for this discussion. The most general conclusion from these studies is that the various forms of complexity are related to different, even opposing, forces within the organization.

In an early report from the larger study, Blau et al. found that expert qualifications on the part of the personnel in 156 public personnel agencies were associated with a high ratio of managers to total personnel (high degree of vertical differentiation).[19] This is consistent with the findings of Hage and Aiken. At the time the research was conducted, this was an unexpected finding; it had been hypothesized that expert qualifications

---

[19] Peter M. Blau, Wolf V. Heydebrand, and Robert E. Stauffer, "The Structure of Small Bureaucracies," *American Sociological Review*, Vol. 31, No. 2 (April 1966). The definition of experts in this case (proportion of the operating staff required to have at least a college degree in a particular specialty) does not approximate professionalization as used by Hage and Aiken and others. Nonetheless, it does differentiate between those who are minimally trained and those who are not.

would be related to a lower ratio of managers, since the experts would not require close supervision. In rethinking their original assumptions, Blau et al. conclude:

> Expert training may be expected to make a man not only more independent in the performance of his duties, but also more aware of the broader implications of his work and more capable of detecting operating problems and finding solutions for them than is an untrained person. Experts are more likely to resent having their discretion limited by managerial directives than employees whose lesser skills make them welcome such guidance. In addition, experts can make greater contributions to the improvement of operating procedures than men without specialized training. Hence feedback communication from the operating staff is especially valuable for management if this staff consists of experts. To take full advantage of the contributions experts can make to operations, management must facilitate the flow of upward communication. [This assumes, of course, some commitment to and operation of rationality norms. R. H. H.] A low ratio of managers tends to discourage upward communication, however, inasmuch as a small contingent of managers can most easily direct operations by issuing orders from a central headquarters to the staff. A high ratio of managers increases opportunities for communication between officials responsible for administrative and those responsible for operating decisions. Such extensive two-way communication is of special importance if the personnel has expert qualifications, not alone because experts tend to be more alienated by one-sided directives but particularly because they make greater contributions through feedback than persons with poorer qualifications.[20]

These findings were reinforced by additional data gathered in 254 finance departments of state and local governments.[21] In departments with personnel having expert qualifications, deeper hierarchies were found, with narrower spans of control for those in the hierarchy. The superiors of experts spent little time in supervision, compared to those of nonexperts. Responsibility is delegated in the departments with experts. In this case, the proliferation of levels in the organization is apparently not a case of "overbureaucratization" with many levels of authority but with no one willing to make decisions. Blau concludes that these levels are not a matter of differentiating authority for authority's sake, but rather a matter of facilitating communications from the bottom to the top of the organization.[22] Although the concern here is not with control within organizations, these findings are important in this regard. The control of the individual employee's behavior is left much more to his own discretion when he is an expert. When he is not, more supervisory time is spent in ensuring that the organization's tasks are

20 *Ibid.,* pp. 458–59.

21 Peter M. Blau, "The Hierarchy of Authority in Organizations," *American Journal of Sociology,* Vol. 73, No. 4 (January 1968).

22 *Ibid.,* p. 461.

being accomplished and that operating decisions are made in accordance with organizational policy. When experts are found in the organization, supervisors (those at the various levels in the hierarchy) are apparently freed from supervisory and routine administrative tasks and can spend more time in planning and coordinating activities.

This interpretation receives strong support from the work of Marshall Meyer. Using data from the same 254 finance departments, Meyer found that in divisions with high levels of expertness, there was a low span of control. Since supervisors had fewer subordinates, the opportunities for communication increased. Meyer concludes:

> The present findings do not mean that expert employees require more supervision than non-experts. It is assumed that experts are responsible for more complex tasks than non-experts, but because of their competence experts are probably better able to complete their task unaided and unsupervised. What the data do indicate is that the kind of work done by expert employees requires freer and more open channels of communication than the work of non-experts demands. Intuition tells one that where spans of control are low, supervisors and subordinates have better access to one another than where spans of control are high. Where spans of control are low, then two-way interchange between superordinates and subordinates becomes possible. Supervisors have a great deal of time to explain complex problems to subordinates, and expert subordinates who are engaged in the composite decision-making process can take solutions as the situation demands. Where working conditions are such that two-way interchange between supervisors and workers is not needed, spans of control will be quite large: Spans of control as high as thirty occur in some industrial settings. . . . Thus it is not expertness in and of itself but rather the need for frequent consultations and communications that produces low spans of control in parts of organizations that employ highly qualified personnel.[23]

These findings have an important implication for the discussion of complexity. Organizations will apparently take either of two basic shapes. They can be wide and relatively flat, with wide spans of control and labor subdivided in a highly specific way; or narrower and deep, with individual members responsible for a wider area of task performance based on their expert qualifications. This conclusion is supported by Meyer's further analysis of data from the 254 finance departments.[24] It would have been useful if this research had included data regarding differentiation among the departments, since this would have provided a test of the idea that the total organizational task, which is translated into the technology utilized, has a major impact on the structure of the total organization. Without such data, this relationship has to be inferred

[23] Marshall W. Meyer, "Expertness and the Span of Control," *American Sociological Review*, Vol. 33, No. 6 (December 1968), 950.
[24] Meyer, "Two Authority Structures."

from other data, as has been done. The Meyer data do demonstrate, however, that organizations do take these two basic forms.

Meyer found that as organizational size increased, the organizations became more complex horizontally *or* vertically. Here again, the general relationship between size and complexity holds. The specific form of complexity, however, is apparently not a function of size. The alternative forms of organization are related to the way in which power is distributed in the organization. In the horizontally differentiated organization, power is centralized with the top management retaining most of the control. In the vertically differentiated organization, on the other hand, lower-level personnel are allowed to make more of the decisions. It was also found that in the horizontally differentiated organizations, there were fewer rules than in the hierarchically differentiated system. Since control is maintained at the top in the former case, there is less need for organizational policies to be made explicit; subordinates are not in a position to engage in the decision-making process and hence do not require the same rules structure. Rocco Carzo, Jr., and John N. Yanouzas found in a laboratory experiment that taller structures performed better than wider ones in terms of profit and rate of return on sales revenue. This is attributed to the fact that the taller structure allowed members of work groups to evaluate their decisions more frequently and that the narrower span of control was more suited to the task being performed.[25] A different task might have led to different results.

In regard to the discussion of forms of complexity at the outset of this chapter, the findings that have been cited indicate some clear patterns. When horizontal differentiation takes the form of division of labor by expertise or high degree of knowledge required, the organization is likely to have a tall hierarchy. If labor is divided into small tasks to reduce the extent of expertise required, the organization will be flatter (wider spans of control) and wider. This conclusion is generally consistent with Joan Woodward's findings from an analysis of English production organizations.[26] The two forms of horizontal differentiation are thus incompatible and differentially related to vertical differentiation.

Two additional points should be made before turning to other research findings. The first is that the research we have discussed, while many steps ahead of the case-study approach, has been concentrated in

[25] Rocco Carzo, Jr., and John N. Yanouzas, "Effects of Flat and Tall Organizational Structures," *Administrative Science Quarterly*, Vol. 14, No. 2 (June 1969), 178–91.

[26] Joan Woodward, *Industrial Organizations* (London: Oxford University Press, 1962).

organizations that perform services for clients or are governmental units. Despite the variations found on the elements of complexity, it is not certain that the total range of variation was encountered. That is, in organizations other than health and welfare agencies and public personnel and finance departments, there might well be a greater or lesser degree of either form of horizontal differentiation, and more or less extensive vertical differentiation. For the conclusions that have been drawn to be fully acceptable, the findings should be extended to other organizations. On a common-sense basis, however, they do seem applicable.

The second point, one that has been alluded to several times throughout the book, is that there is intraorganizational variation in structure. Empirical verification for this point is provided by Hall's analysis of the degree of perceived bureaucracy in ten organizations of diverse types.[27] The employees of these organizations were asked to indicate the extent to which they perceived their organizations to be bureaucratized on the six bureaucratic dimensions. The departments in these organizations were dichotomized into those that performed uniform, easily routinized tasks and those that performed social or creative tasks, following the suggestion of Eugene Litwak.[28] The findings from the data are not surprising in light of the previous discussion. Those departments that performed routine tasks were generally more bureaucratized than those engaged in nonroutine tasks. There were a less rigid hierarchy of authority, a less intensive division of labor, and fewer exact procedural specifications in the nonroutine departments.

Differences in perceived bureaucratization were also examined according to hierarchical differentiation. Here again the findings are not surprising, in that those in managerial positions perceived a lower degree of bureaucratization than those in nonmanagerial positions. If perceptions correspond at all to reality, and in this case there is good reason to believe that they do, it can be concluded that executives operate in a less bureaucratized environment than do their subordinates. The division of labor is not as intense, there is less emphasis on relying on superiors for decision making, procedures are not as stringent, and there is less impersonalization. Thus there is also vertical differentiation within an organization in terms of how the structure is perceived and also probably in terms of how it operates.

These findings are vital for the discussion of complexity. In an organization in which there are many different tasks being performed,

[27] Richard H. Hall, "Intraorganizational Structure Variation," *Administrative Science Quarterly*, Vol. 7, No. 3 (December 1962).

[28] Eugene Litwak, "Models of Organizations which Permit Conflict," *American Journal of Sociology*, Vol. 67, No. 2 (September 1961), 177–84.

there would undoubtedly be such internal variations between depart-ments and levels. Even in an organization with one primary activity, the subdivision into such functions as accounting, personnel, public relations, and so forth, would be a source of internal differentiation. When the contemporary large-scale organization, such as the corporate conglom-erate, multiversity, or government agency is considered, the range of internal structural variations is undoubtedly enormous. It is reasonable to expect, for example, that the fiscal division of a large religious denomination is structured much like that of some corporation in private industry. This would be even more likely with the advent of com-puterized data-processing systems. The same point would probably hold for other common departmental activities across organizations.

PUGH ET AL. (THE ASTON GROUP).   Additional insights into the nature of organizational complexity can be gleaned from the work of Pugh and his associates. As noted previously, the organizations they studied are predominantly manufacturing organizations, with those that are not in the production process, such as bus companies and retail stores, engaging in relatively routinizable activities. Although they are con-cerned with a wider array of structural characteristics than are being considered in the present chapter, their findings are very important to the overall understanding of organizational structure.

As indicated earlier, this research included the number of specialties represented in the work force. The findings from the data analysis cor-roborate the conclusions reached by Blau and Meyer, when Pugh et al. conclude:

> In other words, an organization with many specialists tends also to have more standard routines, more documentation, and a large supportive hierarchy. A hypothesis on this process is that as specialists increase in num-ber, they introduce procedures to regulate the activities for which they are responsible—the personnel specialist his selection procedure, the inspector his quality control, the application forms for vacancies and the inspection reports. A tall hierarchy results to encompass the specialists and the large number of non-workflow jobs.[29]

There is an important difference in the interpretation of the same basic finding that the presence of specialists is associated with a tall hierarchy. While Blau and Meyer see this as a result of the need for communications and mutual consultation, Pugh et al. appear to view it as a result of vertical differentiation among the specialists themselves. It is at this point that the differences in data-gathering devices and the incompleteness of the data make interpretations difficult. While the

---

[29] Pugh et al., "Dimensions," p. 82.

evidence is clear that the number of levels of hierarchy does in fact increase with specialization, it is not clear what the personnel in these
levels do. In the Blau–Meyer formulation, the implication is that the
members of the various hierarchical levels are communicators in supervisory positions. There is no evidence to indicate whether these communicators are members of the specialty. Common sense suggests that
they would actually have to be if the specialists are to make use of their
superiors in discussing alternative plans of action. A fiscal expert in one
of the financial departments would find it extremely hard to communicate in any meaningful way with someone untrained in his specialty,
particularly when highly technical matters are the subject under discussion.

The perspective of Pugh et al. suggests that the members of the hierarchy are actually engaged in specialists' work. That is, they are participating in the work of the specialty and may or may not be primarily
communicators. As we have mentioned, the tall hierarchy may actually
represent a way to promote specialists, keeping them in the organization,
but without substantially altering their actual work. Accountants at
various levels in the accounting hierarchy may all be engaged in accounting, for example, rather than those in higher positions merely being
sounding-boards for those of lower status. This is, of course, an issue
subject to further investigation, since neither set of data has information
bearing on this issue.

It should be noted, before leaving this issue, that the two research
projects being discussed, while using the same basic definition of horizontal differentiation, do not use exactly the same criterion of specialization. The Blau approach more explicitly uses professionalization, while
the Pugh group is concerned with specialization per se, without directly
considering professionalization. This does not totally explain the differences in interpretation, but may account for part of them.

The English research also found high intercorrelations between the
measure of specialization and measures of formalization and standardization. This suggests that organizations scoring high on these measures
have attempted to structure their activities; that is, "the intended behavior of employees has been structured by the specification of their
specialized roles, the procedures they are to follow in carrying out those
roles, and the documentation of what they have to do." [30] This conclusion is verified when the scores on the numerous measures utilized in the
total project are factor-analyzed. This is a technique by which the indicators that vary together can be isolated mathematically from other
clusters of commonly varying measures. The three components of spe-

[30] *Ibid.*, p. 84.

cialization, standardization, and formalization combine into a major "underlying dimension of structure." If the measure of specialization had been more concerned with professionalization, as was the case with Hage and Aiken and Blau and Meyer, the relationships found with standardization and formalization might not have been as strong, since there is a large amount of evidence indicating that professionals tend to work in rather unstandardized and unformalized settings. Here again, the problem of the lack of common definitions interferes with real comparability.

The discussion thus far has been concerned with relationships between the horizontal and vertical dimensions of complexity. The findings have suggested that when organizations divide their tasks into jobs to be performed by specialists (regardless of whether or not these are professionals), *there is likely to be a tall hierarchy with many levels of supervision* (again, regardless of whether or not the members of these levels actually supervise or engage in communications or perform specialists' work themselves). If, on the other hand, the work is subdivided into minute or highly specialized tasks to be performed by nonspecialists who do not require extensive training for the task, *the organization is likely to be rather flat, with each supervisor having a relatively large span of control.*

This conclusion is congruent with the argument made earlier that the nature of the organization's activities has a major impact on the form of its structure. If the organization is engaged in a task that can be accomplished by subdivision into extremely small units, it will probably do so and have the low, wide structure that characterizes such a technology. Tasks requiring specialists will result in the taller, narrow organizations. This assumes, of course, some rationality on the part of the organization and situations in which there is only one obvious way for the organization's activities to be performed. Many of the tasks that are minutely subdivided, as in the case of the assembly line, could in fact be performed by personnel trained to become experts in a wider variety of skills than those commonly used in most assembly-line work. This has been done in cases of "job enlargement"—attempts to increase the amount of responsibility for the person on the assembly line or in the office.[31] These efforts have been somewhat successful in terms of the increase in productivity that the total organization exhibits. Job enlargement would probably entail increased supervisory costs, since the span of control for each supervisor would decrease and more supervisory levels would be developed. The philosophy of management of the particular organization and the nature of the technologies available for use would be the critical factors in determining if job enlargement is possible and desirable.

[31] For a discussion of this phenomenon, see Georges Friedman, *The Anatomy of Work* (New York: The Free Press, 1961), pp. 40–67.

The Effects of Technology

The importance of the effect of technology on the form of complexity taken by an organization can be seen in studies of the automation of industry and offices. Woodward's study found that in process industries, such as petroleum or chemicals, there was a low span of control and a tall hierarchy.[32] This finding is corroborated by Robert Blauner's analysis of the same type of industry.[33] In both cases, the need for consultation with superiors and the ramifications of serious errors necessitate close interactions between supervisors and first-line workers. The supervisors have to know exactly what is going on and interact frequently with personnel at the workflow level. Here the line workers have a major impact on the work process itself, and their decisions are vital in the smooth functioning of the organization.

A contrasting impact of automation is seen in Meyer's analysis of the consequences of automation in the office.[34] Here, automation takes the form of introducing data-processing units into the organization. The structural consequence in this case is different from that in the continuous-flow production organizations. While a tall hierarchy is evident, the span of control of the first-line supervision is large. The lower-level employees in such a division actually perform simple tasks, such as IBM card punching and verifying and simple machine operations. Errors in this case do not have the ramifications that they do in the process manufacturing setting and can be detected later with less potential damage to the whole system. The members of the tall hierarchy in this case do not really engage themselves in supervision of the work force, but rather act as consultants with other divisions in the organization that utilize, but may not be familiar with, the intricacies of the data-processing section. In this case, the data-processing division of an organization probably has a different form from that of the rest of the organization, emphasizing again the importance of intraorganizational differences in structural arrangements.

The Spatial Dispersion Factor

Before turning to a broader consideration of the implications of varying degrees of complexity, let us discuss the issue of spatial disper-

---

32 Woodward, *Industrial Organizations.*

33 Robert Blauner, *Alienation and Freedom* (Chicago: University of Chicago Press, 1964).

34 Marshall W. Meyer, "Automation and Bureaucratic Structure," *American Journal of Sociology,* Vol. 74, No. 3 (November 1968), 256-64.

sion. This will serve as a prelude to the discussion of the implications of complexity, since the findings from spatial-dispersion studies begin to give indications of the conditions facing complex organizations. Anderson and Warkow, in their examination of the size of the administrative component of organizations that was discussed in the previous chapter, considered the spatial-dispersion factor. One of their major findings was that the "relative size of the administrative component *increases* as the number of places at which work is performed increases." [35]

This finding was not upheld in Raphael's study of labor union locals. In this case, spatial dispersion was associated with a decrease in the size of the administrative component. Raphael attributes the difference in findings to the fact that labor unions are voluntary associations, and the dispersed locals are semiautonomous from centralized control and operate on their own. She also points out that the dispersed locals tend to be less democratic than those that are centralized and have a larger administrative apparatus.[36] In the centralized setting, according to this analysis, there is a greater likelihood of intensive communication networks developing, thus enhancing the possibility of the operation of democratic processes. The differences in the control mechanism of the voluntary association lead to a more oligarchic situation in the dispersed voluntary association, since a managerial clique can be formed containing elected leaders and selected members who perform many of the administrative functions. This lowers the size of the administrative component in the dispersed unions, but at the same time decreases the opportunities for participation of the rank and file.

These findings reemphasize the fact that voluntary organizations are qualitatively different in many important attributes from nonvoluntary organizations. The differences in control and administrative mechanisms found by Raphael are only part of the picture. Such organizations obviously require a different form of attachment of members and consistent efforts to maintain member support.[37] These differences make generalizations comparing nonvoluntary to voluntary organizations extremely dangerous. It is fairly clear that they are not exact opposites in every characteristic, but the structure and processes in voluntary organizations clearly require careful analysis to determine where the two forms of organizations coincide and where they do not.

Another examination of spatial dispersion is contained in the research of Pugh et al. As in the case of size, they treat number of operating sites

[35] Theodore Anderson and Seymour Warkov, "Organizational Size and Functional Complexity," *American Sociological Review,* Vol. 26, No. 1 (February 1961), 27.

[36] Raphael, "Anderson–Warkov Hypothesis," pp. 773–76.

[37] See Amitai Etzioni, *A Comparative Analysis of Complex Organizations* (New York: The Free Press, 1961), pp. 40–67, for an extended discussion of this point.

as a contextual variable rather than as an element of the organization's structure, but as was also the case with size, spatial dispersion can perhaps more legitimately be treated as a structural characteristic. The research setting here, it will be remembered, is the English Midlands, and the organizations themselves do not represent the spectrum of organizations, being concentrated in engineering and metal industries.[38] Nevertheless, the organizations did vary in dispersion, with service-oriented organizations having the greatest degree of dispersion.

The relationships with other structural characteristics provide a further indication of the consequences of complexity in general. Spatial dispersion was inversely related to structuring of activities. Activities are structured when work roles are predefined; and in dispersed organizations, the workers have more discretion in how they are to carry on their day-to-day activities. Spatial dispersion was positively related to concentration of authority. Important organizational decisions dispersed to multiple operating sites. Since the work is specialized and a taller hierarchy is found in such situations, the finding that authority is concentrated in these settings is consistent with the earlier findings. There was also a positive relationship between dispersion and line control of workflow, which, as was indicated earlier, refers to the fact that the actual work being performed is controlled by the workers in direct contact with the product, clients, or customers. In situations in which there is line control of workflow, there are centrally controlled personnel policies to ensure that the workers are selected on the basis of their ability to carry out the work, without a lot of variation among them. In the case of spatial dispersion, therefore, while the workers on the "line" do not have specific operating procedures spelled out for them and have a rather large degree of control of what they do on the job, the basic decisions regarding what they work on and who will be employed in the first place are retained by the organization. Dispersion is thus accompanied by the retention of certain kinds of control by the central organizations.[39]

An assumption throughout this discussion is that most organizations are complex in one of the various configurations discussed. Another assumption, verifiable from a variety of forms of evidence, is that *there is a strong tendency for organizations to become more complex as their own activities and the environment around them become more complex.* Since organizations grow in size, and since size and complexity are related, this is a moderately well supported assumption. Organizations that survive become more complex.

Simple knowledge about complexity is useful in and of itself. This

---

[38] D. S. Pugh et al., "The Context of Organization Structures," *Administrative Science Quarterly*, Vol. 14, No. 1 (March 1969), 104.

[39] *Ibid.*, pp. 108–12.

knowledge becomes applicable for analysis and practice when the consequences of complexity for the organization are considered. It has been suggested throughout this discussion that increased complexity leads to greater problems of coordination and control. Now let us examine these problems in more detail.

THE CONSEQUENCES OF COMPLEXITY

In one of the most significant studies of organizations in the past decade, *Organization and Environment,* Lawrence and Lorsch examined the sources and consequences of complexity. Their approach to complexity is through the term *differentiation.*[40] In this study, the term means the division of organizations into parts to perform their activities (horizontal differentiation, in our terms), such as sales, production, or research. To this rather standard approach to differentiation, Lawrence and Lorsch add some additional components that are implicit in the discussions of complexity that have been presented here. They note that structural differentiation includes differences in attitude and behavior on the part of members of the differentiated departments. These include orientations toward the particular goals of the department, differing emphases on interpersonal skills, varied time perspectives, and the type and extent of formalization of the structure. Departments, therefore, vary not only in the specific tasks they perform, but also in the underlying behavior and outlooks of their members.

The data for the analysis of differentiation come from firms in three industries in the United States. The first set of industries was firms making and selling plastics in the form of powder, pellets, and sheets.

> Their products went to industrial customers of all sizes, from the large automobile, appliance, furniture, paint, textile, and paper companies to the smaller firms making toys, containers, and household items. The organizations studied emphasized specialty plastics tailored to specific uses rather than standardized commodity plastics. They all built their product-development work on the science of polymer chemistry. Production was continuous, with relatively few workers needed to monitor the automatic and semiautomatic processing equipment.[41]

[40] Paul R. Lawrence and Jay W. Lorsch, *Organization and Environment: Managing Differentiation and Integration* (Cambridge: Harvard Garduate School of Business Administration, 1967). It should be noted that differentiation is not identical to complexity as used in this discussion. It is close enough, however, for comparability.

[41] *Ibid.,* p. 24.

These organizations were in a highly competitive market situation. The major competitive issue, according to the executives interviewed, was the development of new and revised products and processes. The life cycle of any product was likely to be short, since competitors were all engaged in intensive research and could make even a very successful product quickly obsolete. The executives noted that "the most hazardous aspect of the industrial environment revolved around the relevant scientific knowledge." [42] These organizations were in a changing and "turbulent" environment, with both input—in the form of scientific knowledge—and the consumption of output—in the form of customer satisfaction by purchasing the product—highly uncertain. On the other hand, the production process itself was characterized by its certainty. Once the original technical specifications for a particular product were developed, the production process could proceed quite automatically, since the mix between such production variables as pressure, temperature, and chemical composition could be easily measured, and monitoring was part of the production process itself.

The six organizations studied within the plastics industry each had four basic functional departments—sales, production, applied research, and fundamental research—that differed in their own structures. The production departments were the most formalized, and the fundamental research units the least. Sales department personnel were the most concerned with interpersonal relationships, and production departments were the least, with the two research units falling in between. The interesting dimension of the time perspective taken shows the departments falling into a predictable pattern. The ordering, from shortest to longest time perspective, was sales, production, applied research, and fundamental research.[43] The members of the various departments were also differentiated in terms of personal goals, with sale personnel concerned with customer problems and the marketplace; production personnel with cost reduction and efficiency; and the research personnel concerned with scientific matters, as well as the more immediately practical issues of process improvement and modification. The scientific personnel were not as concerned with purely scientific matters as the authors had anticipated, but they did have clearly different goals from those of the members of other departments.

Differentiation in these organizations thus clearly involves more than

42 *Ibid.*, p. 25.

43 The importance of the time perspective has been particularly stressed by Elliot Jaques in *Equitable Payment* (London: Heinemann Educational Books, Ltd., 1961). The differences between departments are important in the utilization of a "time-span of discretion" as a basis for payment, as formulated by Jaques. The same criterion should not be used across departments.

sheer differentiation by task. The members of the departments were differentiated according to organizationally important behaviors and attitudes. Equally or perhaps more important for the general discussion is the fact that these differences in task, behavior, and attitude are directly related to the kind of environment that the various departments must work with in their short- and long-run activities. *A high degree of differentiation (complexity) is therefore related to a highly complex and differentiated environment.*[44] In this case the complexity refers to the competitive situation in which the organizations find themselves (this degree of competition is not limited to profit-making organizations) and to the rapidly changing and complicated technological world in which they must survive.

To provide contrasts for the plastics firms, Lawrence and Lorsch studied two other industries; the major factor in their selection was the rate of environmental change. The second one chosen was the standardized container industry. The rate of sales increase in this industry was at about the level of the rate of population growth and the growth of the gross national product, so the organizations in the industry were approximately keeping even with the environment in these respects. More important for the purposes of their study, no significant new products had been introduced in two decades. The major competitive factors were "operational issues of maintaining customer service through prompt delivery and consistent product quality while minimizing operating costs." [45] While these are not easy or simple tasks to perform, they are stable; and the problems and prospects for the future are much more certain than in the plastics field.

The third set of organizations studied was in the packaged foods industry. In terms of environmental conditions, these organizations were intermediate between the plastics and container firms. While they engaged heavily in innovations, the rate of new-product introduction and the growth of sales were less than in the plastics industry, but more than in the container field.

When the differentiation within the organizations in these three industries was examined, the findings were as predicted—the plastics firms were the most differentiated, followed by the food firms, and then by the container firms. From this evidence and that presented earlier, the role of the environment in shaping an organization becomes obvious. The specific form an organization takes is dependent upon the environmental conditions it faces. Added to this, of course, are the considera-

[44] This conclusion builds on and is supported by the work of Tom Burns and G. M. Stalker in *The Management of Innovation* (London: Tavistock Publications, 1961).

[45] Lawrence and Lorsch, *Organizations and Environment*, p. 86.

tions of size, traditions within a particular organization or set of organizations, and the idiosyncrasies of individual organizations. These latter factors are "added on" after the environmental considerations, since the environment provides the basic requirements for shaping the organization, and the other considerations appear to be limited to variations on the central theme provided by the environment.

If this interpretation of the sources of complexity is taken as correct (and even if it is not), the major question remains. What does complexity do to an organization? Lawrence and Lorsch provide some important indications of the consequences in their further analysis of organizations in these three industries. They base their analysis on the concept of *integration,* which they define as "the quality of the state of collaboration that exists among departments that are required to achieve unity of effort by the demands of the environment." [46] The authors are also concerned with the effectiveness of the organizations. Here they use rather standard and appropriate market and economic measures. Organizations are more effective when they meet environmental pressures and when they allow their members to achieve their individual goals. Lawrence and Lorsch do not have direct evidence on the individual and his reactions to the organizations, but their findings imply that an organization that is successful in terms of market and economic factors is also successful in adapting to its environment and in providing its members with appropriate incentives and rewards.

Complexity, Conflict, and Performance

The results of the analysis of integration and effectiveness are in some ways surprising. In the plastics industry, the most effective organizations are those with the greatest degree of differentiation, and these also face the most severe integration problems. Their effectiveness in the face of high differentiation is explained by their successful conflict resolution. It is not the idea of successful conflict resolution that is surprising; it is the fact that the effective organizations were characterized by a high degree of conflict in the first place—that they were not totally harmonious, with all personnel working as members of one happy team. From the data discussed earlier, it is apparent that the differentiation in terms of departmental and individual attitudinal and behavioral differences would lead inevitably to conflict. In these organizations, such conflict contributes to effectiveness.

Conflict per se, of course, would make negative contributions to the

46 *Ibid.,* p. 47.

organization if it were not resolved. So another important contribution of this research is its analysis of conflict resolution. The authors do not suggest that there is one best form of such resolution. Rather, they provide evidence that conflict-resolution processes vary according to the specific conflict situations that are faced in a particular form of organization. In the case of the highly differentiated plastics organizations, integration is achieved by departments or individuals who are in a position, and have the knowledge available, to work with the departments involved in conflict situations. In this case, the position is at a relatively low level in the managerial hierarchy, rather than at the top of the organization. This lower position is necessary because of the specific knowledge required to deal with the departments and issues involved. The highly differentiated and effective organization thus anticipates conflict and establishes integrating (conflict-resolving) departments and individuals whose primary purpose is to work with the departments in (inherent) conflict. Another important consideration is that the integrating departments or individuals are equidistant between the conflicting departments in terms of their time, goal, interpersonal, and structural orientations. This middle position leads to effective resolution not through simple compromise, but rather through direct confrontations between the conflicting parties. Conflict resolution in this setting thus becomes a process whereby the parties thrash out their differences in the open with the assistance of integrators who understand both their positions.[47]

In the container corporations, with their lesser degree of differentiation, conflicts also arise, but not to the extent found in the plastics firms, owing to the lesser differentiation. Conflicts are resolved here at the top of the effective organization.[48] In the container industry, those at the top of the organization have greater knowledge because of the stable environment and the lack of differentiation between organizational segments. This lack of differentiation means that the knowledge involved is not as specialized, and a top executive can have a good grasp of what is going on in the major divisions. Lawrence and Lorsch suggest that in this case, and in others like it, decentralization of influence would be harmful.[49] The food-processing firms generally fall between the plastics and the container firms in the extent of their differentiation and in the integration problems faced.

A major conclusion from this analysis is that *effectiveness is not achieved through following one organizational model.* While our concern here is with neither effectiveness nor organizational models, this conclusion is vitally important for understanding organizations. Said in

47 *Ibid.,* pp. 54–83.
48 Two organizations each were studied in the food and container industries.
49 *Ibid.,* pp. 131–58.

other words, *there is no one best way to organize for the purpose of achieving the highly varied goals of organizations within a highly varied environment.* Particular kinds of goals coupled with specific kinds of activities within particular kinds of environments do call for particular organizational structures if effectiveness is a major criterion for the organization. Organizational structure is thus not a random phenomenon, but is based on the factors that have been stressed throughout this analysis.

This conclusion is strengthened when Blau and Schoenherr's findings are considered.[50] This study is based on government finance and public personnel agencies. They also find that increased complexity engenders problems of communication and coordination. More of the time of the personnel in the managerial hierarchy is spent in dealing with these problems than in direct supervision in a highly complex organization. There is also pressure in complex organizations to add personnel to handle the increased control and coordination activities, increasing the proportion of the total personnel devoted to such activities.

This fact introduces an interesting paradox into the analysis of organizations. While large organizations can experience savings through the economics of large size, the complexity that is related to large size creates cross-pressures to add managerial personnel for control, coordination, and conflict-reduction functions. Decisions to physically disperse, add divisions, or add hierarchical levels may be made in the interests of economy. At the same time, the economies realized may be counterbalanced by the added burdens of keeping the organization together. Complex organizations are thus complex in more ways than just their structure. The processes within such organizations are also complex. The techniques that are effective and efficient within a simple structure just may not be effective or efficient in a more complex case.

SUMMARY AND CONCLUSIONS

This chapter has dealt with a central variable in organizational analysis. The discussion has been based on research carried out in a wide variety of organizational settings. The emphasis has been on comparative research rather than case studies, in the belief that while case studies can generate interesting hypotheses, firm conclusions can be drawn only from a more widely based test of the hypotheses derived. Despite the

[50] Blau and Schoenherr, *The Structure of Organizations.*

soundness of the research that has been cited in the discussion, it is still premature to accept the results without reservations. Additional research in a wider variety of settings, including the vast array of voluntary organizations, is necessary before any form of definite conclusions are really warranted. The degree of disparity must be determined between formal specifications of relationships and the manner in which they are actually carried out. In spite of these reservations and problems, this chapter has revealed several important points about complexity and, more important, about organizations.

Complexity takes several forms: horizontal differentiation—through an intense division of labor or through the performance of tasks by specialists—vertical differentiation, and spatial dispersion. It was emphasized that organizations can vary internally in the degree to which complexity on these various axes is present. In terms of structure, organizations with an intense subdivision of labor tend to have less vertical differentiation. Those with horizontal differentiation by specialists usually have rather tall hierarchies. These differences are largely attributable to the nature of the technology being employed in the organization.

Complexity is related to important internal and external processes. The Aiken–Hage research pointed out that high complexity (specialization) is related to decentralized decision making, higher rates of change, and the presence of more joint programs with other organizations. The Blau–Meyer research pointed out that the presence of experts is accompanied by more managers to assist in the control, communications, and coordination processes. Pugh et al. suggest that the tall hierarchy that is found when specialists are present may actually reflect a division of labor among the specialists themselves. The specific situation may determine which explanation is correct, since the kinds of specialists included in the two studies were different. The important point is that specialization by expertise is strongly associated with such vertical differentiation. Spatial dispersion was found to be related to a larger administrative staff in hospitals, but not in labor unions. The important distinctions between voluntary and nonvoluntary organizations are undoubtedly the major factor in these differences. In spatially dispersed English firms, it was found that the workers on the line had a high degree of control over their day-to-day operations, with major decisions being retained by the central headquarters of the organizations.

Regardless of the form, high degrees of complexity introduce coordination, control, and communication problems for the organization. The Lawrence and Lorsch research indicates that such problems are sources of conflict for the organization, but that such conflict is positively related to effectiveness if it is resolved in the appropriate manner. Indirectly, therefore, complexity is also related to eflectiveness. This conclusion only holds, of course, when the technology and environment require complexity. In those cases where less internal differentiation is demanded, high levels of complexity would not contribute to organizational effectiveness.

The evidence presented strengthens the theme of the entire analysis. Environmental and technological factors, together with the related consideration of the nature of the personnel, traditions, decision making, and other internal conditions, determine the form of an organization at any particular point in time.[51] As these factors change, the form of the organization will also change.

From this perspective, then, complexity becomes more important than the size factor in understanding organizations. In the words of Zelditch and Hopkins, "Large size, in our view, is not in itself a critical characteristic of organizations. Rather what appears to be important here is complexity, which is often indicated by size but is quite distinct from it." [52] An organization's complexity is therefore a good predictor of many of its other characteristics.

[51] Support for this conclusion is found in Jack P. Gibbs and Harley L. Browning, "The Division of Labor, Technology, and the Organization of Production in Twelve Countries," *American Sociological Review*, Vol. 31, No. 1, (February 1966), 81 92.

[52] Morris Zelditch, Jr., and Terrence K. Hopkins, "Laboratory Experiments with Organizations," in Amitai Etzioni, ed., *Complex Organizations: A Sociological Reader* (New York: Holt, Rinehart & Winston, Inc., 1961), p. 470.

FORMALIZATION

6

We have considered formalization before in our analysis, both explicitly and implicitly. In this chapter we will follow the same format as in the past—defining the subject matter and then tracing its antecedents and consequences—but we will add to this basic approach a greater concern with the individual. His reactions and behavior are vitally affected by the degree of formalization of an organization. His freedom of discretion is enhanced or limited by the extent to which his expected behavior is preprogrammed by the organization.

No assumption will be made that a high degree of formalization is either organizationally or individually good or bad. Instead, the position will be that circumstances determine the appropriate degree of formalization. The nature of the individuals involved and the technological–environmental conditions under which the organization operates will be shown to be the important determinants of the appropriate extent of formalization.

The introduction of the individual into the analysis will not mean that the emphasis will shift totally away from the organizational level. On the contrary, formalization has important consequences for the organization as a whole and for its subunits. As in the case of the individual, these consequences are contingent upon the conditions under which the organization is operating.

THE NATURE OF FORMALIZATION

Much of the essence of the nature of formalization has already been discussed under the subject of the Weberian model of bureaucracy. The rules and procedures designed to handle contingencies faced by the organization are part of what is called formalization. As we noted in the previous discussion, the extent to which rules and procedures are present varies. The simple matter of what time a person gets to work can differ widely among and within organizations in regard to the degree to which this act is formally specified. At the high end of the formalization continuum are organizations that specify that a person must be at his desk or other work spot at 8:00 A.M. or he will be "docked" a half-hour's pay. Close to the other end is the case where there are no rules about being in the office or shop at a particular time, just as long as the work gets done. This is typified by many academic institutions.[1] The variation in the presence of such rules is not a matter of the professionalization of the labor force, as might be assumed. Many law firms, for example, require their members to register with their secretaries exactly where they will be going when they leave the office and how long they will be gone.

MAXIMAL FORMALIZATION. Rules, therefore, can vary from highly stringent to extremely lax. These variations exist on the whole range of behaviors covered by organizational rules. The same kinds of variations exist in terms of procedures. A simple example of highly formalized procedures is the assembly line, where a piece of material is *always* passed in the same direction, with the same work being performed on it. A similar case in an office setting is where letters requesting a certain type of information are *always* processed in the same way, with the same type of information returned to the requester. The extreme examples of this, of course, are the computer-prepared responses to inquiries about such things as under- or overpayments of credit-card bills. This is one example of a highly formalized procedure in which the organization has been able to preprogram its responses to a wide variety of contingencies. Much of the frustration that a person feels when he receives a computer

---

[1] There may well be informal norms operative in this area that are quite strong. For example, I once worked in a situation where, for a period of time, the informal expectation was that Saturday mornings were to be spent at the office, even if this meant only a token appearance. For the moment, however, the informal aspect of rules, procedures, etc., will be ignored.

printout rather than a personal letter is due to his feeling that his request was apparently just like everyone else's—that he is not an unusual case and therefore can be treated in a highly formalized way. The real frustration comes, of course, when his is in fact an unusual case and the computer procedures are inappropriate to his request. Despite the personal exasperation that this can develop, the fact remains that a large proportion of the communications into an organization can be handled by such formalized procedures.

MINIMAL FORMALIZATION.   At the other end of the formalization-of-procedures continuum would be cases that are unique and for which no procedures have been developed. In these cases, members of the organization must utilize their own discretion in deciding what to do. At the extreme would come the cases Perrow has referred to as calling for intuition, and even perhaps inspiration, in solving—unique situations with no preprogrammed answers.[2] In terms of our concern with organizational structures, such uniqueness must be a regular part of the organization's (or subunit's) activities. That is, a unique situation become routine if it is repeated over time, and formalized procedures can then be developed to handle this once-unique situation. Thus, nonformalized organizations are those that deal constantly with new situations for which precedents do not exist. Examples here would be organizations engaging in frontier areas of scientific research of which the forthcoming results are not known. Organizations dealing with human problems, such as mental health clinics, would be in a similar situation.

At this point it should be noted that it usually doesn't matter whether the procedures or rules are formalized in written form. Unwritten norms and standards can frequently be just as binding as written ones.[3] Nevertheless, most research utilizes the written system as the basis for assessment and analysis.

Jerald Hage makes essentially the same point when he states:

> Organizations learn from past experiences and employ rules as a repository of that experience. Some organizations carefully codify each job, describing the specific details, and then ensure conformity to the job prescription. Other organizations have loosely defined jobs and do not carefully control work behavior. *Formalization*, or standardization, is measured by the proportion of codified jobs and the range of variation that is tolerated within the rules defining the jobs. The higher the proportion of codified jobs and the less the range of variation allowed, the more formalized the organization.[4]

[2] Charles Perrow, "A Framework for the Comparative Analysis of Organizations," *American Sociological Review*, Vol. 32, No. 2 (April 1967), 196.

[3] See Jerald Hage and Michael Aiken, *Social Change in Complex Organizations* (New York: Random House, Inc., 1970), pp. 22–23.

[4] Jerald Hage, "An Axiomatic Theory of Organizations," *Administrative Science Quarterly*, Vol. 10, No. 3 (December 1965), 295.

Hage and Aiken, in their later research, follow essentially the same definition of formalization. They state:

> Formalization represents the use of rules in an organization. Job codification is a measure of how many rules define what the occupants of positions are to do, while rule observation is a measure of whether or not the rules are employed. In other words, the variable of job codification represents the degree to which the job descriptions are specified, and the variable, rule observation, refers to the degree to which job occupants are supervised in conforming to the standards established by job codification. Job codification represents the degree of work standardization while rule observation is a measure of the latitude of behavior that is tolerated from standards.[5]

These variables are operationalized by asking the members of organizations to respond to a series of questions bearing directly on these issues. Measures of their perceptions of their own organization are thus used to determine the extent to which the organizations are formalized.

A similar definitional perspective is found in the work of Pugh et al. They define formalization as "the extent to which rules, procedures, instructions, and communications are written."[6] They also include "standardization" (the extent to which "there are rules or definitions that purport to cover all circumstances and that apply invariably"[7]) as one of their basic dimensions of organizational structure. These variables are operationalized by using official records and documents from the organization to determine such matters as the number of procedures of various kinds and the proportion of employees who have handbooks describing their tasks. An analysis of the data from the English firms studied reveals that standardization and formalization combine with specialization when the component scales are factor-analyzed. The authors call this factor the "structuring of activities."[8] They note that this brings the issue of role specificity to the forefront as an important organizational consideration. In highly formalized, standardized, and specialized situations, the occupant of the role has his behavior highly specified, leaving him few options that he can exercise in carrying out his job.[9]

The similarities between these definitions point up the general consensus about the meaning of formalization. Even when quite different measures of this variable are used in research, the same meaning is

---

[5] Jerald Hage and Michael Aiken, "Relationship of Centralization to Other Structural Properties," *Administrative Science Quarterly,* Vol. 12, No. 1 (June 1967), 79.

[6] D. S. Pugh et al., "Dimensions of Organizational Structure," *Administrative Science Quarterly,* Vol. 13, No. 1 (June 1968), 75.

[7] *Ibid.,* p. 74.

[8] *Ibid.,* p. 84.

[9] *Ibid.,* p. 86.

utilized, an all too rare occurrence in organizational analysis. The methodological differences deserve some comment at this point. Formalization has been approached from two basic perspectives. The utilization of members' perceptions, as exemplified by the Hage and Aiken work, relies upon the average or median score on responses to a question or set of questions to determine the degree of formalization for the organization (or subunit) as a whole.[10] The alternative approach, as followed by Pugh et al., is the utilization of official records and information from key informants about the organization. This also yields a formalization score for the organization. Unfortunately, despite the similar conceptualizations, these methods apparently yield somewhat different results.

There are several possible reasons for these differences. In the perceptual approach, members of the organizations may not be giving their actual perceptions, possibly because of some fear of reprisal by the organization even though the researchers assure the anonymity of the respondent. While this undoubtedly occurs in some cases, it does not seem to be a major factor. Other research using the same approach has demonstrated that the scores from the perceptual scales are quite valid when other indicators are used as validity checks.[11] A much more likely explanation is that perceptions of organizations do in fact differ from the officially described patterns. The many valuable studies that have shown the existence of "informal" procedures and work-group structures in organizations suggest that what actually goes on in an organization can differ markedly from what is officially described and prescribed.

Scores on perceptual scales may thus represent an accurate portrayal of an organization's degree of formalization or other structural features. This would imply that the use of official records or statements is of no use. This is *not* the case. The official system sets the parameters for any deviance that does occur. A prescribed degree of formalization is the starting point from which actual behavior begins. As a general rule, organizations that are more formalized on paper are more formalized in practice. Both methods can be used in ranking a set of organizations on their degree of formalization, even though the exact scores for each organization are not the same. The ideal method, of course, would be to measure rates of behavior to determine any aspect of organizational life; but the costs involved would be so tremendous that little more than a case study would be possible. The more economical measures

10 The questionnaire items used are taken from scales developed by Richard Hall. The indices are found in Hage and Aiken, "Relationship of Centralization," p. 79.

11 See Richard H. Hall, "The Concept of Bureaucracy," *American Journal of Sociology,* Vol. 72, No. 3 (November 1966).

described are used in order to obtain data that, although somewhat less accurate, do allow comparisons across organizations.

Another interesting point here is that deviations from the officially prescribed patterns are undoubtedly not random. That is, in some organizations, the deviance will be more pronounced and widespread than in others. It would be interesting and important to determine the factors associated with these varying patterns of deviance in organizations. It would appear that the cruciality of the norms and the strength with which they are enforced are decisive here. The extent to which the members *believe* in the norms would also be important. Policies are carried out by individuals. At the same time, the establishment of procedures and policies by an organization essentially sets its course for future activities. The organization and its members perform in accordance with the established policies.

Formalization has received a great deal of attention in recent research. We will examine the relationships between formalization and other organizational properties before going on to a consideration of the individual.

FORMALIZATION AND OTHER ORGANIZATIONAL PROPERTIES

Centralization of Power

Power is an important component in any social system. As we shall see in detail in the next chapter, the distribution of power has major consequences for the performance of an organization and the behavior of its members. An important consideration in dealing with power is the manner in which it is distributed in the organization. Hage and Aiken, in their study of social welfare agencies, found that formalization was rather weakly associated with a centralized decision-making system.[12] Organizations in which the decisions were made by only a few people at the top relied on rules and close supervision as a means of ensuring consistent performance by the workers. These organizations were also characterized by a less professionalized staff. Thus, the presence of a well-trained staff is related to a reduced need for extensive rules and policies.

This interpretation is supported in Blau's analysis of public personnel agencies. Blau found that in those organizations with highly formalized personnel procedures and rigid conformity to these procedures, there

---

[12] Hage and Aiken, "Relationship of Centralization," pp. 80–90.

was a decentralization of authority.[13] This is at first glance contradictory, since the evidence seems to say that formalization and decentralization are related. A closer examination reveals strong compatibility with the Hage and Aiken findings. In this case, adherence to merit-based personnel procedures ensures the presence of highly qualified personnel at the local (decentralized) level. These people are then entrusted with more power than are personnel with questionable qualifications. Formalization in one area of operations is thus associated with flexibility in another.

On this point Blau states:

> Rigidity in some respects may breed flexibility in others. Not all aspects of bureaucratization are concomitant. The bureaucratic elaboration of formalized personnel procedures and rigid conformity with these personnel standards do not necessarily occur together, and neither aspect of bureaucratization of procedures gives rise to a more rigid authority structure, at least not in employment security agencies. Indeed, both strict conformity with civil service standards and the elaboration of these formalized standards have the opposite effect of fostering decentralization, which permits greater flexibility.[14]

This rather simple set of findings reinforces a notion expressed earlier —complex organizations are complex. Formalization in one area brings pressures to bear to decrease formalization in another area. Organizations are thus constantly in conflict, not only between individuals or subunits, but also between and within the processes and structures that make up the organization.

It is important to note that the research of Hage and Aiken and of Blau deals with relatively professionalized work forces. One of the hallmarks of professionalization is the ability and willingness to make decisions based upon professional training and experience. It is not surprising to find lower levels of formalization in such situations. When the work force under consideration does not or is assumed not to have this decision-making capacity, the implications of the Blau findings have to be reexamined. In that case, formalized personnel procedures would probably be associated with a more centralized decision-making system, with the formalization level probably more consistent in all phases of the operation.

Program Change

Further research by Hage and Aiken into the rate of program change in the agencies reveals that formalization is also related to the num-

---

[13] Peter M. Blau, "Decentralization in Bureaucracies," in Mayer N. Zald, ed., *Power in Organizations* (Nashville, Tenn.: Vanderbilt University Press, 1970), p. 160.
[14] *Ibid.*

ber of new programs added in the organizations.[15] In this case, formalization is negatively associated with the adoption of new programs. The reduction of individual initiative in the more formalized setting is suggested as the major reason for this relationship. In organizations that establish highly specific routines for the members to follow, there is likely to be little time, support, or reward for involvement in new ideas and new programs.

In their analysis of organizational interdependence, Aiken and Hage found that formalization was not very important in explaining the number of joint programs in which the agencies under investigation were engaged.[16] Apparently, factors other than formalization come to be important for this type of linkage. This is somewhat inconsistent with the idea expressed earlier that formalization would tend to impede innovativeness, which the existence of joint programs would seem to require. Aiken and Hage suggest that the development of joint programs has increased suddenly, so that organizational procedures might be in a state of flux. They also believe that the diversity of occupations (complexity) is by far the dominant influence here, actually overriding other considerations.

Technology

In their continuing research in these sixteen agencies, Hage and Aiken then looked at the relationship between technology and facets of organizational structure. They follow the suggestions of Perrow and Litwak and divide the organizations into "routine" and "nonroutine" categories on the basis of scores derived from the responses of members to a series of questions.[17] Even though these are all social agencies, there is a marked difference in the degree of routineness.

> The highest on routineness is a family agency in which the case-workers use a standard client interview that takes less than fifteen minutes. The purpose of the interview is to ascertain the eligibility of clients for county, federal, or state medical aid. An interviewee said: ". . . somewhat routine—even though each patient is individual, the type of thing you do with them is the same. . . ." The organization at the other extreme is an elite psychiatric

[15] Jerald Hage and Michael Aiken, "Program Change and Organizational Properties," *American Journal of Sociology*, Vol. 72, No. 5 (March 1967), 511–17.

[16] Michael Aiken and Jerald Hage, "Organizational Interdependence and Intraorganizational Structure," *American Sociological Review*, Vol. 33, No. 6 (December, 1968), 925–26.

[17] See Perrow, "A Framework," and Eugene Litwak, "Models of Bureaucracy Which Permit Conflict," *American Journal of Sociology*, Vol. 67, No. 2 (September 1961).

family agency in which each member is an experienced therapist and allowed to work with no supervision at all.[18]

The relationship between routinization and formalization is in the expected direction. *"Organizations with routine work are more likely to have greater formalization of organizational roles."* [19] Since these organizations tend to be on the nonroutine end of an overall continuum of routineness, the findings are even more striking: Had organizations more toward the routine end of the continuum been included, the differences observed would probably have been greater. These findings strengthen, of course, the general argument that has been made throughout this book.

Hage and Aiken's research, one of the most thorough and systematic pieces of ongoing research available in the literature, is based on data from a limited number of organizations of relatively similar characteristics. The limitations inherent in using this type of data base are difficult to avoid, given the intrinsic difficulties in organizational research. But despite these limitations, their findings are generally consistent with those of Pugh's research team, which proceeded independently and with very different measures.

It will be remembered that the Pugh research was carried out with English work organizations as the sample. These researchers were interested in obtaining "hard" indicators of the organizations and the contexts in which they operated. Their major indicator of technology was *workflow integration.*

> Among organizations scoring high, with very integrated, automated, and rather rigid technologies, were an automobile factory, a food manufacturer, and a swimming baths department. Among those scoring low, with diverse, nonautomated, flexible technologies, were retail stores, an education department, and a building firm.[20]

While they contain more diversity than those in the Aiken and Hage study, these organizations are clustered toward the routine end of the routine–nonroutine continuum. As would be expected from the previous discussion, technology emerges as an important predictor of the degree to which activities are structured in these organizations. It is not as

---

[18] Jerald Hage and Michael Aiken, "Routine Technology, Social Structure and Organizational Tools," *Administrative Science Quarterly,* Vol. 14, No. 3 (September 1969), 369.

[19] *Ibid.,* p. 371. [Italics in original.]

[20] D. S. Pugh et al., "The Context of Organizational Structures," *Administrative Science Quarterly,* Vol. 14, No. 1 (March 1969), 103.

closely associated with structuring as is the size factor, but as Chapter 4 pointed out, size is misleading as a predictor in these circumstances.

In a later examination of the same data, Hickson et al. subdivide the technology concept into three components.[21] "Operations technology" refers to the techniques used in workflow activities, ranging from automated equipment to pens and pencils, and includes the ideas of the degree of automation of equipment, the rigidity of the sequence of operations, and the specificity of the evaluation of the operations. The second component is "materials technology," which concerns the materials processed in the workflow. Perrow has pointed out the importance of the perceived uniformity and stability of the materials, and Rushing has shown that the "hardness" of materials makes an important difference in the division of labor in organizations.[22] The third component is "knowledge technology," and refers to the characteristics of the knowledge used in the workflow. The approach of Perrow is again used, with the primary indicators the number of exceptional cases encountered and the degree of logical analysis used in solving problems.

This appears to be a useful set of distinctions for the technology concept. Unfortunately, the British researchers have data on only the operations technology phase. Nevertheless, their findings and interpretations are vital additions to the understanding of what leads to important organizational structural characteristics. The primary conclusion from this analysis is that technology is *not* the major "cause" of structure. Using only the operations-technology component, the finding remains that size predominates as a predictor of structure. The authors conclude:

> . . . *variables of operations technology will be related only to those structural variables that are centered on the workflow.* The smaller the organization, the wider the structural effects of technology; the larger the organization, the more such effects are confined to particular variables, and size and dependence and similar factors make the greater overall impact. In the smaller organizations, everyone is closer to the "shop-floor," and structural responses to the problems of size (for example) have not begun to show. In larger organizations, managers and administrators are buffered from the technology itself by the specialist departments, standards procedures, and formalized paperwork that size brings with it.[23]

[21] D. J. Hickson, D. S. Pugh, and Diana C. Pheysey, "Operations Technology and Organization Structure: An Empirical Reappraisal," *Administrative Science Quarterly*, Vol. 14, No. 3 (September 1969), 378–97.

[22] William A. Rushing, "Hardness of Material as Related to Division of Labor in Manufacturing Industries," *Administrative Science Quarterly*, Vol. 13, No. 2 (September 1968), 229–45.

[23] Hickson et al., "Operations Technology," p. 395.

These conclusions seem extremely reasonable, given all the arguments that have preceded these findings. While the role of technology is discounted from the evidence at hand, it appears quite logical that the material and knowledge phases of the technological concept would come into play among those organizational units "buffered" from the operations technology. A knowledge of an organization's size, types of technology, and other such factors will thus permit a prediction of the type of organizational structure it will have.

Tradition

There is one additional component that should be added to these considerations. Organizations emerge at different historical eras, face varying contingencies, and develop different traditions. These differences affect the way in which factors such as size and technology affect the degree of formalization and other such characteristics. For example, if an organization for some reason—such as the belief system of an important early top executive—became highly formalized in its codification of job descriptions in writing, it would probably continue to be more formalized over time than other factors would predict.

Organizations cannot be viewed as solely subject to the pressures of size, technology, environment, and so on. They develop characteristics that are embedded in formal and informal system of the organization. These traditional factors have largely been ignored by organizational analysts, perhaps because they are so difficult to codify. At the commonsense level, they are important and deserve more attention than they have received.

We have seen from the total discussion that formalization is related to several important organizational characteristics. The very nature of formalization is such that it is central to the life of and in organizations. The specification of rules, procedures, penalties, and so on, predetermines much of what goes on in an organization. Indeed, formalization is a major defining characteristic of organizations, since behavior is not random and is directed by some degree of formalization toward a goal.

We have examined the relationships between formalization and other organizational properties. The focus will now shift to the individual in the organization. Like formalization, individuals too must be treated as variables, since they bring different abilities, habits, and other behaviors with them into the organization and develop their own styles of behavior once they are in. While our focus here will be on the individual, the consequences for the organization will also be noted.

FORMALIZATION AND THE INDIVIDUAL

Members

An extreme example of formalization can be found in Crozier's analysis of the two French organizations.[24] He notes, "Impersonal rules delimit, in great detail, all the functions of every individual within the organization. They prescribe the behavior to be followed in all possible events. Equally impersonal rules determine who shall be chosen for each job and the career patterns that can be followed." [25] This extremely high degree of formalization, plus several other characteristics of the organizations, create a "vicious circle" in which the workers follow the rules for the sake of the rules themselves, since this is the basis on which they are evaluated. The rules become more important than the goals they were designed to help accomplish. The organization becomes very rigid and has difficulties dealing with customers and other aspects of the environment. Since the rules prescribe the kinds of decisions to be made, those in decision-making positions tend to create more rules when situations arise for which there are no precedents. Rules become security for the employees. There is no drive for greater autonomy, since that would be threatening. There is a strong desire to build safeguards through increased rigidity. The personnel in such a system become increasingly less free to operate on the basis of their own initiative and, in fact, seek to reduce the amount of freedom to which they are subject. To one who values individual freedom, this is a tragedy. It would be presumptuous to say that it is such for the individuals involved, even though the argument could be made that the long-run consequences for them and for the total social system may indeed be tragic from several moral and ethical perspectives. For the organization, the consequences are clear. It becomes maladaptive to changes of any sort.

The personal and organizational dysfunctions were recognized some thirty years ago in Robert Merton's seminal discussion of the "bureaucratic personality." Merton notes that a trained incapacity can develop in the kind of situation under discussion. Actions and decisions based on past training and experience may be very inappropriate under different conditions. Merton suggests that the process whereby these conditions develop is part of the system itself.

24 Michel Crozier, *The Bureaucratic Phenomenon* (Chicago: University of Chicago Press, 1964).
25 *Ibid.*, pp. 187–88.

The bureaucrat's official life is planned for him in terms of a graded career, through the organization devices of promotion by seniority, pensions, incremental salaries, etc., all of which are designed to provide incentives for disciplined action and conformity to the official regulations. The official is tacitly expected to and largely does adapt his thoughts, feelings, and actions to the prospect of this career. But *these very devices* which increase the probability of conformance also lead to an over-concern with strict adherence to regulations which induces timidity, conservatism, and technicism. Displacement of sentiments from goals onto means is fostered by the tremendous symbolic significance of the means (rules).[26]

Nonmembers

This strict and even excessive adherence to the rules can also have negative consequences for persons not in the organization itself. Clients who have regular contact with the organization, such as welfare recipients or students in registration lines at colleges and universities, are constantly dismayed and angered by the impersonal and rule-bound treatment they all too often receive. The individual feels like a number, or a "hole in an IBM card."

Reactions to Formalization

This rather dismal view of life in a highly formalized organization is extended by Victor Thompson's description of "bureaupathic" and "bureautic" behavior. Thompson suggests that the kinds of behavior discussed by Merton are caused by feelings of insecurity. Bureaupathic behavior "starts" with a need on the part of the person in an authority position to control those subordinate to himself." [27] Superordinates themselves, except at the very top of the organization, are subordinate to someone else, and so this control can tend to be the too-rigid adherence to rules that has been discussed, since this protects the individual from making possibly erroneous decisions and actions on his own. According to Thompson, the most significant source of insecurity in modern organization is

. . . the growing gap between the rights of authority (to review, to veto, to affirm) and the specialized ability or skill required to solve most organizational problems. The intellectual, problem-solving content of executive

[26] Robert K. Merton, "Bureaucratic Structure and Personality," in Merton, *Social Theory and Social Structure,* rev. ed. (New York: The Free Press, 1957), pp. 200–201. [Italics in original.]

[27] Victor Thompson, *Modern Organizations* (New York: Alfred A. Knopf, Inc., 1961), p. 154.

offices is being increasingly diverted to specialists, leaving hierarchical rights (and duties) as the principal components of executive posts. Persons in hierarchical positions are therefore increasingly dependent upon subordinate and nonsubordinate specialists for the achievement of organizational (or unit) goals. The superior tends to be caught between the two horns of a dilemma. He must satisfy the nonexplicit and nonoperational demands of a superior through the agency of specialized subordinates and nonsubordinates whose skills he only dimly understands. And yet, to be counted a success he must accept this dilemma and live with its increasing viciousness throughout his life. He must live with increasing insecurity and anxiety.[28]

Thompson suggests that these pressures lead to a "drift" toward the introduction of more and more rules to protect the incumbents of offices, exaggerated aloofness, resistance to change, and an overinsistence on the rights of office. These reactions are organizationally and personally damaging.

The second form of behavior—bureautic—is also personally and organizationally dysfunctional. This type of reaction involves striking out at the system, personalizing every encounter, and taking every rule as one designed to lead to one's own personal frustration.

> The bureautic employee is not likely to get into the hierarchy, and so may come to be regarded as a failure. Because of his inability to enter intelligently into abstract, complex, cooperative relationships, he tends to be pushed to one side, unless he has some unusual skill that the organization badly needs. He is often regarded as "queer." All of these facts add to his bitterness and increase his suspiciousness. He projects his failures onto the organization and the impersonal "others" who are his enemies. He feels he is surrounded by stupidity and maliciousness. He feels powerless and alienated from the system.[29]

While some would argue with the psychological mechanisms that Thompson uses in his development of these reactions to the organization, the reactions themselves do exist.

From the discussion thus far, it seems that life in an organization almost inevitably leads to some form of personal and organizational malfunctioning. But these negative reactions are not inevitable and universal. There are critics of the total system who suggest that it is too corrupt and corrupting and should be abolished. A more reasoned approach is to ask under what circumstances and with what consequences such conditions exist.

Some clues to the answers can be found in the literature on professionals in organizations. There is a growing interest in this topic since increasing numbers of professionals of all sorts are working in organiza-

---

28 *Ibid.,* pp. 156–57.
29 *Ibid.,* p. 176.

tions, and many occupations are attempting to professionalize. Analyses of the relationships between professionals and their employing organizations formerly proceeded from the premise that there are built-in strains between professional and organizational principles and values.[30] Recent research has looked at this relationship more closely, attempting to discover the conditions under which strain is felt, since it assumes that there can be situations in which the professional is able to carry out his work with a minimum amount of interference from the organization, while the organization is able to integrate the work of the professionals for its own benefit.

This approach is followed in George Miller's analysis of the degree of alienation experienced by scientists and engineers employed in a large corporation in the aerospace industry.[31] These professionals reported that they felt more alienation when their supervisor used directive, rather than participative or laissez-faire, supervisory practices, and less alienation in situations in which they themselves had some control over the decisions affecting their work. The same general pattern was found in regard to other incentives that the organization provided professionals. There was less alienation when the scientists and engineers had some part in deciding the nature of their own research efforts, when the company provided opportunities and a climate for the pursuit of their own professional careers, and when the company encouraged purely professional activities, such as the publication of papers or pursuit of additional training.

Miller also found that the length of professional training was associated with the extent of alienation felt. The more training a person has, the more he is likely to feel alienation under those conditions that produce it for the group of professionals as a whole. That is, for a Ph.D. scientist, the absence of encouragement of professional activities is more likely to produce alienation than it is for an M.A. scientist.[32] Utilizing the idea of intraorganizational variations in structure, Miller examined the extent of alienation felt by the professionals when the specific work location was controlled. Some of the professionals worked in a basic-research laboratory in the company, but most were employed in research and development in one of the major production units. As might be expected, the personnel in the basic-research laboratory ex-

---

[30] See, for example, William Kornhauser, *Scientists in Industry* (Berkeley: University of California Press, 1963); and Peter M. Blau and W. Richard Scott, *Formal Organizations* (San Francisco: Chandler Publishing Co., 1962).

[31] George A. Miller, "Professionals in Bureaucracy, Alienation Among Industrial Scientists and Engineers," *American Sociological Review*, Vol. 32, No. 5 (October 1967), 755–68.

[32] Some differences were also found between the scientists and engineers, but this is not of importance in the present discussion.

perienced much less alienation than those in the production-oriented unit.

The organizational structure in which these professionals worked was related to their degree of alienation from work. Professionals were chosen as a group to examine because professionals bring to the organization a set of externally (professionally) derived standards by which they can guide their own behavior. The presence of organizational guidelines (formalization) is thus a duplication and probably perceived as less valid than are the norms of the profession involved. *For professionals, therefore, the greater the degree of formalization in the organization, the greater the likelihood of alienation from work.*

This point is supported further when two additional research reports are considered. Part of the research of Aiken and Hage has been concerned with the degree of alienation felt by the professionals in the sixteen social welfare agencies they examined.[33] They too were concerned with alienation from work—although their measurement of this variable was quite different from that used by Miller—but they also looked at alienation from expressive relations. This was measured by responses to questions asking the degree of satisfaction felt about superiors and co-workers. The less satisfaction felt, the more the individual is alienated from expressive relations.

As would be expected from the direction of this discussion, the greater the degree of job codification of the organization, the more alienated were the workers, in both areas of alienation. Alienation was much more strongly felt in terms of the job itself. "This means that there is great dissatisfaction with work in those organizations in which jobs are rigidly structured; rigidity may lead to strong feelings of work dissatisfaction but does not appear to have such a deleterious impact on social relations in the organization."[34] Strict enforcement of rules was strongly related to both forms of alienation; social relations are also disturbed when rules are strictly enforced. It was also found that both forms of alienation were high when authority in the organizations was centralized and the members had little opportunity to participate in decision making. Again, it must be stressed that these findings hold for the psychiatrists, social workers, and rehabilitation counselors included in this study.

A different approach was taken by me in my analysis of the relationships between professionalization and bureaucratization.[35] Bureaucratiza-

[33] Michael Aiken and Jerald Hage, "Organizational Alienation: A Comparative Analysis," *American Sociological Review*, Vol. 31, No. 4 (August 1966), 497–507.

[34] *Ibid.*, p. 504.

[35] Richard H. Hall, "Professionalization and Bureaucratization," *American Sociological Review*, Vol. 33, No. 1 (February 1968), 92–104.

tion is a broader concept than formalization, but it contains many of the same implications, as indicated in earlier discussions of the topic. I attempted to demonstrate that professionalization, like formalization, is a continuous variable, with some occupations being more professionalized than others. The study included physicians, nurses, accountants, teachers, lawyers, social workers, stockbrokers, librarians, engineers, personnel managers, and advertising account executives. After the occupations were ranked according to their attitudes toward several professional values, the average scores for each occupation were matched with the scores on bureaucratization measures for the organizational units in which these people worked. The results of the rank-order correlational analysis are shown in Table 6–1.

TABLE 6–1 RANK-ORDER CORRELATION COEFFICIENTS BETWEEN PROFESSIONALISM SCALES AND BUREAUCRACY SCALES

	Professional Organization Reference	*Belief in Service to Public*	*Belief in Self-Regulation*	*Sense of Calling to Field*	*Feeling of Autonomy*
Hierarchy of Authority	−.029	−.262	−.149	.148	−.767 **
Division of Labor	−.236	−.260	−.234	−.115	−.575 **
Rules	−.144	−.121	−.107	.113	−.554
Procedures	−.360 **	−.212	−.096	.000	−.603 **
Impersonality	−.256	−.099	−.018	−.343 *	−.489 **
Technical Competence	.593 **	.332 *	.420 **	.440 **	.121

$* = p < .05.$
$** = p < .01.$
Source: *Richard H. Hall, "Professionalization and Bureaucratization,"* American Sociological Review, *Vol. 33, No. 1 (February 1968), 102.*

These results indicate that in general, bureaucratization is inversely related to professionalization. This is consistent with the argument in this section. Examined more closely, these findings reveal some interesting patterns. There is a relatively weak inverse relationship between the hierarchy-of-authority dimension and the professional attitudes. The presence of a relatively rigid hierarchy may not adversely affect the work of professionals if the hierarchy is recognized as legitimate. This is similar to the findings of Blau, who suggests that the presence of a hierarchy may facilitate communications from the professionals to the top of the organization. If the hierarchy of authority is legitimate and does facilitate communications, it apparently does not matter whether or not decisions are made in a prestructured way—and particularly if the work of the professionals can be carried out without extensive interference by the organization.

A stronger negative relationship is found on the division-of-labor dimension. This means that the presence of professionals impedes minute specialization of tasks within the organization. A weaker relationship is found on the presence-of-rules dimension. The kinds of rules the organizations develop in these cases apparently do not interfere with the work of the professional. There is a stronger negative relationship on the procedural-specifications dimension. As more procedures are specified by the organization, the burden on the professionals apparently is stronger. In this case, the professionals are likely to want to utilize procedures that they themselves develop on the job or through their professional training. The inverse relationship between degree of professionalization and the organizational emphasis on impersonality is indicative of the fact that the professional personnel are inclined to deal face-to-face with fellow professionals and develop strong colleague ties. These strong ties are the exact opposite of organizationally desired impersonality, which implies an absence of affective relationships within the organization. The strong positive relationship between the professional variables and the organizations' utilization of technical competence as the basis for their personnel procedures is not surprising. The professions themselves verbalize and practice the idea that a person should be judged by his performance and other rational criteria. This is clearly compatible with organizational usage of the same idea.

Viewing these findings from another perspective, the strong negative relationships between the "feeling of autonomy" professional variable and the first five bureaucratic dimensions is an important indicator of the relationship between bureaucratization and professionalization. This finding indicates that ". . . increased bureaucratization threatens professional autonomy. It is in these relationships that a potential source of conflict between the professional and the organization can be found. The strong drive for autonomy on the part of a professional may come into direct conflict with organizationally based job requirements. At the same time, the organization may be threatened by strong professional desires on the part of at least some of its members." [36]

Formalization and Professionalization

All the studies that have been discussed have concluded that professionalization and formalization are incompatible. The more professional-

[36] *Ibid.*, pp. 102–3.

ized the work force, the more likely that formalization will lead to conflict and alienation. A major implication of these findings is that *formalization and professionalization are actually designed to do the same thing—organize and regularize the behavior of the members of the organization.* Formalization is a process in which the organization sets the rules and procedures and the means of ensuring that they are followed. Professionalization, on the other hand, is a nonorganizationally based means of doing the same thing. From the organization's point of view, either technique would be appropriate, as long as the work gets done.

It is exactly at this point that the organization faces a major internal dilemma. If it allows too little freedom for its members, they are likely to feel oppressed, alienated, and "bureautic," and to engage in rule following for its own sake. If, on the other hand, it allows more freedom, behavior is apt to become erratic and organizationally irrelevant. A basic factor here appears to be the kind of guidelines for behavior that the individual himself brings to the organization. The more work standards he brings with him, the less the need for organizationally based standards.

It is difficult, of course, for the organization to know what kind of standards a person brings with him. Even the use of a relatively common criterion, such as membership in a recognized profession, is not a perfect predictor, since not all members of a profession act in accordance with the profession's standards. And when the organization moves into other personnel areas, away from the professions or established crafts, the availability of such external criteria may disappear. Even well-developed external criteria such as professionalization may at times be organizationally irrelevant, so that the organization has to develop its own system of rules and procedures to accomplish what it is attempting to do.

A basic problem here is that the organization may have uncertain and inaccurate knowledge about its personnel. It may, for example, assume that its female workers are interested only in finding a husband and getting married, and may thereby rigidly structure the positions involved. This conceivably could make the work so unenjoyable that marriage would look like an attractive alternative to the women involved.

Here, one point should be mentioned that is obvious but often ignored. There is nothing inherently more moral or excellent in professional or craft standards than in organizational norms. Many analyses of the relationships between professionals and their employing organizations seem to imply that the professional standards are somehow better than those of the organizations. Unless there are available specific criteria of what the organization and the professionals are trying to accomplish, such an assumption is unwarranted.

Before moving to a broader look at the implications of formalization for the individual and the organization, we must draw one additional conclusion from the analysis of professionals in organizations. The emphasis in much of the research in this area is on conflict between the professional and his employing organization. Evidence from the Hall research suggests that such conflict is not inevitable and should not be assumed without demonstration. This research found, for example, that the legal departments of large organizations are not necessarily more bureaucratized than law firms of comparable size. The lawyer working in the trust department of a bank may actually be working in an organizational environment similar, and perhaps even identical, to the one he would find in a law firm. This suggests that it is very possible to find organizational structures that are compatible with the degree of professionalization of their members.

Professionals and nonprofessionals bring behavioral guidelines with them into the organization. These guidelines can potentially mesh nicely with those provided by the organization. Some people are very satisfied in a highly formalized situation, while others find such a setting completely frustrating. By the same token, a low degree of formalization would be a satisfying condition to some, but not to others. A convenient way to conceptualize this issue is through the idea of *role* as it has been used in the organizational literature.

FORMALIZATION AND ROLES

Robert Kahn et al. have provided the most widely used and systematic framework for the understanding of the phenomena under discussion. It was developed in their work on the factors associated with role stress.[37] The framework is illustrated in figure 6–1. The authors begin their discussion of this model by noting:

> To a considerable extent, the role expectations held by the members of a role set—the prescriptions and proscriptions associated with a particular position—are determined by the broader organizational context. The organizational structure, the functional specialization and division of labor, and the formal reward system dictate the major content of a given office. What the occupant of that office is supposed to do, with and for whom, is given by

[37] Robert L. Kahn, Donald M. Wolfe, Robert P. Quinn, J. Diedrick Snoek, and Robert A. Rosenthal, *Organizational Stress: Studies in Role Conflict and Ambiguity* (New York: John Wiley & Sons, Inc., 1964).

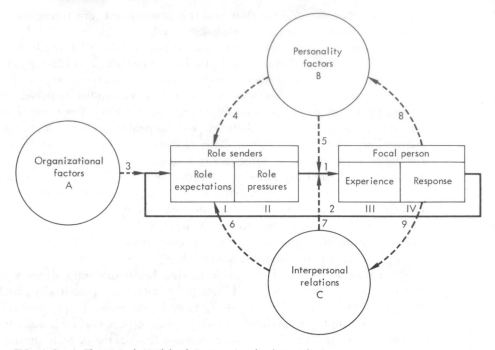

FIG. 6–1   A Theoretical Model of Factors Involved in Adjustment to Role Conflict and Ambiguity

Source: Robert L. Kahn et al., Organizational Stress: Studies in Role Conflict and Ambiguity *(New York: John Wiley & Sons, Inc., 1964), p. 30.*

these and other properties of the organization itself. Although other human beings are doing the "supposing" and the rewarding, the structural properties of organizations are sufficiently stable so that they can be treated as independent of the particular persons in the role set. For such properties as size, number of echelons, and rate of growth, the justifiable abstraction of organizational properties from individual behavior is even more obvious.

The organizational circle (*A*) in Figure [6–1], then represents a set of variables. Some of them characterize the organization as a whole; for example, its size, number of ranks or status levels, the products it produces, or its financial base. Other variables in this set are ecological, in that they represent the relation of a certain position or person to the organization; for example, his rank, his responsibilities for certain services in the division of labor, or the number and positions of others who are directly concerned with his performance.

Arrow 3 asserts a causal relationship between various organizational variables and the role expectations and pressures which are held about and exerted toward a particular position. For example, a person in a liaison position linking two departments is likely to be subjected to many conflicting role pressures because his role set includes persons in two separate units, each having its own goals, objectives, and norms. In general, the organizational conditions surrounding and defining the positions of one's role senders will determine in part their organizational experience, their expectations, and the pressures they impose.

[The personality circle (*B*)] is used broadly to refer to all those factors that describe a person's propensities to behave in certain ways, his motives and values, his sensitivities and fears, his habits, and the like. . . . [The interpersonal relations circle (*C*) refers to] the more or less stable patterns of interaction between a person and his role senders and to their orientations toward each other. These patterns of relationships may be characterized along several dimensions, some of them stemming from the formal structure of the organization, others from informal interaction and the sharing of common experiences. The following dimensions are seen as particularly important in the present context: (1) *power* or ability to influence; (2) *affective bonds,* such as respect, trust in the cooperativeness and benevolence of the other, and attraction or liking; (3) *dependence* of one on the other; and (4) the style of *communication* between the focal person and his associates.

As Figure [6–1] indicates, interpersonal relations (Circle *C*) fulfill some functions parallel to those described in connection with personality factors. The kind of pressure exerted by role senders upon the focal person depends to some degree upon the nature of relations between them (Arrow 6). Role senders who are superior in the formal hierarchy will present their demands in a different manner from subordinates or peers. Pressures will also be interpreted differently depending on the relationship between focal person and role senders (Arrow 7). For example, pressures from relatively powerful associates arouse more tension than similar pressures from others. Finally, the nature of a person's behavioral reactions to a given experience may be affected by interpersonal relations in the situation. For example, such coping responses as overt aggression may be virtually ruled out when the pressures are exerted by a hierarchical superior.[38]

Sources of and Role Conflict and Ambiguity

An important consideration, implied in this model but not made sufficiently clear, is that the input into behavior from the three major sources (organizational, personality, and interpersonal) is not constant and equal. In a highly formalized organization, for example, the organizational factor is designed to and usually does outweigh the other factors. In the less formalized situation, personality and interpersonal factors would be more dominant.

This model and the research from which it emerged assume that the "mix" between these factors is not always perfect. One kind of improper mix occurs when there are too many role messages being sent to an individual, with role conflict resulting. There may be incompatible expectations being sent to a person: on the one hand, by the organization in terms of formal requirements of his job; on the other, from members

[38] *Ibid.,* pp. 31–33.

of his role set, who attempt through interpersonal means to make him behave in accordance with their own desires, which may be different from the organizationally demanded behaviors. In some cases, the organizational demands themselves may be in conflict, as when a "supervisor requests a man to acquire material which is unavailable through normal channels and at the same time prohibits violations of normal channels." [39]

When a person is asked to perform a series of tasks that are incompatible with one another, he is experiencing "role overload." It is impossible for the person to complete all his assigned tasks at one time. "He is likely to experience overload as a conflict of priorities; he must decide which pressures to comply with and which to hold off. If it is impossible to deny any of the pressures, he may be taxed beyond the limit of his ability." [40] This conclusion is verified by Stephen Sales' analysis of organizational factors associated with coronary disease.[41] He finds that it is among personnel in overloaded positions that the risk of coronary problems is the highest. Dissatisfaction with one's work is also related to coronary problems, but this is not our concern here. Role overload and role conflict result from the combination of organizational, interpersonal, and personal demands that are in excess of capacity and ask competing behaviors on the part of the individual.

Essentially the opposite condition is present when *role ambiguity* occurs—that is, when there is insufficient information sent to a person on how he is to perform his role. As in the case of conflict, the effects of ambiguity on the individual can be severe. He may not know what he is to do and may undergo stress because of this uncertainty. The absence of information can be based in any of the three sources of behavior.

Formalization and Role Behavior

This discussion of role behavior has been designed to indicate the interplay between organizational and other factors in determining the behavior of individuals in organizations. From the discussion, it should be clear that the degree of formalization of the expectations about how a particular role is to be played is an important component of how the role is played and how the individual reacts to his situation in the organization. From the standpoint of improving performance of individuals within the organization, increasing their morale, and improving the overall performance of the organization, the proper mix between

---

[39] *Ibid.*, p. 20.
[40] *Ibid.*
[41] Stephen M. Sales, "Organizational Role as a Risk Factor in Coronary Disease," *Administrative Science Quarterly*, Vol. 14, No. 3 (September 1969), 325–37.

formalization and the personal and interpersonal characteristics has to be achieved. Since personnel vary, it is impossible to come up with a single prescription of how to do this. What is required, apparently, is sufficient flexibility on the part of the organization to enable it to adapt to developments in its personnel. If it adds highly trained people in a research and development section, for example, it should not expect to impose the same structure on these personnel that it does on another section of the organization.[42] Similarly, if the personnel in any section of the organization for one reason or another are able to provide more personal guidelines for their behavior than they initially could, the organization should be able to relax its own set of rules and procedures. Since most people do in fact learn, it would follow that this relaxation should be a rather normal and expected kind of phenomenon.

The role concept is a useful device for understanding the interplay among personal, interpersonal, and organizational factors as they impinge upon the behavior of organizational members. One author, David Hickson, maintains that role theory may be the key to understanding the various perspectives on organizations. According to Hickson, "Theory has converged upon the specificity (or precision) of role prescription and its obverse, the range of legitimate discretion." [43] This convergence takes the form of criticism and advocacy of alternative ways of specifying role behavior. The formalization or specificity continuum extends from situations where "prescription is in general terms and goes no further than outlining the boundaries of legitimate discretion to roles where all but a fraction of role behavior is minutely described. Somewhere near the latter extreme comes the semi-skilled assembly-line operator, as well as particular activities in the performance of some roles, for example the first violin player while on stage." [44]

Hickson goes on to list, among others, most of the authors we discussed in the section on perspectives on organizations, in terms of how they think roles ought to be prescribed by the organization. He then notes that the concentration on the degree of role specification, while useful as a means of structuring various organizational theorists and a useful exercise in its own right, *may have led to a situation in which other important questions are ignored.* He states:

> Grouping writers by the variables they have associated with role specificity draws attention to other ranges of variables, where little or nothing has

[42] The importance of not imposing a rigid structure on people who are to be innovative is strongly made by Victor Thompson in "Bureaucracy and Innovation," *Administrative Science Quarterly*, Vol. 10, No. 1 (June 1965), 1–20.

[43] David J. Hickson, "A Convergence in Organizational Theory," *Administrative Science Quarterly*, Vol. 11, No. 2 (September 1966), 225.

[44] *Ibid.*

> been done; for example, small-group formation in organizations, and small-group processes from sociometric choice to tension-release mechanisms. It could be asked whether there are more groups per organization if specificity is lower: Are they smaller? Are they more cohesive? Do they show more tension? And so on. Nor have possible relationships been tested with personality traits, attitudes, or ways of thinking. For example, does not organizational innovation presuppose individual creativity? If so, then the low specificity associated with innovation must also be related to creativity. But, in addition, it is hypothesized that low specificity is related to anxiety and power conflict. Drawing these several hypotheses together, if innovation is associated with low specificity, then the underlying individual creativity must not only survive conditions of anxiety and power conflict but even derive stimulation from them. Can this be tested in the field in organizations? [45]

This last question is still to be answered. Hickson is correct in noting that a premature sense of closure can be felt if organizational theorists look only at the role concept. It is an extremely useful tool, however, for examining the interface between the individual and the organization. The attention paid to specificity or formalization is also not unwarranted, since it is so crucial to the understanding of organizations.

The Importance of Formalization

Formalization is the organizational technique of prescribing how, when, and by whom tasks are to be performed. This specification can be rigid or loose. The pattern it takes depends on several factors. The task being performed, the knowledge base from which task performance emerges, and the nature of the personnel have all been shown to be related to the degree of formalization. Lawrence and Lorsch's research has indicated that an optimal mix between the degree of formalization and these other factors is important for organizational effectiveness. This research also partially answers Hickson's query regarding the place of conflict in the innovative process, since in this case conflict was inherent and beneficial in the organizations involved in the innovative process. All these considerations suggest that formalization cannot be viewed as an evil or a good, but rather as an element of organizational structure that does and should vary from situation to situation and over time within any one situation.

Like other facets of organizational structure, formalization is subject to and dependent upon changing conditions. These changes can come from outside the organization in terms of environmental and technological shifts. They can also come from within the organization as the na-

---

[45] *Ibid.*, pp. 234–35.

ture of the organization's members changes and the relationships between the parts of the organization are altered. Despite the dynamic nature of structure, it must be reemphasized that it is from structure and as a reaction to structure that the processes within organizations occur. The sstructure, including size, complexity, and formalization, is a "given" at any point in time.

SUMMARY AND CONCLUSIONS

This chapter and the entire section began with the premise that an organization's structure, including its degree of formalization, makes an important difference in how the organization and its members perform. While none of the studies that were discussed attributed causal primacy to structural factors, it is clear from the analysis that structural characteristics have important relationships with other major organizational features, such as rate of change, the distribution of power within the organization, and relationships with the environment. We have also seen that the degree of formalization has important consequences for the individual. He can overreact, becoming a slave to the rules or fighting them for the sake of fighting. The individual can be dulled by an over-specification of how he is to perform in the organization. At the same time, the behavior of individuals, if inappropriately guided by the organization by either too much or too little specification, can have extremely negative consequences for the organization.

The entire discussion has been guided by evidence suggesting strongly that organizational structure is formed by influences from outside and inside the organization. A major external influence is certainly the technological environment in which the organization operates. This would include the material, operations, and knowledge facets of the technology concept. While technology appears to be the key environmental variable, others would include relationships with other such general environmental factors.

Internally, the role of the professional was stressed, largely owing to the amount of evidence that has been amassed regarding the professional in the organization. Since they probably constitute the most conspicuous occupational group in organizations—with the possible exception of some of the crafts, which would have similar characteristics for the purposes of this discussion—and since more and more occupations are attempting to professionalize and more and more professionals are working in organizations, it is understandable that the work of professionals would be so highly emphasized.

Although the evidence discussed comes largely from the realm of the professions, the major point made was that the individual brings guidelines for his own behavior with him. It is the degree of congruence between these individual guidelines and those that the organization needs for the fulfillment of its tasks that is critical in determining the appropriate degree of formalization. These personal guidelines can obviously vary in terms of their strength, saliency, and content within any occupational grouping in the organization. The amount of previous training and experience, whether a person is a professional or not, is probably a major factor in determining how self-guiding he can be.

Formalization is necessary in organizations. The degree of formalization is the variable that should be kept under constant scrutiny as an important practical matter. For the organizational analyst, the degree of formalization is a major variable for understanding both the organization and the performance and thoughts of its members.

An extremely useful tool for bridging the organizational and individual levels of analysis is the role concept. Roles contain individual, interpersonal, and organizational components as they are enacted. As Hickson has demonstrated, role specification has been a major focus for many of the students of organizations. While, as he suggests, it might be useful to move beyond this point, the role concept would appear to be of continued utility in understanding behavior in organizations.

The discussion of complexity indicated that organizations have many different parts. These parts, whether along the vertical or the horizontal axis, can and do vary in their degree of formalization. It has been amply demonstrated, for example, that research and development departments, or others that employ highly specialized personnel, typically are less formalized than their counterparts in the rest of the organization. It also appears that the degree of formalization declines as one moves up an organization's hierarchy. Complexity and formalization are thus interrelated and should be considered together in analyses of organizational structure.

This section began with a consideration of organizational size, often taken to be a major structural characteristic. The evidence presented indicates that size is important, although not to the degree that has often been posited. An organization's size and changes in size present problems of coordination and control. Growth is often accompanied by increased formalization and growing complexity. According to this analysis, size should not be taken as the cause of these shifts in organizational structure. Rather, attention should be paid to the conditions that lead to an increase in size. These conditions appear to be the factors that have formed the basis for the entire discussion in this section—environment, technology, and the characteristics of members of the organization.

The analysis of organizational structure can be, and often is, somewhat dry and unnecessarily static; but it is vital for understanding what goes on in an organization, for behavior is an outgrowth of structure. Organizational processes occur within a structured framework. At the same time, of course, processes transform structure. This transformation can be abrupt or gradual. Whatever the pace of change, a new structure emerges within which the continuing processes of organizational behavior are found. The next section will examine the vital processes of power, decision making, and communication.

part three

INTERNAL ORGANIZATIONAL PROCESSES

At this point in our analysis, we turn from looking at *what* an organization is like to *why* it is the way it is. The subjects of this section—power, conflict, leadership, decision making, and communications—are the major ways in which an organization moves from one state to the next. The organizational structure sets the stage for these processes to occur. When they occur, the organization is usually transformed into a new condition, which sets the stage for the processes to continue, and so on. Since the processes occur constantly, this is oversimplified, but each power act or communication situation comes out of the existing structural arrangement and contributes to any changes in the organization.

We will be concerned with many questions that are important to members of any organization. For example, who has power in an organization and why? The answer here is more complex than simple rank. The products of the use of power are more complex than simple compliance. Is power something that only emerges from interpersonal interactions, or can there be power differentials between organizational units as well? Do power differences lead inevitably to conflict within the organization? If and when conflict occurs, is it most reasonable to try to eliminate it as quickly as possible, or is conflict good for the organization? Does leadership make any difference at all in what happens to the organization, or are organizations subject only to the demands of the situation? Can there be rationality in the decision-making process? What is needed to make even moderately good decisions? Is the answer to almost every organizational problem more and better communications?

Questions like these will occupy our attention for the next several chapters. As might be expected, the answers to these questions will not be crystal clear for several reasons. The questions themselves deal with issues for which the answers are often complex, containing contradictory elements. The evidence for the answers is weak, in fact much weaker than the evidence that was available for the structural analysis. Much of the writing in this area is in the form of advocacy, which is an excellent thing in many cases, but not much use in careful analyses. Our concern will continue to be the organization, with less interest in the individuals involved. As will be seen, however, individual variations make a tremendous difference in what happens to the organization as these processes occur.

POWER
AND
CONFLICT

7

Power and conflict are processes in organizations. When we say this, we mean that they are important elements in the social relationships that occur. They are part of the *dynamics* of organizational life, in that they are a major component of change. Our concern will be with the nature and consequences of these related processes. The processes are said to be related because conflict often occurs as a result of a power relationship—often, but not inevitably, since a power relationship can exist without conflict and conflict can occur without power having been a precedent event.

Both processes are also important outside the organizational context. Both, in and out of the organization, have been the topics of many discussions, but too little actual research. The evidence we will use will be suggestive, rather than definitive, in most cases. It would be nice to have a complete set of research findings from which propositions regarding these processes could be derived. Instead, we will have to rely on rather incomplete information and make our interpretations on a more tentative basis than in the earlier discussions.

THE NATURE OF POWER IN ORGANIZATIONS

Power can usually be rather simply defined. There are many treatises dealing with the concept, and most are in general agreement that it has to do with relationships between two or more actors in which the behavior of one is affected by the other. The political scientist Robert Dahl defines power as "*A* has power over *B* to the extent that he can get *B* to do something *B* would not otherwise do." [1] This simple definition really contains the essence of the power concept. It also implies an important point that is often left out of considerations of power—that the power variable is a relational one. Power is meaningless unless it is exercised. A person or group cannot have power in isolation; it has to be in relationship to some other person or collectivity.

Power Relationships

The importance of the relational aspect of power is specifically developed in Richard Emerson's comments on the importance of dependency relationships in the total power constellation. He suggests that power resides *"implicitly in the other's dependency"* [2]; in other words, that the parties in a power relationship are tied to each other by mutual dependency.

> Social relations commonly entail *ties of mutual dependence* between the parties. A *depends* upon B if he aspires to goals or gratifications whose achievement is facilitated by appropriate actions on B's part. By virtue of mutual dependency, it is more or less imperative to each party that he be able to control or influence the other's conduct. At the same time, these ties of mutual dependence imply that each party is in a position, to some degree, to grant or deny, facilitate or hinder, the other's gratification. Thus,

[1] Robert Dahl, "The Concept of Power," *Behavioral Science,* 2 (July 1957), 202–3. For other general discussions of power, see Robert Bierstedt, "An Analysis of Social Power," *American Sociological Review,* Vol. 15, No. 6 (December 1950), 730–38; Peter M. Blau, *Exchange and Power in Social Life* (New York: John Wiley & Sons, Inc., 1967); Abraham Kaplan, "Power in Perspective," in Robert L. Kahn and Elise Boulding, eds., *Power and Conflict in Organizations* (New York: Basic Books, Inc., Publishers, 1964), pp. 11–32; and Max Weber, *The Theory of Social and Economic Organizations,* trans. A. M. Henderson and Talcott Parsons (New York: The Free Press, 1947), pp. 152–93.

[2] Richard M. Emerson, "Power Dependence Relations," *American Sociological Review,* Vol. 27, No. 1 (February 1962), 32.

it would appear that the power to control or influence the other resides in control over the things he values, which may range all the way from oil resources to ego-support, depending on the relation in question.[3]

Dependency is particularly easy to see in organizations, since the very nature of organizations requires interdependence of personnel and subunits. The existence of power relationships is also generally easy to see. Gary Wamsley notes that in highly bureaucratized organizations, ". . . power or authority would tend to be hierarchic: each level would have just that amount of power necessary to carry out its responsibilities; ascendant levels in the hierarchy would have increasing power based on broader knowledge about the organization and/or greater task expertise. . . ." [4] The design of these types of organizations rests largely on the power variable, with the intent of ensuring that each level in the organization has sufficient power. When an issue arises that is out of the purview of an office at a particular level, it is passed up the organization until it reaches the level where the decision can appropriately be made. Of course, few organizations approximate this ideal type, in that the power arrangements are affected by informal patterns worked out over time and by personal differences in the exercise of the power available in an office. Nevertheless, in many organizations, power relationships are tightly prescribed and followed, and they are highly visible to all who enter the organization.

While power is very easily seen and experienced in such settings, in others it is more obscure. In some situations it is extremely hard to isolate. Rue Bucher tells the following anecdote as an example of this:

> According to the students' statements, the dean asserted that "nobody in the university has the authority to negotiate with the students. . . ." "Obviously somebody in the university makes policy decisions," the statement said, "and until an official body comes forward, we consider the present situation a refusal to negotiate our demands." [5]

In the situation described, neither the students nor the university administration in question could locate an office or individual who had the power to negotiate with students. The students' perception that this constitutes a refusal to negotiate is only partially accurate. This type of matter had not arisen before, and there was undoubtedly no established way to handle such situations because the power relationship was yet to

[3] *Ibid.*

[4] Gary L. Wamsley, "Power and the Crisis of the Universities," in Mayer N. Zald, ed., *Power in Organizations* (Nashville, Tenn.: Vanderbilt University Press, 1970), p. 53.

[5] Rue Bucher, "Social Process and Power in a Medical School," in Zald, ed., *Power in Organizations*, p. 3.

be determined. Wamsley notes that in such situations, power is "variable; situationally or issue specific; surrounded by checks and balances; an interdependent relationship, often employing negotiation and persuasion and often found in changing coalitions." [6]

Power is as much a fact of university life as of corporate life. It takes a different form and is expressed in different ways, but it is still there. In campus situations such as student–administration confrontations, issues and relationships are being explored that had not really been part of the preexisting power system. (It is interesting that it is usually the administration that is involved in such confrontations, when the issues the students are most concerned about generally have their origins in faculty actions or inactions.) In this sense, more power is introduced into the system as arrangements are made to handle such incidents in the future. So we see that there is not a fixed amount of power (zero-sum game) in the system for all time and that the amount of power can contract or expand.

Implied in the discussion of the relative clarity of power relationships in organizations is the important point that power must be viewed as more than merely interpersonal. The subunits in an organization also have varying amounts of power. Perrow, for example, in a study of industrial firms, found that the sales departments were overwhelmingly regarded as the most powerful units in the organizations involved.[7] The members of the other departments regarded them that way and apparently behaved accordingly. While the tendency is to look only at interpersonal power, ignoring interdepartmental power relationships obscures an important facet of the organizational power issue.

Types of Power

The discussion thus far has treated power as a rather unitary concept, but there is a long history of distinguishing *types* of power. Probably the best-known and most widely used classification system is Weber's.[8] Weber makes a basic distinction between power and *authority*. The former involves force or coercion and would not be an important factor as an internal process in organizations except in cases such as slave-labor camps, some prisons, some schools, and so on. Authority, on the other hand, is a form of power that does not carry the force implica-

6 Wamsley, "Power and the Crisis," p. 53.

7 Charles Perrow, "Departmental Power and Perspective in Industrial Firms," in Zald, *Power in Organizations*, pp. 59–89.

8 Max Weber, *Theory of Social and Economic Organization* (New York: The Free Press, 1947), pp. 324–28.

tion. Rather, it involves a "suspension of judgment" on the part of its recipients. Directives or orders are followed because of the belief that they ought to be followed. Compliance is voluntary. This requires a common value system among organizational members, as Scott notes, and this condition is usually met.[9]

It is useful at this point to distinguish between authority and persuasion or personal influence. Authority involves an acceptance of the power system as one enters the organization, while persuasion or influence are power situations in which the decision is made, consciously or unconsciously, at the particular moment the power appeal is sent from the power holder. When a persuader becomes institutionalized, in the sense of being always accepted and thus legitimated by the recipient, this becomes authority.

Many current social controversies revolve around the authority issue. When members of a system do not accept the values of the system, as in the case of the radical movement, authority as expressed by the police, courts, or organizational rules becomes nonlegitimate for the people involved. A whole new frame of reference is brought into play, as are other forms of power, such as coercion and persuasion. The fact that such situations are noteworthy is indirect evidence of the overwhelming dominance of authority as the form of power in organizations.

Weber goes on to distinguish between types of authority, developing his well-known typology of traditional, charismatic, and legal authority.[10] *Legal authority* is the type of most power relationships in modern organizations; it is based on a belief in the right of those in higher offices to have power over subordinates. *Charismatic authority* stems from devotion to a particular power holder and is based on his personal characteristics. This type is certainly found in modern organizations, to which it can be either a threat or a benefit. If a person in an authority position can extend his legal powers through the exercise of charismatic authority, he has more power over his subordinates than that prescribed by the organization. If the performance of the subordinates is enhanced (assuming for the moment that their performance enhancement is also beneficial to the actors themselves), such an addition is beneficial. If, on the other hand, charismatic authority is present in persons outside the formal authority system, distortions in that system will be evident. As we will see later, it is unlikely that a person with legal authority will be able to extend his power through the exercise of charisma. The third form, *traditional authority,* is based on belief in the established traditional order and is best exemplified by operating monar-

---

[9] W. Richard Scott, "Theory of Organizations," in Robert E. L. Faris, ed., *Handbook of Modern Sociology* (Chicago: Paul McNally and Co., 1964), p. 497.
[10] Weber, *Theory of Social and Economic Organization,* p. 328.

chies. Vestiges of this form can be found in organizations in which the founder or a dominant figure is still present, when terms such as "the old man wants it that way" are verbalized and the wishes of the "old man" are followed.

Power Bases

Since Weber's time, there have been several attempts to classify the power concept into still more useful categories. One of the approaches that has attracted a good deal of attention is that of John French and Bertram Raven.[11] Their concern is primarily with the bases of interpersonal power, but their conclusions can easily be extended to the organizational level. Their typology is based on the nature of the relationship between the power holder and the power recipient. *Reward* power, or "power whose basis is the ability to reward," is limited to those situations in which the reward is meaningful for the power recipient. The second power basis is *coercive* power, based on the recipient's perceptions of the ability of the power holder to distribute punishments. French and Raven note that the same social relationship could be viewed as one of reward power in one instance and coercive power in a second. If a worker obeys a foreman's order because of a fear of punishment, it is coercive power; if another worker obeys in the same way in anticipation of a future reward, it is reward power.

The third form of power is very close to the implication of the Weberian distinction between power and authority. This type is called *legitimate* power. The recipient acknowledges that the power holder has the right to influence him and he has an obligation to follow the directions of the influence. *Referent* power is present when a power recipient identifies with a power holder and tries to behave like him. In this case the power holder may be unaware that he is in fact a power holder. The final form, *expert* power, is based on the special knowledge attributed to the power holder by the recipient. The power recipient behaves in a particular way because he believes that the information possessed by the holder is relevant and that he himself does not have that sort of information available. The simplest example here, of course, is in the professional–client relationship, when the client follows the "doctor's orders."

All these forms of power are found in organizations. All are also, or can be, part of the legitimate authority system, except for referent

---

[11] John R. P. French and Bertram Raven, "The Bases of Social Power," in Dorwin Cartwright and Alvin Zander, eds., *Group Dynamics*, 3rd ed. (New York: Harper and Row, Publishers, 1968), pp. 259–69.

power. The ability to reward or coerce is often viewed as legitimate, even though at times coercion is distasteful. The presence of staff experts in almost all organizations is in essence a recognition of the legitimacy of expert power. Thus, while French and Raven distinguish legitimate power from the other bases, all the bases with the exception of referent power are legitimate within the organizational framework.

Distinguishing between the forms of power is an empty exercise unless it means something for the organization and its participants. In the next section, some of these consequences will be identified.

SOME CONSEQUENCES OF POWER RELATIONSHIPS

Compliance and Involvement

Using a typology of power quite similar to French and Raven's, Etzioni has attempted to develop both a typology and an analytical scheme for organizational analysis built around the power variable.[12] As indicated in Chapter 2, Etzioni identifies three forms of power—coercive, remunerative, and normative. Normative power "rests on the allocation and manipulation of symbolic rewards and deprivations through employment of leaders, manipulation of mass media, alloaction of esteem and prestige symbols, administration of ritual, and influence over the distribution of 'acceptance' and 'positive response.' "[13] This form of power is quite close to French and Raven's referent power, and the other two categories proposed by Etzioni are almost identical to coercive and reward power in the French and Raven discussion. Expert and legitimate power are omitted; Etzioni suggests that legitimate authority is based on one of the three power bases, anyway, and that legitimate authority has been overused in organizational analyses. This is an oversimplification, but the formulation itself is useful for the purposes here, since it does indicate the range of consequences that can be linked to the different forms of power.

Etzioni links the three forms of power to the kinds of involvement that the lower participants in organizations have with the organization. By lower participants, he means those who are subject to the power in the organization. In using the simple dichotomy of elites or organizational representatives and lower participants, Etzioni glosses over the important fact that most people in most organizations are both power

---

[12] Amitai Etzioni, *A Comparative Analysis of Complex Organizations* (New York: The Free Press, 1961).

[13] *Ibid.*, p. 5.

holders and power recipients, since they are between the very top and the very bottom of the organization. The lower participants in an organization that uses coercive power are characterized as having an *alienative* involvement with the organization. This is an intense negative orientation, most easily seen in cases of "inmates in prisons, prisoners of war, people in concentration camps, enlisted men in basic training, [where] all tend to be alienated from their respective organizations." [14]

In organizations using remunerative power, the involvement is neither positive nor negative and is generally of low intensity. "*Calculative* orientations are predominant in relationships of merchants who have continuous business contacts. Attitudes of (and toward) permanent customers are often predominantly calculative, as are relationships among entrepreneurs in modern (rational) capitalism. Inmates in prisons who have established contact with prison authorities, such as 'rats' and 'peddlers,' often have predominantly calculative attitudes toward those in power." [15] This same form of involvement would characterize many workers in production and clerical positions, if their work is viewed as a means to ends that are found outside the work situation; and it would also be characteristic of the guards in the prison setting where alienation is found among the inmates.

Moral involvement characterizes those in organizations utilizing normative power. This is a high-intensity form of involvement and can be seen in the behavior of a "parishioner in his church, the devoted member in his party, and the loyal follower [in following] his leader. . . ." [16] Etzioni notes that moral involvement can take two forms. Pure moral commitments are based on an internalization of norms and an identification with the authority of the organization. Social commitment, on the other hand, is based on a sensitivity to pressures from members of the individual's primary group. In the latter case, the person has not internalized the norms to any great extent, but rather goes along with the beliefs and behaviors of people who are significant to him.

The forms of power and kinds of involvement form the basis for the organizational typology. Etzioni recognizes the presence of mixed types in which more than one form of power and involvement are found. In primary and secondary schools, for example, coercion is a secondary pattern to the normative power that is more often utilized. Coercion largely disappears in higher education. Therapeutic mental hospitals similarly use coercion as a supplemental process. Professional organizations, such as law firms, universities, and research organizations, utilize normative compliance patterns, with utilitarian compliance a

---

[14] *Ibid.,* p. 10.
[15] *Ibid.*
[16] *Ibid.*

close second. Newspapers are an interesting combination, also, in that the production side of the operation is characteristically utilitarian, while the editorial side is predominantly normative. The same pattern would characterize other parts of the mass media. Labor unions are a heterogeneous category, with all forms of power being represented. Most are utilitarian–normative, according to Etzioni. These combinations and difficulties in placement weaken this formulation as a typological effort; but the correlates of these compliance patterns that Etzioni identifies are important for our uses here.

The first set of correlates is concerned with goals and effectiveness. There are three major types of goals: *"order, economic,* and *culture."* The typical form of compliance structure for each type of goal is as would be expected: coercive, utilitarian, and normative. The same pattern holds for the effectiveness issue. Effectiveness is enhanced if organizations can move toward congruent compliance systems.

A second major concern is with the manner in which power is distributed in organizations. Etzioni notes that both instrumental and expressive leaders are found in most organizations and that the way these forms of leadership interact is highly dependent on the basic power system. In coercive organizations, inmates develop a separate social system in which expressive leadership predominates, although instrumental factors are present in the case of persons who engage in merchandising, "escape-engineering," and so on. In normative organizations, where few boundaries exist between upper and lower participants, there is a tight integration between the levels in the organization. In utilitarian organizations, expressive and instrumental leaderships are usually separated, with the instrumental leader's orders generally followed without too much dissension. Forms of leadership are related to organizational effectiveness, according to Etzioni.

> In normative organizations it is functional for the expressive elite to subordinate the instrumental one; this seems indeed to be the case in the Jesuit order, the Episcopalian church, and in some labor unions, but not in other normative organizations, particularly egalitarian churches. In utilitarian organizations, high productivity is associated with subordination of the expressive elite by the instrumental elite, and cooperation between the two. In coercive organizations the antagonism between organizational and informal elites makes for an unstable relationship instead of a clear pattern of subordination.[17]

Etzioni then examines the kind of integration of members found in the three forms of organizations. Consensus is highest in normative organizations, lowest in coercive, and intermediate in utilitarian. Com-

[17] *Ibid.*, p. 126.

munications in the three types of organizations are also quite different. There are many blockages to communications between ranks in coercive organizations, few in normative, with the utilitarian organizations again holding an intermediate position. There is a high rate of horizontal expressive communication in coercive organizations and egalitarian normative organizations, while in hierarchical normative organizations there is a high rate of downward expressive communications. In utilitarian organizations, there is a high rate of downward and upward instrumental communications. The socialization of members is carried out primarily by fellow inmates in coercive systems, particularly in the expressive sphere. Normative organizations are heavily involved in the socialization process, since they rely tremendously on the commitment of their members. Utilitarian organizations are in the position of having to engage in less direct socialization, since they rely on outside agencies for a supply of trained personnel.[18]

Attention is then focused on the relationships between these compliance patterns and the organizations' environment. Coercive organizations have few activities outside the organization itself, while normative organizations are much more likely to be involved in a series of activities in the wider environment. Utilitarian systems, unless they bring in normative patterns, are likely to be rather narrow in their activities in the wider environment.[19]

Etzioni's treatment of the correlates of the power system relies upon secondary data and logical analysis. While other variables related to the power system could be identified, the discussion has indicated the importance of the power system as a means by which people are linked to their organizations.

Conformity

Donald Warren has utilized the French–Raven power typology in his analysis of the manner in which schoolteachers conform to organizational controls.[20] Warren is concerned with behavioral as opposed to attitudinal conformity as the dependent variable in the power relationship. Behavioral conformity is compliance "in overt behavior, but without internalization of norms." [21] Attitudinal conformity involves both compliance and internalization. Warren also deals with the visibility of the

---

18 *Ibid.,* pp. 127–50.
19 *Ibid.,* pp. 151–74.
20 Donald I. Warren, "Power, Visibility, and Conformity in Formal Organizations," *American Sociological Review,* Vol. 33, No. 6 (December 1968), 951–70.
21 *Ibid.,* p. 954.

power recipients. He suggests that those recipients subject to coercive and reward power must be highly visible, since their performance must be constantly under surveillance by the power holder. On the other hand, referent and expert power recipients are much less visible, since they share the same social goals as the power holder. In these latter power forms, the recipients are motivated to conform and there is less need for direct surveillance.

Warren finds that in most of the schools studied, more than one form of power was used. The combinations of power forms are consistent in terms of what would be normally expected. Expert and referent power tend to be found together and are closely related, while coercive and legitimate have a minimal relationship. Coercive power was the type found alone most often, while referent and expert power were most often combined with one of the other forms. These combinations are important from a theoretical standpoint; they suggest that in these cases, power is not something that is available in a social system in a fixed amount (zero-sum game). Power is a variable within the system, as to both type and amount.

The findings in regard to conformity are particularly interesting. Table 7–1 indicates the types of conformity associated with the different power bases. The differences between behavioral conformity and attitudinal conformity are particularly striking, in that the form of power that is successful in one form of conformity tends to be very unsuccessful in the other. The contribution of referent power to conformity is also interesting to note, since it is "particularly decisive in achieving social control, regardless of its combination with other power bases." [22] The most important conclusions to be reached from this data, according to Warren, are that "effective social control is the result of diverse processes of individual conformity, and that there are systematic linkages of those processes to different bases of social power." [23]

Warren then adds the professionalism of the teachers to his analysis. He finds that in highly professionalized settings, coercive power is weak, whereas it is a stronger base in less professionalized settings. The addition of the professional variable weakens the impact of reward power, which apparently is not a major basis for control in these school settings. Legitimate, expert, and referent power are all linked to professionalism, with legitimate power having the strongest association. The control system in a highly professionalized school, then, appears to be most effective when these three forms of power are present and utilized. Control would tend to be ineffective when coercive or reward power is

22 *Ibid.,* p. 961.
23 *Ibid.,* p. 962.

TABLE 7–1   RANK-ORDER CORRELATIONS BETWEEN SOCIAL POWER BASES AND TYPES OF CONFORMITY: 18 SCHOOL AVERAGES

Type of Conformity	*Coercive Power*	*Reward Power*	*Expert Power*	*Legiti- mate Power*	*Referent Power*	*All Bases*
Total Conformity	+.337 *	+.362 *	+.255	+.368	+.753 *	+.703 *
Behavioral Conformity	+.661 *	+.335 *	−.147	+.015	+.136	+.488 *
Attitudinal Conformity	+.151	+.306	+.395 *	+.509 *	+.718 *	+.654 *
Attitude Socialization	+.113	+.256	+.015	+.216	+.636	+.480

* Significant at .05 level.

In total conformity, teachers use approach preferred by the principal.

Behavioral conformity represents teacher use of approach preferred by the principal but would prefer another approach.

Attitudinal conformity represents teacher use of approach preferred by the principal which is also preferred by teacher.

Attitude socialization represents a shift in teacher attitude closer to the principal's approach.

Source: Donald I. Warren, "Power, Visibility, and Conformity in Formal Organizations," American Sociological Review, Vol. 33, No. 6 (December 1968), 961.

the major basis used. This is consistent with most of the discussions of professionals in organizations.

The findings in regard to the forms of power and of behavioral and attitudinal conformity and to the role of professionalism have some important implications. The major one is that the form of power used will vary in its effectiveness according to the type of conformity sought and the kinds of personnel over which the power is wielded. Since not all personnel are professional and since attitudinal conformity is at times both unnecessary and almost impossible to achieve, coercive and reward power cannot be viewed as inherently dysfunctional. On the other hand, since attitudinal conformity can reduce the need for surveillance and hence the costs (behavioral and financial) of power, the other forms of power can in some cases be viewed as being more effective in a wide variety of organizational situations.

Any one of the forms of power discussed can also be viewed as a socially negative or positive process. There is a rather constant implication (not necessarily implied by Warren) that referent, legitimate, and expert power are somehow better and more democratic than coercive or reward power. It should be clear that power holders or power systems can be viewed as legitimate, expert, or referent for reasons that in the long or short run are organizationally or societally dysfunctional or disastrous. This latter point, of course, is almost impossible to document while the system is in operation. At the same time, it is important not to assume inherent goodness in any of the power forms discussed.

Perceptions of Authority

A related approach has been taken by Robert Peabody in his analysis of perceptions of organizational authority.[24] Peabody distinguishes four forms of authority. Authority of *position* is similar to a combination of French and Raven's coercive and reward power bases, since it involves the right to hire and fire, promote or demote, and distribute rewards. Peabody uses essentially the same definition in his concept of *legitimacy* as do French and Raven, while his terms *competence* and *person* are almost identical with expert and referent power. Peabody examined the perceptions of authority among members of a social welfare agency, a police department, and an elementary school. His interview data provide some insights into the way power recipients view those in a position of authority.

Some comments reflecting legitimate authority were:

> "Authority to me is something you are bound to obey. It's something that I respect."
> "A lot of authority is in the manual—it's the law." [25]

References to the authority of position have a slightly different flavor:

> "The person with the rank has the final say. Whether you agree with him or not, you go along with him."
> "Authority is mostly our supervisor and grade-II supervisor." [26]

A quite different frame of reference is evident when authority is seen to be based on competence. Here the respondents are talking about their own authority rather than that of their superiors, but the point is made clear:

> "I have the final word in licensing. There is no written law as to what a good foster home or what a bad foster home is, except as we have defined it in our experience and knowledge. We have the authority to deny the

[24] Robert L. Peabody, "Perceptions of Organizational Authority: A Comparative Analysis," *Administrative Science Quarterly*, Vol. 6, No. 4 (March 1962), 463–82.
    [25] *Ibid.*, p. 476.
    [26] *Ibid.*, p. 478.

license entirely. And it's based on this knowledge and experience rather than the manual."

"Well, my authority is completely within my classroom, and I'm given a great deal of authority there. And I'm appreciative of this. I'm given a complete reign. I can use my own philosophy, mainly because it's the philosophy of the district. With a good teacher, *that's O.K. With a bad teacher it's not."* [27]

Authority of the person can be easily seen in the next comment:

"Authority is based on someone to lead . . . so a person in authority would have to be a leader. He would have to have the ability to command and other traits of leadership. . . ." [28]

Although this form of data is not the strongest in the world, the findings from this study are interesting in that they show how authority patterns form configurations in the organizations studied. In the police department, authority of position was emphasized, as might be expected from the ever-present reminders of official rankings, such as uniforms and quasi-military behaviors. A rather surprising finding is that authority of person also proved to be extremely important in this setting. Human-relations skills were constantly noted here as being important, more so than for the social workers and teachers in the study. Peabody attributes this finding to the fact that particular kinds of people are attracted to the kind of work that policemen do, although he does not specify what kinds of people these are. Another interpretation offered by Peabody is that skill in interpersonal relations is emphasized as a basis for authority in the absence of clear criteria of technical competence. He suggests that as ". . . younger, career-oriented police officers with college training in police administration replace older, 'small-town cops,' the importance attached to authority of competence in this police department will probably increase." [29] Whether this does in fact happen, of course, still remains to be seen.

The social workers also exhibited a rather surprising pattern. They emphasized authority of position overwhelmingly. According to Peabody, this is a function of this particular organization. Very few members had had graduate training in social work, so that the overall competence level was relatively low; and the organization was headed by a matriarchal figure. The teachers, on the other hand, 75 percent of whom had had some graduate training, emphasized authority of competence over the other forms.

The Peabody and Warren studies emphasize two important points. The first is that the nature of the personnel, in this case their degree

27 *Ibid.* [Emphasis added.]
28 *Ibid.,* p. 479.
29 *Ibid.,* p. 480.

of professionalization, is strongly related to the form of power utilized in the organization. One would predict that when inappropriate forms are used, the likelihood of disruptive conflict would be increased. Although the professionalization variable was used in these two studies and indeed seems to be a crucial factor in many organizations, other components of the characteristics of the power recipients besides professionalization would surely be important in regard to the kinds of power that can most effectively be used.

The second point is that in both studies there were multiple power forms present and utilized. Organizational power apparently involves more than a simple utilization of one or the other of the forms of power that have been discussed. Power forms tend to exist in combination in the kinds of organizations studied. In both studies, of course, it is to the organization's advantage to obtain more than sheer behavioral conformity, since it would be extremely beneficial if the members of the organization also had attitudes corresponding to their behavior. Power through legitimacy, coercion, or position must apparently be supplemented by factors such as competence or human-relations skills.

It would be erroneous to generalize from these two studies about all organizations and all power relationships. There are many situations, for example, in which more than one form of power is found, but *not* within the same person or position. Etzioni has pursued this issue in his analysis of patterns of dual leadership in organizations.[30] He took his lead from laboratory studies that found that in task-oriented groups, expressive (or socio-emotional) leaders emerge who rank high in interpersonal dealings, in addition to instrumental (or task) leaders who rank high in stressing task performance; Etzioni suggests that these two forms of leadership are seldom combined in one person. Although there are undoubtedly a few "great men" who successfully carry out both forms of leadership, in most situations these roles are separated. From this analysis, Etzioni notes that the familiar distinction between the formal and informal leaders receives strong empirical support from the laboratory studies. More important, the instrumental leader is the one appointed by the organization, except where the organization itself is primarily expressively oriented, while the expressive leader emerges in the course of social interaction among work groups.

From this point, Etzioni goes on to apply his familiar distinctions between organizations, suggesting that in socializing and other expressive organizations, the organization is dependent upon expressive leadership; in segregating organizations, such as prisons, expressive leadership is not required; and in producing organizations, expressive leadership is of secondary importance. This argument is consistent with Etzioni's

[30] Amitai Etzioni, "Dual Leadership in Complex Organizations," *American Sociological Review,* Vol. 30, No. 5 (October 1965), 688–98.

distinctions, mentioned earlier, between forms of power. What is important here is the application of these ideas to the power relationships under discussion. Etzioni suggests that in coercive or segregating organizations, attempts at utilizing expressive leadership—such as in rehabilitation of prisoners—are likely to fail, given the predominance of instrumental power sources. A few rehabilitation personnel scattered over a large number of prisons have their power dissipated against the force of the existing power structure.

A more important consideration in terms of the preceding discussion is the fact that a first-line supervisor in a producing organization is unlikely to be able to play both the expressive and the instrumental role. He is appointed to his position as an instrumental leader. From the evidence available, informal or expressive leaders emerge in such situations. If the supervisor is exposed to and expected to exercise human-relations skills, he is probably doomed to failure, according to Etzioni. If he attempts to engage in expressive leadership, he will be confronting a preexisting expressive leader. At some point in time he will have to choose between expressive and instrumental activities, as when his own superiors want to see production increased or some other instrumental task accomplished. If he attempts to implement the instrumental directive, his role as an expressive leader is severely threatened, since he can no longer be "one of the boys."

While the Warren and Peabody studies identified multiple power patterns within the same organizations, the power relationships analyzed were general, rather than situation specific. If Etzioni is correct, it is unlikely that multiple forms of power that are incompatible can be successfully used over time. For example, a holder of expert power may also serve as a referent in some cases, whereas reward and referent power would appear to be incompatible. In the kinds of organizations studied, it is conceivable that the power patterns described involved more than the one-to-one power relationship among the individuals involved. The types of organizations studied—schools, police departments, and social welfare agencies—can probably be characterized as organizations with multiple power relationships, and thus the findings are not surprising. It would be extremely useful to have information on the relative strength of the identified power bases linked to specific situations, so that a clearer picture of the nature of power in organizations would be available.

Power and Communications

So far, we have focused principally on the manner in which individuals are controlled within various power systems. But power systems involve more than the control of individuals. A study by Joseph Julian indicates that the communication system within an organization is also affected by the power arrangements.[31] Using data from five hospitals, Julian found that the hospitals utilized differing power systems. The differences were largely attributed to the nature of the hospitals. In voluntary general hospitals, the power system tended to be normative, while in a tuberculosis sanatorium and a veteran's hospital, coercive patterns were a more evident part of the power relationship. Julian obtained his information about the power relationships from the patients in the hospitals. Obviously, patients are only one of several groups in hospitals subject to the power system. The "semi-professional" staff, including nurses and technicians, and the nonprofessional staff (orderlies and kitchen help) also are subject to the established power system. Data are not available to determine if the power relationships with patients are the same as those with the paid staff. They are probably not exactly equivalent, especially since remuneration enters the picture with regard to the staff personnel. This indicates again the fact that multiple power relationships probably characterize most organizations. This would particularly be the case when the organization contains such members as clients or students.

Some good insights are supplied by Julian into the nature of normative and coercive power as applied through sanctions on the patients. Normative sanctions include "explaining the situation to the patients again in more detail," and "asking relatives or friends to talk to the patient." The explanations and talks are designed to make the patient comply with the hospital's (doctor's) wishes. Coercive sanctions include "putting a patient under sedation to keep him quiet and restricting the patient's activity . . ."[32]

When the communication patterns between hospital staff members and the patients are analyzed, it is found that there are more communication blockages under the more coercive system. These communication blockages are actually functional for the organizations. Julian states:

> Within the framework of this study, normative–coercive hospitals, which control and block patient activities to a greater extent than normative hospitals, restrict communication for coordinative purposes. In a more general way, normative–coercive organizations have more communication blocks because they are more effective for realizing the goal of control or coordination.[33]

---

[31] Joseph Julian, "Compliance Patterns and Communication Blocks in Complex Organizations," *American Sociological Research,* Vol. 31, No. 3 (June 1966), 382–89.

[32] *Ibid.,* p. 385.

[33] *Ibid.,* p. 386.

Another important finding from the Julian study is the fact that the hospitals varied not only in the *type* of control utilized, but also the *amount*. One of the general hospitals was larger than the others. In this hospital, more coercive sanctions were employed than in the other general hospitals,[34] and the overall amount of control exercised was also higher. At any one point in time, the amount of power is undoubtedly fixed, but over time and across organizations the amount varies.

In our discussion thus far, we have been concerned with the power relationships between upper and lower participants in organizations—the vertical dimension of power. As indicated earlier, these relationships can occur at any point in the vertical structure of an organization. That is, vertical power can be found between a president and the vice-presidents of a university, as well as between faculty and students. Much of this relationship involves the way in which a superior interacts with his subordinates. The behavior and attitudes of both parties in a vertical relationship have been a primary focus of studies of "leadership" or management "styles," and will be dealt with in the next chapter.

HORIZONTAL POWER RELATIONSHIPS

The vertical dimension is only one part of power relationships in organizations. Power relationships between individuals and units horizontal to each other are another important, but less systematically studied, component of total power systems. Interdepartmental, staff–line, and professional–organizational relationships are all familiar loci of the horizontal dimension.

Before we look at some of the research in this area, an apparent contradiction must be clarified. The term "horizontal power relationships" seems to represent an inconceivable situation. If the parties in the relationship have exactly equal amounts of power, then as soon as one gains power at the expense of the other, a vertical element is introduced. But the concern here is with relationships among units and persons who have positions relative to each other that are basically lateral. In these lateral relationships, the power variable can become a major part of the total relationship. It is conceivable that power will not enter the relationship if the parties have no reason to attempt to influence each other's behavior. However, the power variable would almost inevitably

34 One of the other general hospitals was a university hospital. This makes it somewhat different from the typical general hospital, but for the purposes here it can be grouped with general hospitals.

enter such relationships when issues such as budgetary allocations, output quotas, priorities for personnel, and other such matters come into the picture.

While some would claim that power is the basis for all social relationships, this is not the position taken here. Let us rather say that there is a potential for power to enter all relationships. The research to be discussed focuses on these horizontal power relationships. The fact that particular relationships are clearly arenas of power and others do not receive attention demonstrates the variable nature of power. While potentially present, it does not enter every situation.

Staff–Line Relationships

Horizontal or lateral power relationships have been carefully analyzed by Melville Dalton.[35] Perhaps his best-known contribution is the analysis of staff–line conflict. (The staff is roughly equivalent to what has been called the supportive or administrative component in earlier discussions, while the line in this case is engaged in the production-output activities of the organization.) Dalton found that these personnel were in rather constant conflict in several areas. The staff personnel tend to be younger, have more formal education, be more concerned with proper dress and manners, and be more theoretically oriented than the line managers in the organizations studied. This is a basis for conflict, but it is also part of the power relationship. The power aspect, aside from its importance in actual conflict situations, comes in when the staff attempts to get some of its ideas implemented (expert power).

Power is also exerted in terms of the personal ambitions of the people involved. Dalton assumes that both sets of managers seek income, promotions, power in the organization, and so on. In the organizations studied, the line personnel held the power in controlling the promotion process; but at the same time, they feared that the staff might come up with ideas that would put the line's modes of operations under serious scrutiny as being outmoded or unimaginative. In this instance we have an example of two different forms of power as a part of one power relationship. The outcome is a series of conflicts between line and staff that, viewed from outside the organization, are costly to the organization. There is a fairly high turnover among staff personnel, who apparently feel that they are not getting anywhere in the organization. The staff resents the line, and vice versa.

In order to accomplish anything, the staff must secure some coopera-

---

[35] Melville Dalton, *Men Who Manage* (New York: John Wiley & Sons, Inc., 1959), pp. 71–109.

tion from the line. This requires giving in to the line by moderating proposals, overlooking practices that do not correspond to rigid technical standards, and in general playing a rather subservient role in dealing with the line. If this is not done, the staff's suggestions would probably go unheeded. This in turn would make their output zero for the time period, and their general relevance for the organization would then be questioned.[36] This, of course, is not a unique situation. The exact extent of such conflicts and conditions under which they occur are unfortunately not clear, since Dalton had a small sample of manufacturing organizations only. But that this sort of phenomenon is a major component of traditional manufacturing firms and that variations of the patterns described are found in every organization does seem to be generally accepted.

Professional-Organizational Relationships

The analysis of staff–line relationships has been largely replaced in recent years by a concern with professional–organizational relationships. These are usually expressed in terms of conflict, as we noted in Chapter 6. The power components of this type of relationship are similar in many ways to the staff–line conflicts discussed by Dalton. A major difference would appear to be that the organizational members with whom the professionals interact, while not professionals in the traditional sense, are usually not poorly educated people who have come up through the ranks. The modern executive is also well educated and is likely to show the same kinds of interest in general social values as the professional.[37]

It is commonly noted in discussions of professionals in organizations that the "reward" power system for them is more complicated than for other organization members.[38] The professional typically desires the same kinds of rewards as other people, in terms of money and other extrinsic factors, but he is also likely to want recognition from his fellow professionals as a good lawyer, scientist, or whatever. In addition to this, evaluation of his work is difficult for someone not in the profession himself, and yet it is likely to be made by personnel who are not familiar

---

36 *Ibid.,* pp. 104–10.

37 See Renato Tagiuri, "Value Orientations and the Relationship of Managers and Scientists," *Administrative Science Quarterly,* Vol. 10, No. 1 (June 1965), 39–51.

38 For extended discussions of these points see William Kornhauser, *Scientists in Industry* (Berkeley: University of California Press, 1963); *Administrative Science Quarterly,* Vol. 10, No. 1 (June 1965), entire issue; and Howard M. Vollmer and Donald L. Mills, eds., *Professionalization* (Englewood Cliffs, N.J.: Prentice-Hall, Inc., 1966), Chapter 8.

with his special area of competence. This is true in many cases even if the evaluator, in an administrative position, is a member of the same profession. For example, a research scientist in an organization is likely to be under the supervision of another scientist who has been promoted to research administration. The very fact that the latter is now working in administration prevents him from keeping up with his scientific discipline, since developments occur rapidly and it is difficult even for the practicing scientist to keep abreast of what is occurring in his field.

Since the organization must in some way control all its members, the issue becomes very difficult with respect to the professional. If it tries to exert legitimate control through the hierarchy, the professional is apt to resist it. If it turns over the control of the professional to other professionals, the organization not only loses control, but is uncertain as to whether the professionals involved are contributing to the organization exactly what the organization thinks they should. This dilemma is frequently resolved by allowing the professionals to control themselves, with a fellow professional (for example, the research administrator) held accountable for the work of his unit as a collectivity. This allows the professional to work in a situation of less direct scrutiny, but provides the organization with a system of accountability.

The reward system in these situations is also frequently altered. Instead of promoting a professional by moving him higher in the administrative system, organizations are developing "dual ladders" for their promotion system, whereby professionals can advance either by being promoted in the traditional way or by staying in their professional unit and with their work, but at increasingly higher salaries.[39] Additional rewards for the professional can come through publication and participation in the affairs of his profession. Organizations can also provide these kinds of incentives. As the professional becomes better known in his field, his own power increases. At the same time, the organization continues to have power over him, by providing the reward system as a whole.

This discussion has involved ways in which the power issue may be resolved. But obviously, in many cases the issues are not resolved and the professional is in conflict with the rest of the organization. He may feel that the organization is intruding into his work through unnecessary rules and regulations, or that this contributions are receiving insufficient attention and reward. The members of the organization in contact with the professional, on the other hand, may view him as hopelessly impractical and out of touch with what is really important for the

---

[39] For a criticism of this technique, see Chris Argyris, "On the Effectiveness of Research and Development Organizations," *American Scientist*, Vol. 56, No. 4 (1969), 344–55.

organization. These lateral power relationships will probably increase, as professionals and professionalizing occupations are becoming increasingly important to organizations of every variety.

Another form of lateral power relationship that would often involve professionals is in the area of expertise. Since there is no one universal organizational or societal truth system, experts can take differing views on what is good, rational, legal, or effective for the organization. When the perspectives of accountants, lawyers, research scientists, management consultants, and executives are combined, it is extremely unlikely that a common viewpoint will emerge even after serious discussions. As the level of training and expertise increases in organizations, such differences will probably increase, also, and so the power of expertise may well become a greater source of conflict for organizations.

CLIQUES.   A different view of lateral power relationships is provided by Dalton, in his analysis of the formation and interaction of cliques in industrial organizations.[40] Dalton shows that personal self-interest can take the form of clique formation across organizational lines. Cliques can form vertically as well as horizontally, of course. In either case, coalitions are formed for the purpose of gaining something for the members involved. "Horizontal defensive" cliques, for example, develop when members of an organization at the same level band together in the face of real or imagined threats to their security by automation or reorganization. The "horizontal aggressive" clique is formed to accomplish a purpose—perhaps to halt the expansion of a staff or professional department that is seen as usurping some of the power of the members of the clique. Dalton's analysis shows that organizations are constantly filled with interpersonal power situations as events and conditions shift over time. These power relationships do not necessarily, and in fact usually do not, follow the established organizational hierarchical or horizontal system.

Dalton's analysis tends to lead one to view organizations as a "bewildering mosaic of swiftly changing and conflicting cliques, which cut across departmental and traditional loyalties. . . ."[41] While this view is warranted as a check on an overformalistic view of organizations, it is an overreaction. Cliques would not form unless there were a common base for interaction or if the members were not already in interaction. Rather than being random, clique formation obviously begins from the established organizational order and then becomes variations from that order. The fact that these cliques can form vertically or

[40] Dalton, *Men Who Manage*, pp. 57–65.
[41] Nicos P. Mouzelis, *Organization and Bureaucracy* (Chicago: Aldine Publishing Company, 1968), p. 159.

horizontally and represent personal and subunit interests reflects the constant interplay of the power variables within the organization.

Uncertainty and Dependency

Crozier's analysis of the French organizations gives another view of conflict along the horizontal dimension. Departments in the tobacco firms were in a constant power struggle, with the maintenance men holding the most power because of their knowledge in repairing the equipment necessary to the production process. Production workers and their supervisors were essentially helpless unless the maintenance personnel performed their work. This, of course, gave the maintenance men a great deal of power in the organization. Crozier states:

> With machine stoppages, a general uncertainty about what will happen next develops in a world totally dominated by the value of security. It is not surprising, therefore, that the behavior of the maintenance man—the man who alone can handle the situation, and who by preventing these unpleasant consequences gives workers the necessary security—has a tremendous importance for production workers, and that they try to please him and he to influence them.[42]

In analyzing this situation, Nicos Mouzelis notes:

> The strategy consists in the manipulation of rules as means of enhancing group prerogatives and independence from every direct and arbitrary interference from those higher up. But as rules can never regulate everything and eliminate all arbitrariness, areas of uncertainty always emerge which constitute the focal structural points around which collective conflicts become acute and instances of direct dominance and subordination re-emerge. In such cases the group which by its position in the occupational structure can control the unregulated area has a great strategic advantage which is naturally used in order to improve its power position and ensure a greater share of the organizational rewards.[43]

This is a vivid example of the dependence relationship inherent in a power situation. If it were not for the essential expertise of the maintenance men in this situation, the production workers would not be so dependent. Although the Crozier study is perhaps an extreme case, it does illustrate how lateral relationships can become built around the power of the parties involved.

[42] Michel Crozier, *The Bureaucratic Phenomenon* (Chicago: University of Chicago Press, 1964), p. 109.
[43] Mouzelis, *Organization and Bureaucracy,* p. 160.

Additional insights into this kind of power relationship are provided by Perrow, in a study directly concerned with the power of different departments in organizations.[44] Using data from twelve industrial firms based on answers to the question, "Which group has the most power?" Perrow found that the firms were overwhelmingly dominated by their sales departments. This domination is shown in figure 7–1. Although

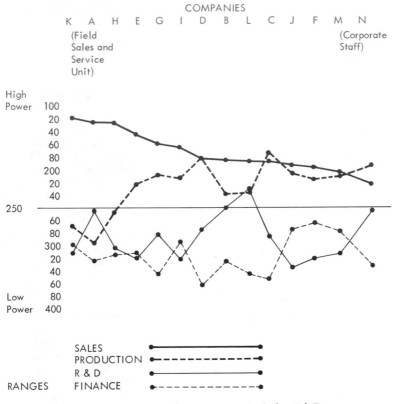

FIG. 7–1   Overall Power of Departments in Industrial Firms
(Means of Departmental Means)

Source: Charles Perrow, "Departmental Power and Perspective in Industrial Firms," in Mayer N. Zald, ed., Power in Organizations *(Nashville, Tenn.: Vanderbilt University Press, 1970), p. 64.*

he does not have direct evidence, Perrow believes that this would be the case in most industrial firms in the United States.

Since manufacturing firms must sell their products, and since customers (institutional or individual) "determine the cost, quality, and

44 Perrow, "Departmental Power."

type of goods that will be produced and distributed," [45] the customer determines organizational success. While all departments in the organization contribute to customer satisfaction, it is sales that has the most direct contact with this important group.

> . . . sales is the main gate between the organization and the customer. As gatekeeper, it determines how important will be prompt delivery, quality, product-improvement, or new products, and the cost at which goods can be sold. Sales determines the relative importance of these variables for the other groups and indicates the values which these variables will take. It has the ability, in addition, of changing the values of these variables, since it sets pricing (and in most firms adjusts it temporarily to meet changes in opportunity and competition), determines which markets will be utilized, the services that will be provided, and the changes in products that must be made. As the link between the customer and producer, it absorbs most of the uncertainty about the diffuse and changing environment of customers.[46]

Perrow then gets on to generalize that the most critical function in an organization tends to have the most power, linking his analysis to Crozier's. He notes that in the one firm that was production-dominated, the production department was able to get control of the computer and inventory and purchasing. It was in a position to tell the sales department what could or could not be done under existing conditions. These same functions could be handled in the finance department, as was the case in another firm, with finance passing the information along to sales, thus giving sales power over production. The combination of critical function and dependence gives sales its power position in these organizations.[47]

Horizontal Power Distribution

Horizontal or lateral power relationships have thus far been approached through studies indicating the unplanned but natural growth of power differentials and coalitions among organizational subunits. As in the case of the vertical forms of power relationships, lateral patterns can also be established by the organization itself. It can decide to centralize or decentralize the holding of legitimate forms of power. When power is decentralized, it is distributed among the various units of an

---

45 *Ibid.*, p. 65.

46 *Ibid.*

47 These findings are similar, except in terms of who holds the power, to those of Paul R. Lawrence and Jay W. Lorsch, *Organization and Environment: Managing Differentiation and Integration* (Cambridge: Harvard Graduate School of Business Administration, 1967).

organization on the basis of the organization's own discretion in the matter. It is evident that decentralization can also have a vertical dimension when power operations are passed *down* to lower levels in the organization. This is probably more accurately labeled the delegation of power. Decentralization as used here is the power given to organizational subunits (departments or separate operating units) that could be retained by the central organization hierarchy at the same level as the subunits to which it is distributed.

Blau's research provides an excellent example of some of the issues involved in this form of lateral power distribution.[48] The data are from employment security agencies (public personnel agencies) in the United States. Blau was concerned with the patterns of decentralization within the state headquarters of these agencies, as well as to the managers of local offices distributed throughout each state. An important finding is that "delegation of responsibilities to the managers of local offices is apparently not related to delegation of responsibilities within the state headquarters."[49] In the terms we are using here, power can be delegated within the state headquarters, as lower ranks are authorized to carry out hiring responsibilities, budget preparation, or policy changes. At the same time, these areas and others can be decentralized out from the main headquarters to the organizational units in the field.

Several factors are associated with delegation and decentralization. A primary one is the use of merit standards of civil service and the formalization of personnel procedures. While these appear on the one hand to increase the rigidity of the organization, on the other hand they allow increased flexibility and discretion, in that reliability of performance is increased. The organization decreases its risks in decentralizing by ensuring that those to whom power is decentralized meet at least minimal competence standards. "The better qualified the employees, the greater reliance management can place in the performance of their duties."[50] Another factor related to the distribution of power throughout the organization was the amount of automation present in the organization. Automation serves as an impersonal mechanism of control, since the performance of personnel must comply with the computer system in operation. The risks of delegation and decentralization are thus further minimized with these procedures.

Blau suggests that as the number of exceptional issues or cases increases, personnel standards should be modified to ensure that qualified personnel are present to handle increasingly complicated tasks. This

---

[48] Peter M. Blau, "Decentralization in Bureaucracies," in Zald, *Power Organizations,* pp. 150–74.

[49] *Ibid.,* p. 156.

[50] *Ibid.,* p. 161.

implies that increasing the rigidity in one phase of an organization's operations may actually encourage flexibility in others.

As might be expected, organizational size is also found to be related to the extent of decentralization and delegation. Increasing size apparently makes it impossible for those at the top of an organization to cope with the greater import of the decisions that must be made and at the same time to encompass all the relevant information into the decision-making process. While the importance of decisions increases, leading to a tendency to retain power, the impossibility of doing everything makes distributing the power more attractive. Increasing the control through more formalization of personnel procedures and automation appears to be the typical way out of this dilemma.

Many of the basic issues regarding decentralization were discussed in Chapter 5, when the various combinations of horizontal and vertical forms of complexity were compared. As was indicated in that section (pp. 164–69), the organizationally optimal form of complexity is linked to the tasks the organization is performing. Since the decentralization of power is linked so closely to the structural arrangements, the same generalizations probably hold true. When the tasks to be performed involve and require the commitment of the members of the organization, delegation and decentralization are probably effective devices. The effectiveness, however, depends upon the degree of competence the personnel in question bring to their tasks. As Blau's study indicates, when the quality of the personnel can be assured, decentralization and delegation can probably operate well. Without this assurance, they become more risky. Decentralization is not the organizational panacea.

LOWER PARTICIPANTS

We have focused on vertical and horizontal components of power relationships in organizations. Before attempting to bring together the findings of the studies examined and developing an overview of power, a final form of the power relationship should be examined. This type is organizationally strange, but anyone who has had any contact with an organization has confronted it from time to time. The power of "lower participants" in organizations can be a source of both frustration and wonder; secretaries are capable of causing extreme frustration and embarrassment, among other things, for their bosses, and hospital attendants can in some cases make physicians dependent upon them.[51]

[51] Thomas J. Scheff, "Control over Policy by Attendants in a Mental Hospital," *Journal of Health and Human Behavior,* 2 (1961), 93–105.

David Mechanic has identified some of the sources of power of lower participants.[52] As we shall see, these are not too different from the general sources of power that have been discussed in the earlier sections. What is different is that the lower members of organizations are able to amass the resources that a purely structural analysis would suggest should not be theirs. The first source of power is expertise coupled with the difficulty of replacing the person in question. The maintenance men in Crozier's study had this form of power over the managers in the tobacco industry. Another example is a person in a clerical position who gains power by being the only one in an organization who knows how to perform a particular operation. This person thus becomes indispensable, with all work having to go through his hands. In some cases, patterns of personal likes and dislikes can make or break another person in the organization who ostensibly has a higher position; for example, requests for information can be conveniently "lost."

A second source of power is the amount of effort and interest expressed on the job. Mechanic notes the example of university departmental secretaries who can have "power to make decisions about the purchase and allocation of supplies, the allocation of their services, the scheduling of classes, and, at times, the disposition of student complaints. Such control may in some instances lead to sanctions against a professor by polite reluctance to furnish supplies, ignoring his preferences for the scheduling of classes, and giving others preference in the allocation of services." [53] Removal of this power from secretaries itself involves the expenditure of time and effort. A departmental chairman is unlikely to come down hard on a trusted secretary, whereas he might with younger or disfavored faculty.

There are several other factors associated with lower participants' power. One is the attractiveness of the individual involved; personal or physical attractiveness can lead to relationships that are outside the organization's (or individual's) intent. Physical location and position within an organization can make one person more critical than another; a major information processor can have strong control over those who are dependent on him for accurate information. Coalitions among lower participants can also increase their power. Rules themselves can provide a source of power, in that strict adherence to a highly formalized rules system can hold up operations in the organization. A supervisor cannot really criticize his subordinates if they point out to him that they are following the letter of the law.

[52] David Mechanic, "Sources of Power of Lower Participants in Complex Organizations," *Administrative Science Quarterly*, Vol. 7, No. 3 (December 1962), 349–64.

[53] *Ibid.*, p. 359.

These sources of power of lower participants are close to the earlier discussion of the French–Raven and Etzioni conceptualizations. The importance of the Mechanic discussion lies not so much in pointing out that lower participants can and do have power in organizations, but rather in indicating that the forms of power in these instances are not very different from what is organizationally based and intended. Power in organizations exists in several "directions" and in multiple forms. That it is important should be evident from the discussion thus far. The next task is to try to bring these various findings together into some kind of coherent overview of organizational power.

A PERSPECTIVE ON POWER IN ORGANIZATIONS

Amount of Power

The first point to be made here is a quantitative one, concerning the amount of power in an organization. This would appear to be a rather simple issue, since someone in a management position has a specified amount of power over a person beneath him. The matter is not that simple, however, when the presence of multiple bases of power is considered. C. J. Lammers deals with this issue when he states, "To sum up, managers and managed in organizations at the same time come to influence each other more effectively and thereby generate joint power as the outcome of a better command by the organization over its technological, economic, and human resources in the service of certain objectives." [54] Lammers assumes that the members are seeking the same basic goals. This joint influence is actually a condition of more power in the organization than was the case before mutual influence entered the picture. If the French and Raven classification of power bases is utilized, it is obvious that the amount of power in an organization, as well as in a single interpersonal situation, is a variable. The amount of power in an organization changes over time. [55]

In summarizing a series of studies on the amount of power in organizations, Arnold Tannenbaum notes that the expansion of power

. . . may occur under either of two classes of conditions. The first is that of an external expansion of power into the organization's environment. The

[54] C. J. Lammers, "Power and Participation in Decision Making," *American Journal of Sociology,* Vol. 73, No. 2 (September 1967), 204.
[55] Although most discussions deal with increases in the amount of power in a system, it is entirely plausible that the amount could also decrease.

second concerns a number of internal conditions that subsume: (1) structural conditions expediting interaction and influence among members, and (2) motivational conditions implying increased interest by members in exercising control and a greater amenability by members to being controlled. These conditions may sometimes be related. For example, extending control by the organization into its environment may bring more decisions within the purview of the organization that are subject to the control of its members, thus increasing the possibility of a greater total amount of control. At the same time such increased opportunities to exercise control within the organization may increase the members' involvement in and identification with the organization and hence increase their interest in exercising control and their amenability to being controlled. Members, then, as possible control agents, engage in more frequent influence attempts, and as possible objects of control, provide new opportunities to one another to exercise control. Thus external developments may affect social and psychological processes within the organization conducive to a high level of internal control, just as conditions of a high level of involvement by members and of a high level of control within the organization may contribute to the strength of the organization and hence to its power in the environment. . . .[56]

This view of power as varying in the amount present in organizations has to be approached with some caution. First of all, the amount of power is not something that varies dramatically from situation to situation. The kinds of factors leading to an increase or decrease would typically not be rapid or sudden in their impact. An exception here would be the case of something like a disaster, in which the change in the amount of power in the organization could be very dramatic. Generally, however, changes in the amount of power will be gradual. A second caution is that at any one point in time the amount of power in an organization is fixed—a zero-sum game. If one person or group gains in power, another loses. Power acts are carried out within a fixed-amount framework. It is the framework that is altered over time.

The Distribution of Power

When the focus is shifted from the amount of power to the reasons *why* power is distributed as it is, several points stand out. The ability to cope with uncertainty leads to power differentials.[57] The less specific a person's role or the greater the uncertainty, the greater the power of the individual (or unit) involved.[58] The more central the function

---

[56] Arnold S. Tannenbaum, *Control in Organizations* (New York: McGraw-Hill Book Company, 1968), pp. 14–15.

[57] D. J. Hickson, C. R. Hinings, C. A. Lee, R. E. Schneck, and J. M. Pennings, "A Strategic Contingencies' Theory of Power" (unpublished paper, University of Alberta, Edmonton, Canada, 1969).

[58] Dennis J. Palumbo, "Power and Role Specificity in Organization Theory," *Public Administration Review*, Vol. 29, No. 3 (May/June 1969), 237–48.

for the organization, the more power the person or unit will have. If a person or unit is difficult to replace, more power will be present. These arguments are similar to analyses of the power in the wider society; at the same time, they suggest the factors that would be associated with alterations in the power distribution. Conditions change; thus the centrality, uncertainty, and ease of replacement will also change.

As Robert Michels reminds us, power has a self-perpetuating aspect.[59] Thus, those in power in an organization tend to remain in power. They have resources, and the power recipients do not. The very fact that legitimacy is such an important consideration in organizational power arrangements sets the stage for the perpetuation of existing power distributions.

Most of the discussion of power in organizations has been concerned with the manner in which an individual or unit is able to control the behavior of others in the organization. The emphasis has been on the idea that power is not a static phenomenon, even with the same personnel involved. But the issue becomes more complicated if problems of succession of personnel at all levels are considered. Studies by Alvin Gouldner, Robert Guest, and Oscar Grusky have indicated that changes in the top management can have important repercussions for the total organization, particularly when the new leader tries to utilize a different power basis than did his predecessor.[60] The turnover of personnel also contributes to the instability of power relationships.

The distribution of power in organizations has ramifications beyond those already discussed. The distribution of resources within an organization, including rewards, budget items, and personnel, is affected by the power system.[61] Since the allocation system is affected by the existing power system, it tends to perpetuate the existing system. Zald points out that the accounting and information systems within organizations are important agents of power; they determine the emphasis given to particular kinds of activities and the information that is available to various members of the organization. Zald also notes that the nature of the incentive system within the organization is an important power consideration, since it provides the basis, both in nature and extent, on which rewards are distributed.

[59] Robert Michels, *Political Parties* (New York: Thomas Y. Crowell Company, 1962).

[60] Alvin Gouldner, *Patterns of Industrial Bureaucracy* (New York: The Free Press, 1954); Robert Guest, "Managerial Succession in Complex Organizations," *American Journal of Sociology*, Vol. 68, No. 1 (July 1962), 47–54; and Oscar Grusky, "Corporate Size, Bureaucratization, and Managerial Succession," *American Journal of Sociology*, Vol. 67, No. 3 (November 1961), 355–59.

[61] See Mayer N. Zald, "Political Economy: A Framework for Comparative Analysis," and Louis R. Pondy, "Toward a Theory of Internal Resource Allocation," in Zald, ed., *Power in Organizations*, pp. 221–61 and 270–311.

External Factors

The focus of our discussion has been primarily on factors internal to the organization. Zald points out that external considerations also play an important role in the power system of the organization.[62] Here, factors such as associations of similar organizations (trade associations or baseball leagues), relationships with suppliers and users of the organization's output, regulatory agencies, and other indirectly involved parties affect the amount and distribution of power within the organization. An example of this is provided by Richard Peterson, who notes that the National Labor Relations Board, after its establishment in the 1930s facilitated the growth in power of labor unions. At the same time, the increasing complexity of labor laws and regulations led to the development of specialists in labor relations, and these personnel also gained in power in the organization, largely as a consequence of these external factors.[63] External economic conditions also affect the power system in organizations as markets for labor and outputs shift, the source of "raw materials" is altered, and the nature of the organization's clientele varies.

Power in Voluntary Organizations

This analysis appears to be applicable to all organizations. But before we conclude this section, a brief consideration of power in voluntary organizations is in order. Voluntary organizations have all the characteristics of other organizations in regard to the nature and importance of power as an internal process. They are somewhat different, however, because of the apparent need for membership participation in order for the organization to remain viable. Most analyses point to the cruciality of the democratic process for voluntary organizations, since this form of power determination tends to assure continued participation. John Craig and Edward Gross suggest that in addition, voluntary organizations must remain permeable to new ideas and interests if democracy is to be maintained.[64] This permeability assures continued participation by maintaining membership interest in issues that are new and around

---

62 Zald, "Political Economy," pp. 229–36.

63 Richard A. Peterson, "Some Consequences of Differentiation," in Zald, ed., *Power in Organizations,* p. 146.

64 John G. Craig and Edward Gross, "The Forum Theory of Organizational Democracy: Structural Guarantees as Time Related Variables," *American Sociological Review,* Vol. 35, No. 1 (February 1970), 19–33.

which power can cluster, thus preventing the tendency toward oligarchy. Maintaining membership involvement is crucial for such organizations. From most of the evidence, it is apparent that this involves distributing some form of power among all the organizational participants, regardless of the power form and other considerations.

This last point about voluntary organizations raises another issue, which has been implicit in the total discussion. As in the case of organizational structural arrangements, it is apparent that there is no one optimal power arrangement for organizations in terms of performance and effectiveness. The kinds of considerations stressed in the earlier discussion are also relevant here. *The nature of the personnel of the organization, its task, and the general technological–environmental conditions appear to be the key determinants of the form of power most appropriate for various kinds of organizations.*

This discussion concerning the nature and consequences of power relationships in organizations has intentionally omitted, except by inference, the link between power and conflict. The reason for this omission is that while power often leads to conflict, the existence of power relationships does not inevitably lead to conflict situations. In those cases where power is viewed as legitimate (referent, expert, or legitimate), conflict is not usually part of the picture, since the power recipient feels that his own interests coincide with those of the power holder. If the power base shifts or the basis for legitimacy is altered, then, of course, conflict is a distinct possibility. Regardless of this limitation, conflict is an evident part of organizational life and as such is a vital process.

CONFLICT IN ORGANIZATIONS

Many of the important forms of conflict within organizations are already well known to anyone concerned with organizations or the society in general. Labor–management conflict is a prominent part of our social heritage, as well as of organizational life. The existence of professional–organizational and staff–line conflicts has already been amply discussed. Many of the power relationships described in the previous section are also conflict situations.

In this section, the purpose will be to analyze conflict in organizations by examining its bases, forms, and consequences. (The analysis will focus on conflict *within* organizations; conflict between organizations and those between organizations and the wider society will be handled in the last section of the book.) The focus will be on the analysis, rather than on providing detailed examples. Most such examples are well known, and most also can be extrapolated from the discussions of power. As in the case of power, there have been relatively few empirical studies of conflict that are more than ex post facto case studies.

Conflict in organizations involves more than simple interpersonal conflict. (Not that interpersonal conflict is necessarily simple, given the complexities of the human personality, but for our purposes it is only part of the picture.) The psychologist Nevitt Sanford makes this point in a historical perspective when he states, "Twenty years ago, it seemed easy to account for organizational conflict by blaming the problem behavior of individuals. But the simple formula, 'trouble is due to trouble-makers,' is unfortunately inadequate in the light of our present knowledge of the social process." [65] The inadequacy of the individualized approach to conflict is based on the fact that organizational considerations and the very nature of organizations themselves contribute to conflict situations.

Bases of Conflict

Another psychologist, Daniel Katz, has identified three organizational bases of conflict. The first is "functional conflict induced by various subsystems within the organizations." [66] This form of conflict involves the fact that:

> Every subsystem of an organization with its distinctive functions develops its own norms and values and is characterized by its own dynamics. People in the maintenance subsystem have the problem of maintaining the role system and preserving the character of the organization through selection of appropriate personnel, indoctrinating and training them, devising checks for ensuring standard role performance, and so on. These people face *inward* in the organization and are concerned with maintaining the *status quo*. People in the procurement and disposal subsystems, however, face *outward* on the world and develop a different psychological orientation. These differing orientations are one built-in source of conflict. Put in another way, the systems of maintenance, production, and adaptive development each develop their own distinctive norms and frames of reference which contain their own elements of potential conflict.[67]

Although the focus is on the psychological states of the members of the organizations, the point is important, since different subunits in

---

[65] R. Nevitt Sanford, "Individual Conflict and Organizational Interaction," in Kahn and Boulding, eds., *Power and Conflict in Organizations*, p. 95.

[66] Daniel Katz, "Approaches to Managing Conflict," in Kahn and Boulding, *Power and Conflict*, p. 105.

[67] *Ibid.*, pp. 105–6.

organizations perform tasks that come into conflict because they are basically incompatible.

The second source of conflict is the fact that units have similar functions. Conflict here can take the form of "hostile rivalry or good-natured competition. . . ." [68] Such competition can be beneficial, but it can also be destructive. The final form of organizationally based conflict is "hierarchical conflict stemming from interest-group struggles over the organizational rewards of status, prestige, and monetary reward." [69] Since less than total satisfaction with the reward structure is common and subgroups develop with their own communication systems and norms, it is normal that lower-level personnel "try to improve their lot by joining forces as an interest group against the more privileged members of the organization." [70] Although one typically thinks of blue-collar workers and unions in this regard, the process would operate with white-collar workers and subgroups in the management hierarchy.

These organizationally based conflict situations are only part of the picture, of course, since the individual plays an important role here. Just as we cannot assume that the organization will always act rationally, there can be no assumption that individuals will not "depart from rational, reality-based behavior in their individual struggles against one another or in their participation in group struggles." [71] This is a very complicated situation to analyze, since what may seem to be an organizationally based conflict situation may actually be the outcome of individual deviation. The opposite is also possible, of course; what appears to be conflict between individuals may actually be based on their organizational positions.

The Conflict Situation

We have been looking at the bases of and parties in conflict situations. A more complete view includes these components, but adds the conflict process itself and the aftermath. Kenneth Boulding has provided a framework for a composite view of the total conflict situation.[72] He suggests that there are four components in the process. First are the parties involved. Conflict must involve at least two parties—individuals, groups, or organizations. Hypothetically, therefore, there can be nine

68 *Ibid.,* p. 106.
69 *Ibid.*
70 *Ibid.*
71 *Ibid.,* pp. 106–7.
72 Kenneth E. Boulding, "A Pure Theory of Conflict Applied to Organizations," in Kahn and Boulding, *Power and Conflict,* pp. 136–45.

types of conflict—person–person, person–group, and so on. Boulding suggests that there is a tendency for symmetry in these relationships, in that person– or group–organizational conflict tends to move toward organizational–organizational conflict. This is based on the power differentials that are likely to exist between these different levels in the organization.

Boulding then identifies the "field of conflict" as the next component in his framework. This is defined as "the whole set of relevant possible states of the social system. (Any state of the social system which either of the parties to a conflict considers relevant is, of course, a relevant state.)" [73] What Boulding is referring to here are the alternative conditions toward which a conflict could move. If the parties in a conflict have a particular power relationship with one another, with one having more power than the other, the field of conflict involves a continuation of the present state, plus all the alternative conditions. These alternatives include both parties' gaining or losing power or one's gaining at the expense of the other. This concept is indicative of the processual nature of conflict, in that the parties in the situation will seldom retain the same position in relation to one another after the conflict is resolved or continued. The field of conflict includes the directions of the movement as the process occurs.

The third component is the dynamics of the conflict situation. This refers to the fact that each party in a conflict will adjust its own position to one that it feels is congruent with that of its opponent. If one of the parties becomes more militant, the other will probably do the same. This assumes, of course, that the power available to the two parties is at least moderately comparable. A nonorganizational example of the dynamics can be found in international relations, where nations will intensify their own conflict efforts in anticipation of or reaction to their opponents' moves. This can escalate into all-out war and eventually total destruction, or can stabilize at some point along the way. The same phenomenon occurs in organizations, with the equivalent of all-out war in the case of labor–management conflicts that end in the dissolution of the company involved. The dynamic nature of conflict can be seen in the fact that there is an increase and decrease in the intensity of a conflict during its course. While the field of conflict may remain the same, the energies devoted to it vary over time.

The final element in the Boulding model is the "management, control, or resolution of conflict." [74] The terms used suggest that conflict situations are generally not discrete situations with a clear beginning

[73] *Ibid.*, p. 138.
[74] *Ibid.*, p. 142.

and end. They obviously emerge out of preexisting situations and do not end forever with a strike settlement or lowering of the intensity of the conflict. Boulding notes that organizations attempt to prevent conflict from becoming "pathological" and thus destructive of the parties involved and the larger system. One form of conflict resolution is a unilateral move; according to Boulding, a good deal of conflict is resolved through the relatively simple mechanism of the "peaceableness" of one of the participants. While it relates primarily to interpersonal conflict, this idea can be utilized in the organizational setting. Peaceableness simply involves one of the parties' backing off from the conflict. The other party reacts to this in most cases by also backing off, even if he would prefer to continue, and the conflict is at least temporarily resolved. This kind of resolution is seen in labor–management disputes when one of the parties finally decides to concede on some points that were formerly "nonnegotiable."

Reliance upon peaceableness is potentially dangerous, however, because the parties just may not exhibit this kind of behavior. For the peaceable party itself, this strategy has danger if the opponent is operating pathologically or irrationally to any degree. For this reason, organizations develop mechanisms to resolve or control conflict. One technique here is to placate the parties involved by offering them both some form of "side payment" as an inducement to stop the conflict—for example, in the case of professional–organizational conflict, where the professionals are given concessions in the form of relaxing some organizational rules they feel to be excessively burdensome.

Unfortunately, research in this area has not indicated what reactions the rest of the organization has to conflicts with professional units. It is possible that such conflicts are resolved simply by concessions to the professionals, and a realistic view would suggest that something has to be done for the other members of the organization also, since they often resent the greater freedom given to the professionals. Even though the professionals are sometimes physically separated from the rest of the organization in an attempt to minimize comparisons and distinctions between the groups involved, it would seem that increasing benefits for the professional group would lead to a demand from the nonprofessionals for comparable concessions. These could take the form of increases in the rewards offered or greater likelihood of moving up in the organizational hierarchy.

Conflicts in organizations can also be resolved through the offices of a third party. The third party might be a larger organization that simply orders the conflict behavior to cease under the threat of penalties—as in the case of governmental actions to prohibit strikes and lockouts in a labor dispute that threatens the national interest—or might be a mediator. Since intraorganizational conflict takes place within a larger context, the organization can simply prohibit the conflicting behavior. This does not resolve the issues involved, but it reduces the intensity of the conflict behavior. Mediation can do the same, and can even lead to a complete resolution of the conflict by presenting new methods of solution that might not have occurred to the parties involved, or by presenting a solution that would not be acceptable unless it were presented by a third party.

The resolution of a conflict leads to a stage that Louis Pondy calls the aftermath.[75] This is a useful concept, in that conflict resolution does not lead to a condition of total settlement. If the basic issues are not resolved, the potentiality for future and perhaps more serious conflicts is part of the aftermath. If the conflict resolution leads to more open communications and cooperation among the participants, this too is part of the aftermath.[76] Since an organization does not operate in a vacuum, any successful conflict resolution in which the former combatants are now close allies is not guaranteed to last forever. Changes in the environment and altered conditions in the organization can lead to new conflict situations among the same parties or with others.

The contemporary view of conflict is that it is not inherently good or bad for the participants, the organization, or the wider society. Lawrence and Lorsch's research, for example, has indicated that conflict, where it is an integral part of the system and is managed effectively, can contribute to organizational effectiveness. Conflict has multiple bases and takes multiple forms. It also has multiple consequences for the organization. Our focus here has been on internal conflicts. Conflicts between the organization and its environment are also vital for organizations, as will be seen in Chapters 10 and 11. *Power and conflict are major shapers of the state of an organization. A given organizational state sets the stage for the continuing power and conflict processes, thus continually reshaping the organization.*

---

[75] Louis R. Pondy, "Organizational Conflict: Concepts and Models," *Administrative Science Quarterly*, Vol. 12, No. 2 (September 1967), 304. See also Louis Pondy, "Variations of Organizational Conflict," *Administrative Science Quarterly*, Vol. 14, No. 4 (December 1969), 499–505, for an additional categorization of the forms of conflict. This entire issue of *Administrative Science Quarterly* is devoted to organizational conflict of various types.

[76] Much of the thought on the consequences of conflict has been crystallized in the works of Lewis Coser. See Lewis A. Coser, *The Functions of Social Conflict* (New York: The Free Press, 1956), and *Continuities in the Study of Social Conflict* (New York: The Free Press, 1967). Coser notes that despite the attention paid to conflict in recent years, there has been little in the way of empirical research to show for all the attention (*Continuities*, pp. 7–8).

SUMMARY AND CONCLUSIONS

This chapter has attempted to identify and trace the consequences of power and conflict in organizations. Common sense suggests that these are important to the operations of any organization and that the lives and behavior of organizational members are vitally affected by their relative power positions. The discussion concluded that power is a reciprocal relational phenomenon between the parties involved and that each party is dependent on the other. The power relationships can be rigidly specified in advance or can develop as the relationship itself develops. This point reemphasizes the close connection between organizational structure and processes, since it is the structure that sets the original limits on the relationship.

Although power relationships are typically thought to be interpersonal, it has been pointed out that power differentials between organizational units are also important. Interunit power relationships usually take place along the lateral or horizontal axis in the organization. Vertical or hierarchical arrangements by definition involve a power component. Also on the vertical dimension, but not in an organizationally planned way, are the power bases developed by lower participants that allow them to exert power over those farther up the organizational hierarchy.

In addition to this directional aspect of power, we discussed the forms of power in and out of organizations. There is agreement that power in organizations does not take just one form—legitimate authority —and that extraorganizational considerations are important in power relationships. The empirical research reviewed provided additional insights into these relationships. From the outset it became apparent that most power relationships involve the use of more than one form of power. Because individuals and organizational units develop relationships over time, additional elements will almost surely be added to prestructured power arrangements.

The nature of the power system used in the organization has important consequences for the manner in which individuals attach themselves to the organization and for the more general issue of organizational effectiveness. If inappropriate power forms are used, the organization is likely to be less effective than it might otherwise be. Studies of power in organizations reiterate the dominant theme of this book—that organizational structure and processes are in constant and reciprocal inter-action. Power relationships develop out of and then alter existing structural arrangements.

In a broader look at power, it was emphasized that power is not a fixed sum in organizations. The amount of power in the system can increase or decrease. Although a power system is often established by the organization, the considerations discussed above regarding multiple forms of power and the reciprocity involved in the power relationship make a general growth in power almost inevitable.

It was also pointed out in this section that the power variable is vital in determining internal resource allocations. This fact leads to the con-clusion that power relationships in organizations tend to be stable, since the original allocation of resources will be an important determinant of future power relationships. The fact that external considerations affect the power distribution and relationships within an organization is a reaffirmation of the general systems approach that has been taken throughout. Organizational structure and processes are in interaction with the environment and organizational outputs affect the environ-ment, which then in turn becomes a potentially altered form of input.

The discussion of conflict in organizations was somewhat truncated because of the close relationship between this process and power, power being an important, even decisive, element in conflict. The identification of the various forms, stages, conditions, and consequences of conflict point up its endemic nature in organizations. To view organizations as entities in which conflict upsets the equilibrium is to avoid reality. Conflict is part of the normal state of an organization. The consequences of conflict are also normal, in that they are both organizationally and individually positive and negative.

In the next chapter, an issue related to power will be discussed. Leadership involves one or more of the forms of power discussed, since it can be exerted from a position of legitimate authority or expertise, or can develop as a form of referent power. We will analyze alternative forms of leadership and their consequences for the organization.

8

LEADERSHIP AND DECISION MAKING

How To Become A Leader, How To Become A Better Leader, and *Why I Was A Better Leader*—books and articles with such titles perennially lead the best-seller lists of organizational literature, and treatises on decision making come in a close second. There are reasons for this, of course. Personal gain is the primary factor, but leadership and effective decision making are assumed to be crucial for the organization as well.

This assumption will be the basis for the present chapter. We will examine the impact of leadership on the organization and the issue of leadership style. The conditions under which decision making becomes important for the organization and the factors that contribute to effective decision making will also be considered.

As in the past, the focus of the analysis will be on the organization. The individual is also important in this context, of course, since the individual in a leadership or decision-making position makes his own inputs into what he does. Although he is constrained by organizational and external factors, the individual supplies many inputs into these processes. There is some evidence suggesting that the higher a person is in the organizational hierarchy, the fewer such constraints he faces.[1] If this is the case, the input of the individual becomes that much more important.

There is a great deal of literature about leadership and decision making, but the forms it has taken reduce its usefulness for our purposes. The "better leader" material doesn't seem to do anyone much good, except the author. Research on these topics has been largely confined to relatively low levels in the hierarchy; few studies of top leaders are available that take the organization as their focus. The concentration on foremen and other first-line supervisors in leadership studies has generally ignored the fact that this is the organizational level in which constraints on the individual are the greatest. Attempts to improve the leadership abilities of the personnel will probably be largely fruitless, given the narrow range of discretion available.[2] With these caveats in mind, we can now turn to the subject matter itself, acknowledging the fact that much of the evidence to be discussed will have to be more indirect than we would like.

LEADERSHIP

Leadership is a special form of power. It is closely related to the "referent" form referred to in the previous chapter, since it involves, in Etzioni's words, ". . . the ability, based on the personal qualities of the leader, to elicit the followers' voluntary compliance in a broad range of matters. Leadership is distinguished from the concept of power in that it entails influence, i.e., change of preferences, while power implies only that subjects' preferences are held in abeyance." [3]

For our purposes, Etzioni's general definition, if not the specific distinction made, is extremely useful. The fact that the followers do in fact alter their preferences to coincide with those of the leader is an important consideration. The followers *want* to go along with the wishes of the leader. Alvin Gouldner takes essentially the same position when he states that the leader is "any individual whose behavior stimulates patterning of the behavior in some group." [4] The leader therefore is an influence on what the members of the group do and think.

1 Jean Fellows Welling, "Role and Norm Deviation" (unpublished M.A. thesis, University of Minnesota, 1969).

2 See Amitai Etzioni, "Dual Leadership in Complex Organizations," *American Sociological Review*, Vol. 30, No. 5 (October 1965), 688–98.

3 *Ibid.*, pp. 690–91.

4 Alvin Gouldner, in Alvin Gouldner, ed., *Studies in Leadership* (New York: Harper & Row, Publishers, 1950), p. 17.

Functions of Leadership

The differences between leadership and power are still insufficiently developed, however, since leadership can occur in any group at any level within the organization. Phillip Selznick provides the distinction we need when he notes that leadership involves *critical* decisions. It is more than group maintenance.[5] The critical tasks of leadership, according to Selznick, fall into four categories. The first involves the definition of the institutional (organizational) mission and role. This is obviously vital in a rapidly changing world and must be viewed as a dynamic process. The second task is the "institutional embodiment of purpose," which involves building the policy into the structure or deciding upon the means to achieve the ends desired. The third task is to defend the organization's integrity. Here, values and public relations intermix; the leader represents his organization to the public and to its own members as he tries to persuade them to follow his decisions. The final task is the ordering of internal conflict.[6]

Here again it must be pointed out, as Selznick does, that these functions can operate at all organizational levels. The position taken here is that *leadership can occur in any group or organizational situation.* For our purposes, however, most important for the organization is the leadership (or lack of leadership, in some cases) that occurs at the top of the organization. It is here that the tasks of the leader have the real impact on the organization, and it is here that our attention will be primarily focused.

One further set of distinctions should be made before we proceed with an analysis of leadership. Studies carried out in small-group laboratories have consistently found that leadership is actually a differentiated process, with *task* or *instrumental* activities rather clearly separated from *socio-emotional* or *expressive* activities.[7] Drawing on the work of Robert Bales and his associates, Etzioni develops a "dual leadership" approach to organizations, suggesting that in most cases leadership rests in the hands of more than one person, and that the demands of the two forms may conflict. Organizational demands will determine which form will

---

5 Phillip Selznick, *Leadership in Administration* (New York: Harper & Row, Publishers, 1957), p. 29.

6 *Ibid.,* pp. 62–63.

7 See for example, Robert F. Bales, "The Equilibrium Problem in Small Groups," in Talcott Parsons, Robert F. Bales, and Edward A. Shils, eds., *Working Papers in the Theory of Action* (New York: The Free Press, 1953), pp. 111–61; and Robert F. Bales and Phillip E. Slater, "Role Differentiation in Small Decision Making Groups," in Talcott Parsons and Robert F. Bales, eds., *Family Socialization and Interaction Processes* (New York: The Free Press, 1955), pp. 259–306.

be successful, with socio-emotional more effective in normative organizations and task in instrumental organizations. Etzioni concludes that, at least for first-line supervisors, attempts to improve socio-emotional leadership qualities are doomed to failure, since these efforts will run headlong into the existing socio-emotional leader who has risen to his position in the interactions of the work group. This type of interpretation, of course, is counter to the ideas and ideals of the "human-relations" school of management, which stresses the utility of socio-emotional interactions in the leadership process. Although it is concerned with relatively low levels in the hierarchy, this is an important point to keep in mind in the discussion of leadership.

Components of Leadership

Every organization has an individual or set of individuals at the top decision-making level who can exercise power through simply giving orders and making decisions. This is simple power of position and does not involve leadership as we will approach it here. Our view of leadership involves what a person does above and beyond the basic requirements of his position. *It is the persuasion of individuals and innovativeness in ideas and decision making that differentiates leadership from the sheer possession of power.* A mechanical reliance on organizational position would bring about a situation in which the characteristics of the individuals filling top positions would not make any difference whatsoever. The organization would be totally constrained by precedent and its own structure.

The ideas expressed thus far have implied strongly that individual characteristics are crucial for the leadership role. This does appear to be the case. This idea must be approached with extreme care, however, to put it in the proper perspective. There is a very real danger in assuming that because individual characteristics are crucial for the leadership function, there is a set of *traits* that leaders possess. The literature regarding leadership took this approach at one time, with identification of the key leadership traits a major goal of the research. This approach didn't get very far, for two reasons. The basic one was that common leadership traits could not be identified. There is no set of characteristics possessed by leaders and not by followers. This realization led to the second contributing factor in the downfall of the trait approach. Attention increasingly turned to the *situation* in which leadership was exhibited.[8]

[8] For a discussion of this point see Gouldner, *Studies in Leadership.*

The situational approach takes the position that the set of conditions of the moment—the situation—defines by whom and in what manner leadership will be expressed. In one situation, one individual will emerge as the leader; in another situation, another individual. This approach has largely dominated the sociological approach to leadership, especially in small-group studies, but in recent years it has come under fire for its inattention to the characteristics of those who rise into leadership positions. The emergent position is that while different situations demand different forms of leadership and thus generally different individuals, particular skills and behaviors will be called for in each different situation. This is a blending of the trait and situational approaches and appears to avoid the serious pitfalls of each.

This combination approach is used by Edwin Hollander and James Julian. They reject the trait and situational approaches per se, noting that both tell us something about leadership, but not the whole story. To the ideas that have already been stated, they add the important element of interaction between leader and followers.[9] The leader *influences* his followers in the interaction process, and their reactions, of course, have an impact on his own behavior.

Organizational leadership, from the perspective taken here, is a combination of factors. The most obvious is the high *position* in the organization. This gives the leader his power base and leads followers to the expectations that he has a legitimate right to that position and that he will in fact engage in the leadership process by shaping their own thoughts and actions and performing the leadership functions for the organization as a whole.[10] These expectations can be seen even in periods of dissidence within the organization, when there is leadership succession and the followers express the hope that the new person will provide what the old one did not.

In addition to the position held, the leadership role demands that the *individual behave in such a way that the expectations of the followers are fulfilled.* Here the interrelationships between the characteristics of the individual and the position filled become crucial. Rather than suggesting that there is one set of leadership "traits," the evidence

9 Edwin P. Hollander and James W. Julian, "Contemporary Trends in the Analysis of Leadership Processes," *Psychological Bulletin*, Vol. 71, No. 5 (May 1969), 387–97.

10 This is consistent with Cartwright's approach, which suggests that a distinction should be made between the power of a position (power) and the power of a person (leadership). For our purposes, the person must have the position at the top of the organization before he can exercise the type of leadership under discussion. See Dorwin Cartwright, "Influence, Leadership and Control," in James G. March, ed., *Handbook of Organizations* (Chicago: Rand McNally & Co., 1965), pp. 4–5.

indicates that the particular characteristics giving rise to leadership behavior vary with the situation. This conclusion allows a rapprochement
between the trait and situational approaches to leadership. Certainly a
random assignment of persons to positions of leadership would not make
the leadership process occur very frequently. At the same time, it is
clear that a leader in one situation may not be able to do much in
another, different environment. Leadership, therefore, depends on the
congruence between the situation and the characteristics of the person
who is appointed or elected, or who assumes leadership. (Since we are
concerned with organizations, we assume that most persons in leadership
positions are appointed or elected.)

It is after the appointment or election that the *interaction process*
takes over. This process will determine whether or not the person in the
position, with his individual characteristics, will become a leader.

Now let us move to the central issue—what does a leader do for or
to an organization, and how does he do it?

THE IMPACT OF LEADERSHIP ON THE ORGANIZATION

There is very little evidence regarding the effect that top leaders have
on organizations. The ideal situation would be to specify the conditions under which leadership has an impact, pinpointing the direction
and magnitude of the effect, then to put this in juxtaposition with the
other factors affecting organizational operations. These other factors
would include the external and internal considerations under discussion
throughout this volume. We should also know the constraints on the
leader—the structural blockages to his impact, or, put in another way,
the degree of latitude he actually has to set policy and implement decisions.

Since the evidence for this kind of analysis is just not available, we
will have to use more indirect kinds of information. The first kind will
be from the large number of studies of lower-level managers and executives, and the second from examinations of managerial succession. The
intent is to extrapolate from these studies some conclusions regarding
the impact of top leadership on the organization. The conclusions will
have to be viewed as tentative, given the shakiness of the evidence, but
the apparent importance of the leader role warrants this type of approach.

Studies of leadership in organizations are confusing, if not downright chaotic, even to those who are well versed in the literature.[11] A major factor in the confusion, aside from the ideological biases evident in some investigations, is the large number of dependent variables used in leadership analyses. If variations in the amount or style of leadership are taken as the independent variable, then a whole series of variables has been treated as the dependent ones. These run the gamut from hard measures of productivity to the more elusive factors of morale and satisfaction.

Leadership Styles

Research regarding leadership has come to focus around two contrasting styles or approaches to the leadership role. These are the authoritarian (task) and supportive (socio-emotional) approaches. The biases alluded to earlier are evident and understandable when these two terms are brought into the discussion (who would want to support authoritarianism?). The supportive leader is "characterized by . . . employee oriented, democratic behavior, uses general supervision, and is considerate of his subordinates." [12] The authoritarian leader, on the other hand, is much more likely to rely on the power of his position and to be more punishment-centered. A very evident problem for the discussion here is that the authoritarian form actually may not be leadership in the way we have defined it.

The supportive leader utilizes socio-emotional appeals to his subordinates. This involves:

Consideration for Subordinates. The leader considers the needs and preferences of his subordinates, whom he treats with dignity and kindness, and is not punitive in his dealings with them. Such a leader is frequently referred to as "employee-centered" as opposite to "work-centered" or "task-centered."

Consultative Decision Making. The leader asks his subordinates for their opinions before he makes decisions. Such a leader is consultative, participative, or democratic (as opposed to unilateral, autocratic, or arbitrary) in his decision making.

General Supervision. The leader supervises in a general rather than a close manner, delegates authority to his subordinates, and permits them freedom to exercise discretion in their work rather than imposing tight controls and close (frequently overbearing) supervision.[13]

[11] Cartwright, "Influence, Leadership and Control," p. 3.

[12] Alan C. Filley and Robert J. House, *Managerial Processes and Organizational Behavior* (Glenview, Ill.: Scott, Foresman and Company, 1969), p. 399. This book contains an excellent bibliography of leadership studies.

[13] *Ibid.*, pp. 399–400.

In their excellent review of the research in the leadership area, Filley and House find that supportive leadership, as opposed to autocratic leadership, is quite consistently related to several indicators of subordinate satisfaction and productivity:

1. There is less intragroup stress and more cooperation.
2. Turnover and grievance rates are lower.
3. The leader himself is viewed as more desirable.
4. There is frequently greater productivity.

The evidence here is confounded, unfortunately, by the possibility that the workers themselves may contribute to their greater satisfaction and productivity by their own attitudes and behavior, independent of that of the leader. They might just be high-producing, positively oriented employees who "do not require close, autocratic supervision, and therefore it is possible for the supervisor of such employees to be more human-relations oriented." [14] Despite this possibility, the weight of the evidence is that supportive leadership does lead to more positive attitudinal responses, particularly on the part of subordinates.

The productivity issue is not as clear as the attitudinal one. While some evidence does suggest that greater productivity is associated with supportive supervision, other studies report no difference or actually more output when autocratic styles are used.[15] An obviously important question here is, What does the organization want? If satisfied employees are desired, then the supportive approach has clearly rather been shown to be more effective. Short-run output gains, on the other hand, may be more easily achieved under an autocratic system. There is also evidence to suggest that when workers expect to be supervised in an autocratic style, supportive supervision can be counterproductive and satisfaction-threatening.

In summarizing these leadership studies, Filley and House conclude that supportive leadership behavior is most effective when:

1. Decisions are not routine in nature
2. The information required for effective decision making cannot be standardized or centralized
3. Decisions need not be made rapidly, allowing time to involve subordinates in a participative decision-making process

[14] *Ibid.*, p. 402.

[15] See Robert Dubin, "Supervision and Productivity: Empirical Findings and Theoretical Considerations," in Robert Dubin, George Homans, Floyd Mann, and Delbert Miller, *Leadership and Productivity* (San Francisco: Chandler Publishing Co., 1965).

and when subordinates:

4. Feel a strong need for independence
5. Regard their participation in decision making as legitimate
6. See themselves as able to contribute to the decision-making process
7. Are confident of their ability to work without the reassurance of close supervision [16]

This particular kind of organization is similar to some that have already been described in the section on organizational structure. These are the less formalized organizations that must rely on the inputs of their own members if they are to be effective. Their technology is such that there is a constant search for new ideas and answers. The obvious corollary of the findings in regard to the kind of organization in which supportive leadership styles are likely to be effective is that in the opposite kind of organization, such forms of leadership are *least* likely to be effective. That is, in organizations in which decisions are routine, information is standardized, and so on, effective leadership is more likely to take the autocratic form, in that inputs from the individual members of the organization are not so important and there is not the need for time spent in the decision-making process. At the same time, it can be postulated that there are organizational members who either are threatened by the decision-making process or have no wish to participate in it, and for whom the provision of ready-made answers in the form of formal procedures or decisions made for them is a satisfying or at least nonthreatening situation.

These interpretations are strongly buttressed by the findings emerging from Fred Fiedler's continuing studies of the leadership process.[17] Fiedler finds that in stable, structured situations, a more strict, autocratic form of leadership is most likely to be successful, while in a situation of change, external threat, and ambiguity, the more lenient, participative form of supervision would work better. Of course, in some organizations conditions will change in one direction or another, suggesting that an effective leader in one situation may not be such in another.

Factors Affecting Leadership Impact

Several aspects of the research discussed thus far ought to be separated out before the present analysis proceeds. As indicated earlier, most

[16] Filley and House, *Managerial Processes*, pp. 404–5.
[17] Fred E. Fiedler, *A Theory of Leadership Effectiveness* (New York: McGraw-Hill Book Company, 1967).

of the studies have been performed with personnel from relatively lower echelons in the organization. Regardless of the level within the organization, it is clear that the nature of the situation being faced and the personnel being led make an important difference in determining which form of leadership is likely to be most effective. It can be argued that it would be good, from an individual or societal perspective, if all personnel were self-motivating and desirous of participating in the decision making, and that the organization as a whole would be healthier if it were constantly innovating and engaging in continual interactions with its environment; but the facts of the matter suggest that neither condition necessarily exists in practice. This then leads to the conclusion that a revamping of leadership styles in organizations is no panacea to be applied to all organizations and all members therein.

The important aspect of the research, for our purposes here, is the demonstrated fact that leadership at this level does make a difference in terms of objective performance indicators and the attitudes of the personnel involved. The question is not one of style, but of impact. If production can be increased or the acceptance of a new mode of organization quickened, leadership does come to be an important process. The extrapolation from this conclusion to top leadership is relatively easy, if unsupported by existing research. The range of behavior affected by first- or second-line supervisors is actually quite small. If the jump is made to the range of behavior that can be affected by those at the top of the organization, the potential for a real impact of leadership can be readily seen. Even in terms of performance and attitudes, the high-level subordinates of high administrators can be affected, and their performance in turn has an impact right down the organization.

An additional point is that leadership and the total managerial function are apparently vitally affected by one of the major considerations throughout this analysis—the technology of the organization involved. The previously discussed research of Joan Woodward and of Lawrence and Lorsch lends support for this conclusion, as does the research of Elmer Burack.[18] These findings systematically document the interplay between the organization's structure, as affected by the technology, and the management structure. Technological factors set limits on the amount and kinds of variations that can be introduced into the system, thus limiting certain aspects of what a leader can do.

Now that we have formed some conclusions about the impact of leadership at both top and lower levels, let us examine the available evidence concerning changes in personnel at the top of the organization.

18 Elmer H. Burack, "Industrial Management in Advanced Production Systems: Some Theoretical Concepts and Preliminary Findings," *American Sociological Quarterly,* Vol. 12, No. 3 (December 1967), 479–500.

Leader Succession

Analyses of managerial succession have been largely limited to case studies, with the exception of some concern about organizational size and the rate of managerial succession. These latter studies will be touched upon later; for the moment, we shall look at some of the implications from the case studies.

Probably the best known of these is Alvin Gouldner's *Patterns of Industrial Bureaucracy*,[19] an analysis of a gypsum plant and mine that underwent a major and dramatic change in top personnel. The former manager had engaged in loose, almost indulgent practices in regard to rule observance and other standards. The parent organization, concerned about the production record of the plant, replaced the old manager with a new man who had the specific mandate of increasing production. The new man knew he would be judged by his record of production, so his alternatives were to continue the established pattern— a procedure that probably would not have worked in any event, since he did not have the personal ties of his predecessor—or to enforce the already-existing rules of conduct and performance. He chose the latter course, and as a result the total system became "punishment-centered." This led to a severe increase in internal tension and stress.

This example is in direct contrast to a case described by Robert Guest.[20] Guest's study was made from observations in a large automobile factory. He states:

> Both studies [his and Gouldner's] examine the process by which organizational tensions are exacerbated or reduced following the succession of a new leader at the top of the hierarchy. Succession in Gouldner's case resulted in a sharp increase in tension and stress and, by inference, a lowering of overall performance. The succession of a new manager had the opposite results in the present case. Plant Y, as we chose to call it, was one of six identical plants of a large corporation. At one period in time the plant was poorest in virtually all indexes of performance—direct and indirect labor costs, quality of output, absenteeism and turnover, ability to meet schedule changes, labor grievances and in several other measures. Interpersonal relationships were marked by sharp antagonisms within and between all levels.
>
> Three years later, following the succession of a new manager, and with no changes in the formal organizational structure, in the product, in the personnel, or in its basic technology, not only was there a substantial reduc-

[19] Alvin Gouldner, *Patterns of Industrial Bureaucracy* (New York: The Free Press, 1954).

[20] Robert H. Guest, "Managerial Succession in Complex Organizations," *American Journal of Sociology*, Vol. 67, No. 1 (July 1962), 47–54.

tion of interpersonal conflict, but Plant Y became the outstanding performer among all of the plants.[21]

The dramatic differences between these two cases might lead one to some sort of "great-man" theory of leadership, with Gouldner's successor a nongreat man and Guest's the opposite. Guest correctly rejects this approach and instead attributes the differences to the actions each man took when confronted with an existing social structure. A major aspect of this social structure was the expectations of higher management in the organizations involved. While both new managers were expected to improve the situation, the new man at the gypsum plant felt that he was expected to get rid of the personnel who were not performing properly. He felt that he was, and probably actually was, under more severe pressure to turn the organization around in a short period of time.

There were some other important differences in the organizations. The tradition in the gypsum plant was that the new top man came from "inside," and in this case, he did not. In addition, the former manager had been active in the community surrounding the plant. The successor thus came into a situation in which there were negative feelings from the outset. The former manager also had a loyal cadre of subordinates who were tied to him through personal loyalty. The successor had little recourse but to use the more formal bureaucratic mechanisms of control. At the automobile factory, on the other hand, the total social setting was different. The factory was in a large metropolitan area in which the previous managers had not become involved. The history of top management succession was one of relatively rapid turnover (three to five years), with the new men coming from outside the plant itself. The auto plant personnel were thus used to the kind of succession that both plants experienced.

Another, more subtle difference that Gouldner describes is the fact that in the gypsum plant, the indulgency pattern and the developed social structure among the personnel were such that there was no orientation toward cutting costs and improving productivity. The previous system was a comfortable one in which rewards, both intrinsic and extrinsic, came without such an orientation.

The predecessor at the auto plant had attempted to use his formal powers in increasing productivity. Like his successor, he was under great pressure to improve the operation, but he chose to attempt this by close and punitive supervision. The successor decided to move in a different path by using more informal contacts with his subordinates and bringing them into the decision-making process. Also, this man worked

21 *Ibid.*, p. 47.

through the existing organizational hierarchy, whereas the new man at the gypsum plant, after some failures with the established subordinates, brought in some of his own men, thus setting up a formal hierarchy that was in a sense superimposed on the existing social structure.

Rational choice from a range of possible alternative courses of action is probably uncharacteristic of most decisions that are made; but alternative approaches to problems can still be selected, whether unconsciously, by default, or by some form of conscious decision making. In the first case under discussion, the gypsum plant manager chose to try to raise the organization's performance by enforcing rules to the letter of the law—dismissing men, for example, for offenses that had previously been largely ignored. The auto plant man, on the other hand, "relegated rule enforcement to a second level of importance." [22]

Guest moves beyond his data and draws a conclusion from the comparison between his and Gouldner's cases. He suggests that the success of the auto plant manager was due in large part to gaining the consent of the governed, or democratization of the leadership process. Gouldner, in a comment regarding Guest's research, notes that the total situations in which the successions occurred were different. The gypsum plant event occurred during a period of recession, with labor relatively plentiful, but with the pressures for improvement probably more intense.[23] The implication here is that when the total situation is viewed, it is incorrect to conclude that one or another approach to the leadership process is always the correct one, even though in both of these cases the autocratic approach was less successful.

From the evidence presented in these two studies, it should be clear that top management does have the potential for really drastic impacts on the organization, although it cannot be stated at the present time what proportion of the variance of organizational performance can be accounted for by this leadership role. Indeed, it would appear that this would vary according to the situation, since the range of alternatives even formally allowed would vary widely. Nevertheless, leadership can be seen as having a major impact on what happens to and within the organization.

Some indications of the factors associated with leadership's potentiality for major impact emerge from additional studies of managerial succession. There have been several attempts to specify the relationship between organizational size and the rate of succession. Oscar Grusky examined the largest and smallest deciles of the 500 largest companies in the United States (in terms of sales volume), and Louis

22 *Ibid.*, p. 52.

23 Alvin Gouldner, "Comment," *American Journal of Sociology*, Vol. 67, No. 1 (July 1962), 54–56.

Kriesberg looked at state and local mental health agencies and public health departments.[24] Both came to the conclusion that size and rate of succession are related. That is, the larger the organization, the higher the rate of succession. Gerald Gordon and Selwyn Becker, noting some contradictions between these findings and some others, reexamined the Grusky data, adding additional information from a sample of the next 500 largest business organizations.[25] They found an inverse relationship between size and rate of succession, with the smaller companies having a slightly higher turnover rate among top management. In commenting on this finding, Kriesberg notes that the rate of succession is undoubtedly affected by more than the size factor, with the typical career lines within the organization a major consideration. If the organization builds in the expectation of rapid executive turnover, this will obviously increase the rate.

An additional important factor noted by Kriesberg is the likelihood of interindustry differences.[26] An industry-by-industry analysis would be more definitive than a simple lumping together of all organizations. In keeping with the general theme of this analysis, an adequate typology of organizations should allow some prediction of the kinds of organizations in which succession rates will be high. In the absence of such a typology, the technology factor, implied by Kriesberg, would appear to be important. *What the organization does and the environment in which it works have an impact on how rapidly top leadership changes are made and the extent to which such leadership can actually affect the organization.*

But one point in regard to organizational size is clear. Other things being equal, the larger the organization, the less the impact of succession would be. Large organizations are apt to be more complex and formalized, and thus more resistant to change. It would therefore be likely that top leadership would be unable to "turn the organization around" in either direction in a short period of time, unless it were a totally autocratic system. Referring back to the discussion of rationality in organizations, it would appear that the impact of top leadership on the organization would be a matter of rather small differences when compared with past administrations. This assumes, of course, that

24 Oscar Grusky, "Corporate Size, Bureaucratization, and Managerial Succession," *American Journal of Sociology*, Vol. 69, No. 3 (November 1961), 261–69; and Louis Kriesberg, "Careers, Organizational Size, and Succession," *American Journal of Sociology*, Vol. 68, No. 3 (November 1962), 355–59.

25 Gerald Gordon and Selwyn Becker, "Organizational Size and Managerial Succession: A Re-examination," *American Journal of Sociology*, Vol. 70, No. 2 (September 1964), 215–22.

26 Louis Kriesberg, "Reply," *American Journal of Sociology*, Vol. 70, No. 2 (September 1964), p. 223.

the past or present groups do not operate on the basis of total irrationality.

An indication of the extent of the difference that leadership can make on the organization can be found in some rather offbeat research regarding baseball managers. Baseball managers stand in an unusual organizational position. Their role is similar to that of the foreman, when the total baseball organization is considered; it is similar to that of the top executive, relative to just the playing team. Grusky continued his analysis of managerial succession with major league baseball teams. These are convenient units for analysis since they ". . . ideally, were identical in official goals, size, and authority structure." [27] Grusky was concerned with the relationship between managerial succession and organizational effectiveness. Here again, baseball teams are ideal because effectiveness is reflected directly in the won-lost statistics; how you play the game is not a crucial variable in professional sports.

The findings from the analysis were that the teams with the poorest records had the highest rates of succession. In interpreting these findings, Grusky rejects the common-sense notion built around succession as the dependent variable—that low effectiveness leads to a vote of confidence from the owner, then a firing. Instead, he develops a more complicated analysis, which is in keeping with the previous discussion.

> If a team is ineffective, clientele support and profitability decline. Accordingly, strong external pressures for managerial change are set in motion and, concomitantly, the magnitude of managerial role strain increases. A managerial change may be viewed in some quarters as attractive in that it can function to demonstrate publicly that the owners are taking concrete action to remedy an undesirable situation. The public nature of team performance and the close identification of community pride with team behavior combine to establish a strong basis for clientele control over the functioning of the team. These external influences tend to increase the felt discrepancy between managerial responsibility and actual authority. Since the rewards of popularity are controlled externally, individual rather than team performance may be encouraged. Similarly, the availability of objective performance standards decreases managerial control and thereby contributes to role strain. The greater the managerial role strain, the higher the rates of succession. Moreover, the higher the rates of succession, the stronger the expectations of replacement when team performance declines. Frequent managerial change can produce important dysfunctional consequences within the team by affecting style of supervision and disturbing the informal network of interpersonal relationships. New policies and new personnel create the necessity for restructuring primary relationships. The resulting low primary-group stability produces low morale and may thereby contribute to team ineffectiveness. Declining clientele support may encourage a greater de-

[27] Oscar Grusky, "Managerial Succession and Organizational Effectiveness," *American Journal of Sociology*, Vol. 69, No. 1 (July 1963), 21.

cline in team morale and performance. The consequent continued drop in profitability induces pressures for further managerial changes. Such changes, in turn, produce additional disruptive effects on the organization, and the vicious circle continues.[28]

This rather complicated explanation is challenged by William Gamson and Norman Scotch. Based on a different approach to baseball teams' won-and-lost records, Gamson and Scotch advance a "ritual scapegoating no-way casualty theory." [29] This theory essentially suggests that the manager doesn't make any difference.

> In the long run, the policies of the general manager and other front-office personnel are far more important. While judicious trades are helpful (here the field manager may be consulted but does not have the main responsibility), the production of talent through a well-organized scouting and farm system is the most important long-run determinant. The field manager, who is concerned with day-to-day tactical decisions, has minimal responsibility for such management functions.[30]

Gamson and Scotch go on to note that the player personnel are a critical factor, suggesting that at one point in baseball history, regardless of who was manager, ". . . the Yankees would have done as well and the Mets would have (or more accurately, could have) done no worse." [31] When the team is doing poorly, the firing of the field manager is ritual scapegoating. "It is a convenient, anxiety-reducing act which the participants of the ceremony regard as a way of improving performance, even though (as some participants may themselves admit in less stressful moments) real improvements can come only through long-range organizational decisions." [32] Gamson and Scotch add that there does seem to be at least a short-run improvement in team performance in cases where the manager is changed in midseason. They suggest that this might be attributable to the ritual itself.

Grusky, in a reply to the Gamson–Scotch criticism, further analyzes the data regarding midseason changes. He adds the dimension of whether the new manager came from inside or outside the organization and finds that the inside manager is more successful. He takes this as partial evidence that his more complicated theory is more reasonable, since the inside man is likely to be aware of the interpersonal arrange-

28 *Ibid.*, p. 30.
29 William Gamson and Norman Scotch, "Scapegoating in Baseball," *American Journal of Sociology*, Vol. 70, No. 1 (July 1964), 70.
30 *Ibid.*
31 *Ibid.*
32 *Ibid.*, pp. 70–71.

ments and the performance of his predecessor and thus more likely not to make the same mistakes again.[33]

This may seem at first glance a lot of words spilled over a relatively minor matter in the larger scheme of things, but the points that these authors are addressing themselves to are very relevant for the present analysis. While Gamson and Scotch follow the line of reasoning taken here, that those at the very top of the organization have a greater impact than those further down the hierarchy, Grusky's argument that external and internal pressures for success affect performance is directly in line with the evidence presented by Gouldner and Guest. The kinds of personnel available are modified by the social system of which they are a part. It is within this framework that leadership behavior takes place. Although the important question of just how much leadership behavior actually contributes to the organization is left unanswered, the baseball studies do suggest that both positive and negative results ensue with managerial succession. Few cases of neutrality are found in the analyses.

A final research finding on rates of executive succession should be noted. In an analysis of a business firm and a military installation, Grusky came to the conclusion that rapid rates of succession are associated with limitations on executive control.[34] In the military, which is characterized by a high degree of formalization, thereby limiting the discretion of any one individual, there is an intentional high turnover among all ranks.

The implication here is that in organizations that are relatively loosely structured and where it is expected that the leadership will have a great deal to do with what goes on in the organization, leadership behavior will have a large impact. Since most organizations are in fact relatively highly structured, either in terms of the formal system or the more informal interpersonal system, there are finite limits on what the leader can accomplish. Succession in the United States presidency, which is accompanied by pomp, circumstance, and other lavish ceremonies, tends *not* to make as much difference as the partisan supporters of the new incumbent would hope. Indeed, there is good evidence that the total system serves to frustrate the implementation of new policies. The suggestion has recently been made, for example, that each new administration of the United States government be allowed to replace civil servants with their own appointees (assuming that the appointees can

[33] Oscar Grusky, "Reply," *American Journal of Sociology,* Vol. 70, No. 1 (July 1964), 72–76.

[34] Oscar Grusky, "The Effects of Succession: A Comparative Study of Military and Business Organization," in Oscar Grusky and George A. Miller, eds., *The Sociology of Organizations* (New York: The Free Press, 1970), pp. 439–54.

qualify by civil service criteria), so that program implementation can be achieved.[35]

Does Leadership Make a Difference?

The last few points raise the obvious question of whether or not what has been discussed in this chapter makes any difference after all. If the organization can impose such direct limitations on what the leader can do, is it simply a myth that the leader makes a difference? This is a difficult question to answer, since so many factors go into the operation of any organization. The examples of spectacular success or failure following succession have often been attributed to a change in the top administration, when changes in the environmental conditions of the organization, new personnel in some key operation, or technological developments could hypothetically have as much to do with the change. The earlier discussion should make it clear that the question is not easily answered with the data that are currently available. Probably the most satisfactory answer at the present time is that *given the important leadership functions, there is real potential for leadership to affect the organization.* The exact extent and direction of the effect cannot at present be discerned. One source of the variation in the effect is undoubtedly in *the degree to which the organization is already structured and the extent to which this structure is subject to modification.* Another important consideration is *the extent to which the decisions that are to be made are "preprogrammed" because of precedent, technological specificity that does not allow for much variation, or the absence of familiarity with the range of options available in a situation.*

Since decision making is an important leadership function in several areas, another consideration in understanding the extent to which leadership can affect an organization is the likelihood that the leader will be able to convince the rest of the organization to follow his decisions. It is here that the various forms of power, including interpersonal abilities, come into play again. The leader must be able to implement his decisions, through one mechanism or another, in the organization. A factor that would enter the picture here is the extent to which the other members *expect* the leader to influence the organization. If the role is viewed as one with limited power, it is much less likely to have an impact than in cases where the leader is expected to play some form of messianic role.[36]

---

[35] See the *Washington Star,* July 16, 1970, p. 2.

[36] See George Homans, "Effort, Supervision, and Productivity," in Dubin et al., *Leadership and Productivity,* pp. 51–67, for additional discussion of these points.

Leadership in the Voluntary Organization

The discussion thus far has concerned the work organization, in which the leader is appointed on the basis of criteria set up in advance. The situation is somewhat different in the voluntary organization, in which the leader is elected to office. Without getting into the questions of what kinds of persons are likely to be elected and how they perform their duties, some interesting issues should be mentioned. It has long been noted that in voluntary organizations there is a tendency toward oligarchy, in that the group in power wants to stay there and will endeavor to ensure its continued presence in office.[37] In looking at union leadership, Arnold Tannenbaum notes that leaders have higher incomes than the rank and file they represent. In fact, they are more likely to live like their adversaries in management than like their own union members.

> In addition to its clear financial superiority, the leader's job places him in a world of variety, excitement, and broadened horizons which is qualitatively richer and psychologically more stimulating than his old job in the plant. There are also many tensions and frustrations in the leadership role, and long hours are often required. But these are part of the deep involvement which leaders have in their work. By and large, a return to the worker role would represent an intolerable loss to most leaders.[38]

This personal desire to stay in the leadership position is coupled with several other factors that can lead to oligarchy. The leaders may be able to develop a monopoly on the kinds of skills required for leadership, such as verbal ability, persuasive techniques, and so on. They obtain political power within the organization through patronage and other favors. Given their position, it is relatively easy to groom their successors. Since the nature of unions involves a time cycle in regard to contract negotiations, the leaders can provide the membership with continual reminders of what they have achieved and what they are going to try to achieve the next time. The skills developed in this phase of the union's operation are unlikely to be part of the rank and file's repertoire.

The tendency toward oligarchy is apparently found in most voluntary organizations where there is a wide gap between members and leaders

---

[37] The classic statement of this position is found in Robert Michels, *Political Parties* (New York: Thomas Y. Crowell Company, 1962).

[38] Arnold S. Tannenbaum, "Unions," in March, ed., *Handbook of Organizations*, p. 752.

in the rewards (intrinsic and extrinsic) received. Where the gap is not so great, there is a greater tendency toward democracy. Lipset, Trow, and Coleman's analysis of the International Typographical Union demonstrates this point.[39] This union is one in which the members enjoy relatively high pay and a strong sense of community with their fellow members and leaders alike, and it is quite democratic.

Voluntary organizations can also be differentiated from work organizations on the basis of the strong likelihood of a form of "dual leadership." Analyses of political parties have indicated the existence of both public and associational leadership. The public leaders are those who run for and hold public office, while the associational leaders operate behind the scenes. An exception here would be the British parliamentary system, where the two forms of leadership tend to coincide.[40] While unofficial power arrangements certainly exist in work organizations, they appear to be more fully developed in the voluntary organization, since the latter is characterized by much looser structural arrangements. And this looser structuring would appear to be related to another important consideration: In voluntary organizations, the leader is more likely to have a strong impact than in more structured organizations. There are more possibilities for variation in this setting.

DECISION MAKING

One of the most critical things that leaders do is engage in the decision-making process. Their decisions are made about the major functions that leadership is expected to perform—setting goals, deciding upon the means to the end, defending the organization from attacks from the outside, and resolving internal conflict.

Of course, almost every position in an organization involves some decision making. Such a simple matter as the size of paper to insert in a typewriter involves a judgment. It also involves a clear set of alternatives and a clear set of outcomes, together with what are probably already-established preferences for the outcome of this decision-making process. This is not the kind of decision we are concerned with here; it is a tactical decision, which adds little or nothing to the organization.

---

[39] Seymour Martin Lipset, Martin A. Trow, and James S. Coleman, *Union Democracy* (New York: The Free Press, 1956).

[40] See Joseph A. Schlesinger, "Political Party Organization," in March, ed., *Handbook of Organizations*, pp. 766–68.

What we are concerned with are strategic decisions that affect the fate of the enterprise.

Variables and Constraints

A useful approach to the kinds of decisions that have strategic importance for the organization is provided by James Thompson. Thompson notes that "decision issues always involve two major dimensions: (1) beliefs about cause/effect relationships and (2) preferences regarding possible outcomes." [41] These basic variables in the decision-making process can operate at the conscious or the unconscious level. As an aid in understanding the process, Thompson suggests that each variable can be (artificially) dichotomized as indicated in figure 8–1.

Preferences Regarding Possible Outcomes

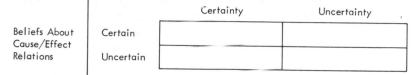

Beliefs About Cause/Effect Relations

Certain

Uncertain

Certainty   Uncertainty

FIG. 8–1 Decision Processes

Source: James D. Thompson, Organizations in Action *(New York: McGraw-Hill Book Co., 1967), p. 134.*

In the cell with certainty on both variables, a "computational" strategy can be used. In this case the decision is obvious and can be performed by a computer with great simplicity. An example here would be simple inventorying, in which, when the supply of a particular item reaches a particular level, it is automatically reordered. Obviously, this is in no way a strategic situation and will not be of concern to us here. The other cells present more problems and are thus more crucial for the organization.

When outcome preferences are clear, but cause/effect relationships are uncertain, we will refer to the *judgmental strategy* for decision making. Where the situation is reversed and there is certainty regarding cause/effect but uncertainty regarding outcome preferences, the issue can be regarded as calling for a *compromise strategy* for decision making. Finally, where there is un-

---

[41] James D. Thompson, *Organizations in Action* (New York: McGraw-Hill Book Company, 1967), p. 134.

certainty on both dimensions, we will speak of the *inspirational strategy* for decision making, if indeed any decision is forthcoming.[42]

A major component of this framework is the amount and kind of information that is available in the system. The more complete the knowledge about cause-and-effect relationships, the more certainty can be brought into the decision-making process. In some areas of knowledge, certainty about cause and effect is quite well developed, while in others the knowledge is probabilistic at best. Since all organizations are social units interacting with society, any involvement of humans in either the cause or the effect part of the equation introduces an element of uncertainty. Complete knowledge is undoubtedly rare in the kinds of decisions with which we are concerned. In discussing the effects of the incompleteness of knowledge and information, Thompson notes that in organizations working at the frontiers of new knowledge—as in the aerospace industry, medical research, and so on—even though all the variables that are known to be relevant are controlled as far as possible, the presence of imperfections and gaps in knowledge lead to the use of the judgmental strategy. Knowledge about cause and effect is further weakened when some elements of the process are beyond the organization's control. Welfare programs, for example, are affected by the people being served and the wider community that supports or rejects the total program. Still another situation in which the cause-and-effect relationship becomes unclear is when the organization is in competition with another organization over which it cannot exercise control. In this case the judgmental strategy is also used, since the organization cannot decide for sure exactly what will happen as a result of its own efforts.

In addition to changes in the nature of the cause/effect knowledge system that occur as new knowledge becomes available—as in the case of new medical discoveries that alter the approach of hospitals to their patients—there is another important component of the system that should be specified. The nature of cause and effect is actually really certain in only a few cases. Cause-and-effect "knowledge" is vitally affected by the belief or truth system that is prevalent in the organization. The importance of this can be seen clearly in the case of welfare systems that have two major alternative truth systems, which can lead to different interpretations of the same knowledge inputs. The organizations can believe, on the one hand, that those on some form of welfare assistance are in that condition because of their own fault; or on the other hand, that the condition exists because of societal imperfections.

---

[42] *Ibid.*, pp. 134–35. The similarity of this approach to Perrow's should be evident.

While there would seldom be a complete acceptance of either extreme position, the dominant truth system would serve as the mechanism by which information coming into the system is interpreted on a cause-and-effect basis, leading to different kinds of decisions being made. Similar examples can be noted concerning the strategies adopted in regard to supervisory practices, international relations, and most other organizational decisions. From the cause/effect standpoint, then, while information is a key factor, the interpretation of the information remains a variable that, while usually constant in most organizations, still affects the outcomes of the decisions that are made. The adoption of a different truth system could lead to entirely different decisions, based on the same information.

The outcome-preference side of the Thompson paradigm contains even more ambiguities for the organization than the cause/effect side. The discussion of goals and rationality in organizations is central here, since it is the decisions that are made about goals that become the outcome preferences. In the operations of an organization, the decisions that are made are obviously among several possible outcomes for the organization. Here the same concerns about knowledge and truth systems are extremely important, since they will help determine exactly what the leadership in the organization will decide in regard to a particular issue.

Outcome preferences are also affected by several other factors. Thompson notes that when human beings are the objects of the organizations' efforts, conflicting desired outcomes can be derived from the subjects themselves. Here again the example of welfare clients can be used. Similarly, in a prison ". . . with therapeutic objectives, some compromise seems inevitable, for conflicting outcome preferences of prisoners force the prison to add custody as an outcome preference." [43] The organization may also be constrained in its choices among outcome preferences by shortages of inputs. If a university would like to develop a national reputation in some field, its preferred outcome may have to be modified if it is unable to secure the kinds of faculty and students to assist it in this endeavor. The case would be similar in the production process if the materials needed were in short or low-quality supply.

Rationality

To these constraints, which are outside the control of the organization and the decision makers, must be added the individual constraint

---

[43] *Ibid.,* p. 137.

of the limited amount of rationality available in the decision-making process. As Simon has so ably pointed out, decisions are made on the basis of "bounded rationality." [44] The reasons for the limits on rationality are linked to the inability of the system as a whole to provide maximum or even adequate information for decision making, and the inability of the decision maker to intellectually handle even the inadequate information that is available. Leaving the issue of information aside for the moment, it is clear that the more important a decision is for the organization, the greater the number of factors contributing to the condition of the organization at the moment that the decision has to be made, and the more far-reaching the consequences of the decision. The intellectual ability to handle these multitudinous factors is just not available among current and past organizational leaders to the degree that they and those affected by the decisions would desire.

The clearest examples of the inability to comprehend and act on the antecedents to the decision-making process and to anticipate the consequences come from the various programs of the federal government. Regardless of the party and leaders in office or behind the scenes, no decision accomplishes totally what it was designed to do—either in domestic or international affairs. The same is true for private industry and other organizational segments of the society. In private industry there are examples of new products, sales campaigns, marketing techniques, and so on, that are labeled "unqualified successes." Realistically, these may be the result of attempts at total rationality or of serendipity, but they are not unqualified successes except on a short-run basis. And even in the short run, a successful program in one phase of an organization's operation may be at the expense of other programs. The intent of this discussion has not been to suggest that we might as well forget about trying to be rational in the decision-making process because it is impossible, but to point out that the complexity of the organization and the situation in which it is operating contain elements that acually work at cross-purposes with each other.

The earlier discussions of rationality and this section on decision making have suggested that organizations attempt to make decisions on as rational a basis as possible. As Thompson so clearly notes, one of the major tasks of the organization is to reduce the constraints on it so that it can operate more rationally. While total rationality is not achieved, it is still reasonable to assume that the desire is to move toward greater rationality rather than away from it. A major consideration in this aim is the amount and quality of information available to the decision

---

[44] Herbert A. Simon, *Models of Men, Social and Rational* (New York: John Wiley & Sons, Inc., 1957).

makers about current conditions and possible future states that might be achieved through the decision-making process. It is at this point that the role of the computer should be brought into the discussion.

The computer is an information-handling device. It obviously handles only that information put in by organizational members. Its role in the decision-making process is to provide more information about the situation concerning which the decision is to be made. Since computers can reduce quantifiable data into summarized statements, a great deal more information can be brought to bear on the issue at hand. A danger here, of course, is overquantification—in the sense that too great an amount of attention can be paid to those facets of the organization's operations that can be assigned a number, and the qualitative aspects ignored. Despite this problem, it is evident that the use of computers can bring greater rationality into the decision-making process by the provision of more information. It should be reiterated, however, that the availability of more information can make the actual decision making more difficult if the information points to alternatives that have conflicting outcomes for the organization. Since it has been shown that changes in one aspect of an organization affect the rest of the organization and that what might be a desirable change in one part may be accompanied by an undesirable change in another, decision making is thus not made easier through more information; but it can be made more rational.

SUMMARY AND CONCLUSIONS

In this chapter, the attempt was made to place the human factor, in the form of leadership behavior, within the larger framework of analysis. We began with the empirical conclusion that leadership behavior affects followers. To this was added the idea that since our concern was with top organizational leadership, the impact on the followers and the organization should therefore be greater. Since there is not as much information about this form of individual input into the organization as would be desirable, the topic had to be approached somewhat indirectly.

It was first noted that the current conceptualization of leadership involves a combination of factors. *The position in the organization itself, the specific situations confronted, the characteristics of the individuals involved, and the nature of the relationships with subordinates all affect leadership behavior and the impact of that behavior.* Since all these variables except the position itself can vary, it is exceedingly difficult to develop single standards or prescriptions for leadership. From the many studies of leadership effectiveness at lower levels in the organization, the conclusion was reached that there is no one style of leadership that is successful at all times. The total situation must be viewed if leadership is to be understood.

The important question of whether or not leadership makes any kind of difference in the organization was of necessity also approached indirectly. Since it has been found that leadership behavior affects both behavior and attitudes at lower levels in the organizations, the extrapolation was made that it is important at the top. A few studies of top management succession led to the same conclusion. It is unfortunate that we do not know exactly in what ways and under what conditions such impacts occur. From the perspective of the total analysis, it is clear that top leadership is important for the organization as a whole. But we cannot specify how much more or less important or under what conditions it is of importance when compared with some of the other factors considered, such as the existing organizational structure, informally derived power relationships, pressures from the environment, relations with other organizations, and so on. We can make the statement, however, that it *is* important, and hope that future research will begin to unravel the relative strength of these factors under various conditions.

Since a large element of the leadership process involves making critical decisions, the nature of decision making was then considered. The importance of information and the nature of the belief systems of those involved was stressed. The complexity of the conditions under which decisions are made and the difficulties in predicting outcomes were also discussed. Decision making, like the rest of organizational life, takes place in a situation of many cross- and conflicting pressures, so that a movement in one direction is likely to trigger countermovements in others. At the same time, it is critical for the organization as new contingencies are continually faced.

Since information is central to decision making, and since communications allow information to flow, we will now examine this process in organizations.

COMMUNICATIONS⁹

Communications are vital to any form of social life. The nature of information and ideas, the means of transmission, the direction of the transmission, the intent of the sender, and the perception of the recipient—all are part of the communication process. In this chapter we will examine research and observations concerning communications to determine the manner in which this process is intertwined with the other processes and with the organizational structure. In keeping with the previous chapter, we will also be concerned with communications effectiveness—in the sense that communications are linked to decision making, which is in turn linked to goal achievement. There is a fairly wide array of literature on the topic, which has come from field research, laboratory experiments, and the experience of practitioners. The intent is to provide an analysis of the sources and consequences of particular communications patterns and an understanding of the factors that lead to blockages or overloading of the communications system. We will also treat the organization's need for accurate information about its outside world.

THE IMPORTANCE OF COMMUNICATIONS

The communication process has already been an implicit consideration of much of the preceding discussion. Organizational structures, with their varying sizes, technological sophistication, and degrees of complexity and formalization, are designed to be or evolve into information-handling systems. The very establishment of an organizational structure is a signal that communications are supposed to follow a particular path. The fact that the officially designated structure is not the operative one indicates only that communications do not always follow the neatly prescribed lines. Power, leadership, and decision making rely upon the communication process either explicitly or implicitly, since these processes would be meaningless in the absence of information.

Organizational analysts have ascribed varying degrees of importance to the communication process. Chester Barnard, for example, states, "In an exhaustive theory of organization, communication would occupy a central place, because the structure, extensiveness, and scope of the organization are almost entirely determined by communication techniques." [1] This approach essentially places communication as the cause of all else that happens in the organization—a rather extreme view that is balanced by others that hardly mention communication at all.[2] The most reasonable approach is one that views communication as varying in centrality according to *where* one is looking in an organization and *what kind* of organization is being studied.

Katz and Kahn note the varying importance of communication when they say:

> When one walks from a factory to the adjoining head-house or office, the contrast is conspicuous. One goes from noise to quiet, from heavy electrical cables and steam pipes to slim telephone lines, from a machine-dominated to a people-dominated environment. One goes, in short, from a sector of the

---

[1] Chester I. Barnard, *The Functions of the Executive* (Cambridge, Mass.: Harvard University Press, 1938), p. 91.

[2] Alan C. Filley and Robert J. House, *Managerial Processes and Organizational Behavior* (Glenview, Ill.: Scott, Foresman and Company, 1969), and Paul R. Lawrence and Jay W. Lorsch, *Organization and Environment: Managing Differentiation and Integration* (Cambridge: Harvard Graduate School of Business Administration, 1967), contain no direct references to communications; while Amitai Etzioni, in *A Comparative Analysis of Complex Organizations* (New York: The Free Press, 1961), and *Modern Organizations* (Englewood Cliffs, N.J.: Prentice-Hall, 1964), gives very little attention to the topic.

organization in which energic exchange is primary and information exchange secondary, to a sector where the priorities are reversed. The closer one gets to the organizational center of control and decision making, the more pronounced is the emphasis on information exchange.[3]

These intraorganizational differences are important. Equally vital are interorganizational differences. Harold Wilensky suggests that four factors are crucial in determining the importance of communications or intelligence for the organization:

> (1) the degree of conflict or competition with the external environment—typically related to the extent of involvement with and dependence on government; (2) the degree of dependence on internal support and unity; (3) the degree to which internal operations and external environment are believed to be rationalized, that is, characterized by predictable uniformities and therefore subject to planned influence; and affecting all of these, (4) the size and structure of the organization, its heterogeneity of membership and diversity of goals, its centrality of authority.[4]

Communication is most important, therefore, in organizations and organizational segments that must deal with uncertainty, are complex, and have a technology that does not permit easy routinization. Both external and internal characteristics affect communication's centrality. The more an organization is people- and idea-oriented, the more important communication becomes. Even in a highly mechanized system, of course, communications underlie the development and use of machines. Workers are instructed on usage, orders are delivered, and so on. At the same time, the routineness of such operations leads to a lack of variability in the communication process. Once procedures are set, few additional communications are required. While communications occur rather continuously in such settings, their organizational importance is limited unless they lead to severe distortions in the operations. The same point can be made in regard to many persons in the communication process itself. The long-distance telephone operator is vital to modern organizations as they attempt to communicate rapidly over wide geographical areas. What is desired of the operator, however, is unvarying performance, so her ideas and personality are irrelevant to the communication process. The current phasing out of the operator is indicative of the

---

[3] Daniel Katz and Robert L. Kahn, *The Social Psychology of Organizations* (New York: John Wiley & Sons, Inc., 1966), p. 223.

[4] Harold L. Wilensky, *Organizational Intelligence: Knowledge and Policy in Government and Industry* (New York: Basic Books, Inc., Publishers, 1967), p. 10. Wilensky's study is very useful as an analysis of the needs of organizations for information from their environment. The focus in this chapter is on communication as an *internal* process. As Wilensky clearly demonstrates, communications are equally important in environmental transactions.

actual unimportance of this role. The important people—and machines—
are those that can, as a matter of design or fact, provide an input into
the communications system.

The process of communication is by definition a relational one; one
party is the sender and the other the receiver at a particular point in
time. As we will see in more detail later, the relational aspect of communication affects the process. At present, the vital point is that the
social relations occurring in the communication process involve the
sender and receiver and their reciprocal effects on each other as they are
communicating. If a sender is intimidated by his receiver during the
process of sending a message, the nature of the message itself and the
interpretation of it will be affected. Intimidation is just one of a myriad
of factors with the potential for interrupting the simple sender–receiver
relationship. Status differences, different perceptual models, sex appeal,
and so on, can enter the picture and lead to distortions of what is being
sent and received.

These sources of distortion and their consequences will occupy a
good deal of attention in the subsequent discussion. A lack of awareness
of the potentiality for distortion has been responsible for the failure
of many organizational attempts to improve operations simply by utilizing more communications. Katz and Kahn point out that once the importance of communications was recognized, many organizations jumped
on a communications bandwagon, believing that if sufficient communications were available to all members of the organization, everyone would
know and understand what was going on and most organizational problems would disappear.[5] Unfortunately, organizational life, like that in
the outside world, is not that simple, and mere reliance on more communications cannot bring about major and positive changes in the
organization itself.

Before we turn to a more comprehensive examination of communications problems and their consequences in organizations, a simple view
of optimal communications should be presented.[6] The view is simple
because it is directly in line with the earlier comments regarding effectiveness and decision making.

Communications in organizations should provide accurate information with the appropriate emotional overtones to all members who
need the communications content. This assumes that neither too much
nor too little information is in the system and that it is clear from the
outset who can utilize what is available. It should be evident that this
is an impossible condition to achieve in a complex organization.

[5] Katz and Kahn, *Social Psychology*, p. 225.
[6] For a discussion of the limitations of a totally rationalistic approach to organizational communications, see Wilensky, *Organizational Intelligence*, pp. x–xi.

In the sections that follow, the factors leading to this impossibility will be examined, from those that are apparently inherent (through learning) in any social grouping to those that are peculiarly organizational.

THE BASES OF EXISTING COMMUNICATIONS SYSTEMS

Social Factors

Since communication involves something being sent to a receiver, what the receiver does with or to the communicated message is perhaps the most vital part of the whole system. Therefore the perceptual process becomes a key element in our understanding of communications in organizations.

The perceptual process in general is subject to many factors, and this may lead to important differences in the way any two people perceive the same person or message. Sheldon Zalkind and Timothy Costello have summarized much of the literature on perception in the organizational setting and have noted that even physical objects differ in the way they are perceived.[7] The perceiver may respond to cues he is not aware of, be influenced by emotional factors, use irrelevant cues, weigh evidence in an unbalanced way, or fail to identify all the factors on which his judgments are based. His own personal needs, values, and interests enter the perceptual process. Most communications take place in interaction with others, and how he perceives the "other" in the interaction process vitally affects how a person will perceive the communication, since other people are more emotion-inducing than physical objects. For example, research has shown that one's interactions, and thus his perceptions, are affected by even the expectations he has of what the other person will look like.

These factors are common to all perceptual situations. For the analysis of perceptions in organizations, they must be taken as basic conditions in the communication process. So it is obvious that perfect perception, in the sense of being uniform across all information recipients, is extremely unlikely, and in fact impossible in any social situation. The addition of organizational factors makes the whole situation just that much more complex.

---

[7] Sheldon Zalkind and Timothy W. Costello, "Perceptions: Some Recent Research and Implications for Administration," *Administrative Science Quarterly*, Vol. 7, No. 2 (September 1962), 218–35. See also Wilensky, *Organizational Intelligence,* for an additional discussion.

Communications in organizations are basically transactions between individuals. Even when communications are in written or broadcast form, the communicator is identified as an individual. The impression that the communication receiver has of the communicator is crucial to how he interprets the communication. Impressions in these instances are not created *de novo;* the receiver utilizes his own learned response set to the individual and the situation. His own motives and values enter the situation. In addition to this, the setting or surroundings of the act of communication affect the impression. A neat, orderly, and luxuriously furnished office contributes to a reaction different from the one given by an office that looks as though a tornado just struck a paper mill. Since the perceptual process itself requires putting ideas and people into categories, the interaction between communicators is also subject to "instant categorization"; that is, you cannot understand another person unless he is placed in some relevant part of your learned perceptual repertoire. Zalkind and Costello point out that this is often done with a very limited amount of evidence.[8] It can also be done with the wrong evidence, as when the receiver notes cues that are wrong or irrelevant to the situation in question.

All these factors are further complicated by the well-known phenomenon of stereotyping. This predisposition to judge can occur before any interaction at all has taken place. It can involve labels such as "labor" or "management" or any other such group membership. The characteristics of the individual involved are thus assumed to be like those of the group of which he is a member—and in probably the vast majority of cases, the characteristics attributed to the group as a whole are also great distortions of the actual world. In the sense being used here, stereotyping involves the imposition of negative characteristics on the members of the communications system. The reverse situation—attributing socially approved characteristics—can also occur, of course, with an equally strong potential for damage to the communication process.

Other factors that enter the communication process in somewhat the same manner are the use of the "halo effect," or the utilization of only one or a few indicators to generalize about a total situation; "projection," or one's assuming that the other member of a communications system has the same characteristics as his own; and "perceptual defense," or altering inconsistent information to put it in line with the conceptual framework already developed. All the factors that have been mentioned here are taken note of in the general literature on perception and must

---

[8] Zalkind and Costello, "Perceptions," p. 221.

be assumed to be present in any communications system. They are not peculiar to organizations.

The literature has also indicated that the characteristics of the perceived person affect what is perceived. Zalkind and Costello cite four conclusions from research regarding the perceiver.

1. Knowing oneself makes it easier to see others accurately.
2. One's own characteristics affect the characteristics he is likely to see in others.
3. The person who accepts himself is more likely to be able to see favorable aspects of other people.
4. Accuracy in perceiving others is not a single skill.[9]

These findings are linked back to the more general considerations—tendencies to stereotype, project, and so on. It is when the characteristics of the perceived are brought into the discussion that organizational conditions become important. Factors such as status differences and departmental memberships affect how a person is perceived. He may be labeled as a sales manager (accurately or not) by a production worker, and the entire communications system is affected until additional information is permitted into the system. The situation in which the communication takes place also has a major impact on what is perceived. This is particularly vital in organizations, since in most cases the situation is easily labeled and identified by the physical location.

Organizational Factors

These rather general conclusions from the literature on perception are directly relevant for the understanding of communications in an organization. All the factors discussed are part of the general characteristics of communications. In the organization, two additional major components of the communications system are evident and must be considered if a composite picture is to be developed. Vertical and horizontal considerations greatly affect the communication process.

Vertical Communications

Patterns of vertical communications have received a good deal of attention, primarily because they are seen as vital in organizational opera-

[9] *Ibid.*, pp. 227–29.

tions. From the lengthy discussions of organizational structure, power, and leadership it should be evident that the vertical element is a crucial organizational fact of life. Since communications are also crucial, the vertical element intersects in a most important way. Vertical communications in organizations involve both downward and upward communication flows.

DOWNWARD COMMUNICATIONS.   Katz and Kahn identify five elements of downward communications.[10] The first is the simple and common *job instruction,* in which a subordinate is told what to do either through direct orders, training sessions, job descriptions, or other such mechanism. The intent of such instructions is to ensure reliable job performance. The more complex and uncertain the task, the more generalized such instructions. As a general rule, the more highly trained the subordinate, the less specific such instructions are, because of the assumption that he will bring with him an internalized knowledge of how to do the job, along with other such job-related knowledge and attitudes.

The second element is more subtle and less often stressed. It involves the *rationale* for the task and its relationships to the rest of the organization. It is here that different philosophies of life affect how much this sort of information is communicated. If the philosophy is to keep the organizational members dumb and happy, little such information will be communicated. The organization may feel either that the subordinates are unable to comprehend the information or that they would misuse it by introducing variations into their performance based on their own best judgment of how the task should be accomplished. Aside from the philosophy-of-life issue, this is a delicate matter. All organizations, even those most interested in the human qualities of their members, have hidden agendas of some sort at some point in time. If the total rationale for all actions were known to all members, the potential for chaos would be high, since not all members would be able to understand and accept the information at the cognitive or emotional levels. This danger of too much communication is matched by that of the opposite type of situation, which also has a strong potential for organizational malfunctioning. If the members are given too little information, and do not and cannot know how their work is related to any larger whole, there is a strong possibility of alienation from the work and the organization. Obviously, the selection of the best path between these extremes is important in the establishment of communications.

The third element of downward communications is *information* regarding procedures and practices within the organization. This is similar to the first element, in that it is relatively straightforward and non-

10 Katz and Kahn, *Social Psychology,* pp. 239–42.

controversial. Here again, whether or not this is linked to the second element is the problematical issue.

Feedback to the individual regarding his performance is the fourth part of the communications system. This is almost by definition a sticky issue, particularly when the feedback has a negative tone to it. If the superior has attempted to utilize socio-emotional ties to his subordinates at all, the issue becomes even more difficult. And it becomes almost impossible when the work roles are so thoroughly set in advance by the organization that the worker has no discretion on the job at all. In these cases, only a totally conscious deviation would result in feedback. In the absence of deviation, there will probably be no feedback other than the paycheck and other routine rewards. Where discretion is part of the picture, the problem of assessment deepens, in that feedback is more difficult to accomplish because of the absence of clear criteria on which to base it. Despite these evident problems, feedback is a consistent part of downward communications.

The final element of this type of communication involves *ideology*. The organization attempts to indoctrinate subordinates into accepting and believing in the organization's (or subunit's) goals. The intent here, of course, is to get the personnel emotionally involved in their work and add this to the motivational system.

These elements, while seemingly simple when the example of the first-line supervisor–worker relationship is contemplated, become more complex when the focus is shifted to a top executive–vice-president situation. While the same elements are present, the kinds of information and range of ideas covered are likely to be much greater in the latter example. Parsons provides a way of understanding these differences when he categorizes organizations by institutional, managerial, and technical levels.[11] The institutional level is concerned with relating the organization to its external world by ensuring that the organization continues to receive support from its constituency and other organizations in contact. Common examples here are boards of directors or trustees whose primary function is often to maintain this sort of support. It has been suggested that the college or university president has had a predominantly institutional role in recent history. Fund raising and legislative relationships occupied a great deal of his time. As student and faculty dissidence grew, the college president was put into the position of attempting to solve internal problems while at the same time playing the institutional role. The incompatibility of these demands can be readily observed through the exceedingly high turnover in this position.

[11] Talcott Parsons, *Structure and Process in Modern Society* (New York: The Free Press, 1960), pp. 63–69.

The managerial level deals with the internal administration of the organization. Once strategic decisions are made, they must be administered, and the managerial level is concerned with the ways in which the organization will carry out these decisions. The technical level is involved with the translation of this information into specific job descriptions and direction.

The existence of these three levels requires that communications be translated as they cross levels. While it can be assumed that all levels speak the same language and indeed that each may understand completely what the others are doing, the fact remains that the tasks are different and the communications' content and intent are also different.

DYSFUNCTIONS OF HIERARCHY.   This broad-level set of differences illustrates the fact that the presence of a hierarchy in an organization introduces communications problems. While the Parsons formulation is basically concerned with the management subsystems of an organization, the problems of translation exist throughout the organization. Blau and Scott point out that hierarchical differences introduce some clear dysfunctions into the communications system.[12] In the first place, such differences inhibit communications. Citing experimental and field evidence, Blau and Scott note the common tendency for people at the same status level to interact more with one another than with those at different levels. There is a tendency for those in lower status positions to look up to and direct friendship overtures toward those in higher status positions. This increases the flow of socio-emotional communications upward, but at the same time leaves those at the bottom of the hierarchy in the position of receiving little of this type of input. This situation is further complicated by the fact that those in higher satus positions also direct such communications upward, rather than reciprocating to their subordinates, thus reducing the amount of satisfaction derived for all parties.

A second dysfunctional consequence is the fact that approval is sought from superiors rather than peers in such situations. Nonperformance criteria enter the communications system, in that respect from peers, which can be earned on the basis of performance, can become secondary to approval-gaining devices that may not be central to the tasks at hand. The plethora of terms ranging from "apple-polishing" to more profane expressions is indicative of this.

The third dysfunction identified by Blau and Scott has to do with the error-correcting function of normal social interaction. It is commonly found that interaction among peers tends to sort out errors and

---

[12] Peter M. Blau and W. Richard Scott, *Formal Organizations* (San Francisco: Chandler Publishing Co., 1962), pp. 121–24.

at least enter a common denominator through the interaction process. This is much less likely to happen in downward communication. The subordinate is unlikely to tell his superior that he thinks an order or an explanation is wrong, for fear of his own status. Criticism of one's superior is not the most popular of communications in organizations.

Another aspect of the hierarchical pattern that can present problems in organizations is the very nature of the hierarchy itself. If the superior is chosen on the basis of his ability, it is likely that he is more able than his subordinates. If this is the case and the ability takes the form of intellectual superiority, a communications gap can exist because of the different levels of thought on which the superior and subordinates operate. The same type of situation occurs when the subordinates are all experts and the superior becomes a generalist because of his administrative duties. Examples here can be found within organizations employing professionals. When the superior communicates downward, he must do so as a nonexpert, and this lack of expertise may limit his credibility to his subordinates.

These problems associated with downward communication in organizations are compounded by the factors affecting perception that have already been discussed. Since rank in an organization is a structural fact, it carries with it a strong tendency for stereotyping. The very terms "management," "worker," "enlisted man," and so on, are indicative of the value loadings associated with rank. As will be seen shortly, these status differences do have their positive side; but the negative connotations attached to many of the stereotypes and the likelihood that communications will be distorted because of real or assumed differences between statuses builds in difficulties for organizational communications.

In keeping with the earlier discussion noting that complex organizations contain characteristics that work in opposition to each other, there are also beneficial aspects to hierarchical patterns for the communication process. The studies of Blau and his associates, cited earlier, are a case in point.[13] It will be recalled that in organizations with highly trained or professionalized personnel, these studies found that a tall hierarchy was associated with effectiveness. The explanation was that the hierarchy provided a continuous source of error detection and correction. When a hierarchy is composed of people of equal or higher ability than the subordinates, their function in this regard is clear. They can make suggestions and offer alternatives that might not be apparent to subordinates. This assumes, of course, that some of the more dys-

13 Peter M. Blau, Wolf V. Heydebrand, and Robert E. Stauffer, "The Structure of Small Bureaucracies," *American Sociological Review*, Vol. 31, No. 2 (April 1966); and Blau, "The Hierarchy of Authority in Organizations," *American Journal of Sociology*, Vol. 73, No. 4 (January 1968).

functional elements of hierarchical arrangements are minimized. Furthermore, unless one assumes that people always rise to a level just above that of their competence, the superiors may in fact be superior.[14] That is, they may actually have more ability than their subordinates. If this is recognized and legitimated by the subordinates, some of the hierarchical problems are again minimized.

Perhaps the most obvious contribution of a hierarchy is coordination. If one accepts the common model of communications spreading out in more detail as they move down the hierarchy, then the role of the hierarchy becomes clear. It is up to the superior to decide who gets what kind of communications and when. He becomes the distribution and filtering center. Given the vast amount of information that is potentially available for the total organization, this role is crucial. In a later section, we will discuss the nature of hierarchical arrangements and how they can be optimally utilized. For the moment, it is sufficient to note that status differences are obviously important for and endemic to downward communications.

UPWARD COMMUNICATIONS.   Contrary to the law of gravity, communications in organizations must also go up, even when nothing is going down. According to Katz and Kahn, "Communication up the line takes many forms. It can be reduced, however, to what the person says (1) about himself, his performance, and his problems, (2) about others and their problems, (3) about organizational practices and policies, and (4) about what needs to be done and how it can be done." [15] The content of these messages can obviously range from the most personal gripe to the most highminded suggestion for the improvement of the organization and the world; and they can have positive or negative consequences, from a promotion or bonus to dismissal. (A case in point is that of a civilian official in the U.S. Department of Defense who attempted to rectify excessively costly procurement procedures and lost his job.) The most obvious problems in upward communications is again the fact of hierarchy. The tendencies we noted regarding downward communications can be turned around here and shown to be impediments also to upward communications.

The situation is even more complex, in some ways, because the person communicating upward can realistically feel threats either to himself or to his work group if certain kinds of information are made available to the superiors in the system. A person is unlikely to pass informa-

14 See Laurence J. Peter and Raymond Hull, *The Peter Principle* (New York: William Morrow & Co., Inc., 1969).
15 Katz and Kahn, *Social Psychology*, p. 245.

tion up if it will be harmful to himself or his peers. Thus the amount and kind of information that is likely to be passed upward is affected by the fact of hierarchy. Anyone who has been in any kind of organization knows that discussions with the boss, chairman, president, foreman, or other superior are, at least initially, filled with something approaching terror, regardless of the source of the superior's power in the organization.

There is another facet of upward communications that is important. Just as communications downward become more detailed and specific, those going up the hierarchy must become condensed and summarized. Indeed, a major function of those in the middle of a hierarchy is the filtering and editing of information. Only really critical pieces of information are supposed to reach the top. This can be seen in clear relief at the national level, where the president of the United States receives capsulized accounts of the huge number of issues with which he is concerned. Regardless of the party in power, the filtering and editing process is vital in the hierarchy, since the basis on which things are "edited out" can have enormous repercussions by the time the information reaches the top. Here, as well as in downward communications, the perceptual limitations we noted earlier are in operation, so there is a very real potential for distorted communications and, more important, for decisions different from those that would have been made if a different editing process were in force.[16]

COMMUNICATIONS IN FLAT HIERARCHIES. The discussion thus far has been built around the typical hierarchical arrangements, with multiple levels in a step-by-step progression up the line. When organizations are flatter, different considerations enter the picture. In the first place, more nonfiltered communications come to the superior in the system. Hypothetically, at least, all persons in a flat structure have equal access to the superior. On the basis of experimental evidence, Carzo and Yanouzas found that while communications took somewhat more time in a taller structure, conflict resolution and coordination were slower in the flat structure.[17] In the flat structure also, the superior must be able to communicate with all his subordinates, so he must be able to understand what they are doing. Since the flat structure is more likely to be found when the subordinates are experts of one kind or another, this is quite unlikely in practice. In these cases, then, upward communications are

---

[16] Wilensky, in *Organizational Intelligence,* is particularly insightful in his historical analysis of intelligence errors and how they affect national policies.

[17] Rocco Carzo, Jr., and John N. Yanouzas, "Effects of Flat and Tall Organizational Structures," *Administrative Science Quarterly,* Vol. 14, No. 2 (June 1969).

inhibited because of the strong potential for inability to communicate.

COMMUNICATIONS WITH "OUTSIDERS." There is an additional form of vertical communications that is too frequently omitted in the organizational literature. Organizations deal with customers and clients. These groups do not necessarily form a vertical relationship, to be sure, since the relationship can actually be in any direction—up, down, or sideways. In the case of clients, the direction is usually downward, in that the client, as a welfare recipient, patient, or student, is typically viewed in this light. Customers can be courted (upward), expected (horizontal), or merely accepted (downward). These are not fixed relationships, as we can see from the recent revolts by students, welfare recipients, and even consumers. Nevertheless, in most cases the direction seems to be downward.

The nature of the communications to these "outsiders" is affected by their relationships with the organization, in terms of the power they hold vis-à-vis the organization. Joseph Julian has shown that the structure of the organization itself also makes a difference in the communications system to clients.[18] Using data from a set of hospitals, Julian related the nature of the compliance patterns in the hospital to the communications system. The hospitals were categorized according to the Etzioni formulation into normative (general hospital) and normative-coercive (sanatorium and veteran's hospital) types. Julian found more communications blockages in the more coercive hospitals; these blockages were used as a means of client control. In the normative hospitals, on the other hand, more open communications were related to greater effectiveness. Here the appeal was to the patients' beliefs that what the hospital was doing for them was the correct thing. The nature of the relationship to the clients in this case was related to the openness of the communications system.

In a somewhat related study, William Rosengren found that in mental hospitals that move to the "therapeutic milieu" approach, the hierarchical tendencies are minimized and the patient becomes much more a part of the communications system.[19] As organizations dealing with clients redefine their relationships with the clients, such alterations in the communications system are inevitable. As clients and paraprofessionals are brought more and more into the decision-making process, previously existing hierarchical arrangements interfere with effective communications.

At this point, a major dilemma must be noted. The introduction of

18 Joseph Julian, "Compliance Patterns and Communication Blocks," *American Sociological Review*, Vol. 31, No. 3 (June 1966), 382–89.

19 William Rosengren, "Communication, Organization, and Conduct," *Administrative Science Quarterly*, Vol. 9, No. 1 (June 1964), 70–90.

clients and paraprofessionals into the communications system of a welfare, medical, or school system increases the range of inputs into the communication and decision-making processes. This helps correct some of the misconceptions and blocked perceptions that can characterize the way in which some professionals and some organizations deal with clients. At the same time, however, if the nonprofessionals for one reason or another begin to dominate the communications and decision-making systems, then the very reason for the presence of the professionals is nullified. This is part of the constant interplay between expertise and the desire for participation. It is a major consideration in understanding the problems associated with vertical communications in organizations.

Horizontal Communications

Communications in organizations go in more directions than up and down. Despite the obvious fact of horizontal communications, organizational analysts for a long time have concentrated more on the vertical aspect. According to Richard Simpson, the major reason for this skewed perspective has been that the classical writers on organizations themselves focused on the vertical, leading to this type of focus by their successors.[20] But whatever the reason, the horizontal component has received relatively less attention, even though a greater proportion of the communications in an organization appear to be of this type. Simpson's study of a textile factory indicates that the lower the level in the hierarchy, the greater the proportion of horizontal communications. This is not surprising; if for no other reason, in most organizations there are simply more people at each descending level. The fact of more people and the already-noted tendency for communications to be affected by hierarchical differences make it natural for people to communicate with those at about the same level in the organization. And those at the same level are more apt to share common characteristics, making communication even more likely.

It is important to distinguish between communications *within* an organizational subunit and those *between* subunits. In later sections, the latter will be examined more closely. For the moment our attention will be turned to communications within subunits.

This type of communication is "critical for effective system functioning."[21] It is impossible in most cases for an organization to work out in

---

[20] Richard L. Simpson, "Vertical and Horizontal Communication in Formal Organizations," *Administrative Science Quarterly*, Vol. 4, No. 2 (September 1969), 188–96.

[21] Katz and Kahn, *Social Psychology*, p. 243.

advance every conceivable facet of every task assigned throughout the organization. At some point there will have to be coordination and discussion among a set of peers as the work proceeds. The interplay between individuals is vital in the coordination process, since the supervisor and the organization cannot anticipate every possible contingency. This is a rather sterile analysis, of course, since people desire—and the communications process contains—much more than task-related information. The long history of research in industrial psychology and sociology has indicated the importance of peer interactions in at least partially meeting the socio-emotional desires of the participants. The fact that the socio-emotional side is brought into the leadership role (or at least is attempted) indicates the recognition of its importance. In peer interactions there is the greatest likelihood of such experiences in the organization. Katz and Kahn state:

> The mutual understanding of colleagues is one reason for the power of the peer group. Experimental findings are clear and convincing about the importance of socio-emotional support for people in both organized and unorganized groups. Psychological forces always push people toward communication with peers: people in the same boat share the same problems. *Hence, if there are no problems of task coordination left to a group of peers, the content of their communication can take forms which are irrelevant to or destructive of organizational functioning.*[22]

The implication here is clear. It is probably beneficial to allow work groups at every level of the organization to have some task-oriented communications left to them, so that the potentially counterproductive communications do not arise to fill the void. This implication must be modified, however, by a reference back to the general model that is being followed here. It will be remembered that organizational, interpersonal, and individual factors are all part of the way people behave in organizations. If the organizational arrangements are such that horizontal communications are next to impossible, then there is little likelihood of any communication. Work in extremely noisy circumstances or in isolated work locales would preclude much interaction. (These situations, of course, contain their own elements of problems for the individual and the organization.) On the other side of the coin, too much coordination and communications responsibility left to those who, because of the absence of training or ability, are unable to come to a reasonable joint decision about some matter would also be individually and organizationally disruptive.

While it is relatively easy, in abstract terms, to describe the optimal

22 *Ibid.*, p. 244. [Italics in original.]

mix between vertical and horizontal communicatons in the sense that they are being described here, there is another element to communication among peers that should be noted. Since the communications among peers tend to be based on common understandings, and since continued communications build up the solidarity of the group, work groups develop a collective response to the world around them. This is true for communications on the vertical axis as well as for other aspects of the work situation. When this occurs, therefore, there is likely to be a collective perception of communications passed to or through the work group. This collective perception can be a collective distortion. It is clear that work groups (as well as any other cohesive collectivity) can perceive communications in a totally different light from the one that was intended. A relatively simple communiqué, such as the fact that there is some likelihood of reorganization, can be interpreted to mean that an entire work force will be eliminated. While this type of response can occur individually, the nature of peer relationships also makes it possible as a collective phenomenon.

Interaction among peers is only one form of horizontal communications. The other major form, obviously vital for the overall coordination of the operations, occurs between members of organizational subunits. While the former has been the subject of some attention, the research concerning the latter has been minimal. The principal reason seems to be that such communications are not supposed to occur. In almost every conceivable form of organization, they are supposed to go through the hierarchy until they reach the "appropriate" office, at the point where the hierarchies of the two units involved come together. That is, the communications are designed to flow through the office that is above the two departments involved, so that the hierarchy is familiar with the intent and content of the communications. In a simple example, problems between production and sales are supposed to be coordinated either through an office designed for that purpose or through the individual in charge of both activities.

Obviously, such a procedure occurs in only a minority of such lateral communications. There is a great deal more face-to-face and memo-to-memo communication throughout the ranks of the subunits involved. A major reason for this form of deviation is that it would totally clog the communications system if all information regarding subunit interaction had to flow all the way up one of the subunits and then all the way back down another. The clogging of the system would result in either painfully slow communications or none at all.

Therefore, the parties involved generally communicate directly with each other. This saves time and can often mean a very reasonable solution worked out at a lower level with good cooperation. However, it may mean also that those further up the hierarchy are unaware of what has happened, and this can be harmful in the long run. A solution to this problem is to record and pass along the information about what has been done; but this too may be neglected, and if it is done, it may not be noticed.

While the emphasis in this discussion has been on coordination between subunits, it should be clear that much of the communication of this sort is actually based on conflict. The earlier discussions of the relationships between professionals and their employing organizations can be brought in at this point. When professionals or experts make up divisions of an organization, their areas of expertise are likely to lead them to different conclusions about the same matter. For example, in a petroleum company it is quite conceivable that the geological, engineering, legal, and public relations divisions could all come to different conclusions about the desirability of starting new oil-well drilling in various locations. Each would be correct in its own area of expertise, and the coordination of top officials would obviously be required when a final decision had to be made. During the period of planning or development, however, communications between these divisions would probably be characterized as nonproductive, since each of the specialists involved would be talking his own language, one that is unfamiliar to those not in the same profession. From the evidence at hand, each division would also be correct in its assessments of the situation and would view the other divisions as not understanding the "true" meanings of the situation.

This type of communications problem is not limited to professionalized divisions. Whenever a subunit has an area of expertise, it will move beyond other divisions in its conceptualization of a problem. Communications between such subunits are inevitably going to contain elements of conflict. The conflict will be greater if the units involved invest values in their understanding and conceptualizations. Horizontal communications across organizational lines thus contain both the seeds and the flower of conflict. Such conflict by definition will contribute to distortion of communications in one form or another. At the same time, passing each message up the line to eliminate such distortion through coordination at the top has the dangers of diluting the message in attempts to avoid conflict and of taking so much time that the message can become meaningless. Here again, the complexities of an organization that are endemic to the situation preclude a totally rational operation.

COMMUNICATIONS NETWORKS.   Before turning to a more systematic examination of the consequences of all these communications problems in organizations, a final bit of evidence should be noted regarding the manner in which communications evolve. The communication process can be studied in laboratory situations; among organizational character- istics, it is perhaps the most amenable to such experimentation. There has been a long history (Bavelas, Leavitt, etc.) of attempting to isolate the communications system that is most efficient under a variety of cir- cumstances.[23] These laboratory studies are applicable to both the ver- tical and horizontal aspects of communications, since the manner in which the communications tasks are coordinated is the major focus. Three primary communications networks between members of work groups have been studied. The "wheel" pattern is one in which persons at the periphery of the wheel all send their communications to the hub. This is an imposed hierarchy, since those at the periphery cannot send messages to each other; it is the task of the hub to do the coordinating. The "circle" pattern permits each member of the group to talk to those on either side, with no priorities. The "all-channel" system allows every- one to communicate with everyone else.

Using success in arriving at a correct solution as the criterion of ef- ficiency, repeated investigations have found the wheel pattern to be superior. The other patterns can become equally efficient if they develop a hierarchy over time, but this of course takes time, and meanwhile efficiency is reduced. Katz and Kahn and Blau and Scott note that the more complex the task, the more time is required for the communica- tions network to become structured.[24] The importance of these findings for our purposes here is that whether the communications are vertical or horizontal, hierarchical patterns emerge. In the vertical situation, the hierarchy is already there, although the formal hierarchy can be modi- fied through the power considerations of expertise or personal attraction. In the horizontal situation, a hierarchy will emerge. In addition, it is important to note that the task being performed, based on the tech- nology involved, will in part determine where the coordination will occur. It is not a random phenomenon, nor is it necessarily one based on formal position. Instead, the communications network should be built around the specific task. Obviously, this is not always the case.

Now let us examine in more detail the consequences of the com- munications patterns we have discussed.

---

23 See, for example, Alex Bavelas, "Communication Patterns in Task Oriented Groups," *Journal of the Acoustic Society of America*, No. 22 (1950), 725–30; and Harold J. Leavitt, "Some Effects of Certain Communications Patterns on Group Performance," *Journal of Abnormal and Social Psychology*, No. 46 (1951), 38–50.

24 Katz and Kahn, *Social Psychology*, pp. 237–38; and Blau and Scott, *Formal Organizations*, pp. 126–27.

COMMUNICATIONS PROBLEMS

From all that has been said above, it should be clear that communications in organizations are not perfect. The basic consequence of existing communications systems is that messages are transformed or altered as they pass through the system. The fact that they are transformed means that the ultimate recipient of the message receives something different from what was originally sent, thus destroying the intent of the communication process.

Omission

Guetzkow suggests that there are two major forms of transformation —omission and distortion.[25] Omission involves the "deletion of aspects of messages," and it occurs because the recipient may not be able to grasp the entire content of the message and only receives or passes on what he is able to grasp. Communications overload, which will be discussed in more detail later, can also lead to the omission of materials as some messages are not handled because of the overload. Omission may be intentional, as when certain classes of information are deleted from the information passed through particular segments of the organization. Omission is most evident in upward communications, since more messages are generated by the larger number of people lower in the hierarchy. As the communications are filtered on the way up, the omissions are brought into the system. As was indicated earlier, when omissions are intentional, it is vital to know the criteria by which decisions are made to omit some kinds of information and not others. It should be noted that omission can occur simply as a removal of details, with the heart of the message still transmitted upward. This is the ideal, of course, and is not usually achieved, since part of the content of the message is usually omitted also.

Distortion

Distortion refers to altered meanings of messages as they pass through the organization. From the earlier discussion of perceptions, it is clear

---

[25] Harold Guetzkow, "Communications in Organizations," in James G. March, ed., *Handbook of Organizations* (Chicago: Rand McNally & Co., 1965), p. 551. This article contains an excellent bibliography.

that people are selective, intentionally or unintentionally, about what they receive as messages. Guetzkow states:

> . . . because different persons man different points of initiation and reception of messages, there is much assimilation of meanings to the contexts within which transmission occurs. Frames of reference at a multitude of nodes differ because of variety in personal and occupational background, as well as because of difference in viewpoint induced by the communicator's position in the organization.[26]

Distortion is as likely to occur in horizontal communications as in vertical, given the differences between organizational units in objectives and values. Selective omission and distortion, or "coding" in Katz and Kahn's terms, are not unique properties of organizations. They occur in all communications systems, from the family to the total society. They are crucial for organizations, however, since organizations depend upon accurate communications as a basis for approaching rationality.

Overload

A communications problem that is perhaps more characteristic of organizations than other social entities is communications overload. Overload, of course, leads to omission and contributes to distortion. It also leads to other coping and adjustment mechanisms on the part of the organization. Katz and Kahn note that there are adaptive and maladaptive adjustments to the overload situation.[27] Omission and distortion are maladaptive. They are also normal.

Another device used when overload occurs is queuing. This technique lines up the messages by time of receipt or some other such criterion. Queuing can have positive or negative consequences. If the wrong priority system is used, less important messages may be acted upon before those that are really crucial reach the recipient. At the same time, queuing does allow the recipient to act on the messages as they come in without putting him in a state of inaction because of total overload. An example of this is an anecdote from a disaster following a major earthquake. Organizations dealing with the earthquake were besieged with messages. Those to which the victims could come and plead for help on a face-to-face basis, crowding into an office and all talking at once, quickly brought the organizations involved to a halt. The overload was so great that the communications could not be filtered in any way. Another organization received its messages by telephone, a device provid-

[26] *Ibid.*, p. 555.
[27] Katz and Kahn, *Social Psychology*, pp. 231–35.

ing an arbitrary queuing mechanism based on an operating phone and the luck of finding an open line. This organization was able to keep functioning, because the messages came in one at a time. In a queuing situation, of course, there are no real criteria concerning which messages get through and which do not, other than time phasing and luck in getting a phone line.

A modification of queuing that can be a useful device is the filtering process previously mentioned, which involves setting priorities for messages. The critical factor here is the nature of the priorities.

All the communications problems discussed are based on the fact that communications in organizations require interpretation. If there is a case of extreme overload, the interpretive process becomes inundated with so much material that it becomes inoperative. The other situations involve predispositions to interpret in particular ways, or structured preinterpretations into categories and priorities set in advance.

Possible Solutions

With all the problems, potential and real, in the communication process, it is obvious that a "perfect" communications system is unlikely. But although perfection, like rationality, will not be achieved, organizations do have mechanisms by which they attempt to keep the communications system as clear as they can. Downs suggests several devices that are available to reduce the distortions and other complications in the communication process.[28] Redundancy, or the duplication of reports for verification, while adding to the flow of paper and other communications media in an organization, allows more people to see or hear a particular piece of information and respond to it. This is a correction device. Several means are suggested to bring redundancy about, including the use of information sources external to the situation—such as reports that are generated outside the organization itself—thus ensuring that reporting units and individuals coordinate their communications. This coordination can lead to collusion and thus more distortion, but it can be controlled through other monitoring devices.

Downs also suggests that communications recipients should be aware of the biases of the message senders and develop their own counterbiases as a protection device—a process that, of course, can be carried too far and be overdone, but that is the "grain of salt" that is part of all communications. This technique assumes that the recipient knows what the sender's biases are, which is not a guaranteed situation. Another

[28] Anthony Downs, *Inside Bureaucracy* (Boston: Little, Brown and Company, 1967), pp. 118–20.

method Downs advises is that in vertical communications the superior should often bypass intermediate subordinates and go directly to the source of the communications. While this can help eliminate some distortion, it can also create low morale in those bypassed.

Downs' final suggestion involves the development of distortion-proof messages, by using "predesignated definitions and easily quantifiable information." [29] All organizations use this approach but it becomes dangerous as soon as the communications begin to deal with areas about which there are uncertainties. As we discussed in detail in Chapter 3, overquantification can be a real danger, and the same is true of present categories that do not fit new or emerging situations. At the same time, for many routine events such a communications device is highly rational.

There must be communications in organizations. The nature, problems, and suggested solutions of communications all point to the centrality of this process for much of what happens in an organization. While this is an evident fact, it is also evident that the communications system is vitally affected by other structural and processual factors. Communications do not exist outside the total organizational framework. They cannot be over- or underemphasized. More and more accurate communications do not lead inevitably to greater effectiveness for the organization. The key to the communication process in organizations is to ensure that the correct people get the correct information (in amount and quality) at the correct time. All these factors can be anticipated somewhat in advance. If organizations, their members, and their environments were all in a steady state, the communications tasks would be easier. Since obviously they are not, the communication process must be viewed as a dynamic one, with new actors, new media, and new definitions constantly entering the scene.

SUMMARY AND CONCLUSIONS

This chapter has dealt with a topic of obvious importance in organizations and for human societies in general. The communication process, while not limited to humans, is central to humanity.

In an organization, as on the "outside," the process is affected by the actors in the situation. The whole range of factors contributing to distortion in all communication is evident in organizations. Emotional considerations can have a positive or negative influence in the trans-

29 *Ibid.,* pp. 126–27.

mittal of information. Rationality can obscure important socio-emotional inputs into the process. Organizations add another element to the basic nature of communications, however. Here, the communicators fill positions that have expectations built into them, occupy slots that have more or less status and prestige and specialized expertise expected, and have their relationships with others programmed to some degree in advance, and these facts make communications in organizations a special case of the wider process.

The structural considerations of vertical and horizontal relationships add a set of factors that are not so clearly established in other communications systems and can add problems not generally found elsewhere, but the communication process is vital for organizational operations. Effectiveness, power, leadership, and decision making depend upon communications, simply because there must be inputs into these areas and the input is largely information. The better the information, the better the decision making, power utilization, and so on.

While communications can be improved, the basic facts of organizational life apparently preclude the development of a perfect communications system. Here again, one of the contradictions of organizational life is apparent. The better that the structural and processual system is developed for one set of circumstances, the more poorly it operates for others. A clear differentiation between hierarchical ranks or the separation of tasks into specialties can be highly efficient for certain operations, but they present blockages and other problems in the communication process.

These problems that arise from the organizational arrangements cannot be solved without damage to parts of the rest of the system—another example of the complexity of organizations, in that the oppositional forces cannot be perfectly meshed. As is the case with effectiveness, the most intelligent approach seems to be one of compromise and admission that the system cannot work perfectly. In other words, organizations and their members must live with the fact that improvements in one part of the system will be linked with deterioration in others. Conflict will be present. Mistakes will be made. At the same time, of course, there can be an overall improvement if some of the problems are understood and false issues do not enter the scene (stereotyping, the use of the wrong form of power, etc.).

The primary focus in this chapter has been on internal communications. The last section of the analysis involves communications and other relationships between the organization and its environment. We have seen that the internal system does not and cannot work perfectly, but when attention is turned to external relationships, an even looser and less rational system can be observed. This is not meant to imply that tightness and rationality would necessarily be a good thing, but rather to indicate that the relationships are more random, subject to chance, and outside any control system. The analysis will focus on two major themes, the impact of the environment on the organization and that of the organization on its environment.

part four

ORGANIZATIONS
AND
SOCIETY

Structure and process. These topics have been the primary focus of our analysis thus far. Throughout the analysis we have seen that factors outside the organization play a major role in what happens within the organization. In the next chapter, topics such as political forces, economic conditions, and technological change will be examined specifically. We will also look at the relationships between organizations and see how they affect an organization. The final chapter will turn the issue around by looking at the ways in which organizations affect their environment.

Our interest in organizational analysis must be broad enough to ask the question, *What does society do to organizations?* and *What do organizations do to society?* Complete answers to these questions are not available. Partial answers and polemics have filled and will probably continue to fill the library shelves, as well as the minds of decision makers for organizations and for society. The polemics do very little good, except in those few cases where they turn our interests to new directions that have been ignored in the past. The partial answers reflect the severe limitations of the evidence recorded. The topics of this section have not been well researched, and so our knowledge is spotty and skimpy.

When we move down from an abstract level to the substance of these relationships, we can see how important these topics really are. Wars, pollution, conspiracies, social movements, national development, inflation, political pressures, revolutions, and social control systems are just a few of the topics that make up this subject matter. Wars are a special form of interorganizational relationship; inflation has an impact on all organizations; the developing nation must rely on organizations; and so on. While it certainly does not provide all the answers, organizational analysis does give us some important insights into why things happen as they do.

Such analyses should provide more, however. We don't know, for example, the extent to which a television network is affected by direct attacks from the vice-president of the United States, or whether it would make a bigger difference if adverse judgments were passed against it by the Federal Communications Commission or if advertising revenues suddenly lagged. We also don't know the extent to which the interorganizational network that has been called the military-industrial complex is actually such a complex and how it really affects the total social system. We do hope, however, that analysis will provide partial answers and that future research will tell us more than we have learned in the past.

THE ENVIRONMENT AND THE ORGANIZATION

10

The theme of this chapter has been expressed and documented many times already: Conditions external to the organization contribute to what goes on within the organization, the form that the organization takes, and the consequences of its actions. Much of the previous analysis has focused on the technological aspect of an organization's environment. Obviously, this is only part of the picture. In this chapter, by examining the range of conditions that appear to have important influences on organizations, we will attempt to identify the conditions and the direction and extent of their influences. We will be handicapped by insufficient evidence but will still try to determine the relative importance of the factors to be discussed.

Our basic assumption is that the environment is very important to organizations. A recent paper by Shirley Terreberry argues that environmental conditions are *increasingly* important.[1] She says that environments are becoming more "turbulent," in that there are accelerating

[1] Shirley Terreberry, "The Evolution of Organizational Environments," *Administrative Science Quarterly*, Vol. 12, No. 4 (March 1968), 590–613. This term is taken from F. E. Emery and E. L. Trist, "The Causal Texture of Organizational Environments," *Human Relations*, No. 18 (1965), 24.

rates and new directions of change. In order to survive, organizations must be able to adapt to this turbulence, which is attested to by the recent history of colleges and universities, the aerospace industry, the military, and religious organizations. Environmental factors are a source, therefore, of change in the organization, as well as a source or cause of existing conditions.

In order to approach the topic somewhat systematically, let us divide environmental conditions into two categories.[2] The first contains those *general* conditions that must be of concern to all organizations—the economy, demographic changes, and so on. While particular organizations must respond to these facets of these conditions that are most relevant to them, the conditions themselves are the same for all. The second category contains *specific* environmental influences on the organization, such as other organizations with which it interacts or particular individuals who are crucial to it. In the case of specific environmental factors, the interaction is direct, whereas the general environment is not a concrete entity in interaction, but rather comprises conditions that must be grappled with.[3]

The importance of the various environmental conditions varies over time. A condition that is important at one period may become insignificant at another. All the factors to be discussed have the potential of being critical. At present we do not have the research evidence to permit specification of the circumstances under which one is more important than the others; therefore, most of the discussion to follow will have to be taken as suggestive rather than definitive, and many of the examples will be somewhat hypothetical for the same reason.

THE GENERAL ENVIRONMENT

Technological Conditions

Probably the easiest place to begin the discussion of the general environment is with *technology*. Since this topic and the research sur-

[2] This distinction and much of the last section of the chapter reflect extended discussions and work with Professor John P. Clark. At the present time, Professor Clark and the author are conducting research on interorganizational relationships among agencies dealing with problem youth, under support from NIH Grant No. MH 17508–01.

[3] This is a modification of William Dill's notion of "task environment," which refers to those elements in the environment that are relevant or potentially relevant for the organization. Our approach further specifies the nature of the relevant environment. See Dill, "Environment as an Influence on Managerial Autonomy," *Administrative Science Quarterly,* Vol. 2, No. 4 (March 1958), 409–43.

rounding it have already been the subject of a good deal of attention, it can set the stage for the less systematically researched topics that follow.

It will be remembered, following the works of Perrow, Lawrence and Lorsch, and others, that organizations operating in a technological environment that is uncertain and dynamic have been found to exhibit different structures and internal processes from those operating in a rather certain and unchanging technological situation.[4] While we need not at this point review the direction of the relationships and the supporting evidence, it is important to recognize that the organization responds to this aspect of its environment. In fact, in the case of the business firms Lawrence and Lorsch studied, special organizational divisions were established (research and development) to keep the organization current. In other organizations, departments such as industrial engineering, management analysis, and so on, are so designated.

Beyond the importance of the empirical evidence regarding the salience of technology in the operation of organizations, these findings have implications vital to our understanding of organizational–environmental transactions. In the first place, technology and other environmental characteristics are something "out there." The organization does not exist in a vacuum. A technological development in any sphere of activity will eventually get to the organizations related to it. The process of diffusion of technological developments to organizations would itself be an interesting topic for research. Given the evidence that diffusion of ideas to individuals is a complex process, it is probably even more complex in the case of organizations. (Another interesting question is the one of how innovations become accepted within the organization. This is not our concern here, however.) New ideas come into circulation and become part of the environment as soon as they cease being the private property of any one individual or organization. Since the sciences have a norm of distributing knowledge, scientific developments become part of the public domain as a matter of course. A development that can be patented is a different matter, but if it is thought to be significant, other organizations will seek to copy it or extend the previous development further. In either case, an organization is required to keep up with such developments whenever it is in an activity in which they are crucial to its continued success.

4 Paul R. Lawrence and Jay W. Lorsch, *Organizations and Environment: Managing Differentiation and Integration* (Cambridge: Harvard Graduate School of Business Administration, 1967); Charles Perrow, "A Framework for the Comparative Analysis of Complex Organizations," *American Sociological Review*, Vol. 32, No. 2 (April 1967); and Joan Woodward, *Industrial Organizations* (London: Oxford University Press, 1962).

More subtle forms of the technological environment are found outside the hard sciences and engineering. In management and administration, new ideas are introduced through research, serendipity, or practice. One need only mention sensitivity training, T-groups, participative management, or program–planning–budgeting as an indication of the changing technologies, styles, and even fads in the technological developments available to the administration of organizations. In service-oriented organizations such as schools, social-work agencies, and hospitals, the same types of technological shifts can be seen. The organization in any sphere of activity is made aware, through one mechanism or another, of technological developments that are or can be part of its own activities. An important mechanism appears to be the introduction of new personnel or clients who have had contact with alternative technologies and advocate their use in the organization in question. This, of course, can be a source of conflict in the organization, as can the technology-development and monitoring departments.

Organizations do not respond to technological change through absorption. Instead, the political process operates through the advocacy of change or stability. Organizations of every kind contain their own internal "radicals" and "reactionaries," in terms of their responses to technological and other environmental conditions. Since the rate of technological and other environmental changes is not constant for all organizations, the degree to which they must develop response mechanisms varies. For all, however, technology remains an important consideration.

Legal Conditions

An environmental consideration often overlooked but potentially critical is the *legal conditions* that are part of the organization's surroundings.[5] Most organizations that operate outside the law respond to the legal system by their attempts to evade the law and remain underground. Organizations such as voluntary associations with a strictly local base may be relatively unaffected by legal considerations until laws are passed that affect their operations, or until they become developed to the point that they must register with one or another government agency. Airlines, for instance, must comply with safety, rate, alcoholic beverage, and a host of other laws and regulations. Since almost all organizations are affected directly or indirectly by the legal system, this fact must be introduced into the analysis.

[5] This is a component of Etzioni's discussion in Amitai Etzioni, *Modern Organizations* (Englewood Cliffs, N.J.: Prentice-Hall, Inc., 1964), pp. 110–11.

In many and probably most cases, federal, state, and local laws are constants with which organizations must live. However, they do set many of the operating conditions of many organizations, ranging from specific prohibitions of certain kinds of behavior to regulations requiring reporting of income and staffing at periodic times of the year. The importance of laws is shown by the staffs of legal and other experts who form an important part of many organizations and who are specifically charged with interpreting and protecting the organizations' positions.

While the body of laws as a constant is an interesting analytical point, the dynamic aspect of the legal system points up the importance of laws for organizations. When a new law is passed or an interpretation modified, organizations must make some important changes if the law has relevance for them. Here again, relatively mundane matters such as tax and employment regulations are important. More striking are the cases of major shifts that affect organizations in the public and private sectors. For example, U.S. Supreme Court decisions regarding school desegregation have had tremendous impacts on the school organizations involved. The recent concern with the environment has resulted in laws and regulations concerning pollution that have affected many organizations as they utilize their resources in fighting or complying with the new statutes. Laws are thus important external constraints on organizations.

Political Conditions

Laws are not passed without pressures for their enactment. The *political situation* that brings about new laws also has its effects on organizations. To use the pollution example again, the political pressures brought by various conservation groups concerned about potential pollution has contributed in part to a real shortage of electrical power. The strong political pressures to reduce military and aerospace spending have led to crises of one sort or another for organizations in those areas. Police departments are buffeted back and forth between support for "law and order" and condemnation of "police brutality." School systems have drastically altered parts or all of their curricula in the face of threats from groups concerned with such topics as sex education or left-wing textbooks. Some organizations are directly affected by the political process, in that their hierarchy can be drastically changed because of election results. All government units face this possibility after every election, as top officials are changed at the discretion of a new administration.

Organizations in the private sector are less directly affected than public ones, but they must still be attuned to the political climate. Since lobbying for legislation that will be favorable in terms of tax advantages or international trade agreements is an accepted part of the legislative and administrative system of the United States, organizations must devote resources to the lobbying process. "Institutional advertising" is designed to generate some form of public support for the organization involved, as exemplified by the current effort of American railroads to indicate their importance to the nation, while at the same time seeking legislation that will give them a more favorable competitive position. This anecdotal evidence points up the importance of the political process in the wider society for the organizations contained in it.

Economic Conditions

A societal condition that is more obvious, but again strangely neglected by most sociologists, is the state of the *economy* in which the organization is operating. To most businessmen, this is *the* crucial variable. In universities and in government work, experience also shows the importance of economic conditions when budgets are being prepared, defended, and appropriated in nonindustrial areas. Changing economic conditions serve as important constraints on any organization. Much of the earlier discussion of organizational size was based on the assumption that an organization has the economic capability to increase in size. In periods of economic growth, organizations, in general, also grow—and vice versa.

The economy is important for organizations in more than its relationship to gross size. Changing economic conditions do not affect all parts of an organization equally. In periods of economic distress, an organization is likely to cut back or eliminate those programs it feels are least important to its overall goals. This, in fact, is an excellent indicator of the operative goals of organizations. The fact that organizational programs vary according to the economic conditions that are confronted contributes to a paradox for most organizations. Since total rationality is not part of this analysis, it can be safely assumed that an organization cannot be sure of exactly what contribution each of its parts makes to the whole. For example, research and development can be viewed as one of the luxuries that should go when an organization faces some hard times. But by concentrating on the production and distribution of what R&D has done in the past, the organization may miss the development of a new product that would be of great long-run benefit. People in health-related research sponsored by the federal government have claimed that cutbacks in these activities have come at a time when crucial breakthroughs are about to be made. Here again, the decision is made on the economic ground that other activities are of greater importance. Tragic and sometimes humorous examples such as these could be given for probably every kind of organization, and while they could fill a book of their own as organizations attempt to decide what their priorities are, periods of economic difficulty do force organizations to evaluate themselves and trim off excess fat if any is found. As in the case of the communication process, the criteria by which the evaluations are accomplished are the key variables.

Economic conditions around organizations improve and decline, with the organizations responding to the situation. In their responses in any situation, the important factor of competition is present. Economic competition can be most easily seen in business organizations, where success is measured in the competitive marketplace. While the competition is not "pure," it is still an evident part of the system, and of the general value system, in a private-enterprise economy. What is less evident, but equally real, is economic competition among and within organizations outside the business sphere. From repeated experiences in government agencies at several levels, it is clear that competition is fierce during budget season.[6] Government agencies are all competing for part of the tax revenues, which constitute a finite "pot." Organizations that rely on contributions from members, such as churches, are also affected by the general economic conditions, since the contributors have more or less income available. An interesting research question is the extent to which the severity of economic competition varies among organizations in all sectors of society. It seems almost equal, regardless of the organization's major emphases.

Demographic Conditions

Demography is another factor. The number of people served and their age and sex distributions make a great deal of difference to all organizations. As a general rule, an organization can predict its probable "market" for the future from information in census data, but population shifts are less predictable and make the organization more vulnerable. In a society where race, religion, and ethnicity are important considerations, shifts in these aspects of the demographic condition must also be considered. The most striking examples of the importance of demographic change come from organizations located in the central cities of growing metropolitan areas. Businesses, schools, and police departments have different clientele from what they once had, even though

---

6 See Aaron Wildavsky, *The Politics of the Budgetary Process* (Boston: Little, Brown and Company, 1964).

the organizations themselves might not reflect this. At least in the short run, it is the urban poor and minority-group members who suffer the consequences. The organizations themselves, however, eventually undergo transitions (usually painful) as they begin to realize that their clientele has become different and that they themselves must change.

Ecological Conditions

Related to the demographic scene is the general *ecological situation* surrounding an organization. The number of organizations with which it has contacts and relationships and the environment in which it is located are components of the organization's ecological system. In an intense urban area, an organization is much more likely to have contacts with a myriad of other organizations than is one in a rural area. Since the density of other organizations around any particular organization varies widely, the potential for relationships also varies.

Shifting from social ecology to the physical environment, the relationships between organizations and ecological conditions become more evident because of the recent concerns about the total ecological system. It is increasingly clear that organizations have effects on the environment, as is abundantly demonstrated by the various organizations that pollute and the others that fight pollution. These topics are part of the concern of the next chapter.

A more subtle point is that the environment affects organizations. Factors such as climate and geography set limits on the manner in which they allocate resources. Transportation and communication costs rise if an organization is distant from its market or client. Even such mundane items as heating and cooling expenses must be considered limits on an organization. These factors are generally constants, since only in unusual circumstances are there significant changes here. Nevertheless, in a total organizational analysis, these conditions cannot be ignored when comparisons are made between organizations.

Cultural Conditions

The environmental conditions discussed thus far are fairly easily measured in terms of "hard" indicators of the degree to which they are present or absent. A more difficult task is to determine the extent to which they actually affect the organizations in a social system. For the present time it has to be assumed that they make a difference, even though we cannot specify which is more important than the others in particular situations. Other conditions in the external environment that are vitally important are more difficult to measure. The first of these is the *culture* surrounding an organization. The experiences of organizations that attempt to establish new operating units across national boundaries or in different regions of the United States provide commonsense examples of the importance of cultural differences. Unless the values and behaviors of the indigenous population are understood and appreciated, such projects are likely to fail.

Research in this area, while oriented in a different direction, leads to the same conclusion—that the culture of the system surrounding an organization has a major impact on the way the organization operates. Evidence for this conclusion comes from many studies conducted in various parts of the world. Notable among these are Crozier's analysis of two French bureaucracies and James Abegglen's study of Japanese factories.[7] Both confirm the point that the culture permeates the organizational boundaries through the expectations and actions of the personnel. Norms and behaviors that work in one setting are likely to be ineffective or even counterproductive in another. An understanding of a different culture is an accepted requisite for any move by an organization into new areas.

While the influence of the culture is now an accepted fact, it is not clear whether culture overrides other factors in determining how an organization is shaped and operates. There is some evidence suggesting that organizations at an equivalent technological level—for example, at the same degree of automation of production—are quite similar in most respects. The basic problem here is sorting out the influences of these various environmental factors as they impinge on the organization. Unfortunately, the level of knowledge is not yet sufficient for such fine distinctions to be made. The way the various factors discussed so far probably interrelate in their organizational effects is a rather complex interaction pattern. For example, it appears that the more routine and standardized the technology, the less the impact of cultural factors. The production of children's toy automobiles is probably carried out in similar organizations in Hong Kong, London, Japan, Switzerland, or Tonka, Minnesota. When one moves to less routinized technological operations, such as local government, the administration of justice, or highway construction, the impact of culture is likely to be higher.

The complexity of the issue can be seen when it is realized that we are dealing with only two of the variables we have discussed in these examples. If the other factors are added in, the picture is much more

7 Michel Crozier, *The Bureaucratic Phenomenon* (Chicago: University of Chicago Press, 1964); and James C. Abegglen, *The Japanese Factory* (New York: The Free Press, 1958).

difficult to comprehend. As research proceeds and some quantitative measures of the variables discussed become available, the complex interactions will be more understandable.

There is another aspect of the cultural impact on organizations. Culture is not a constant, even in a single setting. Values and norms change as events occur that affect the population involved. These shifts, where they involve conditions relevant to the organization, are significant for it. Newspaper editorials, letters to the editor, and other colorations of reports in the mass media indicate how values can change in regard to particular organizations or types of organizations. These value shifts may precede or accompany political shifts, which would have a more direct kind of impact. Changes in consumer tastes represent another way that cultural conditions can affect organizations. Examples of this are easily found; a dramatic one is that of the contrasting experiences with the Edsel and Mustang cars by the Ford Motor Company.

We have listed those external factors that appear to be the most crucial for the organization. In the best of all possible worlds, the relative strength and direction of the influence of each factor could be specified. This is not possible, given our present knowledge. The research on technology does suggest that it is of critical importance. Just where it ranks in terms of the other environmental conditions remains an open question. All of them seem to be important, but the exact mix cannot be known until a better research base is available.

We have been concerned with the manner in which contemporary conditions impinge upon particular organizations at a particular point in time. We will now shift our attention to the way the total social structure affects the organizations within it. This analysis will reinforce the conclusions we have already reached regarding the kinds of external factors that are important and the fact that there is a mix between these factors. At the same time, the more general importance of such external conditions will be demonstrated.

THE ENVIRONMENT AND ORGANIZATIONAL DEVELOPMENT

Social Conditions

Arthur Stinchcombe has recently examined the interface between organizations and the social structure.[8] In a discussion of organizational

[8] Arthur L. Stinchcombe, "Social Structure and Organizations," in James G. March, ed., *Handbook of Organizations* (Chicago: Rand McNally & Co., 1965), pp. 142–93.

development and historical conditions, Stinchcombe maintains that:

> . . . it seems that in some societies the *rate* at which special purpose organizations take over various social functions (economic production, policing, education, political action, military action, etc.) is higher than in other societies, and that within societies some population groups are more likely to found new types of organizations to replace or supplement multiple-purpose groups such as families or geographical communities for certain purposes.[9]

According to this approach, in order to develop a new organization a population must be *aware* of alternative techniques for accomplishing some task or set of tasks in the society. This means that the traditional approaches are at least being questioned, the population concerned is in contact with other ideas, and there are some possibilities for change within the society. The alternative of developing a new form of organization must be viewed as *attractive* in terms of a cost-benefit analysis; that is, the social and economic costs associated with starting a new organization must be less than the benefits that are expected to be derived. Stinchcombe also points out that the benefits are expected to go to those engaged in organizational development rather than to other groups in the society. Another important condition is that the people involved have to have sufficient *resources*—such as wealth, power, legitimacy, and people—to get the new organization off the ground.

> In societies where most of the land passes through inheritance and is not freely alienable outside the family, where labor's obedience is to its traditional lord rather than to the highest bidder, where wealth stays in bags in the lord's warehouse to be used to support retainers rather than for investment, the rate of organization formation is low.[10]

The final condition is that those seeking to establish the new organization must have the *power* to defeat those interested in maintaining the older system.

These conditions necessary for the start of a new organization have not been distributed randomly throughout history, but they are present in sufficient degrees to allow many new organizations and new organizational forms to develop at many points in time. Stinchcombe notes that new organizations are more likely to survive over time than are new organizational forms. Similarly, new organizations, and more particularly new organizational forms, have a higher organizational death rate than old organizations or old organizational forms. This "liability of newness" is indicative of the inherently conservative nature of society.

[9] *Ibid.*, p. 143.
[10] *Ibid.*, p. 147.

The reasons for the liability of newness are found in the social relations that are part of the larger society and in the behaviors of the members of the new organizations and organizational forms. In the first place, new *roles* have to be learned in new settings. There cannot be the traditional passing on of skills and behaviors; the new organization must rely on general skills possessed by the population. This again means that the nature of the population surrounding the organization is vital for its development and form. If the number of people with the requisite general skills is insufficient, the new organizations will have extreme difficulties in accomplishing their tasks and thus will probably not survive.

The fact that new roles have to be learned leads to other organizational problems. There is likely to be little of the semiautomatic communication and interaction that characterize mature organizations. In a totally new organization, where the new roles are not yet part of the repertoire of the personnel, the whole system is apt to be barely operative *until the roles and role relationships are learned.* This can be accomplished by the imposition of the organizational structure, but this too must be learned and must also coincide in some degree with the behaviors and expectations of the organization members. Stinchcombe notes that if the people coming into the organization have skills and values that are relevant for the organization, the task of developing the organization is simpler. The liability of newness is reduced when there is a "disciplined and responsible work force." [11]

Another characteristic of new organizations is that they involve *social relations among strangers,* without the trust that is generated by long years of association. Here again, the state of the society makes a difference. If the general social relations are characterized by universalistic religious and legal codes that make oaths sacred and laws binding, and achievement norms that outweigh the importance of kinship ties, the liability of newness will be reduced. Social relations in these situations will be built around the current situation, rather than on past experiences and expectations. Strangers can interact with more trust, allowing the organization to get off the ground more easily.

New organizations suffer another drawback, in that *they do not have established ties with the larger society.* There are no steady customers or clients. If the social system is one in which the use of alternative organizations for common tasks is an accepted thing, new organizations will have an easier time establishing themselves. It will not be as unusual for customers and clients to try alternative organizations for their products and services.

[11] *Ibid.,* p. 149.

This analysis points out the fact that the conditions under which organizations and organizational forms are likely to develop are not constant for all times and places. While the points made are clearest in a cross-cultural and historical perspective, it should also be apparent that within one society and in a relatively short period of time, the conditions can change sufficiently so that there will be intrasocietal differences in the rates of organizational development.

OTHER SOCIETAL CONDITIONS. The conditions just discussed do not exist independent of other societal characteristics. They are in fact intermediate variables between some basic societal characteristics and the rate of organizational development. One social characteristic that is a major factor in determining whether the conditions for organizational development will be present is the general *literacy* and specialized advanced *schooling* of the population. The presence of literacy raises the likelihood that each of the intermediate variables will be present to the degree necessary for organizational development to occur. Stinchcombe states:

> . . . literacy and schooling raise practically every variable which encourages the formation of organizations and increases the staying power of new organizations. It enables more alternatives to be posed to more people. It facilitates learning new roles with no nearby role model. It encourages impersonal contact with customers. It allows money and resources to be distributed more easily to strangers and over distances. It provides records of transactions so that they can be enforced later, making the future more predictable. It increases the predictability of the future environment of an organization by increasing the available information and by making possible a uniform body of law over a large area.[12]

In addition to the key variable of education and literacy, there are several factors that are crucial for the conditions permitting organizational formation. *Urbanization* is a second factor identified by Stinchcombe in this regard. He notes that the rate of urbanization should be slow enough to allow the rural migrants to learn and develop routines of urban living. At the same time, the development of urban life is associated with greater heterogeneity of life style, thus providing more alternative working and living arrangements. The urban scene is one of dealing with strangers, and this too assists organizational development, since ascriptive role relationships are likely to be minimized. Impersonal laws are necessary in urban areas just as they are in organizations. Urbanization, like education, increases the organizational capacity of populations, although not to the same degree, according to Stinchcombe.

12 *Ibid.*, pp. 150–51.

Another important condition, and one that has long been identified, is the presence of a *money economy*. This sort of economy

> . . . liberates resources so that they can be more easily recruited by new organizations, facilitates the formation of free markets so that customers can transfer loyalties, depersonalizes economic social relations, simplifies the calculation of the advantages of alternative ways of doing things, and allows more precise anticipation of the consequences of future conditions on the organization.[13]

The *political base* of a society is also important. For the creation of a new organization, political revolutions are held to be important because of their rearranging of vested interest groups and power systems. Resources are allocated on different bases than in the past.

The final societal condition identified by Stinchcombe is the existing level of *organizational density*. The greater the density, the greater the range of organizational alternatives already available and the greater the likelihood that people will have had experience in organizations. This suggests that there is likely to be an exponential growth curve for organizations in a society. This assumes, of course, that the other conditions are also present.

Stinchcombe's discussion is concerned with the conditions of the society that are important for the development of new organizations and new organizational forms. These conditions are components of those discussed earlier in this chapter—the contemporary environmental conditions that are important for the life of an organization. While the picture is drawn in broader relief with historical data, the factors identified remain important for analyses at any particular point in time.

TECHNOLOGY AND ORGANIZATIONAL FORM.   Stinchcombe's article contains an additional set of ideas that is relevant for our purposes. He maintains that the technological conditions available at the time of the formation of an organization set the limits for the form the organization can take.

> Organizations which have purposes that can be efficiently reached with the socially possible organizational forms tend to be founded during the period in which they become possible. Then, both because they can function effectively with those organizational forms, and because the forms tend to become institutionalized, the basic structure of the organization tends to remain relatively stable.[14]

The emphasis on technology is consistent with the argument here. The new idea introduced is that the organizational form that is once introduced and that is compatible with the technology of the times

13 *Ibid.*, p. 152.
14 *Ibid.*, p. 153.

tends to persist over time regardless of changes in technology that occur over time. This raises the interesting question of whether or not the historical factors based on the technology of the period in which an organizational form develops outweigh later technological developments affecting the same kind of organization.

TRADITION VS. COMPETITION.   Stinchcombe's answer to this question is illustrative of the interplay among the environmental factors that have been identified. He notes that the development of organizational forms is based on the factors suggested above, such as the availability of money, available labor, and so on. These allow the development of the intermediate conditions that in turn permit the development of alternatives from the organizational forms of the past. Once an organizational form is developed, as for railroads, banks, or universities, the questions are: Do these forms persist over time in the face of changes in the environment, and if so, why? The answer to this issue lies in another relationship between organizations and their environment. Stinchcombe notes that organizations develop ideologies by which they can be legitimated in the society. Values are built up around the manner in which the organization operates. These values are transmitted to the external world and become part of the value system of the organizational members.

> Thus, in craft-organized industries, unions can and do appeal to the norms of craftsmanship—the value of the industrial discipline they provide—to defend the closed shop. The powers they use to defend their monopoly in the local labor market they obtained originally because they could in fact provide a skilled labor force on predictable terms. The current effectiveness of their strikes is a function of the degree to which craftsmen are in fact superior to untrained men for the work.[15]

While internal traditions and effective institutionalization provide a basis for the continuation of traditional forms, there is still the element of the competition of new forms within the same general technological base. Stinchcombe notes that the family farm and family retail business have largely disappeared in the face of competition from alternative forms. University medical schools have eliminated proprietary medical schools. Countries with common political backgrounds may contain rather different political party forms. If an organization is able to withstand competition or is in a situation where there is no competition, the power of tradition carries the day. The railroad industry prior to the emergence of truck, auto, and air transit is probably the most conspicuous example. It existed through time with essentially the same structure with which it began. Competition has forced slow, and in this

15 *Ibid.*, pp. 167–68.

case, painful, changes to take place. There is thus an interplay between the force of tradition and the demands of competition and new technologies.

A note relating this discussion to the topic of the next chapter is in order here. Since tradition does play an important role in the way an organization operates, and since organizations are unlikely to change unless there is strong external pressure (in competitive, political, technological, or some other form) to change, organizations will tend to maintain their ways. This means that organizations are basically conservative, and they have a stabilizing, conservative, or even reactionary influence on the society around them. Social unrest at any period of history is directed at the organizations of the period—government, private industry, universities, or whatever is viewed by the segments of the population demanding change as impediments to progress. An understanding of why organizations are unlikely to change is thus a major tool for those who would seek to change the society as a whole. However, the development of new organizations and new organizational forms requires certain conditions to be present. Thus revolution cannot accomplish change without the presence of the appropriate conditions for organizational development.

The examination of the general environmental factors central to organizations has been inconclusive. While the roles of technology, legal patterns, culture, and so on, have been demonstrated to be important, we cannot even assign a ranking to the various factors to indicate their relative importance. The situation is further complicated by the fact that these general environmental factors themselves interact, so that it is difficult to isolate any one thing for analysis. This section must therefore conclude on the note that the relationships between organizations and their environment are complicated, but also crucial.

THE SPECIFIC ENVIRONMENT

The specific environment is composed of the organizations and individuals with which an organization is in direct interaction. Our analysis will be focused on organizations. Particular individuals, such as certain politicians or others who independently attack an organization because of real or imagined evils, can be very important, but in the vast majority of cases such individuals are representatives of another organization.[16]

---

[16] The most conspicuous current example of a single individual is Ralph Nader, who attacked and affected General Motors and the entire automobile industry. This sort of example is the exception, rather than the rule.

The Organization Set

The easiest way to begin the analysis is to introduce the notion of the "organization set." [17] In simple terms, the organization set is composed of organizations in interaction with a focal organization. They provide inputs and receive outputs. The complexity of the organization set can be seen in figures 10–1, 10–2, and 10–3. The example is drawn

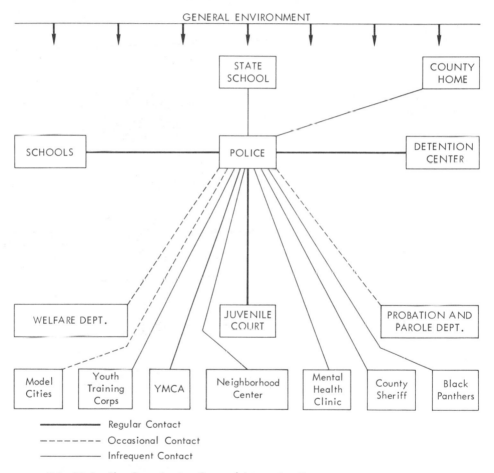

FIG. 10–1   The Organization Set and Interaction Frequency

17 See William M. Evan, "The Organization-Set: Toward a Theory of Interorganizational Relations," in James D. Thompson, ed., *Approaches to Organizational Design* (Pittsburgh: University of Pittsburgh Press, 1966); and Theodore Caplow, *Principles of Organization* (New York: Harcourt Brace Jovanovich, Inc., 1964), pp. 201–28.

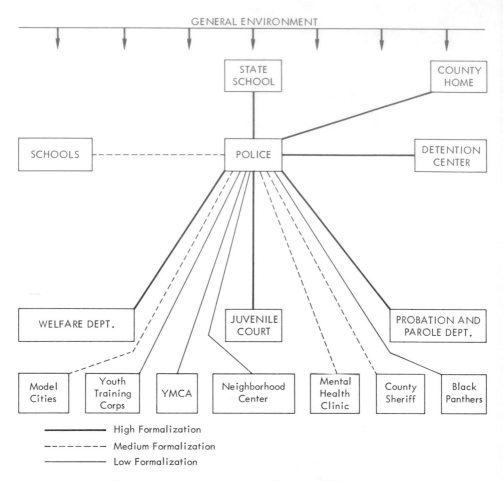

FIG. 10–2 The Organization Set and Formalization of Relationships

from some research underway on the social-control system for problem youths. Figure 10–1 indicates the organizations in interaction with a focal organization, in this case the police. The frequency of the interaction is also indicated. Figure 10–2 indicates the degree of formalization of the relationship, and figure 10–3 indicates whether it is cooperative or conflictual.

These figures include only a few variables and not all the members of the organization set. The complexity of the relationships is indicated by the fact that frequent interactions do not necessarily mean highly formalized or cooperative relations. The total system, of which this particular set is only a part, would include organizations linked to the welfare department, for example, but not to other organizations. The

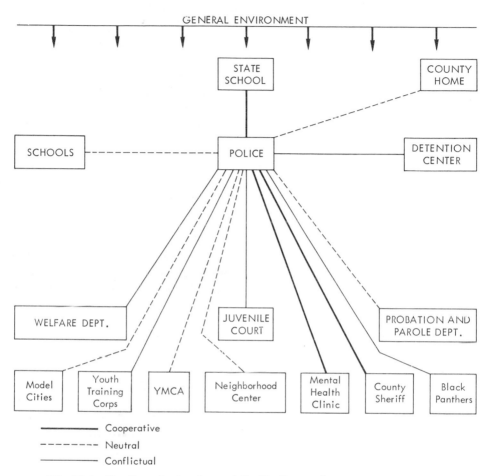

FIG. 10–3   The Organization Set and Conflict-Cooperation

general environmental factors affect each organization as well as the total set of relationships. In this example, the legal requirements for interaction set the stage for much of what goes on.

The illustrations are descriptive of a particular organization set. The analysis of interorganizational relationships is a different and more difficult matter. Relationships vary from routine, highly formalized interactions—such as one business ordering supplies from another or libraries ordering books through an interlibrary loan system—to such an idiosyncratic situation as when members of the boards of directors of two organizations happen to run into each other in the locker room of their athletic club and compare notes about their overlapping interests.

The idea of the "organizational set" was developed by William Evan in a more specific discussion of factors external to an organization.[18] In Evan's concept, every (focal) organization is surrounded by other organizations in interaction. Some of these are input organizations, supplying stimuli in the form of raw materials, personnel, or general expectation, while others are output organizations, receiving things from the focal organization. The autonomy of decision making in the focal organization is affected by the relationships with members of the set. The size of the set, overlapping and interlocking memberships, and the similarity among the members of the set affect the interaction patterns.

The organizational set idea is used somewhat differently by Theodore Caplow. His concept is of organizations of the same type that are visible to each other.[19] Here the interaction may be indirect, as in the case of competing manufacturers or religious organizations that are acutely aware of what their opposite numbers are doing and that, at least partially, shape their own behaviors accordingly. Both conceptualizations of the organizational set idea are useful, as they focus on the specific interactions between organizations.

There is a growing literature about interorganizational relations. There are too few empirical studies for a firm basis of understanding, however. We will attempt to provide some order in the present analysis by suggesting those variables that appear to be crucial and positing the direction of the relationships between them. Most of the examples will come from the youth social-control agencies, and one fact should be made explicit. We are not assuming that a well coordinated system is better than one in which conflicts occur. A highly coordinated system might be much more efficient from the system's perspective, but the youths themselves and ultimately the wider society can suffer.

Patterns

SEQUENCE. There appear to be three basic patterns in interorganizational relations. In the first, there is a definite and regular sequence in the interactions. Physical or social objects are passed from one organization to another. The police apprehend a juvenile and turn him over to the detention center, which turns him over to the juvenile court. Most actual cases are not that simple—disposition decisions are made at each point along the process—and even with a regular sequence, pattern variations can be seen. The police may not like the way the detention center does its job, whereas the detention center and the court are in close accord.

18 Evan, "The Organization-Set."
19 Caplow, *Principles of Organization.*

TIMING.   The second type of pattern differs, in that it occurs at discrete periods of time. This type is exemplified by the multiple organizations concerned with training youths after high school. Both private and public organizations have programs directed toward youths who have not received the kind of education that would prepare them for the jobs that are available. The organizations range from training centers under government auspices, through private corporate efforts, to state and local vocational rehabilitation centers. Added to this complexity are a number of other human-service agencies that often deal with the same clients on a nontraining basis. Interaction patterns here can range from frequent consultation on common clients, an unfortunately rare occurrence, to competition for the clients with the highest chance for success.

ACTIVITY.   The third type of interaction situation is somewhat a mixture of the other two. The example here is the relationships between training agencies that operate while the individual is in the school system and those that "take over" after he leaves. While this is sequential, it is not ordered to the extent of the first type. Some agencies may have a persistent interest in a set of clients over time, while others operate with specific time limitations. Thus there can be overlap of both time and activity.

In all these patterns, there exist other interorganizational relationships besides those discussed. Each organization is in contact with others at any point in time. Formal and informal planning and coordinating efforts are quite common. Formal agencies can be established for coordination. Informal contacts through professional associations, common friends, or even recreational activities must also be considered. Additional relationships exist with organizations such as legal-aid clinics, hospitals, study task forces, model cities programs, and universities concerned with research and application of knowledge.

Impact of General Environment

The discussion thus far has suggested an aura of chaos rather than order. Some order can be imposed by referring back to the general environmental factors that have been discussed. For example, Etzioni has suggested that ecological, cultural, and political conditions have an important effect on these relationships.[20] Burton Clark has identified general economic, demographic, and political arrangements as important.[21]

---

[20] Etzioni, *Modern Organizations,* pp. 110–12.
[21] Burton R. Clark, "Interorganizational Patterns in Education," *Administrative Science Quarterly,* Vol. 10, No. 2 (September 1965), 224–37.

If there is political pressure to cooperate, for example, the organizations dealing with youths are more likely to interact than if the pressure were absent. Technology would also appear to be important. The development of new training or treatment technologies may require that several organizations hire or train specialists in the new technique. It is likely that these specialists will interact with their colleagues in other organizations, thus yielding additional interorganizational linkages. Similarly, organizational members can compare notes on new developments with the same results.

The development of common clients or customers, changing patterns of consumer tastes and desires, shifts in the legal and political bases of the relationships, and the impact of the mass media are additional potentially important factors in the general environment. As in the case of a single organization, specifying the relative strength and direction of these various factors is next to impossible at present. These general conditions certainly would be as important for interorganizational relationships as they are for a single organization.

Internal Conditions

External conditions are vital for interorganizational relationships as they impinge upon a focal organization and affect the manner in which it interacts with other members of its set. At the same time, conditions within an organization are also important. The development of new organizational activities, for example, might bring the organization into contact with other organizations. Members of particular occupations, particularly the professions, have substantial extraorganizational contacts that would bring their own organization into contact with others. Aiken and Hage have found that occupational diversity and professionalization of staff members are related to the presence of joint programs among the social welfare agencies they studied.[22] Organizations with a wide range of activities are likely to have more interorganizational relationships than those with only a few activities.[23] Other internal factors, such as the formalizaiton of roles and the decentralization of decision making, would also seem to be important in determining the extent and quality of relations with members of the set.

22 Michel Aiken and Jerald Hage, "Interorganizational Interdependence and Intra-organizational Structure," *American Sociological Review,* Vol. 33, No. 6 (December 1968), 912–30.

23 See Brian C. Aldrich, "Relations Between Organizations: A Critical Review of the Literature" (unpublished paper, University of Minnesota, 1970).

Conflict/Cooperation

Interorganizational relationships, like all social relationships, take a variety of forms. For our purposes they can be viewed as on a continuum ranging from conflict to cooperation.[24] Neither end of this continuum is as extreme as it conceivably could be. Total conflict, or war, is an interorganizational relationship in which there is very little actual interaction, except by force. Although it is crucial (the interorganizational aspect of war has been strangely ignored), war is so extreme that it would lead us off the track if it were seriously considered here. On the other side of the continuum, extreme cooperation would lead to merger, and the situation would cease to be interorganizational. Thus, for the sake of the analysis and in keeping with reality, conflict and cooperation short of war and merger will be our extremes.

Most interorganizational relationships probably fall somewhere near the middle of this continuum. They take the form of bargaining and exchange relationships, with little in the way of positive or negative emotional connotations. Most relationships occur at the organization's boundaries, often with personnel specifically designated for the purpose. The salesman, public-relations officer, buyer, congressional lobbyist, and front-office receptionist are all boundary personnel who are supposed to participate in interorganizational relationships on behalf of the organization. Quite often supraorganizational units are established to regularize relationships. While established in the name of cooperation, they too are usually rather neutral. Examples of these units are councils of social-welfare agencies, interfraternity conferences, national church councils, manufacturer's associations, and other such coordinating and information-gathering and -disseminating agencies.

In an analysis of interorganizational patterns, Brian Aldrich has at-

---

[24] These distinctions are based on the work of Etzioni (*Modern Organizations*, pp. 111–12), who uses the terms *exchange, conflict, cooperative,* and *bargaining;* Eugene Litwak and Lydia Hylton, "Interorganizational Analysis," *Administrative Science Quarterly*, Vol. 6, No. 4 (March 1962), 395–420, who use *conflict* as their basis; Peter M. Blau and W. Richard Scott, *Formal Organizations* (San Francisco: Chandler Publishing Co., 1962), pp. 214–21, who speak of *symbiotic* and *competitive* relations; James D. Thompson, *Organizations in Action* (New York: McGraw-Hill Book Company, 1967), pp. 31–32, who discusses *cooperative, contractual, co-optative,* and *coalescing relationships;* Sol Levine and Paul White, "Exchange and Inter-Organizational Relationships," *Administrative Science Quarterly*, Vol. 5, No. 3 (March 1961), 600, who use *exchange* relationships; and Harold Guetzkow, "Relations Among Organizations," in Raymond V. Bowers, ed., *Studies on Behavior in Organizations* (Athens, Ga.: University of Georgia Press, 1966), pp. 13–44, who uses *conflict* and *cooperation*.

tempted to identify the sources of conflict- or cooperation-based relationships.[25] The limited evidence that is available suggests that similarities in operating principles, priorities, and structures lead to cooperation, while the absence of these, plus competition for scarce resources, contributes to conflict. Aldrich further notes the frequent but mistaken assumption that cooperative relationships are by definition good. They may indeed lead to greater efficiency but may also be harmful for society, as in the case of a highly cooperative and coordinated control system for deviants that reduces or eliminates individual freedom. Similarly, the recognized dangers of monopoly are in actuality those of cooperating organizations.

Other Components

There are other dimensions of interorganizational relationships. Litwak and Hylton suggest that relationships vary by the degree of standardization, interdependence, and awareness of behavior of the participants.[26] These ideas are expanded in a later paper by Litwak and Rothman, in which they note that interorganizational relationships exist along a continuum of formality.[27] Using confederations of social-welfare agencies as their point of departure, they note that extremely formal ties are found in the larger cities, where formal rules and regulations are common regarding which agency is consulted in regard to particular cases and jurisdictions, and formal directories of social agencies are printed. The point of low formalization can be seen in patterns of occasional lunches or drinks to talk over common interests. Most such relationships would have a medium degree of formalization.

Litwak and Rothman then note that interorganizational relationships can actually only exist with partial interdependence. Merger is likely with total interdependence, while no interdependence would mean no contacts. For the relationship to mean anything to the participating organizations, they must be aware of the relationship and take it into account in their own actions.

Confederations have also been examined by Roland Warren.[28] He identifies four types of agencies for interorganizational interactions. The *unitary* agency is one in which diverse tasks are brought together under

[25] Aldrich, "Relations Between Organizations."

[26] Litwak and Hylton, "Interorganizational Analysis," p. 400.

[27] Eugene Litwak and Jerald Rothman, "Toward a Theory of Coordination Between Formal Organizations" (unpublished paper, University of Michigan, 1969).

[28] Roland L. Warren, "The Interorganizational Field as a Focus for Investigation," *Administrative Science Quarterly*, Vol. 12, No. 3 (December 1967), 396–419.

one administrative unit, as in the case of a city health department or an urban transportation authority. In a sense, this type of agency is actually a single organization, so the analysis actually becomes intraorganizational. Many interorganizational phenomena are undoubtedly present at the intraorganizational level, and vice versa, as problems of coordination, primacy of goals, and budgetary matters among organizational units are considered. For the purposes of this analysis such unitary agencies will be ignored, since interorganizational phenomena are sufficiently distinct from the intraorganizational to warrant a separate approach.

The *federative* context is the second type of agency. It is exemplified by councils of social agencies or church councils. These agencies generally have their own administrative staffs, although the member organizations retain a high level of autonomy. The member organizations themselves have the final authority in determining the actions of the agency. The power of such agencies varies, ranging from those that begin to assume power over their members to those that are almost powerless. Most would have only moderate power.

The third type is the *coalitional* context, which occurs on an *ad hoc* basis when common organizational goals coincide. The organizations involved agree to a division of labor to accomplish their inclusive goal. Warren does not specify how these coalitions are formed and maintained, or the type of interaction among members. The final context is that of *social* choice, which is at the low end of the formalization continuum. The interaction here is on specific issues and can include conflict as well as cooperation.

Effect on the Organization

The effects of interorganizational interactions on the organizations involved has received some attention. (It is interesting to note that there has been almost no attention given to the effects on clients in the case of service organizations.) Thompson says that organizations attempt to "buffer" themselves from external pressures.[29] They try to defend their own domain and acquire power in the interaction process. This can occur in both the conflictual and cooperative situations. Udy notes that external pressures result in increased communications and interactions among members, a higher level of commitment to the organization, more authority exercised at all levels, and a greater cohesiveness on the part of members.[30] This, of course, is very similar to most general formula-

29 Thompson, *Organizations in Action,* p. 20. See also Howard Aldrich, "Organizational Boundaries and Inter-organizational Conflict," *Human Relations,* Vol. 24, No. 4 (August 1971).

30 Stanley H. Udy, Jr., "The Comparative Analysis of Organizations," in March, *Handbook of Organizations,* p. 692.

tions regarding conflict relationships. Both these formulations are built around the conflict perspective, although Thompson's may be applicable in a cooperative situation. It is conceivable that in a federative or coalitional situation, internal cohesiveness and commitment might actually decrease. This might be especially true for those in direct contact with an interaction agency or with other organizations. It is probably true that if one or a set of individuals from an organization are co-opted into another organization, their level of commitment to the first would suffer. These kinds of relationships have not been systematically examined, however.

Guetzkow's approach to the effect on the focal organization might have applicability regardless of the nature of the relationship. He suggests that costs for transportation or communication will increase as the flow of goods or ideas between organizations increases.[31] While this effect is on the focal organization, these costs might also serve as a useful measure of the extent of interaction for both the focal organization and members of its set.

SUMMARY AND CONCLUSIONS

Interorganizational relationships are affected by the wider environment of which they are a part. Political, cultural, ecological, demographic, technological, and economic conditions affect these relationships and, at any one point in time, are a constant consideration for the organizations involved. Shifts in these factors will affect the relationships.

The actual relationships between organizations have multiple sources. These sources can be classified into three categories. The first is external to the organization and the relationship itself; it consists of legal or traditional expectations of contact and the general environmental factors, all of which must be taken into account at any particular point in time.

The second group of sources is within the organizations involved. The development of new programs that overlap with those of another organization is likely to lead to interorganizational relationships, as is complexity, as used by Aiken and Hage to mean occupational diversity. Related to the latter is the professionalization of the employees, since members of common professions have extraorganizational contacts through professional associations and friendships.

The third source category is common units, such as clients, programs,

---

[31] Guetzkow, "Relations Among Organizations," pp. 24–25.

or financial auspices, which lead to interaction. This is related to the sequence factor. Handling common clients in a sequence should lead to heightened interaction; common programs that are nonsequential may lead to minimal interaction, with what does occur being based on competition. Reliance upon a common financial base should lead to heightened interaction, either facilitative or competitive. The degree of awareness would affect the formalization of the relationship. Since organizations can have common clients, programs, and financial auspices, interactions can take place on multiple levels with multiple forms.

The nature of the relationship itself appears to vary along two major continua—formal/informal and conflict/cooperation. A major factor in these relationships is the relative power of the organizations involved. This will affect decision making, allocation of resources, and the kinds of personnel involved in the relationship. The strength of the members' identification with their organizations would also appear to have an impact on the relationship.

This factor is related to the issue of professionalization. Many of the occupations involved in these relationships are professionalized to varying degrees. While Aiken and Hage believe that professionalization facilitates interaction, this appears to be only one side of the picture. Their subjects were predominantly social workers and rehabilitation counselors. When the field is expanded to include schoolteachers, medical doctors, personnel managers, and other specialties, professionalization might preclude effective interaction—assuming professional identification and training, which can lead to an inability to interact effectively with members of other professions. It is proposed that professionalization thus serves as an impediment to interaction and can contribute to competitive relationships. In this regard, the power and status of the professions involved also appear to be important. A profession that is given societal recognition, such as that of the medical doctor, would have more power than that of a social worker. This would affect decision making and other components of the relationship.

Related to the professionalization issue is the nature of the organizations themselves. Their purposes may conflict, coincide, or be complementary. Factors such as centralization/decentralization, the provision of specialists for boundary positions, and other internal organizational characteristics are also important.

Interorganizational relationships affect the *organizations* involved. Attempts to buffer environmental and other organizational factors, costs to the organization, and altered cohesiveness within the organization— all are important, but probably only partial—effects of interaction. Interactions affect the *clients and customers* of the organizations, although it is not clear whether cooperative relationships have positive or negative consequences for the recipients of the organization's actions. Client awareness of interaction patterns would seem to be important but has not been examined. It would appear that a group of aware clients would raise the awareness level of the members of the organizations themselves. Interorganizational relationships also affect the *relationship* itself. The bases and forms of interactions should affect the continuing interactions. Aiken and Hage found that interactions (joint programs) among the agencies they studied tended to further and increase interactions, which were cooperative and rather formal. Competitive interactions, on the other hand, might present blockages to future interactions. They might also lead to informal, conflict-based interactions on a wider basis than the original interactions.

This chapter concludes the basic argument or analytical model around which this book has been organized. After looking at the nature of organizational structure and then the important internal processes, we have seen how external factors impinge upon the organization, altering the structure and affecting the rate and direction of the processes. While this is nice and neat for the purpose of completing a model, the discussion has obviously been unsatisfactory from several perspectives.

The first disappointment is that there is no solid evidence on which to form conclusions regarding the relative strengths of the general and specific environmental factors as they affect organizations. We cannot even be sure that all the relevant factors have been discussed. The second major shortcoming is our inability to determine the extent to which these external factors are more or less important than internal considerations in determining how and why an organization operates as it does. The approach taken here is that they are of essentially equal importance, although they may affect the organization at different times and with different strengths. We have tried to show what some of the external influences apparently do to organizations and how they "enter" the organization. We have also tried to indicate some of the ways in which organizations respond to these external forces.

The final chapter will examine the organization's influence on the environment. A complete analytical model would specify the nature of the reciprocity between the environmental influence on organizations and the organization's on the environment. It would appear, for example, that an organization that is under political pressures might fight back by attempting to alter the political process in its own behalf. Certainly organizations try to influence other organizations. While such a complete analytical model would be nice to have and might be forthcoming in the future, there will be relatively little reference to it here. Future research must examine the issues and perhaps lead us toward a completed model.

11

ORGANIZATIONS AND SOCIAL CHANGE

Whenever the idea of social change is brought up, it is almost automatic to think about organizations. The spread of Christianity or communism, wars on poverty or ignorance, and fights against crime or pollution are all organizationally based. The success of these efforts at large-scale change depends on the successful organization of resources and people. Small-scale changes are also organizationally dependent, whether they are police efforts to slow down the sale of narcotics or attempts to elect a peace candidate. By the same token, each such attempt is met by a countereffort that is also organizationally based.

These self-evident truths must be balanced by another that is less evident. *Organizations are great resisters of change.* The entire discussion in this book has been based on the idea that organizational structures and processes develop that serve as predictors of actions by the organization and its members. Organizations do not act at random; they are therefore conservative by nature, resisting change and the introduction of new patterns. Anyone who has tried to introduce an innovation into a college or university curriculum, alter hospital admitting procedures, improve railroad passenger service, or start a new program within a government agency has been brought face to face with organizational conservatism.

This dual nature of organizations in their relationship to social change will be the topic of this final chapter. We will try to indicate the ways in which organizations contribute to social change, relating this to the nature of the organizations themselves, and then look more closely at the resistance shown by organizations toward the change process. But before we turn to the analysis, a few comments about social change itself are in order.

A major assumption that will soon be evident is that an organizationally dense society is one in which the change process is both rapid and intense. In the discussion in the previous chapter, it was stated that particular social conditions must be ripe if organizations and organizational forms are to emerge. In a society in which a wide variety of organizations and organizational forms exists, as in the contemporary United States, social change is also a constant condition.[1] So we will not spend time discussing whether or not social change is a fact for an organizational society.

This chapter will take a neutral stance toward change; that is, no assumption will be made that change is progress. While everyone probably has a pet change that he would like to see instituted and others that he would resist strongly, it is not the intent here to advocate the kinds of changes that would be most beneficial for the society or the organizations involved. Like anyone else, I have ideas about changes I would like to see in the society, some of which I feel may even be necessary for the survival of the society. However, since the appropriateness of such changes can be demonstrated only by a form of evidence different from the one we are considering here, it would be a disservice to the analysis to get into political, economic, or social advocacy. If the examples and analysis make sense, other examples can be inserted at the reader's will.

The same point holds for the discussion of organizations as resisters of change. Bookshelves are filled with both serious and humorous accounts of the persistence of organizations in the face of extreme demands for change. The negative connotation of the term "bureaucracy" indicates the emotional coloration given to organizational unresponsiveness toward change. Here again, a nonevaluative approach will be taken.

Aside from the general scientific norm that calls for objectivity and dispassionate discussions, there are pragmatic reasons for the position of neutrality taken here. The basic reason is the absence of reliable evidence

---

[1] Phillip Hauser argues that the tempo of change is accelerated in an organizational society such as ours. See Hauser, "The Chaotic Society: Product of the Social Morphological Revolution," *American Sociological Review*, Vol. 34, No. 1 (February 1969), 1–19.

regarding what constitutes a good change, or when an organization is damaging the society around it by its resistance to change. In specific cases, this can be relatively easily determined, but for a total analysis it gets risky. If our knowledge about organizations and social change is at all correct, it should be equally relevant, regardless of the persuasion —left, right, or center—for all organizations, their members, and their publics.

THE ORGANIZATION AND THE SOCIAL STRUCTURE

We will begin with the usual caveat that the analysis is hampered by the absence of good data. Most of the information comes from the limited number of case studies that have been published. Examples of attempts to change society typically deal with successful efforts—as in the case of studies of politicians; we know very little about the losers. While we are concerned with change, and ineffective change attempts therefore are not a central concern, it would be useful to be able to compare successful and unsuccessful efforts. Needless to say, this is an area that is ripe for major research.

Organizations are both agents of change and major sources of societal stability. William Dill notes:

> In countries like the United States and Canada, most of the nations of Western Europe, Australia, or Japan, business organizations are the most powerful. They provide the major source of employment and income and some of the major bases for determining social status. They decide in large measure what shall be produced and how much.[2]

In other societies, government organizations perform the same functions. Regardless of the form of the economy, organizations are the major decision makers for the priorities and actualities of the society.

There is another way in which organizations are important for the social structure. Since modern work is almost exclusively organizational work, and since total life styles are decreasingly influenced by the ascriptive components of age, sex, race, ethnicity, or other such factors, man's occupational roles and the interrelationships between these roles are a major component in determining the overall social structure.[3] The or-

[2] William R. Dill, "Business Organizations," in James G. March, ed., *Handbook of Organizations* (Chicago: Rand McNally & Co., 1965), p. 1101.
[3] For a discussion of this point, see Richard H. Hall, *Occupations and the Social Structure* (Englewood Cliffs, N.J.: Prentice-Hall, Inc., 1969).

ganizations set the occupational rewards that in turn place the individual within the social system. Dill notes:

> One of the greatest areas of impact on the community is in the influence of business on the development and maintenance of social-class distinctions. To a considerable extent, these are based on the hierarchies of job labels and income levels which businesses have institutionalized.[4]

Important considerations in both social history and present operations, such as the master–slave or management–worker relationships, are actually organizational relationships.

At the local-community level, organizations are also important in determining the social structure. In "company towns," the one business organization "not only provides most of the inhabitants of the towns with work, but also undertakes to provide them with housing, schools, stores, recreational programs, and other facilities."[5] The same is true of university towns, military towns, or other such "impacted" communities dominated by one organization. Most communities do not experience this sort of domination, but there are still identifiable patterns in organizationally based communities. Leaving aside for the moment the problems of domination that this discussion suggests, the dependence of the social structure on the organizations in it should be evident. While the society must legitimate its organizations, the organizations develop styles and patterns of their own that are removed from direct societal surveillance and control.

If this position—that organizations are crucial in the determination of the state of a society at any point in time—is acceptable, the argument that organizations are therefore also crucial for social change follows logically. The manner in which organizations can serve as change agents will be approached from three perspectives. The first will involve attempts by organizations to change themselves, which in turn have an effect on the larger social system. The second will involve changes that organizations induce in the behavior of their members, which in turn will affect their performances in society. The third regards direct attempts by organizations to intervene in the social system.

Internal Change and the Society

If the arguments presented above are valid, any shift in organizational staffing patterns will have an effect on the social structure. Decisions to

---

4 Dill, "Business Organizations," p. 1102.
5 *Ibid.*

increase the number of minority-group members in managerial or professional positions, to exclude personnel with long hair, to eliminate certain kinds of employment, and so on, not only alter the internal organizational arrangements but also are reflected in the long and the short run in the surrounding community and total society. Smaller-scale shifts, as in providing "cultural" recreational opportunities, educational programs, and the like, can also be important for the world around the organization, although the impact of these programs is extremely difficult to measure for the organization or the society. On the other hand, the organization can, for one reason or another, drastically alter its total program and thus affect the total social system.[6] A hypothetical case here would be a national government that decides to emphasize its social welfare programs more than foreign alliances and makes budgetary shifts accordingly. Forgetting for the moment the political and emotional appropriateness of such a shift, this organizational rearrangement would have major consequences for the society involved. While this example smacks more of a political shift, it is in fact also an organizational change, which in turn affects society.

The examples cited are obvious shifts for the society. In addition to these, there are more subtle alterations that organizations can accomplish. S. N. Eisenstadt notes that there are situations in which the nature of particular organizations can pervade the rest of the society, through

> . . . the extension of the bureaucracy's spheres of activities and power, either in its own interests or those of some of its elite. It tends toward growing regimentation of different areas of social life and some extent of displacement of its service goals in favor of various power interests and orientations. Examples are military organizations that tend to impose their rules on civilian life, or political parties that exert pressure on their potential supporters in an effort to monopolize their private and occupational life and make them entirely dependent on the political party.[7]

These efforts, which can be conscious or unconscious, involve alterations in the behaviors of members of the society and alterations in the basic social relationships. Eisenstadt also notes that it is possible for organizations to "debureaucratize" as external pressures alter goals or force the organization to change its activities. In these cases, the results on social relationships in the society are similarly affected.

Another example of the way an organization performs its activities and the resultant impact on those in contact with it is found in Merton's

---

6 See Charles Perrow, *Organizational Analysis: A Sociological View* (Belmont, Calif.: Wadsworth Publishing Co., Inc., 1970), pp. 137–40, for a discussion of this situation and some of the attendant problems.

7 S. N. Eisenstadt, "Bureaucracy, Bureaucratization and Debureaucratization," *Administrative Science Quarterly*, Vol. 4, No. 3 (December 1959), 304–32.

classic analysis of "bureaucratic structure and personality." [8] Merton's major interest is in what an organization can do to its own members, a point to which we will return in a moment, but there is also an important implication of what an organization can do to those who have contact with it. Noting that in a bureaucracy there is a strong tendency to use abstract rules and the norm of impersonality in dealing with clients, Merton says that the outsider often finds the bureaucrat to be haughty, arrogant, or harsh. The client is treated as a nobody by a low-level clerk.

> The bureaucrat, in part irrespective of his position with*in* the hierarchy, acts as a representative of the power and prestige of the entire structure. In his official role he is vested with definite authority. This often leads to an actually or apparently domineering attitude, which may only be exaggerated by a discrepancy between his position within the hierarchy and his position with reference to the public. Protest and recourse to other officials on the part of the client are often ineffective or largely precluded by the . . . *esprit de corps* which joins the officials into a more or less solidary ingroup. This source of conflict *may* be minimized in private enterprise, since the client can register an effective protest by transferring his trade to another organization within the competitive system. But with the monopolistic nature of the public organization, no such alternative is possible. Moreover, in this case, tension is increased because of a discrepancy between ideology and fact: The governmental personnel are held to be "servants of the people," but in fact they are often superordinate, and release of tension can seldom be afforded by turning to other agencies for the necessary service. [9]

The considerations in this analysis have undoubtedly contributed in some part to the evident unrest acted out by welfare clients, students, and prisoners. (The reaction of individuals in contact with the organization can be individual or collective. If it is the latter, the "clients'-rights organization" becomes a change agent itself.) While more than the treatment by the organization is involved, this is no small factor in the way people react to the situation in which they constantly find themselves. There are no alternative organizations to turn to in these cases. Somewhat the same form of frustration and tension can be seen in dealings with organizations, private or public, that utilize computerized billing and other services. The client or customer is made to feel like a nonperson in this context. It is impossible to determine whether there is at present a consistent movement toward a more depersonalized form of life. There will undoubtedly be counterforces tending to operate against a total movement in this direction. The important point for

8 Robert M. Merton, *Social Theory and Social Structure* (New York: The Free Press, 1957), pp. 195–206.
9 *Ibid.*, p. 203. [Italics in original.]

our purposes here is that those in contact with an organization are affected by it, both positively and negatively.

Organizational Effects on Members

Merton's analysis contains another important idea that should be examined at this point: The members of the organization itself are affected by its mode of operations. Analyses of the reactions of people to their organizational memberships have taken many forms, from humorous descriptions of life in the organization to bitter denunciations of its dehumanizing effects.[10] The focus of these analyses has run the gamut from the lowest to the highest echelons of the organization. Unfortunately, no firm conclusions can be reached on the basis of the studies, owing primarily to the kinds of data utilized, which tend to be first-hand reports of individual experiences in organizations. These hardly comprise a basis for scientific conclusions, even though they can be fascinating reading.

Some tentative conclusions, however, can be noted. In the first place, work that is very repetitive and that provides little opportunity for individual discretion tends to be highly alienating.[11] While the linkage between alienation from work and alienation from the rest of life is not clear, it is reasonable to expect that the alienated worker may also feel somewhat powerless in and estranged from other forms of social participation. As the occupational situation is varied, giving the individual greater responsibility, the level of alienation tends to go down.

A second conclusion is that organization officials can exhibit "bureaupathic" or "bureautic personality" forms of behavior, which involves excessive aloofness, insistence on the rights of office over and above any regard for competence or new ideas, extreme attachment to ritualized procedures, resistance to change, and an extreme distaste for controversy.[12] This type of response is apparently most prevalent among those who have little other than rules to guide their behavior or who work in a system in which rule observance is the basis for the reward system. While the "Peter Principle" would hold that everyone is fated to rise to one level above his competence, thus making him dependent

---

[10] For a review of this literature, see Hall, *Occupations and the Social Structure,* Chapter 3.

[11] See particularly Robert Blauner, *Alienation and Freedom* (Chicago: University of Chicago Press, 1964).

[12] See Robert M. Merton, "Bureaucratic Structure and Personality," *Social Forces,* Vol. 18, No. 4 (May 1940), 560–68; and Victor Thompson, *Modern Organizations* (New York: Alfred A. Knopf, Inc., 1961), pp. 152–77.

on rules and ritual, there is little evidence that this does in fact occur in all situations.[13] While everyone has his favorite tales of "Bureaucrats I Have Known," experience and common sense suggest that there are people at all levels of all forms of organizations who are competent, happy, and capable of growth in their current positions, as well as in other positions. However, there is a frighteningly large number of organization officials who are totally reliant on the organization for their behavioral cues and responses. While organizational procedures are designed to reduce or even eliminate individual variations in response, there are few who would argue that the total individual should be submerged to the organization. Even in organizations such as the military, with its emphasis on discipline and its need to "socialize into violence," there is no real intent that this should become the sum total of the individual member's repertoire of behavior.[14] In both the long and the short run, the bureaucratic personality is counterproductive for the organization.

It is beyond our current interests to examine why some individuals become subservient to the organization. At the present time it is probably impossible to determine who will and who will not suffer such a fate. What is of concern to us is whether the alienated worker in a routine job or the bureaucratic personality higher up on the official ladder is actually permanently damaged by all this. If we accept the fact that not all organizational employees are happy, the question becomes, Does this unhappiness extend to life outside the organization? The evidence for an answer here is weak, but seems to indicate that those in alienating jobs in an organization can have excitement, fun, and stimulation off the job. In fact, there is good evidence to suggest that assembly-line workers actually think of "life" as being off the job, with the job simply a means to the end of enjoying real life. There is no really solid evidence regarding the nonwork life of the overbureaucratized official. It would seem to follow that his life off the job could also be characterized by a style much different from that on the job. The point here is that the existence of dulling work has *not* been shown to have a carry-over effect on the balance of a man's life. In this perspective, then, organizations per se have minimal societal impact because of their members' taking organizational norms with them into their off-the-job social relations. The question thus remains open as to whether organizational membership of the type being described has any

---

13 See Lawrence J. Peter and Raymond Hull, *The Peter Principle* (New York: William Morrow & Co., Inc., 1969).

14 See Joseph A. Blake, "The Organization as Instrument of Violence: The Military Case," *The Sociological Quarterly*, Vol. 11, No. 3 (Summer 1970), 331–50.

lasting impact on the wider society. Since it is open, however, the possibility remains that the nature of a person's work has important ramifications for the general mental health of the society.

Two additional aspects of the impact of organizations on their members and its relationship with the overall social structure deserve mention. While it is not clear whether a dull or exciting position in an organization leads to a dull or exciting life outside the organization, it is evident that a person's occupation has important consequences for other aspects of his life. For example, his political outlook, patterns of family life, and general life style have been shown to be linked to his occupation. It could therefore be hypothesized that organizations that contain occupations encouraging dissent and controversy, as opposed to conformity and acceptance of the status quo, would have members who carried this style of life outside the organization. Since organizations affect the way in which the various occupations contained therein are oriented, there is an organizational effect on the way people view and act toward the world around them. This effect is balanced by nonorganizational factors as well, but the organization does make a difference. Here again, comparative research is needed to determine exactly how much membership in various forms of organizations contributes to the variance in people's approaches to life.

VOLUNTARY ORGANIZATIONS. The final point in this discussion involves organizations that are *designed* to have an impact on the behaviors and attitudes of their members. The voluntary organization, in most cases, is established to be a force affecting the lives and behaviors of its members. People belong to voluntary organizations because they believe in what the organization stands for and would like to see it promoted. (This ignores that element of voluntary-organization membership that is present for nonnormative reasons.) It is probably very safe to assume that the voluntary-organization membership of an individual is a good indicator of some of his salient values. Even when this assumption is made, however, the question remains as to whether the membership itself makes any difference to his attitudes and behaviors. The answer is that such memberships undoubtedly reinforce predispositions already present when the person joins the organization.

This answer is not very useful, however, since there are insufficient indications of the extent to which such memberships are balanced against other facts of the individual's life. Research into the impact of membership in religious organizations, for example, has led to largely inconclusive results regarding the impact of a person's membership as opposed to that of his place in the social stratification system, his occupation, place of origin, and so on.[15] Without an extended discussion of the importance of such memberships vis-à-vis other important considerations, it is sufficient for our purposes here to note that voluntary-organization memberships have some consequences for the people involved, but it would appear that such consequences are not as strong as those of other conditions under which the person is living. Voluntary-organization memberships thus appear to be modifiers of attitudes and behaviors formed for the individual through his life history.

THE ORGANIZATION AS A CHANGE AGENT

Besides affecting society (largely unintentionally) through their structuring of social life and impacts on members, organizations are also active participants in the social-change process. This can be most easily seen in the political arena, as organizations lobby and fight for legislation and rulings favorable to their own programs. A favorable decision for one organization leads to programs that in turn affect the society. Whenever a government agency is established to carry out a new program, it becomes a social-change agent. We will begin the analysis of change agents with this point, moving from this rather established and accepted form of social change to a consideration of organizations as revolutionary agents.

A classic example of the organization as a change agent is provided by Selznick's study of the Tennessee Valley Authority (TVA) during its formative years.[16] In addition to its pertinence to the analysis of change, this study is also very important for its contribution to the topic of the last chapter—the environmental impact on the organization. There is a reciprocal relationship between organizations and their environments. Each affects the other as they interact.

The TVA Act was passed by the U.S. Congress in 1933.

A great public power project was envisioned mobilizing the "by-product" of dams built for the purpose of flood control and navigation improvement

15 See Gerhard Lenski, *The Religious Factor* (Garden City, N.Y.: Doubleday & Company, Inc., Anchor Books, 1963). See also Howard Schuman, "The Religious Factor in Detroit: Review, Replication, and Reanalysis," *American Sociological Review*, Vol. 36, No. 1 (February 1971), 30–48; and Gerhard Lenski, "The Religious Factor in Detroit: Revisited," *American Sociological Review*, Vol. 36, No. 1 (February 1971), 48–50.

16 Phillip Selznick, *TVA and The Grass Roots* (New York: Harper Torchbook Edition, 1966). Originally published by the University of California Press, Berkeley and Los Angeles, 1949.

on the Tennessee River and its tributaries. Control and operation of the nitrate properties, to be used for fertilizer production, was also authorized, although this aspect was subordinated to electricity. . . . A new regional concept—the river basin as an integral unit—was given effect, so that a government agency was created which has a special responsibility neither national nor state-wide in scope.[17]

That the TVA has had an effect on the physical environment is evident. What is of greater interest for our purposes here is what it has done to the social system into which it was placed. An important consideration in understanding the social effects of the TVA is the fact that the organization was designed to be decentralized. Not only were decisions within the organization to be made at the lowest reasonable levels with participation by members, but local organizations and even local citizens were also to be brought into the decision-making process. For example, the agricultural-extension services of the land-grant colleges were intimately involved with the TVA. This, of course, is one of the prime examples of co-optation, or "the process of absorbing new elements into the leadership or policy-determining structure of an organization as a means of averting threats to its stability or existence." [18]

Co-optation is a two-way process. The organization is affected by the new elements brought into its decision-making process; Selznick documents the manner in which some activities of the TVA were deflected from the original goals because of the new elements in the system. At the same time, the co-optation process affects the system from which the elements were co-opted. The presence of the agricultural-extension element from the land-grant colleges gave this part of the local system much more strength than it had had in the past. The American Farm Bureau Federation was also brought into the process at an early point. In both these cases, the inclusion of one group was associated with the exclusion of another. Negro colleges and non–Farm Bureau farm organizations either lost power or did not benefit to the degree that co-opted organizations did. In addition, the strength of the Farm Bureau in the decision-making process led to the exclusion from the area of other farm programs of the federal government. Regardless of their merits, these programs were therefore unavailable to the system. Selznick notes, "This resulted in the politically paradoxical situation that the eminently New Deal TVA failed to support agencies with which it shared a political communion, and aligned itself with the enemies of those agencies." [19] This becomes a rather complex analysis when one considers the fact that the other government programs involved were also part of the same

17 *Ibid.*, pp. 4–5.
18 *Ibid.*, p. 13.
19 *Ibid.*, p. 263.

larger organization, so that internal politics in one large organization were affected by the external relationships of some of its component parts.

An organization like the TVA affects the social organization around it. Some elements prosper while others suffer. New social relationships arise as alliances among affected individuals and organizations are formed. Thus, an organization specifically designed to be a change agent is exactly that, but in ways that can be most inconsistent with the original intent of the planners. The dynamics of the interactions with the environment affect both the organization and its environment.

In a later reexamination of the study, Selznick notes that the TVA has recently been attacked by conservationists for strip mining.[20] The need for coal for its power productions and the strength of those supporting an expansion of this function within the TVA has led to a further environmental impact. Selznick attributes the current state of the TVA to the internal struggles that occurred in its early history—struggles to obtain environmental support. Since such support is selective, a strong organization such as this rearranges the world around it. If the groups in power in the TVA see the need for a greater capacity for generating electrical power as more important than soil conservation, the internal decision-making process, affected as it is by external pressures, makes a further impact on the social and physical environment.

THE ORGANIZATIONAL WEAPON. In another analysis of organizations as change agents, Selznick studied the bolshevik revolution in Russia.[21] Here he analyzes the nature and role of the "organizational weapon." In defining what he means, Selznick states:

> We shall speak of organizations and organizational practices as weapons when they are used by a power-seeking elite *in a manner unrestrained by the constitutional order of the arena within which the contest takes place.* In this usage, "weapon" is not meant to denote *any* political tool, but one torn from its normal context and unacceptable to the community as a legitimate mode of action. Thus the partisan practices used in an election campaign insofar as they adhere to the written and unwritten rules of the contest—are not weapons in this sense. On the other hand, when members who join an organization in apparent good faith are in fact the agents of an outside elite, then routine affiliation becomes "infiltration."[22]

20 *Ibid.,* pp. xii–xiii.
21 Phillip Selznick, *The Organizational Weapon* (New York: The Free Press, 1960).
22 *Ibid.,* p. 2.

An important component of the organizational weapon is the *"distinctive competence to turn members of a voluntary association into disciplined and deployable political agents."* [23]

THE ORGANIZATION AS THE REQUISITE OF SOCIAL CHANGE. Before turning to some elements of Selznick's analysis, we must point out that the organizational weapon cannot be regarded as just a bolshevik tactic. Indeed, it is the vital component of most major social changes and of change within the organization itself. Stated in another way, in order to achieve change, *there must be organization.* This organization requires the kind of commitment to which Selznick refers. Spontaneous demonstrations or collective emotional responses may be sincere and well-intentioned, but longer-lasting movements toward change must come about through the organizational mode. And Selznick's reference to "constitutionality" can be translated into the *official* and accepted set of organizational arrangements that make up the "constitution" of any organization. The concern here is thus with the organizational weapon as it seeks to change any ongoing existing societal or organizational arrangement.

The scope of the organization as a weapon is determined by its aims. If the change sought is a limited one and one that will not upset the basic system under attack, the change agent still must be viewed as a weapon, but of less scope than one that seeks total organizational or societal change. In the case of bolshevism, the aim was total societal change. The basic means of accomplishing what the movement desired was through the "combat party." Cadres of dedicated men are a basic component of such parties. This dedication requires that the individuals be totally committed to the cause, insulated from other concerns, and absorbed in the movement. Once a core of dedicated personnel is available, the party must protect itself from internal dissension, banning power centers that might threaten the official leadership. The party must be capable of mobilization and manipulation; it must be protected from possible isolation from the people it hopes to convert and also from possible liquidation at the hands of the existing authorities; and it must struggle for power in every possible area of action. This struggle can take place through seeking official recognition, as well through conspiratorial or illegal practices. And at all times, the basic ideology must be kept at the forefront of the members' minds.[24]

The operation of these principles can be seen in the history of the movement that Selznick carefully traces. This manifesto for an or-

[23] *Ibid.,* p. xii.
[24] *Ibid.,* pp. 72–73.

ganizational weapon is potentially applicable at any point in history, in any social setting, and at either the total societal or more microcosmic levels. A revolt of junior high school students exhibits the same characteristics as the bolshevik movement, and so does the history of early Christianity.

For our purposes, the important thing is not the cause being advanced, but rather the fact that having a cause is not enough for social change. The cause must be organized if it is to be successful. The organization can be a successful change agent if it is capable of maintaining dedication and gaining power in the system. The specific means of gaining power will be dependent on the situation. Political or military power is successful only where it is relevant. Selznick says:

> We must conclude, therefore, that in the long view political combat plays only a tactical role. Great social issues such as those which divide communism and democracy are not decided by political combat, perhaps not even by military clashes. They are decided by the relative ability of the contending systems to win and to maintain enduring loyalties. Consequently, no amount of power and cunning in the realm of political combat can avail in the absence of measures which rise to the height of the times.[25]

The implication here is that the specific tactics used in the bolshevik movement may not be effective in another setting, but that the need for a dedicated membership and the concern for power are central to the change process.

SOCIETAL SUPPORT. Throughout the analysis in this book, we have stressed the reciprocal nature of the relationship between an organization and its environment. This is seen in clear relief in the consideration of organizations as change agents. While the basic processes are the same in effective change situations, to be successful an organizational weapon must gain power and support in the society it is attempting to change. The pages of history are filled with abortive efforts that did not gather sufficient support from the society they were trying to change. The basic set of ideas underlying the change effort must therefore be compatible—or become compatible—with the values of the population as a whole. These values of the wider community can be altered during the change process to become more congruent with those of the change agent. At the same time, the change agent itself can become altered as it seeks support from the wider community.

The importance of this form of support can be extrapolated from Joseph Gusfield's analysis of the Women's Christian Temperance

25 *Ibid.,* p. 333.

Union.[26] This organization was highly successful in its attempts to change society through the passage of legislation prohibiting the sale of alcoholic beverages. Its tactics were appropriate for the values of the times, and it succeeded in mobilizing support from a sufficiently large segment of the population. But later, as it became evident that Prohibition was not accomplishing what it was intended to do—and indeed had some unintended consequences that have lasted until the present—and as the originally supportive society changed, the WCTU was faced with a decision regarding its future. It could have altered its stance toward alcohol to keep it in line with the prevailing opinions or maintained its position in favor of total abstinence. The latter course was selected as the result of decisions made within the organization. The consequences of the decision were to isolate the movement from the population, reducing it to virtual ineffectiveness as a force in the wider society.

It is difficult to predict what might have happened if the stance had been altered to one of temperance, rather than abstinence. It well might be that the whole antialcohol movement was one whose time had passed. It might also be that the WCTU would have had a greater educational and social impact if its position had shifted with the times. At any rate, what was once an important social movement became a small, socially insignificant organization.

The social system around it thus affects the social-change agent as much as it does any other form of organization. While such organizations can appear to be revolutionary, deviant, martyred, or in any other emotion-laden category, the fact remains that they are organizations. The critical aspect is the acceptance of the organization by society. This is obviously important for any organization, since it must receive support in one form or another in order to survive, but for these change-oriented ones it is even more so. Unfortunately (or fortunately in some cases), organizational analysts, decision makers, and politicians have not figured out exactly how to determine when an idea's time has come, so that the organization embarking on a change mission is in a precarious position at best.

There are other, more subtle ways in which organizations are change agents. As Perrow notes:

> We tend to forget, or neglect, the fact that organizations have an enormous potential for affecting the lives of all who come into contact with them. They control or can activate a multitude of resources, not just land and machinery and employees, but police, governments, communications, art,

---

[26] Joseph R. Gusfield, *Symbolic Crusade* (Urbana, Ill.: University of Illinois Press, 1963).

and other areas, too. That is, an organization, as a legally constituted entity, can ask for police protection and public prosecution, can sue, and can hire a private police force with considerably wider latitude and power than an individual can command. It can ask the courts to respond to requests and make legal rulings. It can petition for changes in other areas of government —zoning laws, fair-trade laws, consumer labeling, and protection and health laws. It determines the content of advertising, the art work in its products and packages, the shape and color of its buildings. It can move out of a community, and it selects the communities in which it will build. It can invest in times of imminent recession or it can retrench; support or fight government economic policies or fair employment practices. In short, organizations generate a great deal of power that may be used in a way not directly related to producing goods and services or to survival.[27]

Rather obviously, the power potential of organizations is often used to thwart change, as will be seen in the next section. Even in those cases where an organization is an active change agent, if the change is accomplished, the organization tends then to resist further changes. The labor-union movement, which was once considered revolutionary, is now viewed by some as reactionary. National revolutions lead to established governments that in turn are attacked as opponents of social progress. Industries that alter the social composition of a society resist new technologies and social patterns.

CONSTRAINTS.　Organizations do not change the society around them at will. All the environmental influences on organizations also serve as constraints on the organization as a change agent. This point is most graphically seen in the case of organizations in developing nations. If development is a national goal, then almost all organizations in such a society are designed to be change agents. A basic problem, however, is that the organizational forms that work in developed societies do not work in the case of those just developing. For example, R. S. Milne notes that there is a strong tendency for superiors not to delegate authority to subordinates. This is seen as a result of the lack of shared values among the different ranks, differing conceptions of authority, incompetence or lack of training among the subordinates, and the fear of loss of opportunity to earn income corruptly.[28] Similarly, subordinates seem unwilling to accept power. Studies in the Philippines and Latin America have noted the unwillingness of middle-level administrators to make decisions.[29] Milne states that in addition to the shortage of skills, deficiencies in training, lack of resources, and poor communications, the

[27] Perrow, *Organizational Analysis*, pp. 170–71.

[28] R. S. Milne, "Mechanistic and Organic Models of Public Administration in Developing Countries," *Administrative Science Quarterly*, Vol. 15, No. 1 (March 1970), 57.

[29] *Ibid.*, p. 58.

general culture precludes effective administration. Loyalty to the organization, for example, is an alien notion and thus is not present to supplement the formal channels.[30] Milne concludes that effective administration cannot be achieved unless the general cultural conditions also change.

Because of the cultural and other environmental constraints, organizations in developing societies must take a different form from those in more developed situations.[31] It is generally suggested that such an organization must operate in a less formalized manner, taking into account the particular environment in which it is trying to operate.

But despite the constraints, organizations in developing societies do affect those societies. The organizations do things that were not done before, in terms of yielding goods and services and arranging social relationships, and this very simple fact alone affects the surrounding society. Not all such societies will become Westernized or bureaucratized, but they will be different from what they were before the advent of organizations. As in many other situations, the exact direction and extent of the organizational impact is not known, but the impact itself can be seen on the immediate alterations of the social fabric. A more subtle effect is the one occurring between generations. Each succeeding generation will tend to be more accepting of the presence of organizations, creating generation gaps and also altering the organizational environment. A previously hostile environment may become accepting. Here again, the *reciprocity* of the organizational–societal relationship can be seen.

Before we turn to the discussion of organizations as resisters of change, it should be reiterated that organizations have a wide variety of impacts on the environment. These range from the exciting examples of revolution or pollution to the more mundane but equally important matters of establishing and maintaining equilibrium in the system. In a comprehensive analysis, organizations must be viewed as a major stabilizing factor in society. Each kind of output has an impact on society, from the production of goods to the development of ideas. As we have noted repeatedly, this output must be of some value to the society; but it may also have by-products that are harmful to the society. Since an organizational society contains a multitude of values, it must also be recognized that what is of value to one segment of the society may be violently opposed by another segment. Thus it is possible to have organizations that provide drugs or prostitutes. These are still organizations and can only be understood as such.

30 *Ibid.,* p. 62.
31 See particularly Fred W. Riggs, *Administration in Developing Countries* (Boston: Houghton Mifflin Company, 1964); and Victor A. Thompson, "Administrative Objectives for Development Administration," *Administrative Science Quarterly,* Vol. 9, No. 1 (June 1964), 91–108.

The fact that organizations do have outputs that are opposed to or have opposite effects to those of other organizations raises another point about the organizational impact on society. Organizations are at the source of much of the conflict in society. While individual conflict in the form of fights, debates, shootouts, and so on, are the stuff of which movies and newspaper headlines are made, it is conflict between organizations that really alters the fabric of society. The ability to wage a successful conflict is largely tied to the organizational capacities of the parties involved. The outcome of a conflict is usually a situation that is altered from the one that existed before the conflict. Since organizations are such an important component of conflict in society, it follows that organizations are central to social change through this mechanism.

ORGANIZATIONS AS RESISTERS OF CHANGE

An earlier section began with the point that organizations are a major structuring component in society. This structuring takes place because of the work roles of the members of the organizations and the values that organizational membership can impart. Organizations are a means of structuring the activities of the members. This in and of itself is a structuring element. Since our concern in this chapter is with change, it is important to go beyond the basic fact of organizational contributions to social stability. Organizations also actively resist change. This resistance is directed toward change introduced from outside the organization. The organization attempts to protect itself. Obviously, changes that are not important to the organization will not bring an organizational response.

A basic factor in determining the success of the organization in resisting change is the amount of power the organization has in its environment. Except in the isolated cases of communities or regions that are dominated by only one organization, organizations gain and retain power by their participation in interorganizational relationships. Robert Perrucci and Marc Pilisuk have demonstrated that at the community level, interorganizational networks exist in the form of persons who hold executive positions in several organizations.[32] These people can utilize the organizational resources of their multiple organizations during peri-

32 Robert Perrucci and Marc Pilisuk, "Leaders and Ruling Elites: The Interorganizational Bases of Community Power," *American Sociological Review*, Vol. 35, No. 6 (December 1970), 1040–57. This article contains references to the literature on the distribution of power in communities.

ods of community decision making. Persons holding such multiple executive positions tend to have common values and operate as a power bloc. They represent the organizations of which they are members, and thus the organization takes a position on community matters.

At the broader societal level, there are also such organizational linkages. The familiar "military–industrial complex" is such a linkage. In a recent analysis, Stanley Lieberson notes that there are important military–industrial linkages that at least partially explain the maintenance of a war economy and the pattern of governmental expenditures in recent decades.[33] Lieberson goes on to point out that this pattern has been detrimental to much of American industry. At the same time, there are other interorganizational linkages that serve to promote vested interests at the national decision-making level. Lieberson rejects the notion that *all* national decisions are shaped by the military–industrial complex; he says that this is but one of a set of linkages, all of which have a hand in shaping national policy.

These points about decision making at the local and national level are meant to illustrate the power of organizations in the decision-making and policy-setting arenas. In most cases, the decisions and policies are based on attempts to resist changes that are detrimental to the organizational sets involved.

Organizations by their very nature are conservative. This is seen in the political stances taken and in economic policies. When the focus is shifted to the manner in which the organization itself operates, the point becomes even more clear. *Organizations operate conservatively regardless of whether they are viewed as radical or as reactionary by the general population.* In order to document this point, an example will again have to be used, this time from Seymour Martin Lipset's analysis of populist rural socialism in Saskatchewan, Canada.[34] In 1944, the Co-operative Commonwealth Federation (CCF) came to power in the province. The objective was "the social ownership of all resources and the machinery of wealth production to the end that we may establish a Cooperative Commonwealth in which the basic principle regulating production, distribution and exchange will be the supplying of human needs instead of the making of profits." [35] This aim has been only partially realized. One reason has been continued political opposition to the movement; another, consistent with the argument here, is that the move-

[33] Stanley Lieberson, "An Empirical Study of Military Industrial Linkages," *American Journal of Sociology*, Vol. 76, No. 4 (January 1971), 562–84. Lieberson presents a reasoned overview of the literature on this important topic.

[34] Seymour Martin Lipset, *Agrarian Socialism* (Berkeley and Los Angeles: University of California Press, 1950).

[35] *Ibid.*, p. 130.

ment itself apparently became more conservative as power was achieved. An additional important consideration is the fact that the new socialist government utilized the existing government structures in attempting to carry out its program. In explanation Lipset notes:

> Trained in the traditions of a laissez-faire government and belonging to conservative social groups, the civil service contributes significantly to the social inertia which blunts the changes a new radical government can make. Delay in initiating reforms means that the new government becomes absorbed in the process of operating the old institutions. The longer a new government delays making changes, the more responsible it becomes for the old practices and the harder it is to make the changes it originally desired to institute.[36]

The reason for this blunting is quite simple. The new ruling cabinet had to rely on the system already in operation.

> The administratively insecure cabinet ministers were overjoyed at the friendly response they obtained from the civil servants. *To avoid making administrative blunders* [emphasis added] that would injure them in the eyes of the public and the party, the ministers began to depend on the civil servants. As one cabinet minister stated in an interview, "I would have been lost if not for the old members of my staff. I'm only a beginner in this work. B—— has been at it for twenty years. If I couldn't go to him for advice, I couldn't have done a thing. Why now (after two years in office) I am only beginning to find my legs and make my own decisions. . . . I have not done a thing for two years without advice." [37]

It is important to note that this blunting of the aims of the movement can occur without malice or intent. It is not a personal thing, but an organizational one. Certainly, personal motivations can enter the picture in an important way, but the crucial factor is that the new leaders did not understand the organizations they were to head. The organization itself contained rules and procedures that had to be learned along the way, so that the organization became the instrument that deflected the party in power from its goals.

The organization trains its members to follow a system of carrying out its activities. It would require a complete resocialization before the takeover of a new party if this sort of thing were to be prevented. This, of course, is impossible in governmental organizations. An alternative practice would be to purge the entire system, replacing the original members with ones of the appropriate ideology. This would in essence mean that the organization would have to start *de novo* and that nothing

[36] *Ibid.*, pp. 272–73.
[37] *Ibid.*, p. 263.

would be done until the organizational roles were learned and linkages to the society established. Since the organization has clients and customers, as well as a broader constituency in the case of governmental organizations, the expectations of nonmembers would also have to be altered. For these reasons, the likelihood of success is slim, regardless of the technique selected. The tendency for the organization to operate as it has in the past is very strong.

Most governmental organizations in Western democracies operate with a civil service system. An extension of Lipset's analysis suggests, therefore, that changes in the party in power will have less impact on the operation of the government agencies than political rhetoric would suggest. In non-Western societies, the same principles seem to hold. The potentiality for major social change through change in government is therefore modified by the organizational realities that exist. Since social systems do change, of course, the organization must be viewed as something that does not change overnight, but will change with time. The changes that occur may not be in phase with the change in political philosophy of the government in power. A "liberal" party in power may over time be able to introduce more of its adherents into the civil service system. These people can remain in office after a change in the party in power, blunting the efforts of a conservative party, but at the same time increasing the "liberalness" of the agencies involved. In whatever political direction a state, county, or nation is moving, organizational conservatism will remain an important consideration.

Examples from outside the political–government arena can also be readily found. In education, schools in urban areas have seen their constituencies change around them,[38] but there is a strong tendency toward maintenance of the educational programs that were appropriate in the past, despite their growing irrelevancy—and the same change could be documented in higher education. In private industry, the plight of the railroads in the United States is indicative of the resistance of this organizational form to change. Here the resistance is more than the desire to maximize income; in fact, some suggest that the railroads' persistence in their past practices is in spite of the fact that profits could be increased if practices were altered. Organized religions have similarly resisted change, with apparently damaging results for themselves, both as organizations and as social movements.

These examples could be extended. Probably everyone has his favorite case of an organization swallowing up attempts at what seem to be improvements through the continuation of past practices. The point must be reiterated that this is endemic to the nature of organizations. Or-

---

[38] For a discussion of this point, see Morris Janowitz, *Institution Building in Urban Education* (New York: Russell Sage Foundation, 1969), pp. 7–10.

ganizations can and do change. Mechanisms can be set up that help foster change within the organization, as has been shown. At the same time, at some point in its history every organization will resist efforts to make it do something it has not been doing. Individuals in the organization are reinforced by their consistency in behavior in relationship to the organizational norms. Organizational procedures become fixed and valued. Precedent is part of the organizational legal system. All these factors conspire to make the organizations in a society major resisters of change in that society.

SUMMARY AND CONCLUSIONS

This chapter has been intended to accomplish two tasks. The first is the overt one of examining the manner in which organizations are both agents and counteragents of social change. The implicit secondary task is the reconstruction and application of the analysis contained in this volume as a whole. Whatever their position regarding change may be, all organizations have the structural and processual characteristics described in the earlier sections. Future attempts at change must take these facts into consideration if they are to be successful.

The intent behind the entire book has been to analyze organizations from a sociological perspective. In doing this, we have paid less attention to the individual as a member of the organization and to his role within it than may be desirable for a complete understanding of organizational phenomena. It is hoped, however, that the argument and data that have been presented are sufficiently strong to indicate the importance of purely organizational phenomena in our understanding and use of the organizations in society.

The conceptual model used in the analysis stressed that organizations must be viewed as open systems, with their activities organized around the operative goals that have developed during the course of the organization's life. This open system involves inputs from the environment, interpersonal interactions, individual actions, and the effects of the existing organizational structure. The organization engages in activities and contains processes that alter the organization and affect its output. This output in turn affects and is reacted to by the environment. The environmental reactions become in turn further inputs for the ongoing system.

It was argued that the nature of organizations can best be understood by taking organizational characteristics as the basis for any classificatory scheme. From this point it was stated that structural characteristics vary according to the interplay of technology, size, and other factors. Organizations of a like technological base that happen to be of a similar size will tend to exhibit similar characteristics and can thus be classified together. The degrees of complexity and formalization were examined to see the other organizational characteristics with which they are associated. The importance of an organization's structure is that it sets the conditions under which processes take place. Structure by itself has little importance except for the fact that the rest of the nature of organizations begins from the existing structural arrangements.

At this point the processes of power, leadership and decision making, and communications were considered. These processes are the means by which the activities of the organization are carried out and the organization itself changed. These internal sources of change lead to restructured organizations as the reciprocity between structure and process continues. The organizational processes are the action in organizations. Organizational members carry out their rules and the organization does something. What the organization does is to produce an output, which is sent out to the environment. This last section has been concerned with the impact of that output on the environment and the environment's impact on the organization.

It should be obvious that there is a lot yet to be known about organizations. In terms of research and practice, the needs are documented in the kinds of evidence presented in this book. There is much better evidence regarding structural characteristics than about other topics, and although more research is needed here, it is clear that the internal processes and external relations are the areas most in need of understanding. The move from comparative data to case studies is indicative of the state of the art at present.

Research for its own sake is necessary, of course; but there are practical societal problems that organizational analysis can address itself to while continuing to build basic knowledge about organizational phenomena. The increasing demands for participation by clients and consumers in the decision-making process create a natural situation for the further analysis of power and decision making. The concern with the natural environment should furnish analysts a good opportunity to study organizational–environmental transactions. The effect of the growth and decline of the economy on the monies available for public and private organizations is an ideal test for determining the important operative goals of the organizations involved. The concern with education in its various forms and with the fact of multiple constituencies should help develop a more sophisticated approach to the determination of organizational effectiveness, or at least give further documentation to the obsession with easily quantifiable effectiveness measures. The development of the conglomerate corporation should provide opportunities for verification of the ideas presented regarding the impact of alternative technologies, since such conglomerates should demonstrate within their component organizations rather widely different structures and processes. Studies of the multinational organization should further our knowledge about the importance of environmental factors for the organization.

These examples could obviously be multiplied. The evidence that might be forthcoming from such analyses would add to our store of knowledge about organizations and thus make the job of analysis easier and more complete. It should also increase rationality within the organization and the concern and responsibility of the organization for what it is doing to its members, its environment, and itself.

INDEX